Bender, Harold Herman

A Lithuanian Etymological Index

Inktank publishing

Bender, Harold Herman

A Lithuanian Etymological Index

Inktank publishing, 2018

www.inktank-publishing.com

ISBN/EAN: 9783747747117

A LITHUANIAN ETYMOLOGICAL INDEX

Based upon Brugmann's Grundriss and the etymological dictionaries of Uhlenbeck (Sanskrit), Kluge (German), Feist (Gothic), Berneker (Slavic), Walde (Latin), and Boisacq (Greek)

BY

HAROLD H. BENDER, PH.D.

Professor of Indo-Germanic Philology in Princeton University

PRINCETON UNIVERSITY PRESS
PRINCETON
LONDON: HUMPHREY MILFORD
OXFORD UNIVERSITY PRESS
1921

INTRODUCTORY

It has long been recognized that in both Balto-Slavic and Indo-European philology a serious handicap to comparative investigation lies in the fact that the etymological studies that have already been made are not generally available from the standpoint of Lithuanian, in its preservation of sounds and forms the most archaic of all living Indo-European tongues. The present work, which has grown out of an attempt on the part of the author to collect for his own use, both as student and teacher of the language, the most important of these references, will, it is hoped, serve as an immediate and practical key to the bulk of the etymological material offered by Lithuanian, and ultimately form the basis of a formal etymological dictionary.

The difficulties of even a preliminary undertaking of the sort will be recognized by scholars who have worked in Lithuanian from the inside, and I enter court with the plea in confession and avoidance most recently offered by Sommer: "Auf Korrekturen im einzelnen muss ich gefasst sein wie jeder, der auf dem Gebiet des Litauischen arbeitet." The present state of Lithuanian lexicography leaves much to be desired; there is no satisfactory and complete dictionary of the language, and he who would write its etymological dictionary must first become in large measure its lexicographer. A considerable proportion of the words included in the present work are not to be found in the dictionaries. Such words have been traced, so far as possible, to their source, or to within one reference of their source.

Furthermore, the fluidity of the language, its relative want of written or literary traditions, its tendency to secondary formation of words, its subjection internally to numerous dialectic disturbances and externally to various systems of orthography, all frequently interfere with the determination of individual forms under which the etymological material may be conveniently arranged. It would have been desirable to bring more closely together all related material under more readily accessible heads; but at the same time it seemed important for the immediate purpose of the Index to preserve in its alphabetical order the integrity of the Lithuanian vocabulary. However, an effort has been made to lessen by abundant cross references any inconvenience in this direction.

In regard to orthography little need be said save that in recent years standards have tended to establish themselves by fashion and convention, and that I have tried to follow these standards as I saw them. My system differs little from Wiedemann's and but little more from Brugmann's. The discrepancies in the case of the other authors will not, it is believed, interfere with identification, although a little care may be necessary in the use of Kurschat: for example, in alphabetical order; in his writing *iė* (= *ë*), *w* (= *v*); and in his employment of the German digraph ß for Lithuanian *sz*, which, however, is phonetically equivalent to German *sch*. I have given the *Tonqualität* whenever it could be ascertained with a reasonable degree of certainty.

The procedure in each article is as follows: First is given the Lithuanian word with its definition. After the dash come the references to the etymological discussions of the word. But no word has been accepted for the Index without investigation; and so, after the etymological citations, are added references to establish all, or nearly all, words or forms that are not to be found in Kurschat or are included by him within brackets.[1] While this is the

[1] Cf. Kur. p. XI: "Die Einrichtung und Anordnung in diesem meinem Wörterbuche habe ich nun so getroffen: 1) dass ich die mir nicht völlig bekannten Wörter, für deren Richtigkeit ich keine Garantie übernehmen mochte, in eckige Klammern fasste."

main purpose of these additional references, many of them, especially those to Leskien, are also valuable for the light they throw on the internal relations of the word in Lithuanian, and hundreds of references have been inserted for the latter purpose alone. In fact, all of the more important groups in Leskien's *Ablaut* are referred to under at least one word, usually the most frequent representative of the group.

The marks ( ) about an etymological reference indicate that the author referred to rejects explicitly any connection between his title word and the Lithuanian word; or that by way of illustration (grammatical, syntactical, or semantic) he includes the Lithuanian word in an etymology that is unrelated to the word he is discussing.[2] The marks [ ] indicate that the actual Lithuanian word is not found in the article to which reference is made. In such cases, however, there will usually be found either another Lithuanian form which is obviously related, or the establishment of relationship with some other Sanskrit, Slavic, or Greek word, as the case may be, under which the Lithuanian word is mentioned. Absence of ( ) or [ ] implies that the Lithuanian word and the title word referred to are considered by the author to whom reference is made to be related in some way, in whole or in part; or at least that possibility of relationship is admitted.

As an example illustrative of the use of these arbitrary devices we may take the following article:

avìs 'Schaf'—Uh. *áviṣ;* K. *Aue,* (*Schaf*); F. *awēþi,* [*awistr*]; B. I, 94.153.317. II, 1, 169. 2, 129; W. *ovis;* Boi. ὄϊς.

This is to say, being interpreted, that Uhlenbeck, Kluge, Feist, Walde, and Boisacq respectively consider Lithuanian *avìs* related to Sanskrit *áviṣ,* German *Aue,* Gothic *awēþi,* Latin *ovis,* and Greek ὄϊς; that the Lithuanian word is

[2] Inasmuch as Brugmann is indexed by pages and not by words, ( ) are not employed in this way for the *Grundriss.*

treated etymologically on pages 94, 153, and 317 of the first volume of Brugmann, and on page 169 of the first part of the second volume, and on page 129 of the second part of the second volume; that under the heading *Schaf* Kluge discusses Lithuanian *avis* and its cognates as representing the oldest Indo-European designation of the animal, without, however, connecting the stem with German *Schaf;* that Feist, without mentioning *avìs,* connects Gothic *awistr* with Gothic *awēþi,* with which he does compare the Lithuanian word.

An attempt has been made to give the Index some lexicographical value by making the definitions fairly full and complete; by tracing the meanings through the various glossaries, word lists, and dictionaries, both etymological and lexicographical; and by giving the authorities when the meanings differ.

The title words have been chosen independently of the dictionaries, both as to form and arrangement. A few forms that I have been unable to verify (several of which I view with suspicion) are followed by a (?).[3] The relative number of such words is, however, quite insignificant. In numerous instances accent and quality of vowels have been blithely assumed by this author or that with no apparent authority beyond that of general probability. In such cases I have searched for original evidence, and in the event of failure have inserted a (?).

In general a (?) indicates: (a) that the form is evidently assumed and that I find no authority for it; or (b) that the author indexed is apparently mistaken as to the orthography or accent of his Lithuanian form; or (c) that the form is a ἅπαξ λεγόμενον, or nearly so; or (d) that given an infinitive alone or a present indicative alone, the other may

[3] Several words designated in the etymological dictionaries as Lithuanian have been ignored entirely because they were recognized as belonging to some other language, or because they were patently impossible as Lithuanian forms.

be one of two or more forms; or (e) that there is variation or question as to form depending upon dialect, period, dictionary, or other authority; or (f) that in some way the word, in its orthography, accent, *Tonqualität,* inflectional belongings, or meaning, is uncertain. The number of words with a (?) would doubtless be somewhat reduced (though not materially, I believe) if communication were possible with the scholars and the libraries of Germany and Russia. Several important older dictionaries, for example, are, so far as I have been able to ascertain, not available in the institutional libraries of this country; much of their material has, however, been worked over by Leskien and others.

Ordinarily forms that merely illustrate declensional or conjugational endings have been omitted, but they have often been included when the endings are clearly comparative and bring in other languages, or when it seemed important to establish connection with some other indexed word. However, if the root or stem was already indexed and there was no special reason for indexing the termination, a parallel ending in Old Bulgarian, for example, was not sufficient of itself to bring a Lithuanian word into the fold.

Derivative nominal, adjectival, and adverbial stems with familiar and usual suffixes are indexed to references which give no information beyond the suffix that is used only when the basic root or stem is treated elsewhere in the Index, except in a number of cases for special reasons, which will usually be quite apparent: for example, when there is some irregularity in the formation that requires explanation, or when the reference leads to a discussion of the suffix involved, or when the entire word is indexed for at least one other authority, or when a reference is given in the Index to another word that is indexed.

In many cases compound verbs are given, but only when the simple verb is not found, or when the compound forms are specially cited by one or the other of the dictionaries, or when they differ in meaning from the simple verb to such an extent that the connection might be overlooked. Whenever possible they are referred to the simple verb. It should be noted that compound reflexive verbs are given the same alphabetical position that they would have if they were non-reflexive compound verbs; for example, verbs in *at-si-, pa-si-* etc. are indexed in the same position as verbs in *at-, pa-* etc.

No effort has been made to refer each Lithuanian word to every other Lithuanian word with which it may be related. Such relationships will be found variously expressed in the dictionaries. But such references are made in cases in which the relationship is not expressed in the dictionaries or may be easily overlooked; in cases where such references are of more than usual importance; and in a number of examples from a word with little etymological material to a word that is more widely treated in the dictionaries, and with which it is assumed by one or more dictionaries to be related. Usually no cross reference is given when related words are found obviously together in the Index, or when they are immediately connected in one of the references, or when the relationship is otherwise readily apparent. That is to say, each Lithuanian example has been considered and treated on its own merits, with the sole idea of making easily available as much etymological information and opinion as possible.

Some rather obvious things are included, such as occasional plain and regular derivatives from other indexed words, but it was desired to make the book serviceable also to those comparative students who are not at home in Lithuanian. It is impossible to foretell for what each user of the Index will be seeking. One will find too much and the other too little, but the latter will, I trust, not be disappointed so frequently as the former.

Brugmann's *Grundriss* and all the dictionaries (Leskien's *Ablaut* as well) were gone through page by page and line by line, although every word of the exceedingly eclectic Lithuanian indexes in Feist, Walde, and Brugmann has been included; and, in each work, many hundreds more. In the case of Brugmann particularly, the inclusion of his index brought in some words that would otherwise have been excluded, especially references to purely grammatical and syntactical discussions. On the whole, however, my aim has been to include every reference that has real etymological value and at the same time to avoid detracting from the efficiency of the Index by referring, for example, to mere illustrations of case endings, or to more than one citation of exactly the same etymological material.

Usually the index words to each individual dictionary are listed in alphabetical order when more than one appear, but whenever a distinction seems worth noting they are arranged in the order of the etymological importance of the articles to which they refer.

Hundreds of misprints and errors in form in the various dictionaries are corrected in the Index by inference. Where the correction is not obvious, or where there is a difference of opinion, special mention is made. Little attention is paid, however, to differences in writing which belong merely to different systems of orthography.

On a following page will be found a formal list of the works included in the Index. The eighth edition of Kluge appeared after I had worked through the preceding edition, but as the former was going to press, Professor Kluge wrote me: "Eine Vermehrung des sprachvergleichenden Materials und der litauischen Beziehungen ist nicht beabsichtigt." Inasmuch, therefore, as the seventh edition is referred to by title words and not by pages, the Index will apply equally well to the eighth edition. It is a matter of special regret that Berneker's masterly work cannot be included in its entirety, but only one *Lieferung* has reached me since the beginning of the war, and it seems hopeless to wait for the remaining. Several slight typographical variations from Berneker will occasion no difficulty; the most serious is my writing of ĭ and ŭ for the semivowels in his Slavic title words.

Fortunately the last part of Boisacq appeared in time to be included. In December, 1913, Trübner informed me that the second *Lieferung* of Brugmann II, 3 would not appear before 1915. It seems reasonable to suppose that it has been more or less indefinitely postponed; at any rate I have been unable to learn anything further about its appearance.

My hearty thanks are due Professors Brugmann of Leipzig, Uhlenbeck of Leiden, Kluge of Freiburg, Berneker of Munich, Walde of Innsbruck, and Dr. Feist in Berlin, not only for permission to use their works, but also for valuable help and suggestions. The postal inaccessibility of Brussels during the war has frustrated repeated attempts to communicate with Professor Boisacq, so I offer him here my apologies and my belated thanks for the use of his dictionary.

It is a pleasure to add an expression of gratitude to my friend Professor Franklin Edgerton of the University of Pennsylvania for many a helpful hint in these as well as in other philological matters.

HAROLD H. BENDER.

Princeton University,
June, 1921.

ABBREVIATIONS

I

B. = Karl Brugmann, *Grundriss der vergleichenden Grammatik der indogermanischen Sprachen.* Zweite Bearbeitung. Band I (1. & 2. Hälfte, paginated and paragraphed as one); Band II (Teile 1, 2, & 3 [1. Lieferung], each Teil paginated and paragraphed separately). Strassburg 1897 ff.—Indexed by pages, not by paragraphs.

Ber. = Erich Berneker, *Slavisches etymologisches Wörterbuch.* Band I (A—L); Band II (11. Lieferung, M). Heidelberg 1908 ff.

Boi. = Émile Boisacq, *Dictionnaire étymologique de la langue grecque.* Heidelberg-Paris 1916.

F. = Sigmund Feist, *Etymologisches Wörterbuch der gotischen Sprache.* Halle 1909.

K. = Friedrich Kluge, *Etymologisches Wörterbuch der deutschen Sprache.* Siebente Auflage. Strassburg 1910.

Uh. = C. C. Uhlenbeck, *Kurzgefasstes etymologisches Wörterbuch der altindischen Sprache.* Amsterdam 1898-1899.

W. = Alois Walde, *Lateinisches etymologisches Wörterbuch.* Zweite Auflage. Heidelberg 1910.

II

Archiv = Archiv für slavische Philologie, herausg. von V. Jagić. Berlin 1876 ff.

BB. = Beiträge zur Kunde der indogermanischen Sprachen, herausg. von A. Bezzenberger und W. Prellwitz. Göttingen 1877-1906.

Bezz. BGLS. = Beiträge zur Geschichte der litauischen Sprache von A. Bezzenberger. Göttingen 1877.

Bezz. LF. = Litauische Forschungen von A. Bezzenberger. Göttingen 1882.

Brückner SlFw. = Litu-Slavische Studien I. Die slavischen Fremdwörter im Litauischen. Weimar 1877.

Donalitius = Christian Donaleitis: Litauische Dichtungen, herausg. von Aug. Schleicher. St. Petersburg 1865.

Geitler LD. = Beiträge zur litauischen Dialektologie (Sitzungsberichte der Kais. Akad. d. Wiss. in Wien, philol.-hist. Klasse. Bd. CVIII). Wien 1885.

Geitler LS. = Litauische Studien. Prag 1875.

IF. = Indogermanische Forschungen. Zeitschrift für indogermanische Sprach- und Altertumskunde, herausg. von K. Brugmann und W. Streitberg. Strassburg 1892 ff.

Juškevič = Litovskij Slovarĭ. St. Petersburg 1897 ff.

Kur. = Litauisch-deutsches Wörterbuch von Friedrich Kurschat. Halle 1883.

Kur. DLWb. = Deutsch-litauisches Wörterbuch von Friedrich Kurschat. Halle 1870.

Kur. Gram. = Grammatik der litauischen Sprache von Friedrich Kurschat. Halle 1876.

KZ. = Zeitschrift für vergleichende Sprachforschung auf dem Gebiete der indogermanischen Sprachen. Begründet von A. Kuhn. (Berlin und) Gütersloh 1852-1907. Göttingen 1907 ff.

Lalis = Lietuviškos ir angliškos kalbų żodynas. Trečias spaudimas. Chicago 1915.

LBLV. = Litauische Volkslieder und Märchen von A. Leskien und K. Brugmann. Strassburg 1882.

Lesk. Abl. = Der Ablaut der Wurzelsilben im Litauischen (Abhandlungen der philol.-hist. Klasse der Kgl. Sächs. Ges. d. Wiss. Bd. IX) von August Leskien. Leipzig 1884.

Lesk. Nom. = Die Bildung der Nomina im Litauischen (Abhandlungen der philol.-hist. Klasse der Kgl. Sächs. Ges. d. Wiss. Bd. XII) von August Leskien. Leipzig 1891.

Mielcke = Litauisch-deutsches und deutsch-litauisches Wörterbuch. Königsberg 1800.

MLG. = Mitteilungen der Litauischen literarischen Gesellschaft. Heidelberg 1883 ff.

Ness. = Wörterbuch der litauischen Sprache von G. H. F. Nesselmann. Königsberg 1851.

Prell. = Etymologisches Wörterbuch der griechischen Sprache von Walther Prellwitz. 2. Aufl. Göttingen 1905.

Prell. deutsch. Best. in den lett. Spr. = Die deutschen Bestandteile in den lettischen Sprachen. Erstes Heft: Die deutschen Lehnwörter im Preussischen und Lautlehre der deutschen Lehnwörter im Litauischen. Von Walther Prellwitz. Göttingen 1891.

Schleicher LSpr. = Handbuch der litauischen Sprache. I. Bd.: Litauische Grammatik; II. Bd.: Litauisches Lesebuch und Glossar. Prag 1856-1857.

Solmsen = Beiträge zur griechischen Wortforschung. 1. Teil. Strassburg 1909.

Sommer = Die indogermanischen *iā-* und *io*-Stämme im Baltischen (Abhandlungen der philol.-hist. Klasse der Kgl. Sächs. Ges. d. Wiss. Bd. XXX). Leipzig 1914.

Szyr. = Dictionarium trium linguarum in usum studiosae juventutis, auctore R. P. Constantino Szyrwid. Quinta editio. Vilnae 1713.

Wied. = Handbuch der litauischen Sprache von Oskar Wiedemann. Strassburg 1897.

III

acc. = accusative
act. = active
adj. = adjective or adjectival
adv. = adverb or adverbial
bes. = besonders
cf. = confer, compare
cmpd. = compound
comp. = comparative
conj. = conjunction
dat. = dative
dem. = demonstrative
dial. = dialect(ic)
dimin. = diminutive
ed. = edition
e. g. = exempli gratia
end. = ending
etc. = et cetera
f(f). = following
f., fem. = feminine
FN., fn. = footnote
fut. = future
gen. = genitive
gram. = grammar or grammatical
id. = idem
i. e. = id est
impera. = imperative
impers. = impersonal
inf. = infinitive
inst. = instrumental
interj. = interjection
interrog. = interrogative
intr. = intransitive
iter. = iterative
l(l). = line(s)
Lett. = Lettish
Lith. = Lithuanian
loc. = locative
m., masc. = masculine
N., n. = note
neut. = neuter
nom. = nominative

note = footnote (never Brugmann's Anmerkungen in the body of the text)
Ntr. = Nachträge, Berichtigungen, Verbesserungen, additions et corrections, etc.
Old Pruss. = Old Prussian
opt. = optative
p(p). = page(s)
part. = participle
pass. = passive
perf. = perfect
pers. = person or personal
plu. = plural
plu. tant. = plurale tantum
poss. = possessive
prec. = preceding
pref. = prefix
prep. = preposition
pres. = present
pret. = preterit
pron. = pronoun or pronominal
Pruss. = Prussian
q. v. = quod vide
refl. = reflexive
Russ. = Russian
Samog(it). = samogitisch, Samogitian
sing. = singular
suff. = suffix
super. = superlative
supin. = supinum
s. v. = sub verbo
trans. = transitive
usw. = und so weiter
verb. = verbal
voc. = vocative
Wb. = Wörterbuch
z. B. = zum Beispiel
żem. = żemaĩtiszkas, samogitisch, Samogitian

On the use of ( ), [ ], and (?), see pages VII, VIII, IX.

ALPHABETICAL ORDER

All the characters below are used in the Index, and all except those in [ ] represent separate and distinct sounds; but the ones in ( ) and [ ] are not distinguished in alphabetical order from the characters to which they are attached. Those in [ ] are typographical variants, employed chiefly for Old Lithuanian.

a (ą), b, c, cz, d, e (ę ė ë [iė]), g, i (į y), j, k, l, m, n, o, p, r, s, sz [sch], t, u (ų), ů, v [w], z, ż.

A LITHUANIAN ETYMOLOGICAL INDEX

A

á, áá Ausrufe der Verwunderung, des Tadels oder Spottes —W. *ā*.

abejì 'beide'—B. II, 2, 77.80.81.150. See *abù*. Cf. Wied. 158.2.

abypusiaĩ 'beiderseits'—B. II, 2, 929. See *abù* & *pùsė*.

abyszaliaĩ id.—B. II, 2, 929. See *abù* & *szalìs*.

abù 'beide'—Uh. *ubhāu;* K. *beide;* F. *bai;* B. II, 2, 76 (twice).461; W. *ambo;* Boi. ἄμφω. Cf. Wied. 156.2.

adatà 'Nähnadel'—W. *ador*.

adaũ, adýti 'nähen, steppen'—W. *ador*.

adynà 'Zeitpunkt, Stunde'—Ber. *godŭ*.

advos 'kaum'—Ber. *jed(ŭ)va*.

agũnà 'Mohn'—Ber. *makŭ;* Boi. μήκων.

aidinu, aidinti 'reizen'—Ber. *ědŭ*. Cf. Bezz. BGLS. 269-270.

aiksztė 'ebene Fläche, Horizontale'—W. *aequor*. Cf. Bezz. BGLS. 270.

aiksztus 'eben, weit, geräumig'—W. *aequor*. Cf. BB. XXVI, 167, Lalis 3.

ailus 'ätzend, scharf'—B. II, 1, 339.362.

aistra 'heftige Leidenschaft'—W. *īra;* Boi. ἰαίνω, οἶστρος. Cf. Lalis 3.

aisùs 'bitter, traurig'—W. *aerumna*.

aisũju, aisũti 'rufen' (von der Eule)—Ber. *jaskola*.

áiszkus 'deutlich'—Ber. *ěsĭnŭ, iskra*.

aitra 'Strenge, Eifer, Leidenschaft, heftige Begierde'—Ber. *ętrǫ*. Cf. Lesk. Nom. 438.

aitrùs 'bitter, brennend im Munde'—B. II, 1, 339; Ber. *ętrǫ, jarŭ 2;* W. *āter;* Boi. ἀτρύγετος.

aiżaũ, aiżýti 'ausschlauben'—Ber. *ězva*.

ãkas (Kur. also **ãkis**) 'Loch im Eise'—B. II, 1, 160.520; (W. *oculus*); Boi. ὀπή.
akĕczos, ekĕczos plu. tant. 'Egge'—W. 1. *acus, occa;* Boi. ὀξίνᾱ.
akĕju (**ekĕju**), **akĕti** (**ekĕti**) 'eggen'—K. *Egge* 2; W. *occa;* Boi. ὀξίνᾱ, (ὄγμος).
akĕtės plu. tant. 'Egge'—K. *Egge* 2; W. *occa.*
akýlas 'aufmerksam'—B. II, 1, 370.
akìs 'Auge'—Uh. *ákṣi;* K. *Auge;* F. *augō;* B. I, 153.547.589. II, 1, 132.173.577. 2, 202.455; W. *oculus;* Boi. ὄσσε.
ãkis 'Wuhne'—see *ãkas.*
akýtas 'äugig'—B. II, 1, 406. 3, 223.
akyvas 'mit Augen versehen, neugierig'—B. II, 1, 370.
ãklas 'blind'—B. II, 1, 361; W. *aquilus, (cocles);* Boi. ἄκαρον.
aklatis 'Blindheit' (Szyr.; Mielcke 'der Teufel')—B. II, 1, 438.
akmenýnas 'Steinhaufe'—B. II, 1, 278.649.
akmenìngas (B. -íngas) 'voll Steine'—B. II, 1, 510. Cf. Wied. 8.
akmenìnis 'steinern'—B. II, 1, 272.
akmenũtas 'steinig'—B. II, 1, 407.
akmũ 'Stein'—Uh. *áçmā;* K. *Hammer;* B. I, 129.546. II, 1, 238. 2, 295; Ber. *kamy;* W. *ācer, acervus;* Boi. ἄκμων, (κάμῑνος).
ãkrūtas 'Schiff'—Ber. *krǫtŭ.*
ãkstinas 'Stachel'—F. *ahana;* W. *ācer,* 1. *acus;* Boi. 1. ἄκαινα.
akstìs 'spitziges Stöckchen' (auf welches Fische zum Räuchern aufgespiesst werden)—W. *ācer, acus;* Boi. 1. ἄκαινα.
akũtas 'Granne'—K. *Ahne;* F. *ahana;* B. I, 546; W. *acus;* Boi. 1. ἄκαινα.
akũtas, akûtũtas 'hachelig, mit Grannen versehen'—B. I, 863.
aldìmiris 'Lärm'—see *armìderis.*

alẽjus 'Öl'—W. *olea.*
algà 'Lohn'—Uh. *arghás;* B. I, 424.464.591; Boi. ἀλφή.
álkanas 'hungrig'—B. II, 1, 268. See *álkstu.*
alkas 'heiliger Hain'—see *elkas.*
alksna 'Lache'—Uh. (Ntr.) *ṛjīṣás;* (Ber. *lachań*); W. *alga.* Cf. Bezz. BGLS. 270.
aĩksnis 'Eller, Erle'—see *eĩksnis.*
álkstu, álkti 'hungern'—K. *eilige* (*Zähne*); (W. *ulciscor*).
alkúnė, elkúnė 'Ellenbogen'—Uh. *aratníṣ, lakuṭas;* F. *aleina;* B. II, 1, 427; W. *lacertus, ulna;* Boi. λάξ, ὠλένη.
almens 'die aus dem toten Körper fliessende Feuchtigkeit' —see *eĩmės.*
almìderis 'Lärm'—see *armìderis.*
álnė 'Hirschkuh'—W. *alcē;* Boi. ἐλλός. See *élnė.* Cf. Lesk. Nom. 371.
alnis 'Hirsch'—Ber. *elenĭ.* Cf. Juškevič s. v. See *élnis.*
alóju, alóti 'hallo schreien'—W. *lallo.*
alpnas 'schwach, ohnmächtig'—Uh. *álpas;* W. *lepidus;* Boi. ἀλαπάζω.
alpstù, aĩpti 'ohnmächtig werden'— Uh. *álpas;* W. *lepidus;* Boi. ἀλαπάζω. Cf. Lesk. Abl. 374.
alunas 'Alaun'—K. *Alaun.* Cf. Ness. 5[a].
alùs 'Bier'—(K. *Bier*); B. II, 1, 181; W. *alūmen.*
alũju, alũti (Kur.) 'hallo schreien'—see *alóju.*
aĩvas 'Zinn'—B. II, 1, 201.388.
alvẽnas 'ein jeder'—F. *ala-brunsts.*
ãmalas, emalas (**ėmalas?**) 'Mispel'—Ber. *imela.* Cf. Lesk. Nom. 446.
ãmba 'Amme'—Uh. *ambā;* W. *amita.* Cf. Prell. deutsch. Best. in den lett. Spr. 53, BB. XXIII, 298.
anà 'jene'—fem. to *añs,* q. v.
anàs 'jener'—dial. for *añs,* q. v.
añginas 'grosse Schlange'—B. II, 1, 272.601.681.
angìs 'Schlange, Natter'—Uh. *áhiṣ;* B. I, 592. II, 1, 169; W. *anguis;* Boi. ἔγχελυς.
anglìs 'Kohle'—Uh. *áṅgāras;* B. II, 1, 383.

angu Old Lith. 'oder'—Ber. *-go.* Cf. Bezz. BGLS. 270.

anýta 'Schwiegermutter'—K. *Ahn;* W. *anus, amita.*

ánka 'Schlinge'—Uh. *áñcati;* F. *hals-agga;* Ber. *ęčaja;* W. *ancus;* Boi. ἀγκών.

añkstas in **ìsz añksto** 'von früh an'—Uh. *aktúṣ;* F. *ūhtwō;* B. II, 1, 435; W. *nox.* See *ankstì.*

ankstì 'früh, morgens, früh im Jahr'—Uh. *aktúṣ;* F. *ūhtwō;* B. II, 2, 745; W. *nox,* (*aquilus*); Boi. ἀκτίς, νύξ.

ankstýbas 'von früher Art' (e.g. **ankstýbos ropùtės** 'Frühkartoffeln')—F. 2. * *-ba;* B. II, 1, 389.

ankstùs adj. 'früh'—F. *ūhtwō.*

añksztas adj. 'eng'—Uh. *áṁhas;* F. *aggwus;* B. I, 161.387. II, 1, 514.519; W. *ango, angor;* Boi. ἄγχω.

anksztiraĩ plu. 'Finnen, Engerlinge'—K. *Engerling;* W. *anguis.* Cf. Lesk. Abl. 329.

anõks 'von jener Art'—B. II, 1, 498.

anót(e) 'entsprechend, gemäss'—B. II, 2, 732.799; W. *an-.*

añs (dial. **anàs** LBLV. 304), fem. **anà** 'jener, jene'—Uh. *ana-;* F. *anþar, jains;* B. I, 387. II, 2, 336.337; W. *enim;* Boi. ἐκεῖνος.

ansaĩ 'jener'—B. II, 2, 346.

anszas 'Haken'—B. II, 1, 150; (Boi. 1. ὄγκος). See *vą́szas* & Geitler LS. 76.

añt, anta (Old Lith. Cf. Bezz. BGLS. 271) 'auf, zu'—Uh. *ánti;* F. *and;* B. I, 158.719. II, 2, 802.803.805; W. *ante;* Boi. ἀντί.

anta Old Lith. 'auf, zu'—see prec.

antënà 'Entenfleisch'—B. II, 1, 277.278; W. *anas.*

antìkė 'Entchen'—(F. *anda-nēm*); B. II, 1, 488.

añtis 'Busen'—W. *ante.*

ántis 'Ente'—Uh. *ātíṣ;* K. *Ente* 1; B. I, 178.419. II, 1, 171.219; W. *anas;* Boi. νῆσσα.

añtras 'andrer, zweiter'—Uh. 2. *ántaras;* K. *ander;* F. *anþar;* B. II, 1, 326. 2, 53(twice).336.795.

anżûlas dial. 'Eiche'—B. II, 1, 370. See *ążûlas* & cf. Ness. 13[b], Bezz. BGLS. 271.

ap-, api-, apy- 'um'—B. II, 2, 839.840; W. *ob;* Boi. ὄπι-θε(ν).

apaczà 'der untere Teil, Fuss' (des Berges)—B. II, 2, 806; W. *ab.*

apaczõ 'drunten'—B. II, 2, 707.

apdangà 'Kleidung'—Ber. *dǫgŭ.*

apdumiù, apdùmti 'mit Sand oder Schnee betragen' (vom Winde)—see *dumiù.*

apẽ 'circum, de'—B. II, 2, 839.840.843; W. *ob;* Boi. ὄπι-θε(ν).

apgaliù, apgalė́ti 'überwinden, überwältigen'—see *galiù.*

apgintis 'Verteidigung'—B. I, 416. Cf. Lesk. Abl. 326, Lesk. Nom. 548.

apgirtis 'kleiner Rausch, Betrunkener'—B. II, 1, 434.

api-, apy- 'um'—see *ap-.*

apýbrėszkis 'Morgendämmerung'—Uh. *márīciș;* F. *bralv;* Ber. *brěskŭ* 1; W. *flagro;* Boi. φορκός. Cf. Lesk. Abl. 371.

apýdaira 'Vorsicht'—B. II, 1, 350.

apýdairus 'vorsichtig'—B. II, 1, 385. Cf. Ness. 143[b].

apýlanka adv. 'auf Umwegen'—B. II, 2, 713; Ber. *lǫka.*

apýlankomis adv. id.—B. II, 2, 718; Ber. *lǫka.*

apylasus 'wählerisch'—(Ber. *lasŭ*). Cf. Lesk. Abl. 363.

apyneĩ plu. 'Hopfen'—B. I, 339. Cf. Schleicher LSpr. II, 254.

apývaizda 'Vorsehung'—B. II, 1, 155.

apjenkù, apjèkti 'erblinden; verblendet, betört werden'—see *jenkù.*

apkãpinu, apkãpinti (das Land) 'mit Grenzhügeln umgeben'—Ber. *kopa.*

apkė̃żęs perf. act. part. 'im Wachstum zurückgeblieben'—B. II, 3, 276. Cf. Kur. s. v. *kė̃żu* & Lesk. Abl. 371.

apkirė̃ti 'überdrüssig werden'—see *kirė̃ti.*

apsikrutù, apsikrutė̃ti 'seine Arbeit tun'—see *krutù.*

apkurkoti (?) 'mit Wassermoos überzogen werden'—Ber. *krěkŭ.* Cf. Bezz. LF. 131.

aplaidů 'desertor, nefarius'—B. II, 1, 308.
aplaupyti 'berauben'—see *laupyti*.
apliñk prep. 'um'—B. II, 2, 929.
aplinka 'Umgegend'—B. II, 2, 929.
aplinkas adj. 'umliegend'—B. II, 2, 71.
apliñkui 'herum, umher'—B. II, 2, 929.
apmaitinu, apmaitinti 'verwunden'—(Ber. 2. *mělǫ*).
ãpmaudas 'Verdruss'—(F. *af-mauiþs*); Boi. μῦθος.
apmetaĩ plu. tant. 'Aufzuggarn, Schergarn'—Ber. *metǫ* 1; B. II, 1, 155.
apninkù, apnìkti 'überfallen'—see *ninkù*.
appiáuju, appiáuti 'beschneiden'—W. *praepūtium*. See *piáuju*.
appiauklas 'abgeschnittene Vorhaut'—W. *praepūtium*. Cf. Lesk. Abl. 305.
aprėpiu, aprėpti (W. also **aprepėti**) 'umfassen, begreifen' —B. II, 3, 194.365; W. *rapio;* Boi. ἐρέπτομαι. Cf. Bezz. LF. 163.
apskritùs adj. 'rund'—W. *curvus;* Boi. 2. κίρκος. Cf. Lesk. Abl. 283.
ãpstas 'Überfluss, Vorrat'—W. *ops;* Boi. ὄμπνη.
apstùmas 'Fülle, Reichlichkeit'—W. *ops;* Boi. ὄμπνη.
apstùs adj. 'reichlich'—W. *ops;* Boi. ὄμπνη.
apsukalas 'Türangel'—W. 2. *sucula*. Cf. Lesk. Abl. 310-311.
apsisvẽtinu, apsisvẽtinti 'sich bekannt machen'—(W. *satelles*).
apszankinù, apszankìnti (**kumẽlę**) '(eine Stute) bespringen lassen'—see *szankinù*.
apszvaista 'Reinheit'—B. II, 1, 416.
apszvaita id.—F. *hveits;* B. II, 3, 269. Cf. Lesk. Abl. 287.
apszvëczù, apszvẽsti 'umleuchten, beleuchten'—W. *ob*. See *szvëczù*.
aptvaras 'Gehege'—Uh. *toraṇam;* B. II, 1, 150; W. *pariēs;* Boi. σορός.
apurnoju, apurnoti 'bewickeln'—Uh. *ūrṇóti*.

apuszė 'Espe'—Ber. *asika;* B. II, 1, 544. Cf. Lesk. Nom. 599.

apuszis id.—B. II, 1, 544. See prec.

ãpvalkalas 'Anzug'—B. II, 1, 365.619.

apvalùs 'rund'—Uh. *válati;* F. *walus;* B. I, 339; W. *vallēs, volvo;* (Boi. αὐλός (note)). Cf. Lesk. Abl. 354.

apveikiù, apveĩkti 'bezwingen'—see *veikiù.*

àpveizdas 'Vorsehung'—B. II, 1, 155. Cf. Lesk. Abl. 288.

apvìlstu, apvìlti 'täuschen'—Uh. *véllati, (vṛ́thā).* See *privìlstu.*

apvynei plu. 'Hopfen'—B. I, 339. Cf. Schleicher LSpr. II, 256.

apvynióju, apvynióti 'bewickeln, umwinden'—B. I, 339.

ar̃ interrog. particle—Boi. ἆρα.

ãras 'Adler'—see *ẽras.*

arbonas 'Rind'—F. *arbaiþs, (arbi).*

ardaĩ or **ar̃dai** plu. 'Stangengerüst zum Flachstrocknen'—B. II, 3, 138; W. *radius.* Cf. Lesk. Nom. 586, Lesk. Abl. 329.

ardamas 'Spriet, Segelstange'—W. *radius.*

ardaũ, ardýti 'spalten, trennen'—Uh. *árdhas;* B. II, 2, 735 (twice); W. *rārus, radius;* Boi. ἀραιός.

ardìmelis 'Lärm'—see *armìderis.*

ar̃dvas 'geräumig'—B. II, 1, 204. See *er̃dvas.*

arẽlis 'Adler'—B. II, 1, 364; Boi. ὄρνις. See *erẽlis.*

ariù, árti 'pflügen'—(K. *Art*); F. *arjan;* B. I, 285; W. *aro;* Boi. ἀρόω. Cf. Lesk. Abl. 372.

arkė 'Holzbock, Schaflaus'—Uh. *likṣā́.* Cf. Juškevič 107. See *erkė.*

arkilaĩ plu. 'Stangengerüst zum Flachstrocknen'—see next.

arklaĩ plu. id.—B. II, 3, 138; (Boi. ἄρκυς). Cf. Lesk. Abl. 330.

árklas 'Pflug'—F. *arjan;* B. I, 450. II, 1, 341.618; W. *arātrum, aro;* Boi. ἀρόω.

arklÿs 'Pferd'—B. II, 1, 189.197; W. *aro.* Cf. Lesk. Abl. 372.

armìdelis 'Lärm'—see next.
armìderis (**armìdelis, almìderis, ardìmelis, aldìmiris**) id. —Ber. *harmider*. Cf. Brückner SlFw. 82.
artì 'nahe'—B. I, 161. II, 2, 929; W. *ars;* Boi. ἄρτι.
artójis 'Pflüger'—B. II, 1, 196.588.616. See *ariù*.
árżûlas 'Eiche'—W. *argentum* (& Ntr.). Cf. Bezz. LF. 97.
ąsà 'Topfhenkel, Schleife beim Knotenschürzen'—(Uh. *áṁsas*); F. *ans;* B. II, 1, 540; W. *ānsa, ampla;* Boi. 1. ἄμη.
ãsilas 'Esel'—K. *Esel;* W. *asinus*.
asilẽnė 'Eselin'—B. II, 1, 279.
àsys 'Schachtelhalm, Binsen'—W. *arista*. Cf. Bezz. LF. 97.
aslà 'Fussboden'—B. II, 1, 623; (W. *ārea*).
ąsótas 'gehenkelt'—see next.
ąsũtas (W. **ąsótas**) id.—B. II, 1, 407; *ānsātus* (s. v. *ānsa*).
àsz, Old Lith. **esz** 'ich'. Other first pers. pron. forms separately indexed.—Uh. *ahám;* K. *ich;* F. *ik;* B. I, 939. II, 2, 382.427; Ber. *azŭ;* W. *ego;* Boi. ἐγώ.
aszakà 'Fischgräte'—B. II, 1, 494; W. *ācer;* Boi. 1. ἄκαινα.
aszarà 'Träne'—Uh. *áçru;* F. *tagr;* W. *lacrima;* Boi. δάκρυ, (ὀκρυόεις).
aszìs 'Achse'—Uh. *ákṣas;* K. *Achse;* B. I, 158.561.568. II, 1, 170. 2, 129; W. *axis;* Boi. ἄξων, ἅμαξα.
aszmainis 'Achtel'—B. II, 2, 73.
aszmalëkas 'achtzehnter'—B. II, 2, 60. Cf. Ness. 11[a].
ãszmas 'achter'—Uh. *aṣṭā;* B. I, 717. II, 1, 225. 2, 56; W. *octo;* Boi. ὀκτώ.
ãszmens plu. 'Schneide'—see next.
aszmũ, plu. **ãszmens** 'Schneide, Schärfe'—Uh. *áçmā;* B. II, 1, 240; W. *ācer;* Boi. ἄκμων.
aszrùs, asztras, asztrùs 'scharf'—Uh. *açrá-;* F. *ahs, (tagr);* B. I, 160.546.548.568.786. II, 1, 350.385; W. *ācer;* Boi. 1. ἄκαινα. Cf. Lesk. Nom. 440.
asztuñtas 'achter'—B. I, 803. II, 2, 56. Cf. Wied. 157.8.
asztûnerì 'acht'—B. II, 2, 77. Cf. Wied. 158.

asztûnì 'acht'—Uh. *aṣṭā́;* K. *acht;* F. *ahtau;* B. I, 140.548. II, 2, 18.19; W. *octo;* Boi. ὀκτώ.

asztûniólika 'achtzehn'—see prec. & [K. *elf*]; [F. *ainlif*]; B. II, 2, 26.[27]; [Ber. *-lěkŭ*]; [W. *linquo*]. Cf. Wied. 156.

aszvà, Old Lith. **eschwa** (**eszva**) 'Stute'—Uh. *áçvas;* (K. *Ross* 1); F. *aihvatundi;* B. I, 296.338.551 (& Ntr. XLVII).557. II, 1, 161.207. 2, 114; W. *equus;* Boi. ἵππος.

at Ausruf der Verachtung—W. *attāt.*

at-, ata-, ati-, ato- 'zurück-, ab-, her-'—B. II, 2, 844.845. 846; W. *at, (ad).*

atdusas 'Seufzer'—Ber. *duchŭ.* Cf. Lesk. Abl. 296.

ãtdūsis id.—Ber. *dychajǫ.* Cf. Lesk. Abl. 296.

atdvastis 'Atmen'—Ber. *duchŭ.*

ateigà 'Ankunft'—B. II, 1, 507.

atgẽbau (?) pret. 'ich habe hervorgebracht'—Ber. *gabajǫ.* Cf. Lesk. Nom. 253.

atgimas 'Wiedergeburt'—B. II, 1, 155. Cf. Lesk. Nom. 164.

atgrąžas 'Wiederholung'—B. II, 1, 155.

atgrįstù, atgrìsti 'überdrüssig werden'—see *grįstù.*

ati- —see *at-.*

atis 'Steinbutte'—W. *attilus;* Boi. ἐτελίς.

atkaklus 'halsstarrig'—B. II, 1, 385. Cf. Lesk. Nom. 260.

àtkalta, atkaltẽ 'Rückenlehne, Brustlehne'—Uh. 2. *kā́ṭas;* F. *wilja-halþei;* Ber. *kloňǫ;* (W. *clīno*); Boi. κῶλον. Cf. Geitler LS. 78, Bezz. LF. 97, Lesk. Abl. 373, Lesk. Nom. 542.

atkartóju, atkartóti 'wiederholen'—B. II, 3, 215.

atsikõlti (?) 'sich anlehnen'—Uh. 2. *kā́ṭas;* F. *wilja-halþei;* Boi. κῶλον. Cf. Kur. DLWb. s. v. anlehnen, lehnen & Lesk. Abl. 373, 416.

ãtkriczos plu. 'Rückfall'—B. II, 1, 185(twice).635. Cf. Kur. s. v.

atsikustù, atsikùsti 'sich aufrütteln'—see *kuntù.*

atlagaĩ plu. 'lange brach gelegener Acker'—F. *ligan;* Ber. *logŭ;* W. *lectus;* Boi. λέχος.

ãtlaikas 'Überrest'—Uh. *rěkas;* F. *leihvan, iþ;* B. I, 178. II, 1, 150; W. *at;* Ber. *-lěkŭ.*

ãtlankas 'Rückbiegung'—B. II, 1, 152.

ãtlëkas 'Überrest'—B. I, 191.621. II, 1, 150; Ber. *-lěkŭ;* Boi. λείπω. See *ãtlaikas, lẽkas.*

ãtlykis 'Arbeitspause'—Ber. *-lěkŭ.*

atmaina, ãtmainas 'Tausch, Wechsel'—B. II, 1, 257.635; Ber. *měna.* See *maĩnas* & Lesk. Abl. 278, Lesk. Nom. 364.

ãtmigas 'Nachschlaf'—Ber. *migŭ.* Cf. Lesk. Abl. 278.

atmintìs 'Gedächtnis'—Uh. *matíṣ;* F. *ga-minþi, ga-munds;* B. I, 100.398. II, 1, 173.430.633. 2, 100.129; Ber. *-męti;* W. *mens;* Boi. μέμονα.

atmonà 'Andenken'—B. II, 1, 154.168.634. Cf. Lesk. Nom. 217.

ato- —see *at-*.

atólas, *attólas 'Nachheu, Grummet'—W. *tālea;* Boi. τᾶλις. Cf. Lesk. Nom. 179 & B. I, 816: "Baltisch-Slavisch."

atpeñcz 'im Gegenteil, dagegen'—B. II, 2, 742.

atpiauklas 'Abschnitzel'—B. II, 1, 344. See *appiauklas.*

atpirktójis 'Erlöser'—B. II, 1, 196.588. Cf. Kur. s. v.

atsiplaitau, atsiplaityti 'sich breit machen, prahlen'—Boi. πλαίσιον. Cf. Ness. 305[a] & Prell. s. v. πλαίσιον.

ãtrūgos (Lesk.) (Bezz. **àtrugas**) plu. 'das Aufstossen'—K. *räuspern* (the form *atrūgas* cited in K. 7th ed. is Lett., not Lith.). See *rúgiu* & Bezz. LF. 97, Lesk. Abl. 307, Lesk. Nom. 228, K. 8th ed. s. v. räuspern.

àtsailė 'Verbindungsstange (oder -strang) am Wagen'—Uh. *syáti;* F. *in-sailjan;* B. II, 1, 364; W. *saeta;* Boi. ἱμάς. Cf. Bezz. LF. 97 & Lesk. Abl. 282.

atsainus 'nachlässig'—F. *sainjan;* B. II, 1, 291; W. *sērus;* Boi. ἥσυχος.

atsajà 'die Stränge des Pferdes'—B. I, 288. Cf. Geitler LS. 78, Bezz. LF. 97, Lesk. Nom. 224.

ãtsala 'Sandbank im Meere'—W. *insula*. Cf. Juškevič 144.
àtseilis 'das vom Schwengel an die Achse gehende Eisen'—B. II, 1, 364. Cf. *àtsailė* & Bezz. LF. s. v. àtsaile, Lesk. Nom. 458.
atsẽkiu, atsẽkti 'erreichen'—Boi. ἵκω. See *sẽkiu*.
atsektas pret. pass. part. of **sekù**, q. v., 'aufgefunden'—B. II, 1, 396; Boi. ἕπομαι (note).
at-si-(kõlti &c.)—see under *at-(kõlti* &c.).
atskaida 'Abteilung, Kapitel'—B. I, 177. Cf. *skẽdžu* 'scheide' & Geitler LS. 78, Lesk. Nom. 224.
atskirai adv. 'abgesondert'—B. I, 467.
àtskrabai plu. 'Abfall von Zeug'—W. *scrobis*. Cf. Bezz. LF. 97-98, Lesk. Nom. 172.
atsodà 'Absatz am Gebäude'—B. I, 151.485. II, 1, 153. Cf. Lesk. Abl. 341.
atsparas 'Widerstand'—Uh. *spṛṇóti*. Cf. Lesk. Nom. 172.
atstùs adj., **atstù** adv. 'entfernt'—Uh. *suṣṭhús*; B. II, 1, 177; Boi. σταυρός.
atszlaimas 'Vorhof'—B. II, 1, 249; Ber. *klěti, kloňq*. Cf. Lesk. Abl. 286.
atszlainas 'Vorhof, Erker'—B. II, 1, 258. See next & Ness. 12[a], Lesk. Nom. 361.
atszlainis 'Erker', "in Samogitien ein geringer Anbau an ein Gebäude"—B. I, 188; Ber. *klěti, kloňq*; W. *clīno*; Boi. κλίνω. Cf. Lesk. Abl. 286, Lesk. Nom. 361.
atszleĩmas 'Vorhof'—see *atszlaimas*. Cf. LBLV. 331 & Lesk. Abl. 286 (read LB 173 for LB 373).
***attólas** 'Nachheu, Grummet'—see *atólas*.
àtveriu, atvérti 'öffnen'—see *veriù*.
ãtvėtos plu. 'beim Windigen, Worfeln Zurückbleibendes'—B. II, 1, 409. 3, 214. Cf. *vẽtau*.
atżvilga 'Rückblick, Rücksicht'—B. II, 1, 634. See *żvelgiù*.
au- pref.—B. II, 2, 809.
audeklas 'Gewebe'—B. II, 1, 344. On accent cf. Lesk. Nom. 498.
áudmi 'ich webe'—see *áudżu*.

áudra 'Sturm, Tosen, Flut'—Uh. *ódma;* B. II, 1, 379; W. *ventus* (thrice), (*unda*); Boi. αὔρᾱ (& note). Cf. Hirt Ablaut 383, 662.
áudżu (**áudmi**), **áusti** 'weben'—Uh. *ótuṣ;* B. II, 1, 253; W. *vieo;* Boi. ὀθόνη. Cf. Lesk. Abl. 313.
augestis 'Wuchs'—B. II, 1, 439. Cf. Lesk. Nom. 579.
auginù, augìnti 'erziehen'—Uh. *ójas;* B. II, 3, 313.
augla 'Wachstum'—(Ber. *modla*); B. II, 1, 365. Cf. Lesk. Nom. 454.
auglas 'Wachstum, Trieb'—B. II, 1, 365. Cf. Lesk. Nom. 451.
auglis 'Wachstum, Schössling'—B. II, 1, 384.620; Ber. *kašlĭ.* Cf. Lesk. Nom. 460.
augmũ 'Wachstum, Auswuchs'—Uh. *ojmā́;* F. *aukan, aldōma;* B. I, 193.681; W. *augeo;* Boi. αὔξω.
augonis 'Geschwür'—B. II, 1, 638. See *áugu* & Geitler LS. 79, Bezz. LF. 98.
áugu, áugti 'wachsen'—Uh. *ójas;* K. *auch, Wucher;* F. *aukan;* B. I, 211.493.574. II, 1, 435.444. 3, 262.405; Ber. *jugŭ, jutro;* W. *augeo;* Boi. αὔξω. Cf. Lesk. Abl. 314.
auklẽ 'Fussbinde'—B. II, 1, 341; (W. *ocrea*); Boi. ὑφή.
áuksas 'Gold'—W. *aurum.*
áuksinas 'golden'—B. II, 1, 272.665 (twice).
aukszinis 'Rauchloch, Kamin'—F. *auhns;* W. *aulla.*
aukszlis 'Düte oder Schachtel aus Baumrinde'—(W. *aulla*).
áuksztas 'hoch'—Uh. *úkṣati;* F. *auhuma;* B. I, 200.493. 574.785. II, 1, 372.519. 3, 339; Ber. *jugŭ;* W. *augeo, augustus;* Boi. αὔξω, (αἶπος).
auksztỹbė 'Höhe'—B. II, 1, 643. See prec.
auksztimai plu. 'Mieder'—B. II, 1, 251.
auksztỹn adv. 'nach oben, in die Höhe'—see *auksztyniui.*
auksztỹnaika adv. 'rücklings, nach oben gebeugt'—(Ber. *gybǫ*).
auksztyniui, auksztỹn adv. 'nach oben, in die Höhe'—B. II, 2, 703 (twice). Cf. Ness. 16*, Lesk. Nom. 411.

aũksztis 'Höhe'—B. II, 1, 251 (twice).
aũlas 'Stiefelschaft'—B. II, 1, 365; (Ber. *červo*); W. *alvus;* Boi. αὐλός.
aulinkai 'fernerhin, später'—F. *us;* B. II, 2, 809; W. *au;* Boi. αὔτως.
aulỹs 'Bienenstock'—W. *alvus;* Boi. αὐλός.
aunù, aũti 'Fussbekleidung anziehen'—B. II, 3, 320.339; W. *exuo,* (*ocrea*); Boi. ἐνδύμα. Cf. Lesk. Abl. 319.
aurè 'dort, künftighin'—B. II, 2, 337.342; (W. *eccere*).
ausczoju, ausczoti 'schwatzen, munkeln'—see *auszczůju.*
ausìs, dual ausì, 'Ohr'—Uh. *ás;* K. *Ohr;* F. *ausō;* B. I, 193.772. II, 1, 132.157.173. 2, 202.455; W. *auris;* Boi. οὖς.
auszczůju (ausczoju), auszczůti (ausczoti) 'schwatzen, munkeln'—B. I, 173. II, 1, 404; W. *ōs.*
auszrà 'Morgenröte'—Uh. *uṣar-;* K. *Osten;* B. I, 198.493. II, 1, 160.347.625; Ber. *jutro;* W. *aurōra;* Boi. αὔριον.
aũszta 3rd pers. sing., aũszti 'hell werden, tagen'—Uh. *ucchấti;* (F. *wis*); B. I, 558.568.725. II, 3, 75.352; Ber. *jutro;* W. *aurōra;* Boi. 1. ἕως. Cf. Lesk. Abl. 319.
áusztu, áuszti 'kalt oder kühl werden'—W. (Ntr.) *autumnus.* Cf. Lesk. Abl. 319.
autavas, autuvas 'Schuhwerk'—B. II, 1, 162.449.620.
áużůlas 'Eiche'—B. II, 1, 370; W. *argentum* & [Ntr.].
aużůlýnas 'Eichenwäldchen, Eichicht'—B. II, 1, 278.
avikė, avikỹnė 'Schafstall'—B. II, 1, 487. Cf. Lesk. Nom. 512.
avilỹs 'Bienenstock'—W. *alvus* (twice); Boi. αὐλός.
ãvinas 'Widder'—B. II, 1, 272.601; W. *ovis;* Boi. ὄϊς. See *avìs.*
avýnas 'Oheim'—K. *Oheim;* F. *awō;* B. I, 304. II, 1, 278; W. *avus.*
avinẽlis 'Böcklein'—B. II, 1, 370.672.
avìs 'Schaf'—Uh. *áviṣ;* K. *Aue,* (*Schaf*); F. *awēpi,* [*awistr*]; B. I, 94.153.317. II, 1, 169. 2, 129; W. *ovis;* Boi. ὄϊς.

aviù, avė̃ti 'Fussbekleidung tragen'—B. I, 338. II, 3, 153. 180-181.193; W. *exuo;* Boi. ἐννῦμι. Cf. Lesk. Abl. 319.
avižà 'Hafer'—B. II, 1, 506; W. *avēna;* Boi. 2. αἰγίλωψ.
avižáinis adj. 'aus Hafer'—B. II, 1, 279.665.
avižis masc. 'Maikäfer' (Kur. fem. 'Libelle'), plu. **avižiai**— W. (Ntr.) *avis.* Cf. Lesk. Nom. 303.
ażeras 'Teich'—see *ẽżeras.*
ażu East Lith. 'für, hinter'—B. II, 2, 846(twice).847.850. 851.
ażůt 'anstatt'—B. II, 2, 732.846. Cf. Lalis 44.

B

bà 'ja, sehr wohl'—Uh. *bā́ṭ;* F. 1. **-ba;* Ber. *ba;* Boi. φή.
bãbkas 'Lorbeer, Pfeffernuss'—(W. *bāca*). Cf. Ness. 321[a].
bãbras Samog. 'Biber'—Uh. *babhrúṣ;* W. *fiber.* See *bẽbrus* & Kur. s. v. bė̃brus.
bãdas 'Hungersnot, Hunger'—Uh. *bā̆dhate;* F. *bida.*
badaũ, badýti 'stechen'—K. *Bett;* B. I, 156; Ber. *bodǫ;* W. *fodio;* Boi. βόθρος.
badù, badė́ti 'Hunger leiden'—B. I, 156.
baidaũ, baidýti 'scheuchen'—(Uh. *bā̆dhate*); F. *baidjan;* B. II, 1, 542; (Ber. *bědʼǫ*); (W. *boia*).
baigiù, baĩgti 'beendigen'—(W. *fīnis*).
bailùs 'furchtsam, scheu'—Uh. *bhīrúṣ;* B. II, 1, 384.
báimė 'Furcht'—Uh. *bhīmás;* K. *beben;* B. II, 1, 125; Ber. *bojǫ.* Cf. Lesk. Abl. 271.
baisà 'Schrecken'—Uh. *bhīṣáyate;* B. I, 492. II, 1, 542; Ber. *běsŭ;* Boi. πίθηκος. See *baisùs.*
baisỹbė 'Schrecklichkeit'—B. II, 1, 643. Cf. Bezz. LF. 98.
baisioju, baisioti (?) 'beschmieren'—W. *foedus.* Cf. Juškevič 184.
baisùs 'schrecklich, abscheulich'—Uh. *bhīṣáyate;* B. II, 1, 542; Ber. *běsŭ;* W. *foedus, (bellua);* Boi. πίθηκος.
bajùs 'fürchterlich'—Uh. *bháyate;* K. *beben;* B. II, 1, 542; Ber. *bojǫ.*
balà 'Bruch, Torfmoor, sumpfige, öfter mit Gehölz be-

wachsene Strecke'—Uh. *jambālas;* B. I, 519; Ber. *bala, bolna 2, bolto;* W. *palūs.*
balanà 'Splint'—Ber. *bolna* 1.
balañdis (Kur., Lesk., B., W.; **-ánd-** Lesk., B., F.) masc., **balañdė** fem. '(wilde) Taube'—(F. *ahaks*); B. II, 1, 387.467.470; W. *blandus.* Cf. Lesk. Nom. 589.
balandžùkas, balandùkas 'Täubchen'—B. II, 1, 492. Cf. Lesk. Nom. 518.
baldas 'Stössel' (see Kur. s. v.)—Uh. *bhāṇḍam.*
báldau, báldyti 'Gepolter machen'—Uh. *bhāṇḍam.*
balgnas 'Sattel'—B. II, 1, 263. Cf. Bezz. BGLS. 274, Lesk. Nom. 360.
bal̃nas id.—B. I, 719. II, 1, 263.
balnis 'Weissschimmel'—B. II, 1, 256. Cf. Lesk. Nom. 355.
bal̃nius 'Sattler'—B. II, 1, 224.
bal̃sas 'Stimme, Ton, Melodie'—Uh. *bhāṣate;* K. *bellen;* B. I, 430.459.473.778. II, 1, 539.636. 3, 338.340; Ber. *golsŭ.* See *bilstu.*
balsvas 'weisslich'—B. II, 1, 201; Boi. φαλός. Cf. Lesk. Nom. 345.
báltas 'weiss'—Uh. *bhālam;* K. *Belche 2, Gold;* (F. *balþaba*); B. II, 1, 173.413.662; Ber. *bělŭ, (bolto);* W. *fullo, fānum;* Boi. φαλός.
baltẽsnis 'weisser'—B. II, 1, 561.
báltymas 'das Weisse im Auge'—B. II, 1, 250.
baltìnis adj. 'von weisser Art'—B. II, 1, 273.
bal̃tis 'Weisse'—B. II, 1, 173.
baltulis 'candidulus'—B. II, 1, 368.676. Cf. Lesk. Nom. 492.
baltumà 'weisse Stelle'—B. II, 1, 250.
bąlù, bálti (Kur., B., Ber., W.; **bālù** B., Lesk.) 'weiss werden'—Uh. *bhālam;* B. I, 389. II, 3, 137; Ber. *bělŭ;* W. *fullo.* Cf. Lesk. Abl. 372.
balvõnas 'Götze'—Ber. *balvanŭ;* W. *fallo* 1).
balžẽna 'Längebalken an der Egge', **balžẽnas** 'Querbalken an der Egge, am Wagen'—Ber. *bolzĭno;* W. *sufflāmen;* Boi. φάλαγξ. Cf. Ness. 320[b].

bámba 'Nabel'—Uh. *bimbas;* Ber. *bǫbŭlŭ;* Boi. βέμβιξ.
bam̃balas 'Knirps'—Uh. *bimbas;* Ber. *bǫbŭlĭ;* Boi. βέμβιξ.
bambù, bambė́ti 'in den Bart brummen'—Uh. *bambharas;* B. I, 512; Ber. *bǫbĭnŭ;* W. *babit, bombus;* Boi. βαβαί, βόμβος.
bandà 'Viehherde'—Uh. *badhnā́ti, bandhás;* W. *offendimentum;* Boi. πεῖσμα.
bandaũ, bandýti 'versuchen'—B. II, 3, 266.
bañdymas 'das Versuchen'—B. II, 3, 266.
bangà 'Welle'—Uh. *bhañgás, bhanákti;* B. II, 1, 150. 3, 278 (read *bangà* for *bongà*).294; Ber. *bag(ŭ)no;* W. *frango.* Cf. Lesk. Abl. 320.
bãras 'Stück Feld bei den Schnittern, das sie in einem Zuge schneiden'—Ber. *bor̂ǫ;* W. *forus.* See *barù.*
barbõžius 'Summer'—Uh. *barbaras;* B. II, 1, 506.511; W. *balbus;* Boi. βαρβαρόφωνος.
bariù, bárti 'schelten, schmähen'—see *barù.*
bárkszteriu (**bárkszteliu**), **bárkszterėti** (**bárkszteléti**) 'ein wenig klopfen'—B. I, 449. Cf. LBLV. 332.
barnìs 'Zank'—Uh. *bhrīṇā́ti;* F. *ahmateins;* B. II, 1, 287. 634; Ber. *bornĭ.* See *barù.*
barónas 'Schafbock'—Ber. *baranŭ.*
barskutis 'Bartschaber, Schermesser'—see *barzskutis.*
bar̃szczai plu. 'Roterübensuppe'—Ber. *bŭrščĭ.*
barù (**bariù**) (**bármi**), **bárti** 'schelten, schmähen'—Uh. *bhartsati, bhrīṇā́ti;* B. I, 481.513; Ber. *bor̂ǫ;* W. *ferio,* (*bāro*). Cf. Schleicher LSpr. II, 260 & Lesk. Abl. 372.
barzdà 'Bart'—Uh. *bardh-;* F. *bars;* Ber. *borda;* W. *barba.*
barzdótas (Kur. **barzdū́tas**) 'bärtig'—B. II, 1, 204.405. 664; W. *barba.* Cf. Lesk. Nom. 561.
barzskutis, barskutis 'Bartschaber, Schermesser'—B. I, 719. Cf. Schleicher LSpr. II, 260, Ness. 322[a], Bezz. BGLS. 90, 275. See *barzdà.*
bãsas 'barfüssig'—Uh. 1. *bábhasti, bhā́sati;* K. *bar;* B. II, 1, 166.510; Ber. *bosŭ;* (W. *fānum*) ; Boi. ψῆν.
bãsius 'Barfüssler'—B. II, 1, 224.

baubiù, baũbti 'brüllen' (vom Rinde)—W. *baubor;* Boi. βαΰζω.

-baudau, -baudyti—see *pasibaudyti* 'sich erheben, aufbrechen'.

baudinu, baudinti (?) 'exciter, éveiller l'envie de'—Boi. πεύθομαι. Cf. Juškevič 196.

baũdžava 'Scharwerk, Frondienst'—Ber. *bludǫ, buďǫ;* Boi. πεύθομαι.

baudžiù, baũsti 'zurechtweisen, strafen, züchtigen'—Uh. *bódhati;* K. *bieten,* 1. *Beutel;* B. I, 192.202. II, 3, 397; Ber. *bludǫ, buďǫ;* W. (Ntr.) *confūto;* Boi. πεύθομαι.

bauginù, baugìnti 'ängstigen, schrecken, scheuchen'—W. *fugio;* Boi. φεύγω.

baugulis 'Furcht'—B. II, 1, 368. Cf. Lesk. Nom. 491.

baugùs 'furchtsam'—Uh. *bhujáti;* F. *biugan;* B. I, 596.631; (Ber. *lękǫ*); W. *fugio;* Boi. φεύγω.

bausmė̃ 'Zucht, Strafe'—B. II, 1, 253.

bãžmas 'Menge, Masse'—(Uh. *bahúṣ*). Cf. Lesk. Abl. 372.

bè prep. 'ohne'—Uh. *bahíṣ;* B. II, 2, 735.810.811; Ber. *bezŭ.*

be- verb. pref. indicating duration 'noch, immer fort'—B. II, 2, 811; Ber. *besěda.*

bėbrìnis adj. 'vom Biber'—B. II, 1, 272.274; W. *fiber.*

bẽbrus (**bebrùs, bė̃brus,** Samog. **bãbras**) 'Biber'—Uh. *babhrúṣ;* K. *Biber;* B. I, 448.518. II, 1, 129; Ber. *bebrŭ;* W. *fiber.* Cf. Lesk. Nom. 434.

bedu, bedėti (?) 'graben'—K. *Bett;* F. *badi;* B. I, 156 (note); Ber. *bodǫ;* W. *fodio;* Boi. βόθρος, (εὐνή). Cf. Lesk. Abl. 360.

bėgas 'Lauf, Flucht'—B. II, 1, 154; Ber. *běgnǫ;* Boi. φέβομαι. See *bė̃gu.*

bėgìmas 'das Laufen'—B. II, 1, 251.632.

bė̃gis 'Lauf, Flucht'—Ber. *běgnǫ;* Boi. φέβομαι. See *bėgas.*

bė̃gu (**bė̃gmi**), **bė̃gti** 'laufen, fliehen'—F. *and-bahts;* B. I, 590.621. II, 3, 98.123; Ber. *běgnǫ;* W. *fugio;* Boi. φέβομαι. Cf. Ness. 325[a], Lesk. Abl. 370.

beldesis 'Getöse'—B. II, 1, 637. See *beldu* & Bezz. BGLS. 275, Lesk. Nom. 593.

beldu, beldėti 'klopfen'—Uh. *bhāṇḍam.* See *bìldu* & Lesk. Abl. 320.

Lett. **bemberis** 'Tannzapfen'—W. *fimbria* (read lett. for lit.). Cf. Lesk. Nom. 444, BB. XXI, 236.

beñdras 'Teilhaber, Genosse'—Uh. *badhnâti, bándhuṣ;* F. *bindan;* B. I, 345.523. II, 1, 357; W. *offendimentum,* (*necto*); Boi. πεῖσμα.

bendróvė 'Genossenschaft'—see prec. & Ber. *dǫbrava.* Cf. Lesk. Nom. 352.

bengiù, beñgti 'beenden'—(W. *fīnis*). Cf. Lesk. Abl. 320.

bė́ras 'braun'—Uh. *babhrúṣ,* 1. *bhallas;* K. *Bär* 2, *braun,* [*Biber*]; Ber. *bebrŭ, bronŭ;* W. *fiber;* Boi. φρύνη, φορκός, ὀφρῦς.

beriù, beȓti 'streuen'—Ber. *bĭrlogŭ;* (W. 2. *frons*). Cf. Lesk. Abl. 321.

bérnas 'Jüngling, Knecht'—F. *barn;* B. II, 1, 261; W. *fero;* Boi. φερνή, -φρήσω.

berniokas 'Bursche'—B. II, 1, 501. Cf. Lesk. Nom. 514.

bérniszkas 'knechtisch'—F. *barnisks;* B. II, 1, 667. See *bérnas.*

bėrokas 'Brauner' (Pferd)—B. II, 1, 501. Cf. Lesk. Nom. 513 & *bė́ras.*

bérszta, bérszti (?) 3rd pers. pres. 'es (das Getreide) fängt an weiss zu werden'—Uh. *bhrâjati;* F. *bairhts;* B. I, 493.545.566. II, 1, 413; Ber. *berza;* W. *flagro;* Boi. φορκός. Cf. Lesk. Abl. 368.

béržas 'Birke'—Uh. *bhūrjas;* K. *Birke;* B. I, 450.548.991; Ber. *berza;* W. *fraxinus.* Cf. Lesk. Abl. 321.

berždžà 'gelt, unfruchtbar'—Ber. *berďa.*

bėskõgi 'also darum; es ist klar, warum . . .'—(W. *fānum*).

bėt 'aber, sondern'—B. II, 2, 811.

bẽzas 'Holunder'—Ber. *bŭzŭ.*

bẽzdas id.—Ber. *bŭzŭ.*

bẽzdas 'crepitus ventris'—B. II, 1, 155. Cf. Lesk. Abl. 321.

bezdù, bezdė́ti 'pedere'—W. *pēdo.*
bezmė̃nas 'Schnellwage'—Ber. *bezmen.*
biaurė̃stis 'Greuel, Scheusal'—B. II, 1, 439. See *biaurùs.*
biaurétuvas 'contaminator'—B. II, 1, 449. Cf. Lesk. Nom. 567.
biaurùs 'hässlich, unrein, greuelhaft'—W. *fū.*
biczùkas 'Bienchen'—B. II, 1, 672. See *bitìs* & Lesk. Nom. 518.
bijaũs, bijótis 'sich fürchten'—Uh. *bháyate;* K. *beben;* B. I, 521. II, 2, 76. 3, 168; Ber. *boję;* (W. *fūcus*). Cf. Lesk. Abl. 271.
bylà 'Rede'—B. II, 3, 215.266. See *bylóju.*
bildesis 'Gepolter'—B. II, 1, 637. See *bìldu.* On accent cf. Lesk. Abl. 320 & Lesk. Nom. 593.
bìldinu, bìldinti 'klopfen'—Uh. *bhāṇḍam;* Ber. *bĭltaję.* See *bìldu.*
bìldu, bildė́ti 'poltern'—Uh. *bhāṇḍam,* (*bháṇḍate*); K. *poltern;* Ber. *bĭltaję.* Cf. Lesk. Abl. 320.
bildùkas 'Polterer, Poltergeist'—Uh. *bhāṇḍam;* B. II, 1, 493. 616.
bilè, bìle " 'etwa, ob, vielleicht'; in Verbindung mit Interrogativa 'irgend', z. B. **bilè kàs** 'irgend wer.' "—Ber. *lc.*
bylóju, bylóti 'reden'—(Uh. *bháṇati*); B. II, 3, 215.266; (W. *fleo*). Cf. Lesk. Abl. 320.
bilstu, bilti 'zu reden anfangen'—(Uh. *bháṇati*); B. I, 459.778. II, 3, 338.371; (W. *fleo*). See *bal̃sas* & Lesk. Abl. 320.
bim̃balas 'Rosskäfer, Bremse'—Uh. *bambharas;* Ber. *bębĭnŭ;* W. *bombus;* Boi. *βόμβος, πεμφρηδών.* See *bambù* & Lesk. Abl. 320.
bim̃bilas id.—Uh. *bambharas;* Ber. *bębĭnŭ;* Boi. *βόμβος, πεμφρηδών.* See prec.
-bime opt. 1st plu. end.—Ber. *bytĭ.*
bingùs 'stattlich, mutig' (von Pferden)—(Uh. *bahúṣ*); B. I, 545; Boi. *παχύς.* Cf. Lesk. Abl. 320.
bir̃binas 'Schmeissfliege'—B. II, 1, 260; Ber. *bŭrbotŭ.*

birbỹnė 'Blaseinstrument, das einen schnarrenden oder summenden Ton gibt'—B. II, 1, 621. See next.
birbiù, biȓbti 'summen'—Uh. *barbaras;* Ber. *bŭrbotŭ;* W. *balbus, (fremo);* Boi. βαρβαρόφωνος, φόρμιγξ, (βάρβιτος). Cf. Lesk. Abl. 321.
bìrgelas 'une bière légère'—Boi. φρύγω. Cf. Juškevič 211.
birkal̃s 'Schiffspfund'—Ber. *berkovec.* Cf. Brückner SlFw. 72.
birkavas id.—see prec. Cf. Juškevič 211.
byrù, bìrti (B. bįrù, bírti) 'ausgestreut werden, ausfallen' —B. I, 389; Ber. *bĭrlogŭ.* Cf. Lesk. Abl. 321.
biȓžlis 'Birkenzweig'—Ber. *berza.* See *béržas* & Lesk. Abl. 321.
bìt 'er war'—see *biti.*
bìtė 'Biene'—see *bitìs.*
biti, bìt old & dial. pret. 3rd sing. (**esmì**) 'er war'—B. I, 294.339.518; Ber. *bytĭ;* W. *fio;* Boi. φῖτυ. See *búti* & Kur. Gram. 1106 & note.
bitìkė 'Bienchen'—B. II, 1, 488. Cf. Lesk. Nom. 511.
bìtinas 'Weisel'—B. II, 1, 272.
bitìs, bìtė 'Biene'—K. *Biene;* Ber. *bĭčela;* W. 2. *fūcus;* Boi. (Ntr.) βύκτης.
bitùkas 'Bienchen'—B. II, 1, 672. Cf. Lesk. Nom. 518.
blágnyjůs, blágnytis 'sich ausnüchtern; sich aufhellen'—Boi. φλέγω Cf. Juškevič 213.
blaiksztaũs, blaiksztýtis 'sich aufklären' (vom Himmel)—B. II, 3, 284; Ber. *blěskŭ.*
blaisvas 'nüchtern'—B. II, 1, 202. Cf. Lesk. Nom. 345-6.
blaivas 'hell, licht, nüchtern'—K. *Blei;* B. I, 718. II, 1, 201; Ber. *blědŭ.* Cf. Lesk. Nom. 345.
blaivaũs, blaivýtis 'sich aufklären' (vom Himmel)—Ber. *blědŭ.* See prec.
blakà 'schlechte Stelle in der Leinwand'—W. *flaccus;* Boi. βλάξ. Cf. Lesk. Nom. 214.
blãkė 'Wanze'—Ber. *bloska;* W. 1. *blatta.*

blandaũ, blandýti (akìs) '(die Augen) niederschlagen'—(Uh. *bradhnás*); K. *blind;* F. *blinds;* B. II, 3, 122. 251; Ber. *blędǫ, blǫdŭ.* Cf. Lesk. Abl. 321.
blandùs "bündig", 'nicht wässerig' (von der Suppe): see Lesk.—Ber. *blędǫ.* Cf. Lesk. Abl. 322.
blaszkaũ, blaszkýti 'hin und her, seitwärts schleudern'—W. *flagrum.* Cf. Lesk. Abl. 372.
blebenù, blebénti 'plappern, schwatzen'—Uh. *balbalākaroti;* Ber. *bĭlbŭ;* W. *balbus, blatero;* Boi. *βαβαί.*
blendżũs, blę̃stis 'sich verfinstern'—(Uh. *bradhnás*); K. *blind;* F. *blinds;* B. I, 422.449.521. II, 3, 122.138; Ber. *blędǫ.* Cf. Lesk. Abl. 321.
bliáuju, bliáuti 'brüllen'—Ber. *blujǫ;* (W. *spuo*). Cf. Lesk. Abl. 293.
blìgstu, blìgsti 'aufleuchten'—Uh. *bhrājati;* F. *bairhts;* W. *flagro.* See *blizgù* & Lesk. Abl. 290.
blyksztù, blỹkszti 'erbleichen'—B. II, 3, 284; Ber. *blĭskŭ;* Boi. *φλέγω.* See *blizgù* & Lesk. Abl. 271.
blynai plu. 'von feinem Buchweizen- oder Gerstenmehl bereitete Kuchen'—Ber. *mlinŭ.* Cf. Brückner SlFw. 72.
blį̃sta (3rd pers. sing.), **blį̃sti** 'Abend (dunkel) werden'—(Uh. *bradhnás*); K. *blind;* F. *blinds;* B. II, 3, 75; Ber. *blędǫ.* Cf. Lesk. Abl. 321.
blýszkiu, blyszkė́ti 'funkeln'—Ber. *blĭskŭ;* W. *flagro.* See *blizgù.*
bliũdas 'Schüssel'—F. *biuþs.* Cf. Brückner SlFw. 72.
bliũvù, bliúti 'in Brüllen oder Blöken ausbrechen'—B. II, 3, 137; Ber. *blujǫ.* Cf. Lesk. Abl. 293.
blìzgis 'Flitter'—W. *flagro.* See next.
blizgù, blizgė́ti 'flimmern'—Uh. *bhrājati;* F. *bairhts;* Ber. *blĭskŭ;* W. *flagro;* Boi. *φλέγω.* Cf. Lesk. Abl. 290.
blyzgũju, blyzgũti id.—Ber. *blĭskŭ.* See prec.
blõgas 'schwach, krank, schlecht'—Ber. *blagŭ;* W. *flaccus;* Boi. *βλάξ.*
bloszkiù, blõkszti 'seitwärts schleudern'—W. *flagrum.* Cf. Lesk. Abl. 372.

blúkstu (**blúksztu**), **blúkti** (**blúkszti**) 'schlaff, welk werden' (von den Muskeln)—Ber. *blĭknǫ;* W. *flaccus.* Cf. Ness. 342[a].

blusà 'Floh'—B. I, 873-4; Ber. *blŭcha;* W. *pūlex;* Boi. ψύλλα.

blužnãžolė 'Milzkraut'—B. II, 1, 91.

blužnẽ 'Milz'—W. *lien.* See next & Ness. 342[b], Sommer 178.

blužnìs id.—Uh. *plīhā́;* W. *lien;* Boi. σπλήν.

bóba 'altes Weib'—Ber. *baba;* W. *babit;* Boi. βαβαί. Cf. Brückner SlFw. 73.

bõbkas 'Pfeffernuss'—(W. *bāca*). Cf. Kur. s. v. *bãpkas.*

bodus 'ekelhaft'—B. II, 3, 349. See next.

bódžiůs (Ness., Kur., Uh., W.; **bodžũs** Schleicher, Lesk.), **bóstis** (**bodė̃tis**) 'sich vor etwas ekeln'—Uh. *bībhatsate;* W. *fastīdium.* Cf. Lesk. Abl. 376.

boginù, bogìnti 'flüchten, wohin jagen'—B. I, 621; (Ber. *bagajǫ*). Cf. Lesk. Abl. 370.

bóju, bóti 'wonach fragen, Rücksicht nehmen, beachten'—B. I, 166. II, 3, 409; W. *fābula.* Cf. Lesk. Nom. 457.

bõstras 'Bastard'—Ber. *baster.*

bostrukė id.—see prec. & Kur. s. v.

bradà 'Waten, Pfütze'—Ber. *bredǫ, brodŭ.* See *bredù* & Lesk. Abl. 322.

brãdas 'Watnetz; Fischereigesellschaft, mit beiden Kähnen, dem Netz und allem Gerät'; **bradaĩs žvejũti** 'mit dem Schleppnetz fischen'—B. II, 1, 152; Ber. *brodŭ,* [*bredǫ*]. See *bredù* & Lesk. Nom. 167.

bradaũ, bradýti 'waten'—B. II, 3, 214; Ber. *bredǫ, brodŭ.* See *bredù* & Lesk. Abl. 322.

brádžoju—see *bráidžoju.*

braidaũ, braidýti 'fortgesetzt umherwaten'—Ber. *bredǫ.* See *bredù* & Lesk. Abl. 322.

bráidžoju (**brádžoju**), **bráidžoti** (**brádžoti**) 'waten'—B. II, 3, 240. See *bredù* & Lesk. Abl. 322.

brangumȳnai plu. 'Kostbarkeiten'—B. II, 1, 278.

brangùs 'teuer, kostbar'—Uh. *bhṛ́ngāras.*

brankstù, brañkti 'teuer werden'—B. II, 3, 370. Cf. prec.

brañktas, brantas 'Knüttel'—(Ber. *brutŭ*).

brantas id.—see prec.

brastà 'Durchwatung, Furt'—B. II, 1, 416.635. Cf. Lesk. Abl. 322.

brastva 'Furt'—F. *fijaþwa* (s. v. *fijan*); B. I, 339. II, 1, 449. Cf. Lesk. Nom. 564.

braszkesis 'Dröhnen, Klappern'—B. II, 1, 637. See next & Lesk. Nom. 592.

braszkù, braszkëti 'prasseln, krachen'—W. *frāgor.* Cf. Lesk. Abl. 372.

braukaũ, braukýti 'wiederholt streichen'—Ber. *brŭsnǫ.* See next.

braukiù, braũkti 'wischen, streichen, scharren'—Ber. *brusĭnića, brutŭ, brŭsnǫ, brykajǫ;* W. *farcio;* Boi. φαρκίς. Cf. Lesk. Abl. 293.

brêdis, brëdis 'Elentier'—(K. *Elentier*); (Boi. βρενθύομαι). Cf. Sommer 254 & 256.

bredù (brendù), brìsti 'waten'—B. I, 394.472. II, 3, 136. 321; Ber. *bredǫ,* [*brodŭ*]. Cf. Lesk. Abl. 322.

brëkszta, pret. **brëszko, brëkszti** impers. 'anbrechen' (vom Tage)—Uh. *márīciṣ;* F. *braiv;* Ber. *brěskŭ* 1; W. *flagro;* Boi. ἀμαρύσσω (& Ntr.), φορκός. Cf. Lesk. Abl. 371.

brendù 'wate'—see *bredù.*

brendůlỹs 'Kern'—Ber. *brědŭ.* Cf. Lesk. Abl. 322.

bręstu, bręsti 'einen Fruchtkern gewinnen, reifen'—Ber. *brědŭ, berďa, bĭrdo* 2. Cf. Lesk. Abl. 322.

brëszko—see *brëkszta.*

brëžiu, brëžti (Kur. **brëžiu, brëszti**) 'kratzen'—Boi. φαρκίς. Cf. Lesk. Abl. 271.

briáujůs, briáutis 'sich mit Gewalt vordrängen'—Uh. *bhrūṇás;* F. *brunna;* Ber. *bruja;* W. *dēfrŭtum;* Boi. βρύω, φρέαρ. Cf. Lesk. Abl. 293.

briáukszt, brúkszt interj. "ripps rapps!"—Ber. *brykają*. Cf. IF. XIII, 188-9.

briaunà 'stumpfe Kante' (Messer, Topf usw.)—Boi. ὀφρῦς.

brýdau, brýdoti 'im Wasser stehen'—B. II, 3, 168; Ber. *bredą*. See *bredù* & Lesk. Abl. 322.

brìngstu, brìngti (Uh., Kur.: **brìnkstu, brìnkti**) 'teuer werden'—Uh. *bhṛṅgāras*. Cf. Lesk. Abl. 322.

brìnkstu, brìnkti 'quellen, schwellen'—Ber. *bręknǫ, berka*. Cf. Lesk. Abl. 322.

brìnkszteriu, brìnkszterėti 'Schnippchen schlagen'; **brįnkterėti** 'klirrend fallen'—Uh. *bhṛṅgas;* Ber. *bręčą;* W. 1. *frigo*. Cf. Lesk. Abl. 322, IF. XIII, 188.

brįnkt Interjektion beim klirrenden Fall—Ber. *bręčą*. See prec. & IF. XIII, 188.

brįnkterėti 'klirrend fallen'—see *brìnkszteriu*.

brìsti 'waten'—inf. of *bredù*, q. v.

brįstu, brįsti 'quellen'—Ber. *berďa, (grǫdĭ)*. Cf. Lesk. Abl. 322.

brìzgilas 'Zaum'—Ber. *brŭzda*. Cf. Lesk. Abl. 359.

brõgas 'Schlampe, die bei Branntwein- oder Bierbereitung zurückbleibende Masse'—Ber. *braga;* W. *fertum*.

brolė́nas 'Brudersssohn'—B. II, 1, 308.604. See next & Lesk. Nom. 388-9.

brólis 'Bruder'—Uh. *bhrātā;* K. *Bruder, Buhle;* Ber. *bratrŭ;* W. *frāter;* Boi. φράτωρ. See *broterė̃lis*.

bróliszkas 'brüderlich'—B. II, 1, 667.

broliùkas 'Brüderchen'—B. II, 1, 492. Cf. Ness. 346[a], Lesk. Nom. 518.

broterė̃lis 'Brüderchen'—Uh. *bhrātā;* F. *brōþar;* B. I, 165. 509. II, 1, 334; Ber. *bratrŭ;* W. *frāter;* Boi. φράτωρ. See *brólis*.

brotuszis 'Vetter, Cousin, Brudersssohn'—W. *frāter*. Cf. Ness. 346[b], Lesk. Nom. 598.

brũkis 'Strich'—Boi. φαρκίς.

brùknė 'Preiselbeere'—K. *Preiselbeere;* Ber. *brusnića*.

brũkszmis 'Strich, Streifen'—see next.

brũksznis (**brũkszmis**) masc., **brũksznìs** fem. id.—B. II, 1, 289 (twice); Ber. *brykają;* Boi. φαρκίς. Cf. Lesk. Abl. 293.

brúkszt interj. "ripps rapps!"—see *briáukszt.*

brukù, brùkti 'einzwängen, mit Gewalt hineinstecken'—Ber. *brutŭ, brykają;* W. *farcio;* Boi. φράσσω. Cf. Lesk. Abl. 293.

brúnas (Kur. **briúnas**) 'braun'—K. *braun.* Cf. Ness. 347ᵃ.

brunjas (? Notice Old Pruss. *brunyos* 'Brünne', Brückner SlFw. 196, Prell. deutsch. Best. in den lett. Spr. 3) 'Panzer'—F. *brunjō.*

brùnklis, brunklỹs 'Knebel', "ein kurzes dickes Stück Holz, zum Zusammendrehen eines Strickes"—W. *farcio;* Boi. φράσσω.

bruvis 'Augenbraue'—Uh. *bhrūṣ;* F. *brusts;* B. I, 507; Ber. *brŭvĭ* 1; (W. 2. *frons*); Boi. ὀφρῦς.

bruzduklas 'Zaum'—Ber. *brŭzda.* Cf. Bezz. BGLS. 277.

brùzga 'Rauschen'—Ber. *bŕuzgają.* See next.

bruzgù, bruzgė́ti 'rascheln'—Uh. *bhṛjjáti;* Ber. *bŕuzgają.* Cf. Lesk. Abl. 315.

bubenù, bubénti 'dumpf dröhnen' (vom Donner)—Boi. βύας. Cf. Lesk. Abl. 293.

bùbyju, bùbyti 'etwas mit dumpfen Schlägen tun' (z. B. 'dreschen')—Boi. βύας. Cf. Lesk. Abl. 293.

bũbnas 'Trommel'—B. I, 521.

buczũju, buczũti 'küssen'—Ber. *búza* 2.

budėlė eine Art Pilz—Ber. *bŭdŭla.*

bùdinu, bùdinti 'wecken'—Uh. *bódhati;* F. *ana-biudan.* Cf. Lesk. Abl. 294.

budrùs 'wachsam'—Uh. *bódhati;* F. *ana-biudan;* B. I, 838. II, 1, 348.385; Ber. *bŭdrŭ;* Boi. πεύθομαι. Cf. Lesk. Abl. 294.

bũgnas 'Trommel'—B. I, 521.

búgstu, búgti (Kur., F., B.: **búkstu, búkti**) intr. 'erschrecken'—Uh. *bhujáti;* F. *biugan;* B. II, 3, 128.

(**búgęs**: II, 1, 567. 3, 444); Ber. *bĕgnǫ*, (*lękǫ*); W. *fugio;* Boi. φεύγω. Cf. Lesk. Abl. 294.

búk impera. 2nd pers. sing. (**esmì**) 'sei'—B. I, 503. II, 3, 149; W. *fui;* Boi. φύω. See *búti*.

bukas 'Holunder, Buche'—Ber. *bŭzŭ;* W. *fāgus*. Cf. Ness. 336[b], Brückner SlFw. 74.

bùkczus 'Stammler'—Uh. *bukkāras;* Ber. *bukajǫ;* W. *bucca;* Boi. βύκτης.

būklà, būklė̃ 'Statt, Aufenthaltsort, Wohnung, Heimat'—Uh. *bhavítram;* K. *Bude;* B. II, 1, 340.344.622; Ber. *bydlo;* W. *fui;* Boi. φύω, (φωλεός). Cf. Lesk. Abl. 315.

buklas 'Lager eines Tieres'—Uh. *bhavítram;* Ber. *bydlo*. See prec.

būklė̃ 'Aufenthaltsort' usw.—see *būklà*.

buklùs 'listig, schlau'—F. *biugan;* W. *fugio;* Boi. φεύγω.

búkstu 'erschrecke'—see *búgstu*.

bukùs 'spitzlos, stumpf'—F. *bauþs*. Cf. Lesk. Abl. 315.

bulbė 'Kartoffel'—W. *bulbus;* Boi. βολβός. Cf. Brückner SlFw. 75.

bulìs 'Hinterbacke'—Uh. *buliṣ;* B. I, 508; W. *bulbus, (follis);* Boi. βολβός.

bùlius 'Stier'—W. *follis*.

bulvis 'Kartoffel'—W. *bulbus;* Boi. βολβός. Cf. Brückner SlFw. 75.

bumbolys 'Steckrübe'—Ber. *bǫbŭlĭ*.

bum̃bulas 'knotenartige Verdickung' (z. B. am Stock, im Garn)—Uh. *buliṣ;* Ber. *bǫbŭlĭ;* W. *bulbus;* Boi. βολβός.

bumbulis 'Wasserblase'—Ber. *bǫbŭlĭ*.

bumbulȳs 'Steckrübe'—Uh. *buliṣ;* Ber. *bǫbŭlĭ;* W. *bulbus;* Boi. βολβός.

bundù, budė́ti 'wachen'—Uh. *bódhati;* K. *bieten;* F. *anabiudan;* B. I, 109.539. II, 3, 74; Ber. *bŭďǫ;* Boi. πεύθομαι. Cf. Lesk. Abl. 294.

bundù, bùsti 'erwachen'—Uh. *bódhati;* B. II, 3, 280.397. 444; Ber. *bŭďǫ;* Boi. πεύθομαι. Cf. Lesk. Abl. 294.

burblenù, burblénti 'gluckern, murmeln'—Ber. *bŭrbotŭ*.

burblỹs 'Kollerhahn'—Ber. *bŭrbotŭ*.
burbu, burbėti 'balzen' usw. (see Ness.)—Ber. *bŭrbotŭ*. Cf. Ness. 337[b].
bur̃bulas 'Wasserblase'—Uh. *budbudas;* Ber. *bŭrbotŭ;* W. *bulbus;* Boi. βομβυλίς.
buris (ū?) 'Haufe, Herde'—F. *uf-bauljan;* B. II, 1, 355. 382. 2, 656; (W. *folium*); Boi. (Ntr.) θήρ. Cf. Geitler LS. 80, Bezz. LF. 103-4, Lesk. Nom. 299, 437.
būrỹs (**lytaũs**) '(Regen-) Schauer'—Uh. *bhuráti;* Ber. *bura;* W. *furo* 1. Cf. BB. XXVI, 188, Sommer 181, note.
-buryti—see *užsiburyti* 'sich ereifern'.
buriù, bùrti 'wahrsagen, zaubern'—B. II, 1, 485; Boi. φάρμακον (& note). Cf. Lesk. Abl. 315.
burklenù, burklénti 'unter dem Bart undeutlich murmeln' —Ber. *burkają*.
burksznóju, burksznóti 'prasseln, rasseln' (vom Regen oder Hagel gegen das Fenster)—Ber. *burkają, bŭrkają*.
búrkszt Interjektion bei rasselnden, rasch klappernden Geräuschen: "burr!"—Ber. *bŭrkają*. Cf. IF. XIII, 190.
bùrkteriu, bùrkterėti 'undeutlich sprechen'—Ber. *bŭrkają*. Cf. IF. XIII, 190, Juškevič 254.
burkũju, burkũti 'girren' (von der männlichen Taube)—Ber. *burkają, bŭrkają*.
burlõkas 'ein russischer oder polnischer Herr'—Ber. *burlak*.
burmìstras 'Bürgermeister'—B. I, 719. Cf. Prell. deutsch. Best. in den lett. Spr. 27.
burnà 'Mund'—F. *fōtu-baurd;* B. I, 454; W. *ferio, frūmen;* Boi. φάρος.
bùrszkiu, bùrkszti (**ożỹs õżką bùrszkia**; Kur. **burszkiûs, burksztis** 'sich begatten') von der Begattung der Ziegen und Schafe—Ber. *bŭrkają*. Cf. IF. XIII, 190.
burva eine Art Kleidungsstück—B. II, 1, 527; Boi. φᾶρος. Cf. Lesk. Nom. 346.
búsęs fut. part. (**esmì**)—B. II, 3, 384.386. See *búti*.

búsiu fut. (**esmì**) 'ich werde sein'—B. I, 503. II, 3, 384. 386.441; Ber. *bytĭ;* Boi. φύω. See *búti.*

búta pret. pass. part. neut. 'gewesen'—Ber. *bytŭ;* Boi. φύω; B. II, 1, 398. See *búti* & Kur. Gram. 1347.

bùtas 'Wohnung, Haus'—Uh. *bhūtás;* K. *Bude;* F. *bauan;* B. I, 106.487.489. II, 1, 398; Ber. *bytŭ, bytĭ;* W. *fui;* Boi. φύω.

búti inf. (**esmì**) 'sein'. Other forms also indexed separately.—Uh. *bhávati;* F. *bauan;* B. I, 111.294.338.339. 487.503.509.518. II, 1, 398.434.443.568. 3, 149.384. 386.412.441; Ber. *bytĭ, bytŭ;* W. *fui;* Boi. φύω, φῖτυ. Cf. Lesk. Abl. 315; Ness. s. v. *Bu* (333[b]); Kur. Gram. 1106; Wied. 221.

būtinaĩ adv. 'wesentlich, gänzlich, bleibend, zum Bleiben'—B. II, 1, 269. See next.

bútinas 'seiend, bleibend, wesentlich'—B. II, 1, 269. See *búti.*

bútų supin. (**esmì**) 'zu sein'—B. II, 1, 443; Boi. φῖτυ. See *búti.*

buvaũ 'ich war', **bùvo** 'er war' pret. (**esmì**)—B. I, 338; Ber. *bytĭ;* W. *fui;* Boi. φύω. See *búti* & Lesk. Abl. 315.

bùvęs perf. act. part. (**esmì**)—B. I, 294. II, 1, 568. 3, 441. See *búti.*

buvinė́ju, buvinė́ti 'hie und da ein Weilchen bleiben'—Ber. *bytĭ.* Cf. Lesk. Abl. 315.

bũvis 'bleibender Aufenthalt'—Ber. *bytĭ.*

bùvo 'er war'—see *buvaũ.*

bůdu, bůdėti 'Ekel empfinden'—B. I, 156. Cf. BB. XVIII, 250; Kur. s. v. *bódu.* See *bódžiũs.*

bũžė 'Keule, Klöppel am Dreschflegel, Nadelkopf'—B. II, 3, 292; Boi. φωΐδες. Cf. Lesk. Abl. 372.

C

cam̃pyti (?) 'scharf zuschlagen'—Ber. *capają.* Cf. IF. XIII, 190.

capnóju, capnóti 'tastend etwas ergreifen'—Ber. *capają.* Cf. IF. XIII, 190, Juškevič 259.

càpt Interjektion bei schnellem Erhaschen—Ber. *capaję*. Cf. IF. XIII, 190.

CZ

czà 'da, hier'—see *czè*.
czameriaĩ plu. 'Enzian'—Ber. *čemerĭ*.
czamerýczos plu. 'Nieswurz, Enzian'—Ber. *čemerĭ*.
czáudżu, czáudėti 'niesen'—Uh. *kṣâuti;* Ber. *kŭchnǫ*. Cf. Lesk. Abl. 294.
czè, czà 'da, hier'—Uh. *tyá-;* B. II, 2, 320.
czemereĩ 'Enzian'—Ber. *čemerĭ*. Cf. Ness. 162[b].
czẽsais adv. inst. plu. 'zu Zeiten, zuweilen'—B. II, 2, 719.
czeslyvas 'ehrenvoll, prächtig'—B. I, 719. Cf. Ness. 164[a].
czėsù adv. inst. sing. 'zu rechter Zeit, zeitig'—B. II, 2, 714.
czìcze 'hier'—B. I, 849. See *szìcze* & Ness. 164[b].
czirksz 'ritsch ratsch'. Interjektion beim Reissen vom Gewebe.—Ber. *čirkaję*. Cf. IF. XIII, 192.
czirkszlỹs 'Wespe'—Ber. *čvĭrčę*.
czirszkiù, czir̃kszti 'einen summenden Ton von sich geben' —Ber. *čvĭrčę*. Cf. Lesk. Abl. 322.
czón (B. czõn) 'hier' (B. 'hierher')—B. II, 2, 320.
czùrinu, czùrinti 'harnen'—Ber. *curę*. Cf. IF. XIII, 192.
czurszkiù, czur̃kszti 'rieseln'—Ber. *curę*. Cf. IF. XIII, 170, 192.
czuru, czurẽti 'rieseln'—Ber. *curę*. Cf. IF. XIII, 192, Juškevič 278.

D

da- pref.—K. *zu;* W. *dē*. Cf. Kur. s. v.
daba 'Art, Weise, Charakter'—Ber. *doba*. Cf. Geitler LS. 80, Brückner SlFw. 79.
dabartinas 'gegenwärtig, jetzig'—B. I, 399. II, 1, 285; W. *diūtinus* (s. v. *diū*), *prīstinus* (s. v. *prīscus*), 2. *tenus;* Boi. *ἐπηετανός*.
dabinė́ju, dabinė́ti 'schmücken'—F. *ga-daban*
dabinù, dabìnti id.—F. *ga-daban;* Ber. *doba;* W. *faber*.

dabnùs 'zierlich'—F. *ga-daban;* Ber. *doba;* W. *faber.*
dãbras 'Biber'—Uh. *babhrúṣ;* K. *Biber;* Ber. *bebrŭ.* See *bẽbrus* & Lesk. Nom. 434.
dãgas m., **dagà** f. 'Erntezeit, Ernte'—Uh. *dāhas;* K. *Tag;* F. *dags;* B. II, 1, 150; Ber. *degŭtĭ, (lěto);* W. *favilla;* Boi. τέφρā. Cf. Lesk. Abl. 361.
dagỹs 'Klette, Dorn, Distel'—W. *fīgo, (digitus);* (Boi. θήγω). Cf. Lesk. Abl. 361.
dãglas 'weiss und schwarz gefleckt oder gestreift' (bes. von Schweinen)—B. II, 1, 362. Cf. Lesk. Abl. 361.
daigaũ, daigýti 'stechen'—Ber. *dĭgna.* Cf. Lesk. Abl. 272.
dáiktas 'Stelle, Ding'—B. I, 209. Cf. Lesk. Abl. 272, Lesk. Nom. 533 (read Abl. 272 for Abl. 27).
dáilinu, dáilinti 'verfeinern, glätten, verzieren'—Ber. *dělo.*
dailùs 'zierlich, geschickt'—Ber. *dělo.* Cf. Lesk. Nom. 256.
dainà 'Volkslied'—Uh. *dī́yati;* (F. *tains*); B. II, 1, 263; Ber. *dikŭ;* Boi. δῖνος. Cf. Lesk. Abl. 271.
daĩnius 'Barde'—B. II, 1, 224. Cf. Lesk. Nom. 325.
dairaũs, dairýtis 'umhergaffen'—Uh. (*dhī́ras*), [*dī́deti*]. Cf. Lesk. Abl. 272.
dáktas 'Stelle, Ding'—B. I, 209. See *dáiktas.*
dalgis 'Sense' (not, as e. g. Lesk., 'Sichel')—B. II, 3, 290; Ber. *dolga;* W. 1. *dolo, (falx)*; Boi. δαίδαλος. Cf. Lesk. Abl. 323.
dalybas 'teilhaftig'—B. II, 1, 388.390. Cf. Lesk. Nom. 592.
dalýbos plu. 'Erbteilung, Auktion' (cf. Ness. 125[a])—B. II, 1, 388.636.638.
dalyjù, dalýti 'teilen, zuteilen'—Uh. *dálati;* B. II, 3, 222; Ber. *dola.*
dalỹkas 'Teil, Sache'—B. II, 1, 388.
dalìs 'Teil, Erbteil, Almosen'—Uh. *dálati;* F. *dails;* B. I, 261; Ber. *dola;* W. 1. *dolo;* Boi. δαίδαλος.
dalýtas 'geteilt'—B. II, 1, 400. See *dalyjù.*
dalývas 'teilhaft'—B. II, 1, 388.
dálna 'flache Hand'—see under *délna*

dañgalas 'Decke, Kleidung'—B. II, 1, 366.619; Ber. *dǫgŭ*. Cf. Lesk. Abl. 323.

danginũs, dangìntis 'sich wohin bewegen'—Ber. *dǫgŭ;* (Boi. ταχύς). Cf. Geitler LS. 86, 88; Bezz. LF. 106; Lesk. Abl. 323. Notice also Ness. 137[b]: *danginu* 'bedecke'.

dañgiszkas 'himmlisch'—B. II, 1, 666. See *dangùs*.

dañgtis 'Deckel'—Ber. *dǫgŭ*. Cf. Lesk. Abl. 323.

dangujejis 'himmlisch'—B. II, 1, 34.124.196. Cf. Bezz. BGLS. 279; Lesk. Nom. 340-341; Sommer 320.

dangùs 'Himmel', (**burnõs**) **dangùs** 'Gaumen'—F. *tuggl;* B. II, 1, 181; Ber. *dǫgŭ*.

dantìs 'Zahn'—Uh. *dán;* K. *Zahn;* F. *tunþus;* B. II, 1, 171. 460; Ber. *dęgna;* W. *dens;* Boi. ὀδών.

dantýtas 'gezahnt'—B. II, 1, 406.

dantótas id.—W. *dens*. Cf. Ness. 126[a].

daraũ, darýti 'machen, tun'—B. II, 3, 199.267.318; Boi δράω. See *derìù* & Lesk. Abl. 361.

dárbas 'Arbeit'—(F. *arbaiþs*); B. II, 1, 389; Boi. δράω, (κῶμος). Cf. Lesk. Abl. 324.

darbas 'Laubgeflechtwerk'—Uh. *darbhás, dṛbháti;* Ber. *dorbŭ*. Cf. Bezz. BGLS. 279.

darbýmetis 'Arbeitszeit'—B. II, 1, 21.

darbininkas 'Arbeiter'—B. II, 1, 486-7.616. Cf. Lesk. Nom. 521 [& 520].

darbùs 'arbeitsam'—(F. *arbaiþs*); B. II, 1, 389.

dárga 'regnerisches, schlechtes Wetter'—Ber. *-dorga* 3. Cf. Lesk. Abl. 324, Ness. 128[b].

dárgana id.—Ber. *-dorga* 3; (W. *furvus*).

dargus 'garstig, schmutzig'—Ber. *-dorga* 3; (W. *furvus*). Cf. Ness. 128[b].

dar̃ktas 'hässlicher, schmutziger Mensch'—B. II, 1, 409 (FN). Cf. Lesk. Abl. 361.

darkùs 'hässlich, garstig, schändlich'—(Ber. *dročǫ*). See *dargus* & Lesk. Abl. 361.

darva 'Kienholz'—see *dervà*.

daržas 'Garten'—Uh. *dṛhyati;* K. *Zarge;* W. *cohors, (fortis);* Boi. δράσσομαι.
daržẽlėlis 'Gärtchen'—B. II, 1, 377. Cf. Lesk. Nom. 481.
daržẽlis id.—B. II, 1, 377.
daržinykas dial. 'Gärtner'—B. II, 1, 497. Cf. LBLV. 289, [Lesk. Nom. 520-1].
daržininkas 'Gärtner'—B. II, 1, 487.
daubà 'Schlucht'—K. *Döbel, Tobel, [tief], [Topf], [Tümpel];* F. *diups;* Ber. *dupa.* Cf. Lesk. Abl. 295.
dauburà id.—K. *Tobel;* B. II, 1, 358. See prec. & Ness. 148[a].
dauburỹs id.—B. II, 1, 358; Ber. *dupa.*
daũg 'viel'—(Uh. *dógdhi*); K. *taugen;* F. *dugan;* B. II, 2, 656; (Ber. *dǫgŭ*); Boi. τεύχω. Cf. Lesk. Abl. 295.
dáuginu, dáuginti 'vermehren'—F. *dugan.* See prec.
daũgsei (B. daũksei) adv. 'reichlich'—B. II, 1, 543.
daugsỹk 'vielmal'—B. II, 2, 67. See *daũg* & *sỹkis.*
dáuksinu, dáuksinti 'vermehren'—K. *taugen;* B. I, 785. Cf. Lesk. Abl. 295.
dausinu, dausinti 'Luft machen'—Uh. *dhūsaras;* Ber. *duchŭ;* W. *bēstia.* Cf. Lesk. Abl. 296.
daũsos plu. 'die obere Luft'—Uh. *dhūsaras;* F. *dius;* B. I, 493.991; Ber. *duchŭ;* W. *bēstia;* Boi. θεός. Cf. Lesk. Abl. 296.
daužiù, daũžti 'heftig stossen'—Ber. *duzajǫ, (dĭgna);* (W. *dūmus*). Cf. Lesk. Abl. 296.
dãvęs perf. act. part. of dúodu, q. v., 'gegeben habend'—B. I, 171.338.489. II, 3, 431.449.493; W. *dō;* Boi. δίδωμι.
daviaũ pret. of dúodu, q. v., 'ich gab'—B. II, 3, 243.317; W. *duim;* Boi. δίδωμι (note).
dažaũ, dažýti 'etwas in Flüssiges tauchen'—(Ber. *dŭždžĭ*); (W. *pollingo*).
debesìs 'Wolke'—Uh. *nábhas;* B. I, 115. II, 1, 518. 2, 301; W. *nebula;* Boi. νέφος, (δνόφος).
dẽbras 'Biber'—Uh. *babhrúṣ;* Ber. *bebrŭ;* W. *fiber.* See *dãbras.*

debrus id.—Uh. *babhrúṣ.* See *dābras.*
dedą̃s pres. act. part. of **dedù**, q. v., 'legend'—B. II, 1, 457.
dė̃das 'Greis'—Ber. *dědŭ.*
dėdė̃ 'des Vaters Bruder, Oheim'—B. I, 136.541. II, 1, 127; Ber. *dědŭ;* Boi. θεῖος.
dedėnos plu. 'Töchter des Vatersbruders'—B. II, 1, 604. See prec. & Lesk. Nom. 389.
dedervinė̃ 'flechtenartiger Ausschlag'—Uh. *dadrúṣ;* K. *Zitteroch;* B. II, 1, 129; W. *derbiōsus.*
dedù (old forms **dėmi, dė̃mi**), **dė́ti** 'legen, setzen, stellen'. Other forms also indexed separately.—Uh. *dádhāti, hitáṣ;* F. *ga-dēþs;* B. I, 131.501.522.718(twice). II, 1, 398.433.442.457.640. 3, 24.99.110.111.143.380.386.409. 493; Ber. *dějǫ, deďǫ;* W. *facio;* Boi. τίθημι. Cf. Kur. Gram. 1175; Wied. 178.2; Lesk. Abl. 371.
degas 'Feuerbrand'—B. II, 1, 524. See *degù* & Lesk. Abl. 361.
dẽgas 'Keim'—W. *fīgo.* See next.
dẽgia, dẽgti impers. 'stechen' (z. B. vom Seitenstechen)—Ber. *dĭgna;* W. *fīgo;* (Boi. θιγγάνω). Cf. Lesk. Abl. 271-2.
degìkas 'Brandstifter'—B. II, 1, 490.
dẽglas 'weiss und schwarz gefleckt oder gestreift' (bes. von Schweinen)—B. II, 1, 362. Cf. Lesk. Abl. 361.
deglas 'Brandmal'—B. II, 1, 365. See *degù* & Bezz. BGLS. 278.
dẽglis 'Stich, Stechen' (Körperschmerz); Name einer Krankheit—B. II, 1, 384.620; Ber. *kašlĭ.* See *dẽgia;* Bezz. LF. 107; Lesk. Abl. 272; Lesk. Nom. 460.
degù, dègti intr.: 'brennen'; trans.: 'etwas durchs Feuer bilden'—Uh. *dáhati;* K. *Tag;* F. *dags;* B. I, 119.129. 542.591. II, 1, 571. 3, 120.250.385.399.447.492; Ber. *degŭtĭ;* W. *favilla;* Boi. τέφρα. Cf. Lesk. Abl. 361.
degùtas 'Birkenteer'—Ber. *degŭtĭ.*
deivė̃ fem. 'Gespenst, Nachtgeist' (Sommer 214: "auch 'Göttin' als regelrechtes Feminin zu *dė̃vas*")—Uh.

devás; B. I, 184.190.299. II, 1, 221; Ber. *divǫ;* W. *deus;* Boi. δῖος. See *dëvẽ.*

deivỹs masc. 'Gespenst, Abgott'—B. I, 190. See prec.

-dẽjas (e. g. in **piktadẽjas** 'Übeltäter', q. v.)—Ber. *dějĭ.* Cf. Lesk. Nom. 309.

dė́jęs perf. act. part. of **dedù**, q. v., 'gelegt habend'—B. II, 3, 493.

dė́k impera. 2nd pers. sing. of **dedù**, q. v., 'lege'—B. II, 3, 99.

deksnìs 'Brandstätte' (cf. Ness. 134[b] & Kur. s. v.)—B. II, 1, 289.540.

dèktinas 'wer zu verbrennen ist'—B. II, 1, 269; Boi. θεπτανός, τέφρα. See *degù* & Wied. 198.

dektìnė 'etwas Gebranntes, Branntwein'—B. II, 1, 269; Boi. θεπτανός, τέφρᾱ. Cf. Lesk. Nom. 406.

dẽl 'wegen'—see *dẽlei.*

délba 'Forkenstiel'—Ber. *dĭlbǫ.* Cf. Lesk. Abl. 323.

delbiù, deĩbti (**akìs**) '(die Augen) niederschlagen'. Kur. s. v.: "nur in der Zusammensetzung mit **nu-**, vielleicht auch nur in dem Part. [perf. act. part.] **nudeĩbęs akìs** 'die Augen niedergeschlagen' in Gebrauch."—Ber. *dĭlbǫ.* See *nudilbstù* & Lesk. Abl. 323.

delczà 'abnehmender Mond'—Ber. *dolnĭ.* Cf. Lesk. Abl. 323.

dėlẽ 'Blutegel'—B. I, 134.203.486.528. II, 1, 364; Ber. *dětę, dojǫ;* W. *fēlo, fīlius;* Boi. θηλή, βδέλλα. Cf. Lesk. Abl. 323.

dẽlei, dẽl prep. with the gen. 'wegen, um . . . willen'—B. II, 2, 929; Ber. *děla.*

délka, délkas 'Angel' (die an Schnüren ins Haff geworfen wird)—Ber. *dolka.*

délna 'innere flache Hand'—B. II, 1, 288; Ber. *dolnĭ;* (W. *dolo*); (Boi. δέλτος, θάλασσα). Cf. Lesk. Abl. 323, Lesk. Nom. 364.

delsiù, deĩsti 'säumen, zögern'—Uh. *dolā.* Cf. Lesk. Abl. 368.

dėmė 'Anschein'—B. II, 1, 247. Cf. Lesk. Nom. 425.

dèmi, dė́mi 'ich lege'—old presents of *dedù*, q. v.

dënà 'Tag'—Uh. *dinam;* K. (*Lenz*), [*Zeit*]; F. *sinteins;* B. II, 1, 264.298.625; Ber. *dĭnĭ;* W. *nundinae.* Cf. Lesk. Nom. 364.

dëna 'trächtig' (von Kühen, Stuten und anderen Tieren)—Uh. *dhénā;* F. *daddjan;* B. I, 172.490. II, 1, 257; Ber. *dětę, doję;* W. *fēlo;* Boi. θῆσθαι. Cf. Lesk. Nom. 355.

denė 'Deckbrett des Kahns' (cf. Ness. 137[a])—K. *Tenne;* (Ber. *lava* 1). Cf. Lesk. Nom. 266, Sommer 63.

dengà 'Decke, Vorhang'—F. *tuggl;* Ber. *dǫgŭ.* See next.

dengiù, deñgti 'decken'—F. *tuggl;* Ber. *dǫgŭ;* (Boi. θάπτω). Cf. Lesk. Abl. 323.

dënõj, dënõ adv. loc. sing. 'bei Tage'—B. II, 2, 708.744. Cf. Wied. 77.

dënõms adv. inst. plu. 'tags'—B. II, 2, 745.

dérgesis 'unflätiger Mensch'—Ber. *-dorga* 3; (W. *furvus*). Cf. Lesk. Abl. 324.

dergėti (dergti ?) (?) Old Lith. 'hassen'—(W. *furvus*). Cf. Bezz. BGLS. 280.

dérgia, dérgti impers. 'schlechtes Wetter sein, stürmend regnen'—Ber. *-dorga* 3; (W. *furvus*). Cf. Lesk. Abl. 324.

deriù, derëti 'feilschen, mieten, in Sold nehmen, einen Vertrag machen; taugen, wozu dienen; gedeihen'—Uh. *driyáte,* (*dharmá*); B. I, 152; Ber. *dorgŭ* 1, (*déra*); W. *firmus;* Boi. θρᾶνος. Cf. Lesk. Abl. 361.

derkiù, deřkti 'mit Unflat besudeln, den After leeren'—W. *foria.* Cf. Lesk. Abl. 361.

dermė 'Vertrag'—(Uh. *dharmá*); W. *firmus;* Boi. θρᾶνος. See *deriù.*

derù, derëti 'wozu dienen, nutzen' usw.—Uh. *driyáte;* Ber. *dorgŭ* 1. See *deriù* & Lesk. Abl. 361.

dervà, darva 'Kienholz'—Uh. *dā́ru;* K. *Teer;* F. *triu;* B.

I, 339.445. II, 1, 157.161.182.199.647; Ber. *dervo, -dorvŭ;* W. *larix;* Boi. δόρυ, δρῦς. Cf. Lesk. Nom. 346.

dĕsiu fut. of **dedù**, q. v., 'ich werde legen'—B. I, 131. II, 3, 386.

deszim̃s dial. 'zehn'—B. I, 719. Cf. LBLV. 309; Bezz. BGLS. 90, 179, 280.

dẽszimt, dẽszimtis 'zehn'—Uh. *dáça, daçát;* F. *taihun, fidwōr-tigjus* (s. v. *fidwōr-taihun*); B. I, 120.522.551. 566.630. II, 1, 438. 2, 22.23.246; Ber. *desętŭ;* W. *decem;* Boi. δέκα. Cf. Kur. Gram. 1009, 1549; Wied. 156.10.

deszim̃tas 'decimus'—Uh. *daçát;* F. *taihunda;* B. I, 407. 415. II, 1, 163.391. 2, 57(twice); Ber. *desętŭ;* W. *decem;* Boi. δέκα. Cf. Wied. 157.10.

deszimterì 'zehn'—B. II, 2, 77. Cf. Kur. Gram. 1033, Wied. 158.

dẽszimtis 'Zehnzahl, zehn'—see *dẽszimt.*

dẽszimts 'zehn'—B. II, 1, 427. 2, 22.23(& note).220; Ber. *desętŭ.* See *dẽszimt* & Kur. Gram. 1009, LBLV. 309.

deszinẽ 'die rechte Hand'—Uh. *dákṣiṇas;* F. *taihswa;* B. I, 548. II, 1, 271; Ber. *desĭnŭ;* W. *dexter, (laevus);* Boi. δεξιός, (λαιός).

dĕtas pret. pass. part. of **dedù**, q. v., 'gelegt'—Uh. *hitás;* B. II, 1, 398; W. *facio.*

dĕtys plu. 'die Lege des Huhns'—B. II, 1, 433.633; Ber. *-dĕtĭ;* Boi. θέσις.

dĕtų supin. of **dedù**, q. v., 'zu legen'—F. *auhjōdus* (s. v. *auhjōn*); B. II, 1, 442.640.

dẽvas 'Gott'—Uh. *devás;* K. *Dienstag;* B. I, 184.190.191. 299. II, 1, 134. 2, 129; Ber. *divǫ;* W. *deus;* Boi. δῖος, Ζεύς. Cf. Lesk. Abl. 272.

dëvẽ 'Göttin'—(Boi. δᾱήρ (note)). See *deivẽ* & prec. Cf. Lesk. Nom. 282, Sommer 10.

dëverìs 'Schwager der Frau, des Ehemanns Bruder'—Uh. *devṛ́;* B. I, 180.296. II, 1, 332; Ber. *dĕverĭ;* W. *lēvir;* Boi. δᾱήρ (& note).

devyneri 'neun'—B. II, 2, 77. Cf. Kur. Gram. 1033, Wied. 158.

devynì 'neun'—Uh. *náva;* K. (8th ed.) *neun;* F. *niun;* B. I, XLII.130. II, 2, 18.20; Ber. *devętŭ;* W. *novem;* Boi. ἐννέα. Cf. Wied. 156.

devyniólika 'neunzehn'—see prec. & [K. *elf*]; F. *ain-lif;* B. II, 2, 26.[27]; [Ber. *-lěkŭ*]; [W. *linquo*]. Cf. Wied. 156.

deviñtas 'neunter'—F. *niunda* (s. v. *niun*); B. I, 294.416. II, 1, 163.391. 2, 20.57; Ber. *devętŭ;* W. *novem;* Boi. ἐννέα. Cf. Wied. 157.9.

dë̄viszkas 'göttlich'—F. *azgō;* B. II, 1, 666.667. See *dē̄vas.*

dëvotas 'religiös'—B. II, 3, 211. Cf. Bezz. BGLS. 280 (s. v. *deiwatas*).

dëvuláitis dimin. 'Göttchen, der liebe Gott'—B. II, 1, 377. Cf. Lesk. Nom. 492.

dëvùlis dimin. id.—B. II, 1, 368. Cf. Lesk. Nom. 492.

dëvulužë̄lis dimin. id.—B. II, 1, 377. Cf. Lesk. Nom. 492.

dëvùžis dimin. id.—B. II, 1, 506.511.676.678. Cf. Ness. 140[a].

dëžti 'durchprügeln'—see *dižu.*

dìdelis 'gross'—B. II, 1, 130.366. Cf. Sommer 325.

didỹbė 'Grösse'—B. II, 1, 643.

dìdis 'gross'—B. II, 1, 130.366. Cf. Sommer 324-5.

didókas 'ziemlich gross'—B. II, 1, 500.680.

didžùlis 'der Grosse, grosser Lümmel'—B. II, 1, 684.

dýgsnis (Kur. & B. dỹksnis) 'Stich, Nadelstich'—B. II, 1, 289 (twice); Ber. *dĭgna;* W. *fīnis.* Cf. Lesk. Abl. 271.

dýgstu, dýgti (Kur. & B. dýkstu, dýkti) 'keimen, aufgehen' (vom Getreide); 'durchbrechen' (von den Zähnen)—B. II, 3, 405; Ber. *dĭgna;* W. *fīgo.* Cf. Lesk. Abl. 271.

dygùs 'scharf, spitzig, stachlig'—(Uh. *dhik*); B. I, 102.603. II, 3, 128; W. *fīgo, (fī);* (Boi. θιγγάνω). Cf. Lesk. Abl. 271.

dygū̃s, dygḗtis 'Widerwillen, Ekel empfinden'—(Uh. *dhik*); (W. *fī, foedus*).

dykà, dykaĩ, ùž dýką adv. 'umsonst, unentgeltlich'—Ber. *dikŭ*. Cf. Lesk. Nom. 220.

dykas adj. 'müssig, unbeschäftigt, unfruchtbar; mutwillig, übermütig; wild'—Ber. *dikŭ*.

añt dýkū 'zum Schein'—Ber. *dikŭ*.

-dilbstù, -dil̃bti—see *nudilbstù* 'ich schlage die Augen nieder'.

dìlės plu. 'Ruderpflöcke' (Stecksel am Bootrande, zwischen denen die Ruder liegen)—(Ber. *dīly*). Cf. Lesk. Nom. 269 & Ness. 149[b]: *Dullas*.

dìlgau, dìlgyti 'mit Nesseln brennen'—(W. *falx*). Cf. Lesk. Abl. 323.

dilgė 'Nessel'—Ber. *dolga*; (W. *falx*). Cf. Ness. 142[b], Lesk. Abl. 323.

dilgẽlė dimin. id.—Ber. *dolga*.

dìlgstu, dìlgti 'von Nesseln verbrannt werden'—Ber. *dolga*. Cf. Lesk. Abl. 323.

dilgus 'stechend, brennend'—Ber. *dolga*. Cf. Lesk. Abl. 323.

dylù, dìlti 'sich abnutzen'—Ber. *dolnĭ*; W. 1. *dolo*; Boi. δαίδαλος. Cf. Lesk. Abl. 323.

dimsta man impers. 'mich dünkt'—Uh. *dhiṣ*. Cf. Ness. 143[a], Lesk. Abl. 323.

dimstis 'Hof, Gut; Hofraum an Gebäuden'—B. II, 1, 136; Ber. *domŭ*; W. *domus*; Boi. δάπεδον. Cf. Lesk. Abl. 323.

dynė (Szyr.) 'Kürbis'—Ber. *dyńa*. Cf. Brückner SlFw. 80.

dìnga, dìngti impers. 'scheinen'; **dìnga mán, mán dìng** 'es scheint mir, mich dünkt'—Uh. *dhiṣ*; (W. *disco* (s. v. *decet*)); (Boi. διδάσκω).

dìngaus, dìngotis 'sich dünken'—(W. *disco* (s. v. *decet*)).

dingstù, diñgti 'wohin geraten, wo bleiben'—Ber. *dǫgŭ*. Cf. Lesk. Abl. 323.

-dingstu, -dingti—see *padingstu* 'ich habe Gefallen'.

dýnis 'Kürbis'—Ber. *dyńa*.

dýrau, dýroti 'gaffen, lauern' (Kur. 'mit gesenktem Kopfe dastehen')—B. II, 1, 350. See *dyru, dyrėti* & Lesk. Abl. 272.

dìrbu, dìrbti (B. dírbu) 'arbeiten'—(F. *arbaiþs*); B. II, 1, 19.389; Boi. δράω. Cf. Lesk. Abl. 324.

dìrgau, dìrgyti '(einen Mechanismus) in Unordnung bringen; (eine Flinte) losgehen machen'—Ber. *-dorga* 3. Cf. Lesk. Abl. 324.

dìrginu, dìrginti id.—Ber. *-dorga* 3.

dìrgstu, dìrgti (von einem Mechanismus) 'in Unordnung geraten'; (vom Gewehr) 'losgehen'—Ber. *-dorga* 3; [W. *furvus*]. Cf. Lesk. Abl. 324.

-dìrlioti—see *nudìrlioti* 'die Haut abziehen'.

dirsztù, diřszti (Kur. etc.) 'hart werden'—see *dirżtù*.

dìrti (?) 'schinden' (Kur. **diru**), 'Rasen abstechen' (Kur. **dyrù**); **nudirtas** pret. pass. part. 'geschunden'—Uh. *dṛṇâti;* F. *dis-tairan;* B. I, 288.463.541. II, 1, 396. 430; Ber. *derǫ, dĭrnŭ, dĭrtŭ;* W. *derbiōsus;* Boi. & Prell. δέρω. Cf. Ness. 143[b]; Kur. s. v.; Lesk. Abl. 323-4, 387; Hirt Ablaut 229; Brückner SlFw. 80.

dyru, dyrėti (?) 'gucken, lauern, heranschleichen' (z. B. auf der Jagd)—Uh. *dīdeti,* (1. *dhīras*); W. *deus;* Boi. ἀθρέω. Cf. Lesk. Abl. 272.

dirvà 'Acker, säbares Ackerland'—Uh. *dūrvā;* Ber. *dervĭńa;* Boi. δαράτᾱ.

dirvõnas 'ehemaliges, jetzt als Wiese benutztes Ackerland' —B. II, 1, 281; Ber. *dervĭńa.*

diřžas 'Riemen, Gürtel'—Uh. *dṛ́hyati;* (Ber: *dĭrzŭ, dĭržǫ*); W. *fortis;* (Boi. δράσσομαι).

dirżmas (?) 'stark'—W. *firmus.* See next.

dirżnas 'stramm, stark, schön gewachsen'—B. II, 1, 258. Cf. Geitler LS. 81, Lesk. Nom. 355.

dirżtù, diřžti (**dirsztù, diřszti** Kur., B., Boi.) 'welk, zähe, hart werden' (z. B. vom Brot)—(F. *trigō*); B. I, 463; (Ber. *dĭrzŭ, dĭržǫ*); W. *fortis;* (Boi. δράσσομαι). Cf. Lesk. Abl. 324.

dižu, dižti; dėžti 'durchprügeln'—Uh. *dehas;* F. *deigan;* B. I, 551; Ber. *děža;* W. *fingo;* Boi. τεῖχος. Cf. Geitler LS. 81, Lesk. Abl. 291.

do Old Lith. prep. & pref. 'zu'—W. *dē.* Cf. Bezz. BGLS. 280.

dorà 'Eintracht'—B. I, 152; Ber. *dorgŭ* 1; W. *firmus;* Boi. θρᾶνος. Cf. Lesk. Abl. 361.

dosnas 'freigebig, mildtätig'—B. II, 1, 265.537.

dosnùs id.—B. II, 1, 265.292.

dovanà 'Gabe, Geschenk, Steuer'—B. I, 204. II, 1, 268. 635. 3, 243; Ber. *davają;* W. *duim;* Boi. δίδωμι (note). See *dúdu* & Lesk. Nom. 387.

dovanóju, dovanóti 'schenken'—B. II, 3, 215.

dõvyju, dõvyti 'zum Springen, Laufen, zu starker, fortgesetzter Bewegung antreiben; abquälen; zunichte machen'. **dõvyjůs, dõvytis** 'herumrasen, toben' (bes. von Kindern im wilden Spiel); 'sich abquälen; verbotenen Umgang pflegen' (von Frauenzimmern)—K. *Tod;* F. *af-dauiþs, dauþs;* Ber. *davą.* Cf. Brückner SlFw. 81.

dovina 'Gabe, Geschenk, Steuer'—B. II, 1, 268. See *dovanà;* Ness. 147[b]; Lesk. Nom. 387.

drabnùs 'leicht anhangend, feist' (Kur. 'leicht ermüdend')—Ber. *droba, drębĭ;* Boi. θρόμβος. Cf. Lesk. Abl. 324.

drabstaũ, drabstýti (Kur. & Uh. -pst-) 'Dickflüssiges oder Breiartiges (z. B. Strassenkot) fortgesetzt umherwerfen; bespritzen'—Uh. 1. *drapsás.* Cf. Lesk. Abl. 324.

drabùs 'zitternd, zittrig'—B. I, 473; (Ber. *drobĭnŭ*). See *drebù* & Kur. s. v. drebùs.

drabùžis, drebùžis 'Kleidungsstück, Kleid, Kleidung' (cf. Ness. 155[b])—B. II, 1, 511; Ber. *drabŭ.* Cf. Kur. s. v.; Lesk. Abl. 324; Lesk. Nom. 600.

dragė Old Lith. 'Hefe'—F. *drōbjan;* Ber. *droždžĭja;* Boi. θράσσω. Cf. Bezz. BGLS. 281, Sommer 154.

draĩkas 'lang gestreckt, schlank' (von Bäumen)—Ber. *drěkŭ.*

draĩkus 'zäh'—Ber. *drěkŭ.* Cf. Lesk. Abl. 272.
drambãžius 'Dickbauch'—B. II, 1, 511. See next and the Lith. words in Ber.
dramblỹs id.—Ber. *drębĭ.*
dranga 'Stange, Wagenbaum' (?)—Ber. *drǫgŭ.* Cf. Lesk. Nom. 208.
drãpanos plu. 'Weisszeug, leinene Unterkleider der Frauen' —Uh. *drāpis;* Ber. *drapajǫ.* Cf. Lesk. Abl. 324.
drapstaũ 'ich bespritze'—see *drabstaũ.*
drąsà 'Dreistigkeit, Kühnheit'—F. *ga-daursan;* Ber. *dĭrzŭ.* Cf. Lesk. Abl. 324.
draskaũ, draskýti iter. 'reissen, zerreissen' (Ness. 155ᵃ also 'rauben, plündern')—B. II, 3, 390; Ber. *drasajǫ.* Cf. Lesk. Abl. 325.
drąsùs 'dreist, kühn'—Uh. *dhṛṣṇóti;* F. *ga-daursan;* B. I, 722; Ber. *dĭrzŭ,* (*dręselŭ*); (W. *faber, fastus*); Boi. *θάρσος.* Cf. Lesk. Abl. 324.
draudžiù, draũsti 'wehren, sperren; verbieten; warnen, drohen'—W. *fraus.* Cf. Lesk. Abl. 294.
draũgalas 'Gefährte, Genosse; Platzmeister bei Hochzeiten' (der den Bräutigam begleitet, um die Gäste einzuladen); (Szyr.) 'Buhler, Ehebrecher'—B. II, 1, 367; Ber. *drugŭ.*
draũgas 'Gefährte, Genosse; Ehemann; Gehilfe; Anhänger'—F. *driugan;* Ber. *drugŭ;* (W. *drungus*).
draugė 'Gefährtin'—B. II, 1, 221. Cf. Lesk. Nom. 282.
draugè, draugià adv. 'mit, zusammen, in Gesellschaft'—B. II, 2, 717; Ber. *drugŭ.* Cf. Lesk. Nom. 283.
drausmė̃ 'Verbot, Drohung, Zucht'—B. II, 1, 252-3.
dravė̃ 'ein Loch im Baum zum Nisten der Vögel'—Boi. *δρῦς.*
dravìs 'Waldbienenstock'—Boi. *δρῦς.* Cf. Ness. 153ᵃ.
drebiù, drẽbti 'mit Dickflüssigem oder Breiartigem (z. B. Strassenschmutz) werfen'—Uh. 1. *drapsás;* (F. *dreiban, drōbjan*); B. II, 1, 540; Ber. *droba;* Boi. *θρόμβος* Cf. Lesk. Abl. 324.

drebù, drebė́ti 'zittern, beben'—Uh. *dṛbháti;* B. I, 473. II, 3, 178; (Ber. *drobĭnŭ*). Cf. Lesk. Abl. 324.

drebulỹs 'Zittern, Fieber, Fieberschauer'—B. I, 441; (W. *febris*).

drebùs 'zitternd, zittrig'—(Ber. *drobĭnŭ*). See *drabùs;* Kur. s. v.; Lesk. Nom. 245.

drebùžis 'Kleidungsstück'—see *drabùžis.*

drëkiù, drẽkti '(Halme) streuen'—Ber. *drěkŭ.* Cf. Lesk. Abl. 272.

drėksztinė (lenta) 'gerissene (Latte), dünn gespaltenes (Brett)'—Ber. *drěska.*

dreskiù, drẽksti 'reissen'—B. I, 868. II, 3, 360.390; Ber. *drasajǫ, drěska.* Cf. Lesk. Abl. 325.

dręsù, drį̃sti 'dreist sein, wagen'—Uh. *dhṛṣṇóti;* F. *gadaursan;* B. I, 452; Ber. *dĭrzŭ, (dręselŭ);* Boi. *θάρσος.* See *drįstù* & Lesk. Abl. 324.

drežóju, drežóti 'streichen, glattstreichen' (z. B. eine gedrehte Schnur)—(Uh. *dhrájati*).

drýbau, drýboti 'dick herabhangen, anhangen'—B. II, 1, 540. See *drebiù* & Lesk. Abl. 324.

drìgnės plu. 'schwarzes Bilsenkraut'—Boi. *τέρχνος.*

drignìs, drignas, drigna, drignus 'Regenbogen, Hof um den Mond'—B. II, 1, 288; (Boi. *θριγκός*). Cf. Ness. 156[a].

drykstù, drỹkti 'sich lang herabhangend ziehen' (von Halmen usw.)—Ber. *drěkŭ.* Cf. Lesk. Abl. 272.

-drykstù, -drìksti—see *sudrykstù* 'ich zerreisse'.

drimbù, drìbti 'in dickflüssigen, breiartigen Stücken langsam fallen', e. g. **snẽgas drim̃ba** 'der Schnee fällt in grossen Flocken'; **sudrìbęs** perf. act. part. 'schlaff in den Gliedern hangend' (von einem Müden)—F. *dreiban;* B. II, 1, 568. 3, 289.446; Ber. *droba, drębĭ;* Boi. *θρόμβος.* Cf. Lesk. Abl. 324.

drį̃sti 'wagen'—inf. of *drįstù* 'ich werde dreist', or of *dręsù* 'ich wage'.

drįstù, drį̃sti 'dreist werden, wagen'—B. I, 452.472.523;

Ber. *dĭrzŭ;* W. *infestus;* Boi. θάρσος. See *dręsù* & Lesk. Abl. 324.

driuktas 'dick, umfangreich'—see *druktas.*

driútas 'fest, stark'—see *drútas.*

dróbė 'Leinwand, Laken'—Ber. *drabŭ.* Cf. Lesk. Abl. 324, Hirt Ablaut 227.

drobùlė 'Umschlagetuch, Laken' (cf. Ness. 156^{b})—Ber. *drabŭ.* Cf. Lesk. Abl. 324.

-droszti—see *padroszti* 'schnell laufen'.

drugỹs 'Fieber; Fiebervogel, Schmetterling'—Ber. *drŭgajǫ;* Boi. ἠπίαλος, τανθαρύζω, τονθορύζω. Cf. Lesk. Nom. 293.

-drugti—see *sudrugti* 'sich gesellen'.

druktas, driuktas dial. 'dick, umfangreich, stark'—W. *fortis, (dūrus).* Cf. Geitler LS. 81, Lesk. Nom. 557.

drumsczù (drumstù), drum̃sti 'trüben'—Ber. *dręselŭ.*

drumstas 'Bodensatz'—Ber. *dręselŭ.*

drumstù, drum̃sti 'trüben'—see *drumsczù.*

drumstùs 'trübe'—Ber. *dręselŭ.*

druskà 'Salz'—(K. *Salz*); F. *drauhsna;* Ber. *drozgajǫ, (krupa);* (W. *frūstum*); Boi. θραύω.

drútas, driútas 'fest, stark, hart'—Uh. *dhruvás;* F. *trauan;* B. II, 1, 201.407; Ber. *-dorvŭ;* W. *dūrus, (fortis);* Boi. δρυμός, (ἀθρέω). Cf. Lesk. Nom. 557.

drūtis masc., **drūtìs** fem. 'Stärke, Festigkeit'—B. II, 1, 172. Cf. Lesk. Nom. 300, 301, 547.

dù masc., **dvì** fem. 'zwei'. Other forms also indexed separately.—Uh. *dvā́;* K. *zwei;* F. *twai;* B. I, XLVI.295. 339.522. II, 1, 163. 2, 10.77(twice); Ber. *dŭva;* W. *duo;* Boi. 1. δύω. Cf. Wied. 156.2.

dubrávas 'ausgefahrenes Loch auf der Strasse'—Ber. *dŭbrĭ.* Cf. Juškevič 357.

dúburas 'Grube voll Wasser, Loch, Tümpel'—Ber. *dŭbrĭ.* Cf. Juškevič 357.

duburỹs (Kur. **dūburỹs**) 'Loch im Boden, Tiefe, Quelle'—B. II, 1, 358. Cf. Lesk. Abl. 295, Lesk. Nom. 448.

dubùrkis 'Grube voll Wasser, Loch, Tümpel'—Ber. *dŭbrĭ*. Cf. Juškevič 357.

dubùs 'tief, hohl'—K. *tief;* F. *diups;* B. I, 109.518.629. II, 1, 358.383; Ber. *dupa;* Boi. πυθμήν. Cf. Lesk. Abl. 295.

dùgnas 'Boden, Grund'—F. *ga-dauka;* B. I, 521. II, 1, 256; Ber. *dŭno;* Boi. πυθμήν. Cf. Lesk. Nom. 360.

dùja 'Staub, Stäubchen; (Kur. DLWb. s. v. Milbe) Käsemilbe'—Uh. *dhūnóti;* F. *dauns, daubs;* Ber. *dują;* W. *fūmus;* Boi. (Ntr.) θίς.

dũkis 'Tollheit, Raserei'—K. *toben*. Cf. Lesk. Abl. 295.

dūkrà 'Tochter'—B. I, 719. II, 1, 162,334; Ber. *dŭkti*.

duksas 'beleibt, völlig'—B. II, 1, 543.

dūkstù, dũkti 'rasend werden, rasen, wüten, böse sein'—K. *toben*. Cf. Lesk. Abl. 295.

duksus 'reich, reichlich versehen'—B. I, 785. II, 1, 543. Cf. Bezz. BGLS. 281, Lesk. Abl. 295.

duktē̃ 'Tochter'—Uh. *duhitā́;* K. *Tochter;* F. *dauhtar;* B. I, 104.109.528.581.628. II, 1, 162.334. 2, 127; Ber. *dŭkti;* Boi. θυγάτηρ.

duktẽlė 'Töchterchen'—B. II, 1, 376. Cf. Ness. 149[a].

dukterė̃lė id.—B. II, 1, 376. Cf. Ness. 149[a].

dulinė́ju, dulinė́ti 'schlendern, bummeln, faulenzen'—Uh. *dolā;* Boi. θολός.

dūlis, dūlỹs 'Räucherwerk zum Forttreiben der Bienen'—Uh. *dhūliṣ;* (F. *dwals*); B. I, 439. II, 1, 382; Ber. *dulo;* W. *fūlīgo;* Boi. θῡμός. Cf. Lesk. Nom. 458.

dùlkė sing. 'Stäubchen', **dùlkės** plu. 'Staub'—Uh. *dhūliṣ;* (F. *dwals*); Ber. *dulo;* W. *fūlīgo;* Boi. θῡμός. Cf. Lesk. Nom. 507.

dùlkėtas (B. **dúlkėtas**) 'staubig'—B. II, 1, 406.

dùlsvas 'schmutzigweiss, rauchfarben, mausgrau'—(W. *flāvus*). Cf. IF. XV, 121 & [Bezz. LF. 109: *dùlas;* Lesk. Nom. 345-6].

dúmas, usually plu. **dúmai** 'Rauch'—Uh. *dhūmás;* F. *dauns;*

B. I, 111.528. II, 1, 246. 2, 430; Ber. *dymŭ;* W. *fūmus;* Boi. *θῦμός, τύφω.*

dumblýnas 'Morast'—B. II, 1, 623. See Lesk. Nom. 409 & next.

dumbù, dùbti 'hohl werden, einsinken'—K. *Tümpel, Döbel;* F. *diups;* Ber. *dupa.* See *dubùs* & Lesk. Abl. 295.

dumburȳs (Bezz. also **dùmburys**) 'Loch, Quelle, gegrabener Teich, vom Strudel ausgehöhlte Tiefe in einem Fluss'—F. *diups;* B. II, 1, 358. Cf. Geitler LS. 82; Bezz. LF. 109; Bezz. BGLS. 40; Lesk. Abl. 295; Lesk. Nom. 448.

dumiù, dùmti 'wehen, blasen, zusammentragen, decken'; **apdumiù, apdùmti** 'mit Sand oder Schnee betragen' (vom Winde)—Uh. *dhámati;* B. I, 410.455; Ber. *dŭmǫ, dymajǫ.* Cf. Lesk. Abl. 315.

dùmplės (B. **dúmplės**) plu. 'Blasebalg'—B. II, 1, 620; Ber. *dŭmǫ.* Cf. Lesk. Nom. 458.

dùndu, dundė́ti 'heftig pochen' (vom Herzen); Ness. 150[b]: 'einen Ton von sich geben, rufen, tönen, murren'—(Uh. *dhúniṣ*).

dùrys plu. tant. 'Tür'—Uh. *dvắr;* K. *Tür;* F. *daur;* B. I, 109.424. II, 1, 133.141.171. 2, 220.245; Ber. *dvĭri;* W. *foris;* Boi. *θύρᾱ.*

duriù, dùrti 'stechen'—Ber. *-darǫ, dira;* Boi. *τέρθρον.* Cf. Lesk. Abl. 316.

dùsas 'Seufzer'; (Mielcke) 'Dunst'; (Kur.) 'Engbrüstigkeit'—Ber. *duchŭ, dŭchŭ;* Boi. *θεῖον, θεός.* See next.

dūsiù, dūsė́ti (Kur. also **dusiù, dusė́ti**) 'atmen, seufzen, keuchen'; Kur.: **dusiù, dusė́ti** 'hüsteln'—Uh. *dhūsaras;* F. *dius;* Ber. *duchŭ, dychajǫ;* W. *bēstia;* Boi. *θεός.* Cf. Lesk. Abl. 296.

dustù, dùsti 'ins schwere Atmen geraten, aufkeuchen'—Uh. *dhūsaras;* F. *dius;* Ber. *duchŭ;* W. *bēstia;* Boi. *θεῖον, θεός.* Cf. Lesk. Abl. 296.

duszimtàsis 'zweihundertster'—B. II, 2, 62. Cf. Schleicher LSpr. I, 63; Kur. Gram. 1029.

dúzgu, dūzgĕti (dų́zgu, dųzgĕti ?) 'einen hohlen, dumpf dröhnenden Schall von sich geben, klappern, tönen'—(Ber. *dŭždžĭ*). Cf. Lesk. Abl. 315.

dů̂bē 'Vertiefung, Loch, Höhle, Grube, Grab'—K. *Döbel;* F. *diups.* Cf. Lesk. Abl. 295.

dů̂bĕtas 'grubig, löcherig' (vom Wege)—B. II, 1, 406.

dū̃biu, dū̃bti 'aushöhlen, ausschnitzen'—Ber. *dupa.* Cf. in Index Berneker's other Lith. examples; Lesk. Abl. 295.

dū̃dąs pres. act. part. of **dū̃du,** q. v., 'gebend'—B. II, 1, 457.

dů̂dlióju, dů̂dlióti 'geben'—B. I, 541.

dū̃du (old form **dū̃mi**), **dū̃ti** 'geben' (with an inf.: 'erlauben, lassen'). Other forms also indexed separately. —Uh. *dádāti;* B. I, 156.158.171.338.339.489.527.717. 718(twice). II, 1, 398.433.442.456.457.458.459. 3, 100.243.317.336.384(twice).386.409.431.449.493; Ber. *damĭ;* W. *dō, duim,* (*cedo*); Boi. δίδωμι (& note). Cf. Kur. Gram. 1176, Wied. 178.1.

dū̃k impera. 2nd pers. sing. of **dū̃du,** q. v., 'gib'—B. II, 3, 100; (W. *cedo*).

dů̂klas 'Korb, in dem den Pferden Futter gegeben wird'—B. II, 1, 340.341. See *dū̃du* & Lesk. Nom. 496.

dū̃mi 'ich gebe'—old pres. of *dū̃du,* q. v.

dū̃na 'Brot'—Uh. *dhānā́s;* (F. *barizeins* (note)); B. I, 156; W. *fēlīx.*

dů̂nis 'Binse'—F. *faura-tani.* Cf. Bezz. LF. 108; Geitler LS. 81; Sommer 256; [Lesk. Nom. 372].

dů̂nis 'Gabe, Almosen, Tribut, Grundzins'—B. II, 1, 287. 634; Ber. *danĭ;* W. *dō.* Cf. Lesk. Nom. 370.

dū̃sęs fut. act. part. of **dū̃du,** q. v., 'daturus'—B. II, 1, 456. 458.459. 3, 384.

dū̃siu fut. of **dū̃du,** q. v., 'ich werde geben'—B. II, 3, 336. 384.386.

dū̃sius dial. fut. act. part. of **dū̃du,** q. v., 'daturus'—B. II, 1, 458.

dů̂slùs 'freigebig, mildtätig, freundlich'—B. II, 1, 373.

důsnis 'Gabe'—F. *ana-būsns;* B. II, 1, 265.289.537. See *dūnis* 'Gabe' & Ness. 145[*].
důsnùs 'freigebig, mildtätig, freundlich'—B. I, 784.
dũtas pret. pass. part. of **dũdu**, q. v., 'datus'—B. II, 1, 398.
důtis (?) 'Gabe'—Uh. *dâtiṣ;* F. *anda-bauhts;* Ber. *datĭ;* W. *dō;* Boi. δίδωμι (note). Cf. Ness. 145[a], Lesk. Nom. 554.
dũtų supin. of **dũdu**, q. v., 'zu geben'—B. II, 1, 442.
dvãras 'Gutshof, Edelhof; Hofraum'—Uh. *dvâr;* F. *daur;* B. II, 1, 156; Ber. *dvorŭ;* W. *foris;* Boi. θύρᾱ. Cf. Lesk. Nom. 170.
dvarinykas dial. (Godlewa) 'Hofmann'—B. II, 1, 487 (read 'Hofmann' after *dvarinykas,* not 'Schuldner'). See prec. & [Ness. 158[a]]; [Bezz. BGLS. 107-8]; [LBLV. 289]; [Lesk. Nom. 520-1].
dvãsė, dvasè, dvasià 'Geist, Seele, Gespenst'; old & dial. 'Hauch, Atem'—Uh. *dhūsaras;* F. *dius;* B. I, 310.493; Ber. *duchŭ;* W. *bēstia, fērālis;* Boi. θεῖον, θεός. Cf. Lesk. Abl. 362; Lesk. Nom. 271, 311; Sommer 148-150.
dvasià 'Geist'—see prec.
dveigỹs 'zweijährig' (von Tieren, nicht von Menschen)—B. II, 1, 513; Ber. *dŭva.*
dvëjau, dvëjaus adv. 'zu zweien, als Paar, selbander'—B. II, 2, 207.208.210.697. Cf. Kur. Gram. 1035, Wied. 158.2.
dvejerì 'zwei'—B. II, 2, 77. Cf. Kur. Gram. 1033, Wied. 158.
dvẽjetas 'Zweiheit'; Ness. 159[a]: "ein Paar, von lebenden Wesen"—F. *bajōþs;* B. II, 2, 24. Cf. Lesk. Nom. 571.
dvejì, fem. **dvẽjos** 'zwei, je zwei'—Uh. *dvayás;* F. *tweifls;* B. I, 288. II, 1, 163. 2, 76.77; Ber. *dŭva;* Boi. δοιός. Cf. Kur. Gram. 1033, Wied. 158.2.
dvejókas 'zweierlei'—B. II, 1, 498. Cf. Wied. 159.
dvejópas id.—F. *tweifls;* B. II, 2, 234. Cf. Kur. Gram. 1036, Wied. 159.

dvējos 'zwei'—fem. of *dvejì*, q. v.
dvējū gen. of dù, q. v., 'duorum'—F. *twai;* B. I, XLVI. II, 1, 163. 2, 10.77 (twice). Cf. Kur. Gram. 1005, Wied. 156.2.
dvēm dat. inst. of dù, q. v., 'duobus'—F. *twai;* B. II, 2, 10. Cf. Kur. Gram. 1005, Wied. 156.2.
dvėsìmas 'das Verenden'—W. *bēstia.* See next.
dvesiù, dvė̃sti 'atmen, hauchen, keuchen'; 'verenden, sterben' (von Tieren)—Uh. *dhūsaras;* F. *dius;* B. I, 493; Ber. *duchŭ,* (*dują*); W. *bēstia;* Boi. θεῖον, θεός. Cf. Lesk. Abl. 361, 296.
dvetas 'Zweiheit'—B. II, 2, 24. Cf. Lesk. Nom. 571.
dvì 'zwei'—fem. of *dù,* q. v.
dvi- (in cmpds.) 'zwei-'—W. *bis;* Boi. δίς.
dvìdeszimt 'zwanzig'—B. II, 2, 37.38. Cf. Wied. 156.
dvìdeszimtas 'zwanzigster'—B. II, 2, 60. Cf. Wied. 157.
dvìdeszimts 'zwanzig'—B. II, 2, 37.38. Cf. Kur. s. v.
dvigubaĩ adv. 'doppelt'—B. II, 2, 72. See next.
dvìgubas 'zweifach, doppelt'—B. II, 2, 71; Ber. *gŭbežĭ;* (Boi. κῦφός).
dvỹlas 'schwarz, schwarzköpfig' (nur von Rindern)—(W. *bīlis*); Boi. θολός.
dvýlika 'zwölf'—K. *zwölf, elf;* F. *twa-lif, ain-lif;* B. II, 2, 5.26.27; [Ber. *-lĕkŭ*]; W. *linquo.* See *dù, dvì* & Kur. Gram. 1010, Wied. 156.11-19, [Lesk. Abl. 277].
dvýliktas 'zwölfter'—B. II, 2, 59. Cf. Wied. 157.11-19.
dvìlinkas adj., **dvilinkaĩ** adv. 'doppelt, zweifach'—B. II, 2, [71].72.
dvilỹpis 'zusammengewachsen, doppelt' (e. g. **dvilỹpis rė̃szutas** 'Doppelnuss')—Ber. *lĕpą.* Cf. Lesk. Abl. 277.
dvỹnas sing. 'Zwilling', **dvynù** dual 'Zwillinge'—K. *Zwilling;* F. *tweihnai;* B. II, 2, 78.79; W. *bīni.* Cf. Lesk. Nom. 363.
dvynùczei plu. 'Zwillinge'—B. II, 2, 78.
dvirãtis 'zweiräderig(er Wagen)'—W. *birotus, rota.*
dvisėdà, dvisėdaĩ adv. 'zweisitzig'—B. II, 2, 717.

dżaugiū̃s, dżaũgtis 'sich freuen'—W. *gaudeo, juvo, (jūbilum)*; Boi. γηθέω. Cf. Lesk. Abl. 295.

dżáuju, dżáuti trans. 'trocknen'—(W. *jējūnus*); (Boi. σκυτάλη). Cf. Lesk. Abl. 295.

dżugus 'schnarrend, quakend, geschwätzig'—W. *jugo*. Cf. Lesk. Abl. 295.

dżungū̃s, dżùgtis (only in composition) 'froh sein'; **prasidżungù, prasidżùgti** 'froh werden, in Freude ausbrechen'—B. I, 280 (note); W. *juvo, (jūbilum)*. Cf. Lesk. Abl. 295.

dżústu, dżúti 'trocken, dürr, mager werden; verdorren; verschmachten'—(W. *jējūnus*). Cf. Lesk. Abl. 295.

E

e (ē) East Lith. 'und, aber'—B. I, 152.941. II, 2, 165; (Ber. *i*). Cf. Geitler LS. 82.

ė̃dęs perf. act. part. of **ė̃du**, q. v., 'gefressen habend'—B. I, 131.495. II, 1, 568. 3, 447.493; W. *edo;* Boi. ἔδω.

ė̄desis (W., Boi., Wied., et alii **ė́desis**) 'Frass, Futter'—K. *Aas;* B. I, 665. II, 1, 478.514.524.542; Ber. *ĕmĭ, ĕsli;* W. *ēsca;* Boi. ἔδω. See *ė́du* & Lesk. Abl. 371.

ėdestis 'Futter'—B. II, 1, 439. Cf. Lesk. Nom. 579.

ėdìmas 'Fressen'—B. II, 1, 251.

ė̄dis 'Frass, Speise'—B. II, 1, 167; Ber. *ĕmĭ;* W. *jējūnus;* Boi. ἔδω. See *ė́du* & Lesk. Abl. 371, Lesk. Nom. 288.

ė̃dmenys plu. 'Fresse, Maul'—Uh. (Ntr.) *ádma*. See *ė́du* & Lesk. Abl. 371, Lesk. Nom. 417.

ė̃dmi 'ich fresse'—old pres. of *ė́du*, q. v.

ėdrà 'Tierfutter'—Boi. ἔδω, εἶδαρ. Cf. Lesk. Abl. 371.

ė̃du (**ė̃dżu**; old forms **ė̃dmi, ė̃mi**), **ė̃sti** 'fressen'. Other forms also indexed separately.—Uh. *átti;* K. *essen;* F. *itan;* B. I, 131.137.148 (& note).495.532.717.718. II, 1, 568. 3, 96.128.373.447.493; Ber. *ĕmĭ;* W. *edo;* Boi. ἔδω. Cf. Kur. Gram. 1177; Wied. 177.3; Lesk. Abl. 371.

ėdža 'Fresser'—B. II, 1, 185; Ber. *ěmĭ*. Cf. Sommer 113, 120.

ědžos plu. 'Futterraufe'—B. II, 1, 185; Ber. *ěmĭ, ěsli*. Cf. Lesk. Abl. 371; Sommer 113, 120; Bezz. LF. 110.

ědžu 'ich fresse'—see *ědu*.

ẽglė 'Tanne'—B. I, 541; Ber. *edla;* W. *ebulum;* (Boi. (Ntr.) ἀκτέα).

egžlỹs 'Kaulbarsch'—see *ežegỹs*.

ei impera. 3rd pers. sing. of **eimì**, q. v., 'gehe er'—B. II, 3, 88. Cf. Wied. 177.2.

eigà 'Gang'—B. II, 1, 506.507; (Ber. *čugają*); Boi. οἴχομαι. Cf. Lesk. Nom. 523.

eĩk impera. 2nd pers. sing. of **eimì**, q. v., 'geh'—B. II, 3, 88.

eilẽ 'Reihe, Zeile, Schicht, Ordnung, Verwandtschaftsglied, Vers, Furche'—B. II, 1, 365.

eĩme pres. 1st pers. plu. of **eimì**, q. v., 'wir gehen'—B. II, 3, 88.

eimì 'ich gehe'—old pres. of *einù*, q. v.

einù (dial. **eitù**; old forms **eimì** 'ich gehe', **eisì** 'du gehst', **eĩti**, dial. **eĩt** 'er geht'), **eĩti** 'gehen'. Other forms also indexed separately.—Uh. *éti;* K. *eilen, gehen;* F. *iddja;* B. I, 178.190. II, 1, 432.441.456. 3, 88.320.362.371. 374.440.493; Ber. *idą;* W. *eo;* Boi. εἶμι. Cf. Kur. Gram. 1178; Wied. 177.2; Lesk. Abl. 272.

eĩsena 'Gang, Gangart'—B. II, 1, 269. Cf. Lesk. Nom. 380.

eismẽ 'Gang, Steig'—Uh. 2. *éṣati;* (Boi. 2. οἶμος). Cf. Lesk. Abl. 272.

eismenė 'Gang'—B. II, 1, 243. Cf. Lesk. Nom. 419.

eitù dial. 'ich gehe'—see *einù*.

eĩtų supin. of **einù** (**eimì**), q. v., 'zu gehen'—F. *blōtinassus;* B. I, 190. II, 1, 441.

ẽjęs perf. act. part. of **einù** (**eimì**) 'ich gehe', q. v.,—B. II, 3, 440.493.

ekěczos 'Egge'—see *akěczos*.

ekěju, ekěti 'eggen'—see *akěju*.

ékszlis 'Kaulbarsch'—see *ežegỹs*.

éldija 'Flusskahn, Lastkahn'—(W. *alvus*). Cf. Lesk. Nom. 317.

elgeta 'Armer, Bettler'—(W. *ulciscor*). Cf. Lesk. Nom. 571.

elgiũs, el̃gtis 'sich betragen, einen Lebenswandel führen'—B. I, 464. Cf. Lesk. Abl. 362.

elkas, alkas Old Lith. 'heiliger Hain'—Uh. *rákṣati;* F. *alhs;* W. *arceo;* Boi. ἀλέξω, (Ntr.) ἄλσος. Cf. Bezz. BGLS. 282, Lesk. Nom. 161.

elksnýnas, elksnỹnė 'Ellerngehölz'—B. II, 1, 278. See next.

el̃ksnis, al̃ksnis 'Eller, Erle'—(Uh. *ṛṣ̥tiṣ*); B. I, 766. II, 1, 265.544; Ber. *jelĭcha;* W. *alnus.*

elkúnė 'Ellenbogen'—see *alkúnė.*

ellenis, ellinis, ellinas Old Lith. 'Hirsch'—K. *Elentier;* Ber. *élenĭ.* Cf. Bezz. BGLS. 282, Sommer 278.

el̃mės, almens 'die aus dem toten Körper (bes. aus dem Munde) fliessende Feuchtigkeit'—(Uh. *lālā*); W. *alga;* Boi. λήμη.

élnė 'Hirschkuh, Hindin'—B. II, 1, 296; Ber. *elenĭ;* W. *alcē;* Boi. ἐλλός. Cf. Lesk. Nom. 371.

élnis 'Hirsch, Elentier'—Uh. *eṇas;* K. *Elentier,* (*Hirsch*); F. *lamb;* B. I, 116.359. II, 1, 264.296; Ber. *elenĭ;* W. *alcē;* Boi. ἐλλός. Cf. Lesk. Nom. 371.

emalas 'Mispel'—see *āmalas.*

ẽmęs perf. act. part. of **imù,** q. v., 'genommen habend'—B. II, 3, 442.493.

ė̃mi 'ich fresse'—old pres. of *ė́du,* q. v.

ėmiaũ pret. of **imù,** q. v., 'ich nahm'—Ber. *emą;* W. *emo* (twice); Boi. νέμω.

éngiu, éngti 'etwas mühsam und schwerfällig tun; schlagen'; **nuéngiu, nuéngti** 'abschaben, abschinden'; **árklį nuéngti** 'ein Pferd abquälen, abtreiben'—B. I, 584. II, 3, 285-6.382 (**énkiu**); Ber. *ęďža;* Boi. νωχελής. Cf. Ness. 19[a]; Kur. s. v.; Geitler LS. 98; Bezz. LF. 110; Lesk. Abl. 329.

ent- pres. part.—see *einù* 'ich gehe' & *iszent-* 'exiens'.
ẽpuszė 'Schwarzpappel'—Ber. *asika*. See *apuszė* & Sommer 123.
ẽras, ãras 'Adler'—Boi. ὄρνις. See *erẽlis* & Lesk. Nom. 162.
ė́ras 'Lamm'—B. II, 1, 207; Ber. *jarŭ* 1; W. *ariēs;* Boi. ἔριφος, (εἶρος (note)). Cf. Lesk. Nom. 165.
ė́rczukas 'Kartoffel'—Ber. *karczoch*.
er̃dvas 'geräumig, weit'—B. I, 718. II, 1, 204; W. *rārus;* Boi. ἀραιός. Cf. Lesk. Abl. 329, Lesk. Nom. 344.
erẽlis, arẽlis 'Adler'—K. *Aar;* F. *ara;* B. I, 445. II, 1, 364; Boi. ὄρνις. Cf. Brückner SlFw. 43 (note 31).
ėrýtis 'Lämmchen, Lamm'—W. *ariēs*. See *ė́ras*.
erkė 'Holzbock, Schaflaus'—Uh. *likṣā;* W. *ricinus*.
erszkė̃tis 'Dornpflanze, Stachel'; plu. **erszkė̃czai** 'Dornen, Dornenhecke'—Uh. *rákṣas;* (Ber. *ežĭ*); W. *ruscum,* (*excetra*). Cf. Bezz. LF. 110.
erszkė̃tras 'Stör'—Ber. *esetrŭ;* W. *excetra*.
erszkė̃tris 'Walfisch'—W. *excetra*. See prec.
ertas 'geräumig'—B. II, 1, 412. Cf. Geitler LS. 82, Lesk. Abl. 329.
ėrubė̃ 'Haselhuhn'—Ber. *ěrębĭ*. Cf. Lesk. Nom. 268-9.
er̃žilas (erželas, eržilis) 'Hengst' (Geitler 'ein junger Mann')—B. I, 565. II, 1, 368; Ber. *kŭnorzŭ,* (*gala*); Boi. ὄρχις. Cf. Geitler LD. 42-43.
ẽsąs, ė̃sąs (old form **sąs**) pres. part. of **esù (esmì)**, q. v., 'seiend'—B. II, 1, 456. 3, 94; Ber. *esmĭ;* W. *sons*. Cf. Wied. 177. 1.
èsiai plu. 'Kannenkraut'—W. *arista*.
esiúklės plu. id.—W. *arista*.
ė̃sk impera. 2nd pers. sing. of **ė́du**, q. v., 'friss'—B. II, 3, 96.
ėska or **ėskas** (acc. sing. **ėską**: fem. or masc.?—very probably nom. **ė̃ska**) 'Aas, Frass, Köder'—B. I, 665.717. 719. II, 1, 477.478.514.524; Ber. *ěmĭ, ěsli;* W. *ēsca;* Boi. ἔδω. See *ė́du* & Lesk. Nom. 504.
eskulus (?) (Szyr., Ness., Kur., s. v.) 'Buche'—there is no

evidence for the existence of the word in Lith. Cf. W. s. v. aesculus; Lesk. Nom. 507; IF. XIII, 279-280.

ẽsme pres. 1st pers. plu. of **esmì**, q. v., 'sumus'—B. I, 343. II, 3, 94; Boi. *εἰμί*.

esmì 'ich bin'—old pres. of *esù*, q. v.

esmù 'ich bin'—see *esù*.

-ẽsnis masc., **-ẽsnė** fem. comp. adj. end. (e.g. **gerẽsnis** 'besser')—B. II, 1, 550.551. Cf. Wied. 165, Lesk. Nom. 598.

ė́stas pret. pass. part. of **ė́du**, q. v.,—B. II, 3, 96; Ber. *ěmĭ*.

èstuba dial. 'Stube'—see *stubà*.

esù (**esmù**; old forms **esmì** 'ich bin', **esì** 'du bist', **ẽsti**, **ẽst** 'er ist') 'ich bin'. Other forms also indexed separately. —Uh. *ásti;* F. *im, is, ist;* B. I, 94.114.339.343.348.783. II, 1, 456. 3, 66.93.94.96; Ber. *esmĭ;* W. *sum, sons;* Boi. *εἰμί* (& note 3). Cf. Kur. Gram. 1106-1110, 1179; Wied. 177.1, 221; Lesk. Abl. 368.

ẽsva pres. 1st pers. dual of **esmì**, q. v., 'wir beide sind'—B. I, 339.

esz Old Lith. 'ich'—see *àsz* & Bezz. BGLS. 283.

eszė 'Äsche, Blei' (Fisch)—(Ber. *jazĭ*).

eszis 'Achse'—W. *axis*. See *aszìs*.

ẽszkau, ëszkóti 'suchen'—see *jẽszkau*.

eschketras (**eszkėtras**) Old Lith. 'Walfisch'—Ber. *esetrŭ;* W. *excetra*. Cf. Bezz. BGLS. 283.

ẽszmas, jẽszmas (Ber., W., Boi. -ẽ-) 'Bratspiess'—B. II, 1, 251; (Ber. *igŭla*); W. *īcio;* Boi. *αἶκλοι, αἰχμή*. Cf. Lesk. Nom. 422.

eschwa (**eszva**) Old Lith. 'Stute'—W. *equus;* Boi. *ἵππος*. See *aszvà* & Bezz. BGLS. 283.

ëvà, jëvà 'Faulbaum'—K. *Eibe;* Ber. *iva;* W. *ūva;* Boi. *οἴα*.

eżẽ 'Rain, Furche, Feldscheide, Grenze, Gartenbeet'; (in der Fischersprache) "flache Stelle des Haffes am Ufer"—Ber. *ězŭ*. Cf. Sommer 146, 156.

eżegỹs, eżgỹs, ė́kszlis, jė́kszlis, egżlỹs 'Kaulbarsch'—Ber. *ězdĭ*.

ẽžeras, ažeras 'See, Teich'—Ber. *jezero;* Boi. ἀχερωίς. Cf. Lalis 43.

ežgỹs 'Kaulbarsch'—see *ežegỹs.*

ežỹs 'Igel'—K. *Igel;* B. I, 565. II, 1, 276; Ber. *ežĭ;* (W. *anguis, ēr*); Boi. ἐχῖνος.

G

gabalas (Ber. **gábala**) (?) 'grösseres Stück' (Fleisch, Brot usw.)—Ber. *kával* 2. Cf. Geitler LS. 83; Bezz. LF. 111; Lesk. Nom. 472.

gabanà 'Armvoll, Last, Bürde'—Uh. *gábhastiṣ;* B. II, 1, 439. 3, 472; Ber. *gabają;* W. *habeo.* Cf. Lesk. Nom. 387.

gabenù, gabénti 'fortschaffen, befördern, bringen, holen'—K. *geben;* F. *giban, gabei;* B. I, 575. II, 3, 175; Ber. *gabają, (gobino)*; W. *habeo.* Cf. Lesk. Abl. 372.

gabl(i)óju, gabl(i)óti 'necken, vexieren'—(Ber. *gabają*).

gablỹs 'wer neckt, vexiert'—(Ber. *gabają*).

gadas 'Vereinigung, Übereinkunft'—K. *gätlich;* Ber. *godŭ.* Cf. Brückner SlFw. 82.

gadynà 'Stunde, Zeit, Zeitverhältnisse'—Ber. *godŭ.* Cf. Ness. 236[a], Brückner SlFw. 83.

gadinù, gadìnti 'beschädigen, unbrauchbar machen, verderben; fälschen, entweihen; töten, hinrichten'—Uh. *gadas;* (F. *gatwō*); (Ber. *gadŭ*); (W. *defendo*). Cf. Lesk. Abl. 326.

gãdnas 'geeignet, brauchbar, tüchtig, würdig'—Ber. *godŭ.* Cf. Ness. 236[b].

gadnùs id.—Ber. *godŭ.*

gagalas East Lith. 'Storch' (or 'Enterich'? See Brückner, below)—Ber. *gogolĭ;* Boi. κίχλη (note). Cf. Geitler LS. 83; Brückner SlFw. 83 (& note 65); Lesk. Nom. 472.

gagù, gagë́ti 'schnattern' (von Gänsen)—Ber. *gagają, gogołą.*

gaidỹs 'Hahn'—Uh. *gā́yati;* (K. *Hahn*); B. I, 177.208.

II, 3, 379; Ber. *gajǫ;* (Boi. κανάσσω). Cf. Lesk. Abl. 273.

gaidrùs 'klar, hell' (bes. vom Wetter; auch vom Wasser)—B. I, 191.591. II, 1, 201.349.539; Boi. φαιδρός, φαιός. Cf. Lesk. Abl. 273.

gaidùs 'erwünscht, lieb'—(Ber. *čakajǫ*). Cf. Ness. (253ᵇ) & Kur. s. v. geidus; Lesk. Abl. 273.

gaĩgalas 'Enterich'—B. II, 1, 128; Ber. *gogolĭ;* Boi. κίχλη (note). Cf. Lesk. Nom. 472, 473.

gailestis 'Mitleid, Reue, Busse, Bekehrung'—B. II, 1, 439. Cf. Lesk. Nom. 580.

gailius 'Reue'—B. II, 1, 225. Cf. Lesk. Nom. 320.

gailiũs, gailė́tis 'Mitleid haben, bereuen'—K. *geil.*

gailùs 'jähzornig, wütend, rachgierig, heftig; giftig, bissig (z. B. von Hunden); beissend, scharf, bitter; mitleidig, kläglich, jämmerlich'—Uh. *helate;* K. *geil;* F. *gailjan* (& Ntr.); B. I, 448; (Boi. φίλος). Cf. Ness. (244ᵃ) s. v. Gailùs & Gailus; Lesk. Nom. 256.

gainióju, gainióti 'treiben, jagen'—Ber. *gańajǫ.* See *genù* & Geitler LS. 83; Bezz. BGLS. 283; Lesk. Abl. 326; Lalis 90; Juškevič 401.

gaĩsas (Ness. also **gaisa**) 'Lichtschein am Himmel' (z. B. Nordlicht, Wiederschein einer Feuersbrunst, Morgendämmerung)—B. II, 1, 201.539; Boi. φαιός. Cf. Ness. 244ᵇ, Lesk. Abl. 273.

gaĩsras (Ness. also **gaisra**) id.—B. II, 1, 355. Cf. Ness. 244ᵇ, Lesk. Abl. 273.

gaiszatis 'Versäumnis, Hindernis'—B. II, 1, 437. Cf. Ness. 244ᵇ, Lesk. Nom. 569-70.

gaiszinù, gaiszìnti 'verzögern, hindern, versäumen; tilgen, vernichten'—W. *haereo;* Boi. βαιός.

gaiszlùs 'säumig, langsam, langwierig, hinderlich'—B. II, 1, 385. Cf. Lesk. Nom. 468.

gaisztù, gaiszaũ, gaĩszti 'säumen, zögern; schwinden, vergehen'—(F. *us-gaisjan*); B. I, 568. II, 3, 262.360.399;

W. *haereo*, (*fīgo*), (*vēscus*); Boi. βαιός (& Ntr.), (σβέννῡμι). Cf. Lesk. Abl. 292.

gaivùs 'frisch, munter, lebhaft'—B. I, 316; W. *vīvo;* Boi. βίος. Cf. Lesk. Abl. 273, Lesk. Nom. 256.

gajùs 'leicht heilend, heilbar; heilsam'—Ber. *gojĭ;* W. *vīvo.*

gajùtės plu. a vulnerary herb (Ness. 'Schöllkraut, Chelidonium majus'; Kur. 'Schafgarbe, Achillea millefolium') —B. II, 1, 418. Cf. Ness. 254[a], Lesk. Nom. 576.

galándu, galą́sti 'wetzen'—W. *glaber*, (*blandus*). Cf. Lesk. Abl. 375.

gãlas 'Ende; Endchen, Stück, Teil'—B. I, 610. II, 1, 527. Cf. Lesk. Abl. 325, Lesk. Nom. 167.

galẽ 'Können, Vermögen'—Ber. *golěmŭ.* Cf. Lesk. Nom. 272, Sommer 55.

galiù, galė́ti 'können, physisch imstande sein'; **apgaliù, apgalė́ti** 'überwinden, überwältigen'; **negaliù, negalė́ti** 'kränklich, unpässlich sein'—Ber. *golěmŭ, golmę* 2; W. *hallus*, (*valeo*). Cf. Lesk. Abl. 374.

galtinis 'Maschenform zum Flechten der Netze'—(Uh. *jāṭā*). Cf. Geitler LS. 83, Hirt Ablaut 619.

galvà 'Kopf, Haupt'—B. II, 1, 208; Ber. *golva;* (W. *calva*); (Boi. κελέβη (& note)).

galvẽlė 'Köpfchen'—B. II, 1, 367. Cf. Ness. 238[b].

galvius 'Grossköpfiger'—B. II, 1, 224.

galvožỹs 'Zwerg'—B. II, 1, 511. Cf. Lesk. Nom. 600.

gaminù, gamìnti 'Kinder erzeugen, Vieh ziehen'—(W. *famulus*). Cf. Lesk. Abl. 326.

gamta 'angeborene Art, Natur, Tugend'—B. II, 1, 415-16. Cf. Geitler LS. 83, Lesk. Abl. 326.

ganà adv. 'genug'—(Uh. *āhanās*); B. I, 591; Ber. *goněją;* (W. *fēnus*); Boi. εὐθένεια. Cf. Lesk. Nom. 214.

ganaũ, ganýti '(Tiere) hüten, weiden'—B. I, 146. II, 3, 267.269; Ber. *gonĭi;* W. *defendo;* Boi. θείνω. Cf. Lesk. Abl. 326.

gañdras 'Storch'—(Ber. *gǫdǫ, gǫsĭ*); (W. *anser*).

gandrýnas 'Masse Störche' (Ness.: "eine Gegend, in der es viele Störche gibt, daher die Dörfernamen Gandrinen usw." On the meaning of the suffix see Lesk. Nom. 408)—B. II, 1, 278.649. Cf. Ness. 239[b], Lesk. Nom. 409.

ganyklà 'Weide, Weideplatz, Trift'—B. I, 541. II, 1, 622.

gãras 'Dampf'—B. I, 144; Ber. *gorę;* W. *formus;* Boi. θέρος, (βορέης). Cf. Lesk. Nom. 167.

garbà 'Ehre'—B. II, 1, 389. Cf. Lesk. Abl. 327, 362; Lesk. Nom. 208.

gárbana 'Locke'—Ber. *gŭrbŭ;* (Boi. γρομφάς (note)). Cf. Lesk. Nom. 387.

garbanũczus 'Lockiger'—B. II, 1, 224.

garbẽ 'Ehre'—B. II, 1, 389; W. (*garrio*), [*grātēs*]. Cf. Lesk. Abl. 362, Lesk. Nom. 590.

garbùs 'ehrwürdig, ehrenvoll'—B. II, 1, 389. Cf. Lesk. Abl. 362, Lesk. Nom. 261.

gar̃das 'eingezäunter Platz, Hürde; Herde'—Uh. *gṛhás;* K. *Garten;* F. *gards;* Ber. *gordŭ;* W. *cohors;* Boi. χόρτος. Cf. Lesk. Nom. 167.

gardùs 'würzig, wohlschmeckend'—Uh. *gṛ́dhyati;* F. *grēdus;* Ber. *goldŭ;* (W. *horior*).

gargaliũju, gargaliũti 'gurgeln, röcheln'—B. I, 425; W. *gurges.*

garnỹs 'Storch, Reiher'—B. I, 583; W. *grūs;* Boi. γέρανος.

gar̃sas 'Schall, Ton, Stimme, Gerücht, Echo'—Uh. *gṛṇā́ti;* F. *kara;* B. I, 575.786. II, 1, 542; Ber. *golsŭ, gorno;* (W. *garrio*); Boi. γῆρυς. Cf. Lesk. Abl. 327, Lesk. Nom. 595.

garsmas 'Gerücht, Ruf, Ruhm, Preis'—B. II, 1, 252. Cf. Lesk. Abl. 327, Lesk. Nom. 422.

garszvà 'Giersch, Aegopodium podagraria' (Mielcke also 'ein magerer Vogel')—Ber. *gorchŭ;* Boi. κρῖθή (note).

gãtavas 'bereit, fertig, willig'—Ber. *gotovŭ.*

gatvė 'Trift, Viehtrift; Strasse'—B. II, 1, 221 (fn.); F. *gatwō.* Cf. Lesk. Nom. 564.

gaubiù, gaũbti: sugaubti 'Getreide einführen, einsammeln' ("im Zem. soll es bedeuten 'von oben her ganz zudecken' "); **užsigaũbti** 'verhüllen'—Ber. *gŭbežĭ;* (Boi. κῦφός). Cf. Geitler LS. 112, Lesk. Abl. 298, Lalis 93, Juškevič 417.

gaudesis 'Summen (der Bienen)'; 'Ton' (überhaupt)—B. II, 1, 636-7. See *gaudžiù* & Lesk. Nom. 593; Geitler LS. 83.

-gaudl(i)oju (?): **užgaudl(i)oju, užgaudl(i)oti** 'anzüglich reden, necken'—B. I, 541. Cf. Ness. 243[a] (užgáudau); Lesk. Abl. 297 (gáudau etc.); Geitler LS. 118; Bezz. LF. 205 (Ntr.).

gaudonė̃ 'Pferdebremse' (Fliege); 'Bremse' ("die den Pferden an das Ohr oder an die Oberlippe angelegt wird, um sie zu bändigen")—Ber. *gǫdǫ.* Cf. Ness. 245[b]; Lesk. Abl. 298; Lesk. Nom. 392.

gaudžiù, gaũsti 'tönen, summen, klingen, heulen, jammern, weinen'—B. II, 1, 540; Ber. *gǫdǫ, (kuzlo)*; W. *fūnus* 1, *(gaudeo)*; Boi. γόος. Cf. Geitler LS. 83, Lesk. Abl. 298.

gaujà 'Rudel von Hunden, Wölfen, Spitzbuben'—K. *Kette* 1; Ber. *govorŭ;* Boi. βόσκω. Cf. Lesk. Abl. 297.

gauju, gauti (?) 'heulen' (von Wölfen)—Ber. *govorŭ.* Cf. Lesk. Abl. 319; Ness. 245[b]; Kur. s. v.

gáunu, gáuti 'erhalten, bekommen'—B. II, 3, 320.328; W. *vola;* Boi. γύαλον. Cf. Lesk. Abl. 297.

gaũras, plu. **gauraĩ** 'Körperhaar'—Ber. *gura;* Boi. γῦρός.

gaurū́tas 'haarig, rauh'—B. II, 1, 407.

gausingas 'freigebig, mildtätig'—B. I, 600; Ber. *govějǫ;* (W. *faveo* 2).

gausùs 'reichlich'—B. I, 600. II, 1, 543; Ber. *govějǫ;* (W. *faveo* 2). Cf. Lesk. Abl. 297, 298.

gaviù (gavė̃ju), gavė̃ti 'fasten'—Ber. *govějǫ.*

-gė̃bau—see *atgė̃bau* 'ich habe hervorgebracht'.

gė́da 'Schande, Unehre, Schimpf, Scham, Schamglied'—K. *Kot* 2; B. I, 137.610.659. II, 1, 265; Ber. *gadŭ;* (W. 2. *foedus*); Boi. δέννος. Cf. Lesk. Abl. 326.

gẽdingas 'schandbar, sich schämend'—B. II, 1, 509; Ber. *gadŭ*.

gẽdinu, gẽdinti 'beschämen, beschimpfen'—Ber. *gadŭ;* (W. 2. *foedus*). See *gė̃da* & Lesk. Abl. 326.

gė̃dmi 'ich singe'—see *gė̃du*.

gëdrà 'helles, andauernd trockenes Wetter; Heiterkeit des Wetters'—see next.

gẽdras 'klar, hell' (bes. vom Wetter; auch vom Wasser)—B. I, 191.591. II, 1, 201.349.[539]; Boi. φαιδρός, φαιός. Cf. Lesk. Abl. 273.

gëdrìngas (B. -íngas) 'heiter, klar' (vom Himmel)—B. II, 1, 509. Cf. Wied. 8.

gëdrùs 'klar, hell' (bes. vom Wetter; auch vom Wasser)—B. II, 1, 349.385. See *gẽdras* & Ness. 246[b].

gedù, gedẽti 'um einen Verstorbenen trauern'—Boi. θέσσασθαι. Cf. Lesk. Abl. 326.

gė̃du (gė̃stu) (gė̃dmi), gëdóti '(ein geistliches Lied) singen; krähen'—Uh. *gâyati;* (K. *Hahn*); (F. *qainōn*); B. I, 208. II, 3, 379; Ber. *gajǫ;* (W. *vīsio*); (Boi. κανάσσω). Cf. Lesk. Abl. 273, Kur. Gram. 1180a.

gegẽ, gega 'Kuckuck'—B. II, 1, 19 (note). Cf. Lesk. Nom. 199, 265.

geida 'Verlangen'—(Ber. *čakajǫ*). See next & cf. Bezz. LF. 112, Lesk. Abl. 273.

geidžù, geĩsti 'verlangen, begehren'—K. *Geiz;* F. *ga-geigan;* B. I, 178.390.577. II, 1, 449.571. 3, 136.492; (Ber. *čakajǫ*); (W. *hērēs, prehendo*); (Boi. 2. κίσσα: read lit. for lat.). Cf. Ness. 253[b] f. & Lesk. Abl. 273.

geinis "der Strick oder das Tau, das die Waldbienenfänger auf den Baum werfen, um an demselben sich hinaufzuschwingen"—B. II, 1, 287 (note); W. *fīlum, fūnis;* Boi. σχοῖνος. See next & Ness. 254[a], Lesk. Nom. 292.

geinis "ein Ast neben einem Stück Holz, behauen wie ein Brettchen, zum Zurückschlagen des Kreisels"—W. *fīlum*. See prec. & Lesk. Abl. 326, Lesk. Nom. 292.

gėlà 'heftiger, stechender, anhaltender Schmerz' (Zahnweh,

Rheumatismus usw.)—K. *Qual;* B. II, 1, 154.168.634; W. *vallessit;* Boi. βέλος. Cf. Lesk. Abl. 325.

gélda 'breiter Trog'—Ber. *galeta.* Cf. Prell. deutsch. Best. in den lett. Spr. 57.

gelė 'Waldveilchen, Viola hirta'—W. *flāvus.* Cf. Sommer 64.

geležìs 'Eisen; die Säge der Brettschneider'—B. I, 583.584; Boi. χαλκός. Cf. Lesk. Nom. 234.

geliù (įgeliù), gélti (įgélti) trans. 'stechen' (von der Biene usw.); intr. **gẽlia** 'es schmerzt', **gélti** 'weh tun, heftig schmerzen'—K. *kalt, Qual;* F. *kalds,* (*naus*); B. I, 593. II, 1, 154.168. 3, 264; W. *gelidus, vallessit,* (*doleo*); Boi. βέλος, γελανδρόν, δέλλῑθες, ὀβελός. Cf. Lesk. Abl. 325.

geliū̃ju, geliū̃ti 'gelten'—Boi. τέλθος.

gelmẽ 'Tiefe, der Grund im Wasser'—(Ber. *glǫbokŭ, golmę* 1); (Boi. θέλυμνα). Cf. Lesk. Abl. 325.

gélmenis 'heftige Kälte'—(Uh. *jaḍas*); F. *kalds;* W. *gelidus* (& Ntr.); Boi. γελανδρόν. Cf. Lesk. Abl. 325.

gelonìs (gelūnìs) 'Stachel (bes. der Bienen); stechender Schmerz; Zahnweh; Eiterstock im Geschwür; eine Krankheit am Finger'—B. I, 469.593; (Ber. *igŭla*); W. *vallessit;* Boi. βέλος, δέλλῑθες. Cf. Ness. 248[b]; Kur. s. v. gelonìs; Schleicher LSpr. I, 51 (p. 123); Kur. Gram. 321; Lesk. Abl. 325; Lesk. Nom. 394.

gelstù, gel̃sti 'gelb werden, reifen'—B. II, 3, 370. See *gel̃tas.*

gel̃svas 'gelblich, blond, fahl'—B. I, 766; Ber. *golǫbŭ;* W. *fel, flāvus,* (*gilvus*); Boi. χέλῡς. See *gel̃tas.*

geltà 'Gelbheit' ("nur bei Menschen, bes. bei gelbsüchtigen")—B. II, 1, 416.644.

gel̃tas 'fahlgelb, blond'—Uh. *háriṣ;* K. *Gold;* B. I, 471. II, 1, 413; Ber. *golǫbŭ;* W. *fel, flāvus;* Boi. χλωρός, χόλος.

geltõnis 'gelbe Farbe'—B. II, 1, 172. Cf. Kur. DLWb. s. v. gelb.

gelumà 'strenge (stechende) Kälte'—K. *kalt;* F. *kalds;* W. *gelidus;* Boi. γελανδρόν. Cf. Lesk. Nom. 431.

gelumbẽ 'feines blaues Tuch; blautuchener Frauenoberrock'—B. II, 1, 388; W. *columba*.

gelũ 'Stachel; Leichdorn'—B. II, 1, 308; (Ber. *kremy*). Cf. Lesk. Abl. 325, Lesk. Nom. 381.

gelùnìs 'Stachel' usw.—see *gelonìs*.

gelžìs 'Eisen'—Boi. χαλκός. See *geležìs*.

gema 'Frühgeburt'—B. II, 1, 155.

gémbė "ein in die Wand etc. geschlagener eiserner oder hölzerner Nagel zum Aufhängen, eine Knagge"—Ber. *gonoba*, *gǫba* 1; Boi. γαμψός, γόμφος (& Ntr.).

gemù, gim̃ti 'geboren werden'—Uh. *jāmiṣ*; F. *qiman*; W. *gener*, [*geminus*], (*famulus*); (Boi. βασιλεύς). Cf. Lesk. Abl. 325.

gendù, gèsti 'entzwei gehen, schadhaft werden (von einem Mechanismus); verderben; verwesen (vom menschlichen Leichnam)'—Uh. *gadas*; F. *qistjan*, (*gatwō*); (Ber. *gadŭ*); (W. *defendo*); (Boi. σβέννῡμι). Cf. Lesk. Abl. 326.

-gendù, -gèsti—see *pasigendù* 'ich vermisse'.

genesis 'Trift, Viehtrift'—B. II, 1, 525. Cf. Lesk. Abl. 326, Lesk. Nom. 593.

genỹs 'Specht'—W. *defendo*; Boi. θείνω. Cf. Lesk. Abl. 368.

geniù, genė́ti 'Zweige abhauen, einen Baum kappen' (Szyr. also 'schlagen, peitschen')—Uh. *hánti*; B. I, 621. II, 3, 184.188; W. *defendo*; Boi. θείνω. See *genù* & Lesk. Abl. 368..

gentãras, gintãras 'Bernstein'—(K. *Bernstein*); Ber. *jantaŕ*. Cf. Ness. 250[a].

gentė 'Schwägerin' usw.—see *jentė*.

gentìs 'Verwandter, Gevatter'—K. *Kind*; W. *gener*, (*janitrīcēs*).

genù, giñti 'jagen, treiben, hüten' (Vieh)—Uh. *hánti*; (F. *banja*); B. I, 129.416.591.621. II, 1, 430.568. 3, 117. 137.396.441.492; W. *defendo*; Boi. θείνω. Cf. Lesk. Abl. 326.

gẽras 'gut' (moralisch und physisch)—F. *qairrus;* B. I, 594; Boi. φέριστος. Cf. Lesk. Abl. 327, Lesk. Nom. 162.

gerbiu, gerbti 'ehren, loben, rühmen'—B. II, 1, 19.389. Cf. Lesk. Abl. 362.

gerdas 'Geschrei, Botschaft'—Ber. *gorno.* Cf. Bezz. BGLS. 284, Lesk. Abl. 327.

gerdenu, gerdenti 'Gerücht verbreiten'—Ber. *gorno.* Cf. Lesk. Abl. 327, Lalis 96.

gėrėjůs, gėrė̃tis (Kur. **gẽrėjůs, gẽrėtis**) 'Wohlbehagen empfinden, sich freuen, sich auf etwas zugute tun'—(W. *horior*); (Boi. χαίρω). Cf. Lesk. Abl. 327.

gerẽsnis 'besser'—B. II, 1, 551. See *gẽras* & *-ẽsnis.*

geriaũs adv. 'besser'—B. II, 1, 545.654. See *gẽras* & Wied. 166.

geriáusias 'bester'—B. II, 1, 545.654. See *gẽras* & *-iáusias.*

gẽrimas 'Trinken, Getränk'—B. II, 1, 251. See *geriù* & Lesk. Abl. 326.

gẽris id.—B. II, 1, 251. See *geriù* & Lesk. Abl. 327.

geriù, gérti 'trinken'—Uh. *giráti;* B. I, 590. II, 1, 435.444. 3, 442; Ber. *grotŭ* 1; W. *voro,* (*bria*); Boi. βορά. Cf. Lesk. Abl. 326.

gerklẽ 'Kehle, Schlund, Speiseröhre, Luftröhre' — Uh. *giráti;* W. *gurges;* Boi. βορά. See prec.

gértas pret. pass. part. of **geriù,** q. v., 'getrunken'—B. II, 1, 399.

gérvė 'Kranich, Grus communis; Quirlhaken' ("das Holz am obern Stein der Handmühle, in welches man den Stock hineinsteckt") — K. *Kranich;* B. I, 571.583 (twice). II, 1, 221 (note); (Ber. *korkŭ*); W. *grūs;* Boi. γέρανος. Cf. Ness. 253[a]; Lesk. Nom. 348; Sommer 220.

ger̃vinas 'männlicher Kranich'—B. II, 1, 601.

gesaũ, gesýti 'löschen'—Uh. *jásate;* (F. *qistjan*); B. I, 590. 727; Ber. *gašǫ;* (W. *sēgnis*); Boi. σβέννῡμι Cf. Lesk. Abl. 327.

gesinù, gesìnti id.—Uh. *jásate;* (F. *qistjan*).

gesmẽ 'kleines eben noch glimmendes Feuer' ("das man eben nur brennen lässt, um die Flamme nicht ausgehen zu lassen")—B. I, 784. Cf. Ness. 253[a], Lesk. Abl. 327.

gësmẽ 'Gesang, geistliches Lied'—B. II, 1, 253; Ber. *gajǫ*. Cf. Lesk. Abl. 273.

gèsti inf.—see 1. *gendù,* 2. *gendù,* or *gestù.*

gestù, gèsti 'erlöschen, ausgehen'—Uh. *jásate;* K. *verquisten;* (F. *qistjan*); B. II, 3, 171 (& note). 268; Ber. *gašǫ;* (W. *sēgnis*); Boi. *σβέννῡμι*. Cf. Lesk. Abl. 327.

gẽstu 'ich singe'—see *gẽdu.*

getis 'Viehtrift'—(Boi. *βόσκω* (note)). Cf. Lesk. Nom. 550.

gëžiù, gẽžti 'grollen'—F. *ga-geigan.* Cf. Lesk. Abl. 273.

gëžiûs, gëžtis 'heftig verlangen'—F. *ga-geigan;* (Boi. 2. *κίσσα*).

-gi strengthening enclitic particle, added to pron., adv., prep., or conj.—F. *mik;* B. I, 985; Ber. *-go;* W. *hic;* Boi. *γε*.

gýdau, gýdyti trans. 'heilen'—B. II, 3, 269; Ber. *gojĭ;* W. *vīvo;* Boi. *βίος*. See *gyjù* & Lesk. Abl. 445.

gijà 'Faden' (beim Weben); 'Masche, Schlinge' (beim Stricken)—Uh. 2. *jyā́;* (K. 8th ed. *Geige*); W. *fīlum;* Boi. *βιός*. Cf. Lesk. Nom. 311.

gyjù (Ness. 254[a]: "veraltet gynu"), **gýti** 'heil werden, aufleben, sich erholen'—Uh. *jinóti;* B. II, 1, 434.443; Ber. *gojĭ;* W. *vīvo;* Boi. *βίος*. Cf. Lesk. Abl. 272-3.

-gyjù, -gýti 'erlangen'—see *įgyjù.*

gìlė 'Eichel'—(Uh. *gaṇḍás*); B. I, 462.472.602. II, 1, 222; W. *glans;* Boi. *βάλανος*. Cf. Lesk. Nom. 235, 269 & Sommer 60.

gilmẽ 'Tiefe'—(Ber. *golmę* 1). See *gelmẽ.*

gìlsta, gìlti impers. 'anfangen zu stechen, zu schmerzen'—B. I, 469 (*gìlo* pret. 3rd pers. sing.). Cf. Lesk. Abl. 325, 382.

giltinẽ 'Todesgöttin, Tod' (cf. Ness. 255[a])—Boi. *βέλος*. Cf. Lesk. Abl. 325.

gilùs 'tief'—(Ber. *glǫbokŭ, golmę* 1); (W. *hio*); (Boi. θέλυμνα). Cf. Lesk. Abl. 325.

gim̃dyvė 'Gebärerin, Mutter; Gebärmutter'—B. II, 1, 204. Cf. Lesk. Nom. 353.

giminẽ 'Abkunft; Stamm, Familie, Geschlecht, Verwandtschaft; Nachkommenschaft'—(W. *famulus*); (Boi. βασιλεύς). Cf. Lesk. Abl. 325.

gimtìs 'natürliches Geschlecht, Geschlechtsunterschied'—(Boi. βασιλεύς). Cf. Lesk. Abl. 325.

ginczà fem. 'Streit'; **gi̇̃nczas** masc. 'Streit; Streiter, Zänker'—Uh. *hatyǎ;* B. I, 416. II, 1, 186.630.635; W. *defendo;* Boi. διφάσιος, θείνω. Cf. Lesk. Abl. 326.

gi̇̃nklas 'Waffe'—B. I, 416; Boi. θείνω. Cf. Lesk. Abl. 326.

gìnsla 'Ader'—see *gýsla*.

gintãras 'Bernstein'—see *gentãras*.

gi̇̃ntas pret. pass. part. of **genù**, q. v., 'gejagt, getrieben'—B. II, 1, 395.

gìntas (B. **gíntas**) pret. pass. part. of **ginù**, q. v., 'abgewehrt'—B. II, 1, 398.

gi̇̃nti 'jagen, treiben'—inf. of *genù*, q. v.

ginù, gìnti (B. **gínti**) 'wehren, schützen'—B. I, 417.423. II, 3, 137; W. *defendo*, (2. *fīlum:* see Lith. *suginù*); Boi. θείνω. See *genù* & Lesk. Abl. 326.

gynù 'ich lebe auf'—see *gyjù*.

gyrà f. 'Ruhm, Prahlerei'; m. 'Prahlhans'—B. II, 1, 611-12. 2, 96. See *giriù* & Lesk. Abl. 327.

girdżù, girdė́ti 'hören, vernehmen'—(F. *kara*); B. II, 3, 182; Ber. *gorno;* (W. *garrio*); (Boi. φράζω). Cf. Lesk. Abl. 327.

gìrė, gìria 'Wald, Forst; Einöde, Wüstenei'—Uh. *giriș;* B. I, 460. II, 1, 170; Ber. *gora;* W. *verŭ;* Boi. βαρύες, βορέης, (δειράς). Cf. Lesk. Nom. 269, Sommer 50-52.

girė̃nai plu. 'Waldleute'—B. II, 1, 308.319.605. Cf. Lesk. Nom. 388.

gìrgżdżu, girgżdė́ti; gùrgżdżu, gurgżdė́ti 'knarren'—Uh. *gárjati;* Ber. *grochotŭ*. Cf. Lesk. Abl. 327.

gìria 'Wald'—see *gìrė*.

gìria 'Trank' (cf. Ness. 251[b])—B. II, 1, 185. See *geriù* & Lesk. Abl. 326; Sommer 51, 186.

giriù, gìrti (B. etc. **gírti**) 'loben, rühmen, preisen'—Uh. *gūrtíṣ, gṛṇā́ti;* (F. *kara*); B. I, 460.465.468.474.571; Ber. *gorno;* W. *grātēs,* (*garrio*); (Boi. γῆρυς). Cf. Lesk. Abl. 327.

gỹrius 'Lob, Ruhm'—B. II, 1, 225.613.

gìrna 'Mühlstein', plu. **gìrnos** (B. **gírnos**) 'Handmühle'—Uh. *grā́vā;* F. *asilu-qairnus;* B. I, 129.606; W. *glārea;* Boi. γῦρις. Cf. Lesk. Nom. 364.

girstù, gir̃sti 'zu hören bekommen, vernehmen'—B. II, 1, 442; Ber. *gorno.* Cf. Lesk. Abl. 327.

gìrtas (B. **gírtas**) pret. pass. part. of **giriù**, q. v., 'gelobt, gerühmt'—B. II, 1, 399.

gìrtas (B. **gírtas**) adj.; old pret. pass. part. of **geriù**, q. v., 'betrunken'—B. I, 418.474.590. II, 1, 399.

girtis 'das Trinken, Trinkgelage'—B. II, 1, 434.

gýsla, gýslė, gìnsla 'Ader, Sehne, Blattrippe'—B. I, 785; W. *filum,* (*vēna*). Cf. Ness. 257[b]; Geitler LS. 84; Lesk. Nom. 455; BB. XXII, 245 ff.

-gýstu, -gýsti 'zu singen, zu krähen anfangen'—see *pragýstu.*

gývas 'lebendig'—Uh. *jīvás;* K. *keck;* F. *qius;* B. I, 101. 294.338.587. II, 1, 202; W. *vīvo;* Boi. βίος. Cf. Lesk. Abl. 273.

gyvatà 'Leben; Lebensunterhalt, Wohnung, Bauerngut; ewiges Leben, ewige Seligkeit'—B. I, 319. II, 1, 416; W. *vīta, vīvo;* Boi. βίος (twice).

gyvena 'Leben, Haushaltung'—B. II, 1, 267.268.635. Cf. Lesk. Nom. 382.

gyvenù, gyvénti 'leben, wohnen, wirtschaften, das Feld bauen'—B. II, 1, 268; W. *vīvo;* Boi. βίος.

gyvis 'lebendiges Wesen, Tier'—B. II, 1, 222.

gyvokas 'lebhaft, lebendig'—W. *vīvo.* Cf. Ness. 258[a], [Lesk. Nom. 515].

glándu 'ich wetze'—(W. *blandus*). See *galándu* & Ness. 236[b], BB. V, 168.

glaudas 'Kurzweil'—B. I, 573; (W. *lūdo*); Boi. χλεύη. Cf. Lesk. Abl. 296.

glaudùs 'glatt anliegend, sich anschmiegend' (z. B. Haar, Pferdeohren); Boi. 'caressant' [sic]—Uh. *golas;* K. (8th ed.) *Klotz;* Ber. *gludŭkŭ;* W. **gluo;* Boi. γλουτός. Cf. Lesk. Abl. 296, Lesk. Nom. 258.

glaudżù, glaũsti 'etwas eng anlegen, anschmiegen'—Uh. *golas;* K. *Klotz;* Ber. *gludŭkŭ;* W. **gluo;* Boi. γλουτός. Cf. Lesk. Abl. 296.

glėbỹs 'Armvoll'—K. *Klafter.* See next & Lesk. Nom. 288.

glė̃biu, glė̃bti 'mit den Armen umfassen; Raum worin haben, enthalten' (z. B. von einem Gefäss)—K. *Klafter;* B. II, 3, 288 (note); Ber. *globǫ;* W. *glēba;* (Boi. βλέπω). Cf. Lesk. Abl. 370.

glėmės (or **glẽmės**?) plu.; **glemis** (?); Boi. **glẽma** (?) 'zäher Schleim'—B. I, 576; W. *glūs;* Boi. (Ntr.) γλοιός. Cf. Kur. DLWb. s. v. Schleim; Geitler LS. 84; Bezz. LF. 113; Lesk. Abl. 328; Lesk. Nom. 425; Sommer 80.

glemżiù, glem̃żti 'knautschen, zusammendrücken, stopfen, fressen' (von Kühen)—Ber. *glenŭ;* W. *glomus.* Cf. Lesk. Abl. 362.

gleżnus 'weich, zart, schwächlich, widerstandslos'—B. II, 1, 475; Ber. *gležǫ.*

gliaumùs 'schleimig, schlüpfrig'—(W. *glūs*). Cf. Lesk. Abl. 296.

glibỹs 'Triefäugiger'—B. I, 473. Cf. Lesk. Abl. 328.

glìnda (B. **glínda**) 'Niss, Ei der Laus'—B. I, 391.852; Ber. *gnida;* W. 2. *lens;* Boi. κονίς. Cf. Lesk. Nom. 201.

glitė 'Klebrigkeit, Fischleim'—W. *glūs;* Boi. γλοιός.

glìtesos plu. 'Schleim'—B. II, 1, 544.

glitùs 'glatt, schlüpfrig, klebrig, schleimig'—Ber. *glista;* W. *glūs, laetus;* Boi. γλοιός. Cf. Lesk. Nom. 557.

glóbiu, glóbti 'umarmen, umhüllen, umfassen'—K. *Klafter;* Ber. *globǫ;* W. *glēba;* (Boi. βλέπω). Cf. Lesk. Abl. 370.

globóju, globóti iter. 'umarmen, liebkosen'—Ber. *globǫ*. See prec.

glodenà (**glůdenà**), **glodìnė** 'Blindschleiche'—B. II, 1, 267; Ber. *gladŭkŭ*. Cf. Brückner SlFw. 83, Lesk. Nom. 383.

glõdnas 'glatt anliegend' (z. B. von Haaren)—(Ber. *lěnŭ*). Cf. Lesk. Nom. 355.

glodùs id.—B. II, 1, 179; Ber. *gladŭkŭ*; W. *glaber*. Cf. Lesk. Nom. 253.

glomóju, glomóti 'umarmen'—Ber. *glenŭ*; W. *glomus*. Notice *globóju*.

glóstau, glóstyti 'streicheln'; **paglóstau, paglóstyti** 'streicheln, schmeicheln'—Ber. *gladŭkŭ*; W. *glaber*, (*blandus*). Cf. Lesk. Nom. 253.

glúdau, glúdoti; glúdoju, glúdoti 'still angeschmiegt daliegen, sich an etwas anlehnen, mit angelehntem Ohre lauschen'—Ber. *gludŭkŭ*; W. **gluo*; Boi. γλουτός. See *glaudżù* & Lesk. Abl. 296.

gludus 'sich anschmiegend'—K. *Klotz*. See *glaudùs* & MLG. I, 388; Lesk. Nom. 257.

glùmas 'hornlos' (vom Vieh); Lesk. also 'schleimig, glatt'(?)—B. II, 1, 388. Cf. Lesk. Abl. 296; Lesk. Nom. 422, 429.

glůdenà 'Blindschleiche'—see *glodenà*.

gnaĩbis 'Kniff'—see *gnỹbis*.

gniáużiu, gniáużti 'die Hand zusammenschliessen, damit drücken'—Ber. *gńavǫ*. Cf. Lesk. Abl. 296.

gniaużtẽ 'Handvoll, Knocke, Faust'—Ber. *gńavǫ*. Cf. Lesk. Abl. 296, Lesk. Nom. 553.

gnỹbis, gnaĩbis 'Kniff; die vom Kneifen zurückgelassene Narbe'—K. *kneipen*; Boi. γνίφων. See next.

gnýbiu, gnýbti 'kneifen' (mit den Fingern, der Zange usw.); 'kränken'—K. *kneipen*; Boi. γνίφων. Cf. Geitler LS. 63-64, Lesk. Abl. 273.

gniūžtẽ 'Handvoll, Knocke, Faust'—Ber. *gńavǫ*. Cf. Lesk. Abl. 296, Lesk. Nom. 547.

gobelẽju, gobelẽti 'sammeln'—Ber. *gabają;* W. *habeo.*

gobėti (?) 'begehren'—B. II, 3, 472; Ber. *gabają;* W. *habeo.* Cf. Geitler LS. 84, Lesk. Abl. 373, Lalis 101, Juškevič 453 f.

gobinu, gobinti 'schachern'; **pragobinti** 'verschachern'— B. II, 3, 175. See *gabenù* & Lesk. Abl. 372.

góbiu, góbti 'einhüllen'. Ber.: "**gobti-si** 'wonach streben'" (?)—Uh. *gábhastiṣ;* Ber. *gabają;* W. *habeo.* Cf. Lesk. Abl. 298, 376.

gocės plu. 'lange Hosen'—Ber. *gata.* Cf. Kur. s. v.; Brückner SlFw. 84; Bezz. BGLS. 283 s. v. gaczos.

gõdas 'Habgier, Geiz'—F. *bi-gitan;* B. II, 3, 294; W. *prehendo.* Cf. Lesk. Nom. 180.

gõdas 'Ochsenzunge, Klette'—B. II, 3, 294; Ber. *gadŭ;* W. *prehendo.* Cf. Bezz. LF. 114.

godau, godyti 'mutmassen, erraten'; **sugodau, sugodyti** 'erwägen'—Ber. *gadają.* Cf. Brückner SlFw. 84.

godẽjůs, godẽtis 'geizig, begierig sein; gierig essen, trinken'—W. *prehendo.*

godỹnė 'Blindschleiche'—Ber. *gadŭ.* Cf. Kur. DLWb. s. v. Blindschleiche; Brückner SlFw. 84.

godoju, godoti 'mutmassen, erraten'—Ber. *gadają.* Cf. Brückner SlFw. 84.

godùs 'habgierig, geizig; gierig, gefrässig'—F. *bi-gitan;* Ber. *gadają;* Boi. χανδάνω.

gõjus 'Busch, Lustwäldchen, Hain'—Ber. *gajĭ.* Cf. Brückner SlFw. 84.

Old Pruss. **golimba-** 'blau'—B. II, 1, 389, l. 15 (read preuss. for lit.). Cf. B. II, 1, 386 (& note 4). 389 (l. 4); Ber. s. v. golǫbŭ; W. s. v. columba etc.

gomuras 'Gaumen'—B. II, 1, 358. See next & Ness. 259[b], Lesk. Nom. 448.

gomur̃ys 'Gaumen, Rachen, Schlund'—K. *Gaumen;* B. I, 174.204.491. II, 1, 358; W. *faux;* Boi. χάος, χήμη. Cf Lesk. Nom. 448.

goslus 'gauklerisch, zauberisch, abergläubisch'—Ber. *kuzlo*. Cf. Brückner SlFw. 84.

grabinĕju, grabinĕti 'hin und her greifen, herumtasten'—Uh. *gṛbhṇâti;* F. *graba;* Ber. *grebą* 1. Cf. Lesk. Abl. 362.

grabùs 'fingerfertig'—Uh. *gṛbhṇâti;* F. *graba;* B. II, 1, 178; Ber. *grebą* 1. Cf. Lesk. Abl. 362.

graibaũ, graibýti 'umhergreifen, haschen, betasten'—F. *greipan*. Cf. Lesk. Abl. 274.

grainu (graju), graiti 'spielen'—Ber. *igra*.

graistaũ, graistýti 'den Rahm abschöpfen'—Ber. *grĕchŭ*.

graju 'ich spiele'—see *grainu*.

grámdau, grámdyti '(ein Gefäss) auskratzend reinigen'—F. *gramst;* B. I, 178.522. II, 1, 468. Cf. Lesk. Abl. 362.

gramózdas 'Gerümpel'—Ber. *gramada*. Cf. Lesk. Nom. 167.

gramzdaũ, gramzdýti 'versenken' (in Wasser, Morast)—F. *qrammiþa;* B. I, 569; Ber. *grązŭ*. Cf. Lesk. Abl. 328.

gramzdinù, gramzdìnti id.—Ber. *grązŭ*. See prec.

gramzdùs 'tief sinkend'; Wied. 'versunken, betrübt'; Boi. 'ayant un fort tirant d'eau'—Ber. *grązŭ;* (Boi. χραίνω (note)). Cf. Lesk. Abl. 328. Notice also Lesk. Nom. 249: "*gramzdùs skaudĕjimas* dumpfer (eigentl. nagender) Schmerz . . . vgl. *grémżdu gṛémszti,* Abl. 362."

grandai plu. "die Latten, Reiser usw., welche auf den Deckbalken des Stalles liegen und auf welchen das Heu liegt"; "die Querstäbe auf den Schlitten, mit welchen Heu geholt wird"—Ber. *gręda;* W. *grunda*. Cf. Bezz. LF. 114; Lesk. Abl. 328; Lesk. Nom. 167-8.

grándau, grándyti '(ein Gefäss) reinschaben'—F. *grinda-fraþjis;* Ber. *grąstokŭ;* W. *frendo*. Cf. Lesk. Abl. 362.

grandẽlė 'Armband'—Ber. *grądają*.

grandìnis 'ringförmig, kreisförmig'—Ber. *grądają*.

grandis 'Ring, Armband, Radschiene; (żem.) ein runder

Käsekuchen'—K. *Kranz;* B. II, 1, 168; Ber. *grędaję,* (*grędĭ*); Boi. γρόνθος (note). Cf. Lesk. Abl. 328.

grasà 'Abscheu, Ekel'—Ber. *groza;* W. *fastīdium.* Cf. Kur. DLWb. s. v. Ekel & Lesk. Abl. 328.

grasaũs, grasýtis 'sich ekeln'—Ber. *groza.*

grasinù, grasìnti 'jemand etwas verekeln'—Ber. *groza.*

grasùs 'ekelhaft, widerwärtig'—(Uh. *bībhatsate*); Ber. *groza;* W. *fastīdium.* Cf. Lesk. Abl. 328.

graudenù, graudénti 'ermahnen'—Ber. *grustĭ.* Cf. Lesk. Abl. 297.

graudinù, graudìnti 'härten, spröde machen, (in der Bibel) ermahnen'; **sugraudìnti** 'betrübt machen'—Ber. *grustĭ;* [W. 1. *rūdus*]. Cf. Lesk. Abl. 297.

graudulis 'Donner'—Ber. *gruda.*

graudùs 'spröde, brüchig; rührend, wehmütig'—F. *kriustan;* Ber. *gruda, grustĭ;* W. 1. *rūdus.* Cf. Lesk. Abl. 297.

graumadas 'Gesellschaft, Reisegesellschaft'—Ber. *gramada.* Cf. Ness. 273[a]; Kur. 138[a]; Brückner SlFw. 86, ll. 1 f.

grausmė 'Warnung, Ermahnung'—Ber. *grustĭ.* Cf. Lesk. Abl. 297.

gráużas 'Kies, Grandacker'—Ber. *gruzla* (Ber.: "Pl. m. 'Graus, Schutt'" apparently should apply to Lett., not Lith. Cf. Lesk.); W. 1. *rūdus.* Cf. Lesk. Abl. 297.

gráużiu, gráużti 'nagen, abbeissen'—(F. *kriustan*); B. I, 590.693; Ber. *gryzę;* W. 1. *rūdus;* Boi. βρύχω. Cf. Lesk. Abl. 297.

grażóju, grażóti 'drohend winken, drohen'—Ber. *groza.*

grążulas 'Deichsel'—B. II, 1, 362. Cf. Lesk. Abl. 328, Lesk. Nom. 484.

grażulis 'Stutzer'—B. II, 1, 368.684. Cf. Lesk. Nom. 491.

grażùmas 'Schönheit, Schmuck; (plu.) schöne Kleider, Putzsachen'—B. II, 1, 250.643.

grażùs 'schön, lieblich, wohlgestattet'—(W. *brevis*). Cf. Lesk. Abl. 362.

grëbas (?) žem. 'Pilz'—Ber. *gribŭ.* Cf. Schleicher LSpr. II, 271; Kur. 132[b].

grëbiu, grëbti 'harken, raffen'—Uh. *gṛbhṇâti;* K. *Garbe* 1; F. *graba;* B. I, 152.480; Ber. *grabǫ, grebǫ* 1; (Boi. γρῖφος (note)). Cf. Lesk. Abl. 362.

grëbiù, grẽbti 'greifen, packen'—K. *greifen;* F. *greipan;* (Ber. *cholǫ*); Boi. ἀγρεῖφνα. Cf. Lesk. Abl. 273-4.

grėblỹs 'Harke'—B. II, 1, 620; Ber. *grabǫ* (twice). See *grẽbiu.*

greĩtas 'geschwind, flink, schnell, hurtig'—(Boi. βριαρός). Cf. Lesk. Nom. 184.

grëjù, grẽti 'Sahne von der Milch abschöpfen'; **użgrëjù, użgrẽti** "beim Fischen mit dem Netz auf etwas stossen, es ins Netz bekommen"—Ber. *grěchŭ;* (W. *frio*). Cf. Geitler LD. 44, Lesk. Abl. 407.

grẽkas 'Sünde'—B. II, 3, 220; Ber. *grěchŭ.* Cf. Brückner SlFw. 85, Wied. s. v.

grëkáuju, grëkáuti 'Sünden in der Beichte vorhalten, Beichte hören; beichten'—B. II, 3, 220.221. See prec.

gremzu, gremsti dial. 'versenken'—Ber. *gręznǫ* (read: mit *z* für *zd*). Cf. Lesk. Abl. 328.

grémżdu, grémszti 'schaben, kratzen'—F. *gramst.* Cf. Lesk. Abl. 362.

gréndu (gréndżu), grę́sti 'reiben, scheuern, abschinden'—F. *grinda-fraþjis;* B. II, 3, 119.373; Ber. *grǫstokŭ;* W. *frendo;* Boi. χόνδρος, χραίνω, (Ntr.) χέραδος. Cf. Lesk. Abl. 362.

gréndżu, grę́sti 'reiben'—see prec.

gresiù, grẽsti 'entwöhnen'. Geitler 'fernhalten, abwehren'; Lesk. '(verekeln) entwöhnen'—Ber. *groza.* Cf. Geitler LS. 84; Lesk. Abl. 328, 400; Juškevič 468.

gretà adv. 'dicht zusammen, nebeneinander'—W. *grex.*

gręžiù, grę̃žti 'wenden, drehen, bohren'—K. *Kring;* B. I, 387.416; Boi. βρόχος. Cf. Lesk. Abl. 328.

grëžiu, grẽžti (Kur., Boi. **grëžiu, grëszti**) 'mit den Zähnen knirschen'—Boi. βρόχθος. Cf. Lesk. Abl. 274.

grëžlě (Kur., Boi. **grėžlě**) 'Schnarrwachtel'—Boi. βρόχθος. Cf. Lesk. Abl. 274, Lesk. Nom. 457.

gręžulě 'Deichsel'—B. II, 1, 362. Cf. Lesk. Abl. 328, Lesk. Nom. 487.

griáuju, griáuti 'umstürzen; donnern'—F. *us-grudja, kriustan;* Ber. *gruchajǫ;* W. *ruo* 1; Boi. *χρα[ϝ]εῖν. Cf. Lesk. Abl. 297.

grỹbas 'Pilz'—Ber. *gribŭ.* Cf. Brückner SlFw. 85.

grìbsznis 'Griff'—(Ber. *chołǫ*). Cf. Ness. 268[a], Lesk. Abl. 273.

grìdyju, grìdyti 'gehen, wandern'—B. II, 3, 222.288; W. *gradior.* Cf. Juškevič 470.

grìkai plu. 'Buchweizen'—(K. *Buchweizen*); Ber. *grĭkŭ.* Cf. Brückner SlFw. 85.

grimstù, grim̃sti 'versinken' (in Wasser, Schlamm)—F. *qrammiþa;* B. I, 376; Ber. *gręznǫ;* W. *grāmiae.* Cf. Lesk. Abl. 328.

grýnas 'kahl, unfruchtbar, armselig; kahl, rein, unvermischt (vom Getreide)'—(Boi. βριαρός).

grindìs 'Dielenbrett, gedielter Fussboden, Strassenpflaster, Zimmerdecke'—F. *grundu-waddjus;* Ber. *gręda;* W. *grunda.* Cf. Ness. 271[a,b]; Bezz. LF. 115; Lesk. Abl. 328; Lesk. Nom. 235.

grindžù, grį̃sti 'dielen, pflastern'—K. *Kranz;* Ber. *gręda.* Cf. Lesk. Abl. 328.

grynicza 'Gesindestube; Räucherkammer'—Ber. *gręda.* Cf. Brückner SlFw. 85.

griovà 'enge Schlucht, Graben, Grube'—Ber. *gruchajǫ.* Cf. Lesk. Abl. 297.

gręstù, grìsti 'überdrüssig werden, Ekel empfinden'—(Uh. *bībhatsate*); Ber. (*grěchŭ*), *groza;* W. *fastīdium.* Cf. Lesk. Abl. 328.

grį̃szas 'Rundung, Kreis'—see *grį̃žas.*

grįsztù, grį̃szti 'zurückkehren'—see *grįžtù.*

griúdžiu, griústi (Kur.) 'stampfen'—F. *us-grudja.* See *grúdžu.*

griūvù, griúti 'einstürzen, zusammenfallen'—F. *us-grudja, kriustan;* B. II, 3, 137; Ber. *gruchają;* W. *ruo* 1; Boi. *χρα[ϝ]εῖν (& Ntr.). Cf. Lesk. Abl. 296-7.

grįžas (B. **grįszas**) 'Rundung, Kreis'—B. II, 1, 155. Cf. Lesk. Nom. 163.

grįžtù, grį̃žti (B. **grįsztù, grį̃szti**) 'sich wenden, zurückkehren; herausbekommen (beim Wechsel)'—B. I, 416. Cf. Lesk. Abl. 328.

grį̃žulas 'Kreis, Reitbahn; der Grosse Bär'—B. I, 416. II, 1, 362. Cf. Lesk. Abl. 328, Lesk. Nom. 484.

grįžulė̃ 'Deichsel'—B. II, 1, 362. Cf. Lesk. Abl. 328, Lesk. Nom. 487.

grobė 'Beute'—B. I, 152; Ber. *grabę̆.* Cf. Geitler LS. 85, Lesk. Abl. 362.

gróbiu, gróbti 'raffen, packen'—K. *Garbe* 1, *grapsen;* B. I, 152.480. II, 1, 178; Ber. *grabę̆.* See *grė́biu* & Lesk. Abl. 362.

gródas 'gefrorener Strassenschmutz'—see *grū́das.*

gróju, gróti 'krächzen; schelten, schmähen'—K. *krähen;* B. II, 1, 435. 3, 202; Ber. *graję;* W. *graculus.*

grõm(i)ata 'Brief'—Ber. *gramata.* Cf. Brückner SlFw. 85.

grubùs 'holperig; grobfingerig'—Ber. *grǫbŭ.* Cf. Lesk. Abl. 316, Lesk. Nom. 257.

grúdas 'Korn; Kern; Korn an einem Gewehre; Tautropfen' —K. *Grütze;* F. *us-grudja;* Ber. *gruda;* W. 1. *rūdus;* Boi. *χραύω, (κάχρυς). Cf. Lesk. Abl. 297.

grūdinù, grūdìnti '(Eisen) härten'—W. 1. *rūdus.* See *graudinù.*

grúdżu, grústi 'stampfen (z. B. Gerste), (Eisen) härten; ermahnen, warnen'—F. *kriustan, us-grudja;* Ber. *gruda, grustĭ;* W. 1. *rūdus;* Boi. *χραύω, (κάχρυς). Cf. Lesk. Abl. 297.

grumadas 'Gesellschaft, Reisegesellschaft'—Ber. *gramada.* Cf. Brückner SlFw. 86.

grumbù, grùbti 'holperig werden; hart oder gefühllos werden (von den Fingern)'—B. II, 3, 287; Ber. *grǫbŭ*. Cf. Lesk. Abl. 316.

grumẽna, gruménti impers. 'aus der Ferne leise und dumpf donnern'—F. *gramjan;* Ber. *grĭmǫ*, (*grŭmŭ*); (W. *fremo*); Boi. χρεμίζω, (βρέμω).

grumodas 'Haufen, Schwarm' (bes. Fliegen)—Ber. *gramada*. Cf. Brückner SlFw. 86.

grumzdżù, grum̃sti 'drohen, warnen'—Boi. χρεμίζω.

gruszia 'Birne, Birnbaum'—Ber. *gruša*. Cf. Brückner SlFw. 86, Sommer 137-8.

grużinẽju, grużinẽti 'nagen'—Ber. *gryzǫ*. See *gráużiu*.

-grużinti—see *sugrużinu* 'ich vernichte'.

grużótas 'uneben, holperig'—Ber. *gruzla*. Cf. Lesk. Abl. 297.

grũdas (Kur. also **gródas**) 'frischer, steif gefrorener Strassenschmutz, der gefrorene ungleiche Boden'—Ber. *gradŭ;* W. *grando*. Cf. Brückner SlFw. 85.

-gu strengthening enclitic particle, added to pron., adv., prep., or conj.—Ber. *-go;* W. *hic;* Boi. γε. See *-gi*.

guba 'Getreideschober'—Ber. *gŭbežĭ;* (Boi. κῦφός). Cf. Geitler LS. 84 & 112 (s. v. sugaubti); Lesk. Abl. 297; Lesk. Nom. 227.

-gubas—see *dvìgubas* 'zweifach' or *trìgubas* 'dreifach'. Cf. also Brückner SlFw. 86 (& note).

gùdras, gudrùs 'klug, schlau, verschmitzt'—B. II, 1, 385; W. *vafer*. See Lesk. Abl. 316, Lesk. Nom. 440-1.

gúdurioju, gúdurioti 'klagen, jammern'—B. II, 1, 358. Cf. MLG. I, 359; Lesk. Abl. 298.

guijù (**guinù**), **gùiti** 'jagen, treiben, trachten'—K. *Kette* 1; Ber. *gonŭ;* Boi. βόσκω. Cf. Lesk. Abl. 297.

guinióju, guinióti 'fortgesetzt hin und her jagen, treiben' —Ber. *gańajǫ*. See prec.

guinù, gùiti 'jagen, treiben'—see *guijù*.

gulbẽ, gulbis fem.; **gùlbas, gùlbis** masc. 'Schwan'—B. II, 1, 386.389; Ber. *kŭlpŭ, golǫbŭ;* W. *columba*. Cf. Ness. 260[b]; Wied. p. 280; Lesk. Nom. 189, 237, 276.

gulýkla (B. gulyklà) 'Lagerstatt, Tierlager'—B. II, 1, 622. Cf. MLG. I, 133; Lesk. Nom. 500.

guliù, gulěti 'liegen, schlafen'—Boi. γωλεός (& note), (βάλλω). Cf. Lesk. Abl. 298.

guliù, gul̃ti 'sich hinlegen, schlafen gehen'—Boi. γωλεός, (θάλαμος). Cf. Lesk. Abl. 298.

gùlkszczoja 'es geht das Gerücht'—Ber. *gŭlkŭ.*

gulta 'Lager, Tierlager, Schlafzimmer'—B. II, 1, 416; (W. *galba*); Boi. γωλεός. Cf. Lesk. Abl. 298.

gum̃bas 'Erhöhung; Knorren; Gewächs an einem organischen Körper, Geschwulst, Pilz; Leibweh, Kolik'—B. I, 390; Ber. *gǫba 2*; Boi. γαμψός, (σπόγγος). Cf. Lesk. Nom. 189, Bezz. LF. 116.

gumbronė 'kröpfige Ente, Anas fuligula'—Boi. γαμψός. Cf. Lesk. Nom. 393.

gumulis 'Klumpen'—Ber. *gomola.* Cf. Lesk. Nom. 486.

gumulis masc., **gumulė** fem. 'Mangelhaftes, Gestutztes' (e.g. **gumulis** 'Bock ohne Hörner'; **gumulė** 'Kuh ohne Hörner, Henne ohne Schwanz')—Ber. *gomola.* Cf. Ness. 262[b], Kur. s. v., Geitler LS. 64.

gunė 'schlechte Pferdedecke'—Ber. *gúna.* Cf. Bezz. BGLS. 286, Brückner SlFw. 86.

gùnga 'Buckel, Ball, Klumpen'—(W. *gingīva*); Boi. (Ntr.) γογγύλος. Cf. Solmsen 221.

gùnyju, gùnyti 'schnell jagen'—Ber. *gonŭ.* Cf. Juškevič 492.

gunžěti 'unter den Flügeln sitzen' usw.—see *gūžěti.*

guñžinu, guñžinti 'gebückt gehen' usw.—see *gūžinu.*

gunžỹs 'Kropf' usw.—see *gūžỹs.*

guñžti 'unter die Flügel setzen' usw.—see *gūžti.*

gurgulẽ fem. 'Menge, Masse' (Leute, Bienen)—Boi. (Ntr.) γυργαθός. See next & Geitler LS. 85, Lesk. Nom. 486.

gurgulỹs 'Wirrwarr von Fäden, dichter Schwarm'—B. I, 449.453.473.572. II, 1, 127; Ber. *gŭrtajǫ; W. grex;* Boi. ἀγείρω, (Ntr.) γυργαθός. Cf. Bezz. LF. 116; Geitler LS. 85; Lesk. Nom. 486.

gùrgżdżu, gurgżdė́ti 'knarren'—see *gìrgżdżu*.
gurklỹs 'Kropf bei Vögeln, Adamsapfel, Kehle'—B. I, 453. 473.474.604. II, 1, 344; Ber. *gŭrdlo;* W. *gurges;* Boi. *βορά*.
gurstu, gurti 'gellen' (von den Ohren)—(W. *garrio*). Cf. Lesk. Abl. 316.
guru, gurti 'bröckeln, schwach werden, nachlassen' — K. *kirre;* (F. *qairrus*); W. *furfur;* Boi. *χέραδος*. Cf. Geitler LS. 85; Bezz. LF. 116; Lesk. Abl. 316.
gurus 'locker, bröckelig' — K. *kirre;* (F. *qairrus*); W. *frendo, furfur;* Boi. *χέραδος*. Cf. Lesk. Abl. 316.
gūsztà fem., **gūsztas** masc. 'Lager eines Hundes, Nest eines Huhns, einer Gans; schlechte Wohnung, Hütte' —Uh. *gûhati;* B. II, 1, 397.416.635; Ber. *gǫzŭ*. Cf. Ness. 263[a]; Lesk. Abl. 316; Solmsen 220.
gùzas 'Buckel, Drüse, Knorren; Knopf am Rock; Spange am Buche'—Ber. *gǫzŭ*. Cf. Brückner SlFw. 86; Lesk. Nom. 190; Solmsen 220-2.
gùzikas id.—Ber. *gǫzŭ*. See prec.
guża 'Haufen Ungeziefer'—Ber. *gŭzŭ*. Cf. Ness. 263[b], Bezz. LF. 116, s. v. gużė́ti.
gùżas 'Storch'—Ber. *gyža, (gǫzŭ)*. Cf. Geitler LS. 85; Lesk. Nom. 192; Solmsen 221.
gużietojis (?) 'Schützer'—Uh. *gûhati*. Cf. Geitler LS. 85, s. v. gużti.
gūżinė́ju, gūżinė́ti (Solmsen, Ber.) 'gebückt gehen'; **gużinė́ju, gużinė́ti** (ŭ or ū? Kur., Bezz., Lesk., B.) 'Blindekuh spielen'—B. I, 558; Ber. *gǫzŭ*. Cf. Bezz. LF. 93; Lesk. Abl. 316; Solmsen 220.
gũżinu, gũżinti; guñżinu, guñżinti "unter die Flügel, an einen warmen Ort setzen; gebückt gehen (von alten Leuten); refl. sich zusammenkrümmen, bucklig sein"—Ber. *gǫzŭ*. Cf. Solmsen 220.
gūżỹs (or **gużỹs**), **gunżỹs** 'Kropf bei Vögeln, Adamsapfel (Boi. 'gésier'; read 'jabot'); Kopf des Oberschenkelknochens; Kohlkopf'—Ber. *gǫzŭ, gyža;* (W. *gingīva*);

Boi. γύγης, (Ntr.) γογγύλος. Cf. Lesk. Nom. 293; Solmsen 220; Sommer 376.

gūžiù, (gūžė́ju), gūžė́ti; gunžù, gunžė́ti 'unter den Flügeln, im Neste, in der Wärme liegen oder sitzen'—Ber. *gǫzŭ*. Cf. Solmsen 220, Juškevič 498.

gūžiù, gū̃žti (Uh., Bezz. gúszti); **gunžiù, guñžti** "unter die Flügel, an einen warmen Ort setzen, dort wärmen; refl. sich zusammenballen, -knäueln, sich einmummeln (in den Pelz); sich zur Erde setzen (vom Huhn, das die Flügel ausbreitet)"; **susigūžiù, susigū̃žti** 'sich zusammenkauern, zusammenhocken'; **susigū̃žęs** (B., Bezz., Lesk. -gúžęs) perf. act. part. 'zusammengekauert'—B. I, 558; Ber. *gǫzŭ*. Cf. Bezz. LF. 116; Lesk. Abl. 316; Solmsen 220.

gūžtù, gū̃žti 'sich verbergen' (Geitler, Uh. 'schützen'); **įsigūžtù, įsigū̃žti** 'sich einhüllen, sich betten'; **įsigū̃sztęs** (**įsigū̃žtęs**) 'sich eingehüllt, eingenistet habend'—Uh. *gûhati;* Ber. *gǫzŭ*. Cf. Geitler LS. 85; Kur. 142; Wied. s. v.; Lesk. Abl. 316, 388; Solmsen 220-1.

gužù, gužė́ti 'im Haufen gehen oder fliegen, sich von allen Seiten sammeln'—Ber. *gŭzŭ*. Cf. Geitler LS. 64; Bezz. BGLS. 286; Bezz. LF. 116; Solmsen 221; Juškevič 498.

gužutys 'Storch'—Ber. *gyža*, (*gǫzŭ*); Boi. γύγης. Cf. Lesk. Nom. 575.

gů̃da (**goda**) 'Lob, Ehre'—Ber. *godŭ*. Cf. Ness. 259[b]; Geitler LS. 64; Brückner SlFw. 84; Lesk. Abl. 379; Lesk. Nom. 232.

gůdė́jůs, gůdė́tis 'gierig sein'—B. I, 288. II, 1, 436.444. 3, 217.

gů̃lis 'Lager, Lagerstätte' (bes. von Tieren)—Boi. γωλεός, (θάλαμος). Cf. Lesk. Abl. 298, Lesk. Nom. 295.

gū̃tas 'Herde Kleinvieh'—K. *Kette* 1; Boi. βόσκω. Cf. Lesk. Nom. 196.

I

į, iñ prep. 'in'; **į-, in-** pref. 'ein-, hinein-'—K. *in;* F. *in,* (*aftarō*); B. I, 388. II, 2, 828.829.831.832.833; W. *in;* Boi. ἐν.

-iáusias super. end. (e.g. **geriáusias** 'bester')—B. II, 1, 545. Cf. Wied. 165; Lesk. Nom. 598; Sommer 301-303, 335-344.

įbraukaĩ 'Füllwände'—W. *farcio.* Cf. Lesk. Abl. 293.

įbraukiù, įbraũkti 'hineinstecken'—W. *farcio.* See *braukiù.*

įdėm 'wirklich'—B. II, 1, 244. Cf. Geitler LS. 85, Lesk. Nom. 428.

ĩeiga 'Eingang'—Boi. οἴχομαι. See *eigà* & Kur. 105ᵇ.

įgaminù, įgamìnti 'einbürgern'—see *gaminù.*

įgeliù, įgélti 'stechen'—see *geliù.*

įgyjù, įgýti 'erreichen, erlangen, erwerben'—Uh. 1. *jinâti;* Ber. *gojĭ;* (W. *viēsco*); Boi. βίā. Cf. Lesk. Abl. 291.

įsigũžtù, įsigũžti 'sich einhüllen'—see *gũžtù.*

ìk 'bis'—see *ikì.*

įsikerė́ju, įsikerė́ti 'sich einnisten'—Ber. *korenĭ.* See *kerė́ju.*

ikì, ìki, ìk prep. 'bis'—W. *aequus.*

ĩkyriu, įkyrė́ti; įkįrù, įkìrti 'sich ekeln, überdrüssig werden; zum Ekel werden'—Ber. *čĭrtŭ.* Cf. Geitler LS. 86; Lesk. Abl. 331; Lalis 111; Juškevič 516, 517.

įkirus 'feindselig'—Ber. *čĭrtŭ.* Cf. Lesk. Abl. 331.

įkyrus 'widerwärtig, ekelhaft, lästig'—Ber. *čĭrtŭ.* Cf. Geitler LS. 86, Lesk. Abl. 331.

įkrypaĩ adv. 'mit halber Wendung, schräg'—Ber. *krěsŭ.*

ikru gen. plu. 'der Waden'—Ber. *ikra* 2. Cf. Bezz. BGLS. 286, Lesk. Nom. 437.

ikszių̃liai 'bis jetzt'—see *szių̃liai.*

iktõl 'bis dahin, bis dann'—B. II, 2, 782. See *ikì* & *tõl.*

ýla 'Ahle, Pfriem'—K. *Ahle;* W. *alica.* Cf. Lesk. Nom. 205.

įlanka 'Einbiegung'—B. II, 1, 153.634; Ber. *lǫka.* See *lankà* & Kur. DLWb. s. v. Beuge, Lesk. Abl. 335.

ìlgas (B., W., Boi. **ílgas**) 'lang' (von Raum und Zeit)—Uh. *dīrghás;* (F. *arbaiþs*); B. I, 476; Ber. *dĭlgŭ;* W. *indulgeo;* Boi. δολιχός. Cf. Lesk. Abl. 386.
il̃gis 'Länge'—B. II, 1, 172.197.251.642. 2, 129 (& fn.).
ilgumèt adv. 'lange Zeit'—B. II, 2, 714.
-imas end. of verbal abstracts (e.g. **sukìmas** 'das Drehen')—B. II, 1, 250.251. Cf. Lesk. Nom. 429-430.
im̃tas pret. pass. part. of **imù**, q. v., 'genommen'—W. *emptus* (s. v. *emo*).
imù, ėmiaũ, im̃ti 'nehmen, beginnen'—(K. *nehmen*); F. *niman;* B. I, 388.783. II, 3, 126.396.442.493; Ber. *emą, imą* (end); W. *emo;* Boi. νέμω. Cf. Lesk. Abl. 329.
iñ prep. 'in'; **in-** pref. 'ein-, hinein-'—see *į*.
įnagis 'Waffe' (cf. Kur. s. v. įnagė)—B. II, 1, 113. Cf. Bezz. LF. 117.
iñdas 'Gefäss'—B. II, 2, 734; Ber. *děją, jandova.*
indauje 'Geschirr'—(Ber. *jandova*). Cf. Geitler LS. 86; Lesk. Nom. 342; Sommer 37; BB. XXI, 120.
indėvai adv. 'künstlich'—B. II, 1, 204. Cf. Lesk. Nom. 344.
indoras 'passend gelegen'—Ber. *dorgŭ* 1. Cf. Bezz. BGLS. 287; Lesk. Nom. 179; [Lesk. Abl. 361].
ìngis (B., Boi. **íngis**) 'Faulenzer'—B. I, 546.584.944. II, 3, 286; Ber. *ęďža;* Boi. νωχελής. Cf. Lesk. Abl. 329.
įnir̃tęs 'ergrimmt'—see *nirstù*.
ýnis 'Reif'—Ber. *inĭjĭ*. Cf. Brückner SlFw. 87.
iñkaras, iñkoras 'Anker'—K. *Anker;* Ber. *ankvra.* Cf. Lesk. Nom. 446, Prell. deutsch. Best. in den lett. Spr. 24.
ìnksta (3rd pers. sing.), **ìnkti** 'verschiessen, verbleichen' (von der Farbe)—W. *aquilus.* Cf. Lesk. Abl. 329.
ìnkstas (B., W. **ínkstas**) 'Niere, testiculus'—B. I, 390.391 (note); Ber. *isto;* W. *inguen,* (*exta*), (*īlia*). Cf. Lesk. Nom. 537.
iñt prep., dial. 'auf, zu'—F. *und;* B. II, 2, 836(twice).837; W. *ante.*
intė East Lith. 'Schwägerin' usw.—see *jentė*.

ýpaczei adv. 'besonders'—B. II, 2, 7; Boi. εἰς, νῦν-ί (s. v. νύ). Cf. Lesk. Nom. 263.

ir̃ 'und, auch'—B. I, 472. II, 2, 997 (Ntr.); W. *arma;* Boi. ἄρα, ῥά.

įrangus 'hurtig, rührig' (bei der Arbeit)—Boi. ῥίμφα. Cf. Ness. 436ᵃ, Lesk. Abl. 340.

įsirę̃żęs (įsirénżęs) perf. act. part. 'sich gereckt habend'—see *-rę̃żti.*

iriù, ìrti (B., W., Boi. **írti**) 'rudern' (den Kahn)—Uh. *arítras;* B. I, 482; W. *rēmus;* Boi. ἐρέ-της. Cf. Lesk. Abl. 329.

ìrklas (B., W., Boi. **írklas**) 'Ruder'—Uh. *arítras;* B. I, 482. II, 1, 341.618; W. *rēmus;* Boi. ἐρέ-της. Cf. Lesk. Abl. 329.

ìrti inf.—see *iriù, ìrti* 'rudern'; or *yrù, ìrti* 'auseinandergehen'.

yrù, ìrti (B. **írti**) 'sich trennen, auseinandergehen, sich auflösen'—Uh. *árdhas, íriṇam, ṛté;* B. II, 2, 709.735. 3, 137.168.379.390; W. *rārus;* Boi. ἀραιός. Cf. Lesk. Abl. 329.

-is end. of definite adj. (e.g. **geràsis** 'der gute')—B. I, 289. II, 2, 331.347; Ber. *i-* (end); W. *is;* Boi. 1. ὅς. Cf. Wied. 146, Sommer 353 ff.

įsakaũ, įsakýti 'sagend einschärfen'—W. *inquam.* See *sakaũ.*

įsekti 'eingraben, einschneiden'—W. *seco.* Cf. Bezz. BGLS. 287, Lesk. Abl. 341.

ìsz, Old Lith. **ìż**, prep. 'aus'; **isz-** pref. 'aus-, hinaus-'—B. II, 2, 824.825; Ber. *iz;* W. *ex;* Boi. ἐξ.

ìszaiżos plu. 'Schlauben'—Ber. *ězva.*

iszblỹszkėlis 'Bleichgesicht, Bleichling'—Ber. *blĭskŭ.* See *blyksztù.*

ìszczos (or **įszczos**? Cf. Bezz. BGLS. 40, 287) plu. 'Eingeweide'—Ber. *isto;* W. *intestīnus,* (*exta*), (*inguen*). Cf. Lesk. Nom. 544.

ìszeiga 'Ausgang'—Boi. οἴχομαι. See *eigà.*

isz-ent- Old Lith. 'exiens'—B. I, 289. II, 1, 456. See *einù* & Wied. 177. 2.

iszganus 'selig, heilbringend'—Ber. *gonŭ.*

isziĩgai 'längs'—B. II, 2, 785. See under *ìsz* & *ìlgas.*

ìszimga 'Leibgedinge, Ausgedinge'—B. II, 1, 507.

iszimtis 'Ausnahme'—B. II, 1, 430. Cf. Bezz. BGLS. 289.

-iszka- adj. suff. (e.g. **dẽviszkas** 'göttlich')—B. II, 1, 502. Cf. Lesk. Nom. 522.

iszkárszęs perf. act. part. as adj. 'vor Alter hinfällig'—Ber. *kŭrsŭ.* See *kársziu.*

iszkéltas participial adj. 'hoch, erhaben'—Ber. *čelo;* W. *celsus.* See *keliù* & Ness. 192[a].

iszkernóju, iszkernóti 'verleumden, schlecht machen'—B. I, 468. II, 3, 308; W. *carino;* Boi. κάρνη. Cf. Geitler LS. 87; Geitler LD. 48; Bezz. LF. 123.

iszkus 'deutlich, klar, offenbar, ausdrücklich; hell (von der Farbe)'—Ber. *ěsĭnŭ, iskra.* Cf. Lesk. Abl. 274, Lesk. Nom. 507.

iszlaivóju, iszlaivóti 'Biegungen machen'—Ber. *lěvŭ* 1. Cf. BB. IX, 290.

iszlẽpėlis 'ein verwöhnter Mensch, Weichling'—B. II, 1, 370. Cf. Ness. 358[a], Lesk. Nom. 465.

ìszliżos fem. plu. 'Zwischenraum zwischen den Zähnen, den Zehen'—Ber. *ližǫ.* Cf. Ness. 360[a], Lesk. Abl. 278.

iszmanaũ, iszmanýti 'verstehen, Einsicht haben'—see *manaũ.*

iszmatrus 'scharfsichtig, vorsichtig'—B. II, 1, 352.385. Cf. Ness. 385[b].

ìszmonis 'Verstand'—B. II, 1, 168. 3, 246. Cf. Lesk. Nom. 237, Lesk. Abl. 336.

ìszmota 'Auswurf, Kehricht; ein ausgeworfenes Feld zum allgemeinen Gebrauch'—Ber. *mětajǫ.* Cf. Lesk. Abl. 364.

iszpaiszaũ, iszpaiszýti 'mit Russ beschmieren; mit einer Kohle zeichnen, adumbrare, primas lineas ducere'—

W. *pingo;* Boi. ποικίλος. Cf. Ness. 281[a], [Lesk. Abl. 280], Juškevič 610.

ìszpleczu, iszplẽsti 'breit machen'—see *pleczù.*

ìszplovos plu. 'Spülicht'—B. I, 338; W. *pluo.* Cf. Lesk. Abl. 304.

iszsirę́żti 'sich ausrecken'—see *-rę́żti.*

iszsekti 'sculpere'—W. *seco.* Cf. Bezz. BGLS. 290, Lesk. Abl. 341.

ìszspleczu, iszsplẽsti 'breiten'—see *spleczù.*

ìszsprogas 'Schössling'—Boi. σπαργᾶν. Cf. Lesk. Abl. 346.

iszsprùkęs perf. act. part. 'entschlüpft'—B. II, 3, 284. Cf. MLG. I, 366; Lesk. Abl. 309.

ìsztaka 'Ablass, Mündung'—B. II, 1, 150.634. Cf. Kur. DLWb. s. v. Ablass; Lesk. Abl. 367.

iszteklis 'Vorrat'—B. II, 1, 383. Cf. Lesk. Nom. 460.

isztẽs adv. 'fürwahr'—B. II, 2, 726.

isztólo 'von fern'—see *tólo.*

isztrypiù, isztrỹpti 'austrampeln'—see *trypiù.*

iszvalaũ, iszvalýti 'fortschaffen'—see *valaũ.*

iszvéngiu, iszvéngti 'vermeiden'—see *véngiu.*

ìszverża 'Raub, Beute'—B. II, 1, 155. Cf. Lesk. Abl. 357.

iszvora 'Suppe, Brei, Mus'—B. I, 151. II, 1, 154. Cf. Ness. 29[b], Lesk. Abl. 356.

ĩtimpas 'Ansatz zum Sprung'—B. II, 1, 155. Cf. Lesk. Abl. 350.

įtoka 'Einlauf des Wassers in die See, Flussmündung'—B. I, 151. Cf. Lesk. Abl. 367.

ĩtranka 'Anstoss'—B. I, 142; Ber. *drǫkŭ;* W. *truncus.* Cf. Lesk. Abl. 352.

įvairas 'mannigfaltig'—B. II, 1, 353. Cf. Lesk. Nom. 442.

įvalaũ, įvalýti 'ernten'—see *valaũ.*

ývas 'Nachteule, Uhu'—W. *jūbilum, (būbo),* Boi. ἰυγή.

ìż Old Lith. 'aus'—see *ìsz.*

įżaizdus 'schädlich, verderblich'—F. *us-gaisjan;* B. I, 723. II, 3, 377. Cf. Lesk. Abl. 290, Lesk. Nom. 261.

iżdas 'Schatz' (bes. einer, der noch verborgen liegt)—Ber. *dějǫ*. Cf. Ness. 29[b], Lesk. Nom. 198-9.

yżià, yżě 'Eisscholle, Grundeis, Treibeis' — B. I, XLV (Ntr.). Cf. Lesk. Abl. 274, Sommer 143-4.

ìżinės plu. 'Schlauben, Hülsen, Schalen'—Ber. *ězva*. Cf. Lesk. Abl. 274.

ìżti 'entzweigehen'; **ìżo** pret. 3rd pers. sing.—Ber. *ěsva;* Boi. ἴξαλος. Cf. Lesk. Abl. 274, 397; Juškevič 676.

J

jà 'ja'—see *jè*.

ją acc. sing. fem. of **jìs**, q. v., 'sie'—W. *jam*.

jalmużnas 'Almosen'—K. *Almosen*. Cf. Ness. 36[a], 4[b]; Kur. s. v.; Brückner SlFw. 87.

jaũ 'schon'—F. *ju;* B. II, 1, 271.326. 2, 707 (note); Ber. *ju;* W. *jam, (aurōra)*.

jauczù, jaũsti 'fühlen, empfinden, merken, wahrnehmen, (Szyr. also) wachen'—W. *vātēs;* (Boi. ζητέω). Cf. Lesk. Abl. 299.

-jaudìnti—see *sujaudìnti* 'in Bewegung setzen'.

jaũdrinu, jaũdrinti 'in Bewegung setzen'; **sujaũdrinu, sujaũdrinti** 'aufhetzen, aufwiegeln'—Ber. *judzę*. Cf. Lesk. Abl. 298.

jáuja 'Flachsbrechstube, wo der Flachs gedörrt und gebrochen wird; (Samog. also) Scheuer mit einem Ofen, in welcher das Getreide noch im Stroh getrocknet wird; grüner Rasenplatz zum Weiden der Kälber'—Ber. *jevinŭ*. Cf. Kur. s. v.; Ness. 37[a]; Bezz. LF. 118.

jáuju, jáuti 'aquam fervidam super infundere'. K.'s "(Teig) anrühren" belongs rather to Lett. *jáuju, jáut*.—(K. *Käse*); Ber. *jucha;* [W. 2. *jūs*]. Cf. Ness. 37[a]; Geitler LD. 47 (s. v. jaukti); Lesk. Abl. 298.

jaukinù, jaukìnti 'gewöhnen, anlocken, zähmen' (nur von Tieren)—Uh. *úcyati*. See *jùnkstu* & Lesk. Abl. 299.

jáunas 'jung'—Uh. *yúvā;* K. *jung;* F. *juggs*, (2. **-ba*); B. II, 1, 271; Ber. *junŭ, ju;* W. *juvenis*.

jaunẽsnis 'jünger'—B. II, 1, 561. See *-ẽsnis*.
jaunỹbė 'Jugend'—F. 2. **-ba.* See *jáunas*.
jaunikáitis 'adulescentulus'—B. II, 1, 677.
jaunìkis 'junger Bursche, Bräutigam'; Bezz. 'Probebräutigam'—B. I, 291-2. II, 1, 489; Ber. *junŭ*. Cf. Bezz. LF. 118.
jaunìmas 'Jugend; Jugendgesellschaft, Ball'—B. II, 1, 250.
jaunulėlis dimin. adj. 'jung'—B. II, 1, 377. Cf. Lesk. Nom. 492.
jaunùmas 'Jugend, das Jungsein'—B. II, 1, 250.
jaurùs 'sumpfig'—Boi. *αὐρ-* (Ntr. p. 1099). Cf. Juškevič 681.
jáutis 'Ochs'—Uh. *yáuti;* W. *jungo,* (*ovis*), (*vetus*); Boi. ζεύγνῡμι. Cf. Lesk. Nom. 540, Sommer 257-8.
javaĩ plu. 'Getreide' (Ness. "bes. solange es noch auf dem Halme steht oder noch nicht gedroschen ist")—Uh. *yávas;* (F. *atisks*); B. I, 130(note).793; Ber. *jevinŭ;* W. *juvenis;* Boi. ζειαί. Cf. Ness. 36-7.
javẽnà 'Getreideacker, Stoppelfeld, Getreidestoppeln'—(F. *atisks*); Ber. *jevinŭ*.
javìnis 'Getreideschober'—Ber. *jevinŭ*.
jè, jà 'ja'—K. *ja*.
jėgà 'Kraft, Besinnung'; **nůjėgà, pajėgà** 'Vermögen, Einsicht, (Szyr. also) Witz, Mutterwitz'—B. I, 270; Ber. *jaglŭ;* Boi. ἥβη. Cf. Lesk. Abl. 371, Lesk. Nom. 206.
jėgiù, jẽgti 'Kraft haben, vermögen, imstande sein'—B. I, 132.602; Ber. *jaglŭ;* Boi. ἥβη. Cf. Lesk. Abl. 371.
jeĩ, jéi 'wenn'—B. I, 262. II, 2, 348; W. *is;* (Boi. εἰ). Cf. Kur. Gram. 1597-1601.
jeknos plu. 'Leber'—Uh. *yákṛt;* B. I, 122.262.589. II, 1, 161.309; Ber. *ikra* 1; W. *jecur;* Boi. ἧπαρ (& note).
jékszlis 'Kaulbarsch'—see *eżegỹs*.
jenkù, jèkti 'erblinden'; **apjenkù, apjèkti** 'erblinden, verblendet, betört werden'—(F. *jiuleis*); (W. *aquilus*). Cf. Lesk. Abl. 329.
jentė, gentė, żentė, East Lith. **intė** 'Frau des Bruders des

Gatten, der Schwester Mannesschwester, des Bruders Frau, Schwägerin'—Uh. 2. *yā́tā;* B. I, 178.270.422. II, 1, 334. 2, 276; Ber. *jętry;* W. *janitrīcēs;* Boi. ἐνάτηρ (& note). Cf. Bezz. BGLS. 93, note 1; Lesk. Nom. 433 (in Ber. read 433 for 483).

jèrubē, jèrublē 'Haselhuhn'—Ber. *ěrębĭ.* Cf. Lesk. Nom. 268-9.

jẽszkau, jëszkóti (ẽszkau, ëszkóti) 'suchen'—Uh. *icchā́ti;* K. *heischen;* F. *fraisan;* B. I, 724.781.940.944. II, 1, 457. 3, 211.352; Ber. *iskǫ;* W. *aerusco;* Boi. ἵμερος. Cf. Lesk. Abl. 274.

jëszkótinas 'quaerendus'—B. II, 1, 269. Cf. Kur. Gram. 1546; Lesk. Nom. 405; Wied. 198.

jẽszmas 'Bratspiess'—see *ẽszmas.*

jëvà 'Faulbaum'—see *ëvà.*

jìs, jì 'er, sie'—Uh. *yás;* F. *is, jabai, jains;* B. I, 94.262. II, 1, 219. 2, 7.325.326.327.328.331.335.390; Ber. *i-* (end); W. *is, jam;* Boi. ἴα (s. v. εἷς), ἰ-δέ, ἴν.

jõ 'eius'—F. *jabai;* B. I, 262. See prec.

jódau, jódyti 'fortgesetzt umherreiten'—Ber. *jaždžǫ.*

jóju, jóti 'reiten'—Uh. *yā́ti;* F. *iddja;* B. I, 288. II, 1, 435. 443. 3, 62.160.161.374.386.418; Ber. *jadǫ* (twice); W. *eo, Jānus.* Cf. Lesk. Abl. 376.

jõks, fem. **jokià** 'irgend welcher, welche'—Ber. 1. *jakŭ* (s. v. *i-*). Cf. Kur. Gram. 904-5.

jómarkas 'Jahrmarkt'; **jomarkaĩ** plu. "die Gewebe der Erdspinne, welche im Herbst von den Stoppelfeldern sich erheben und in Gestalt langer Fäden vom Winde durch die Luft getragen werden" (Nęss.)—B. I, 854. Cf. Ness. 40[a]; Kur. s. v.; Brückner SlFw. 87; Prell. deutsch. Best. in den lett. Spr. 55.

Jõnas 'Johannes'—B. II, 2, 134. Cf. Brückner SlFw. 87, Prell. deutsch. Best. in den lett. Spr. 30.

jotis 'Ritt, Reiterei'—B. II, 1, 435.

jõvalas 'Schweinefutter, Treber'—Uh. *yā́uti;* Ber. *jucha;* W. 2. *jūs;* Boi. ζύμη. Cf. Lesk. Abl. 298.

judinas 'sich regend, beweglich'—B. II, 1, 260. Cf. Ness. 42[a], Lesk. Nom. 398.

jùdinu, jùdinti 'bewegen, schütteln, rütteln; aufmuntern, ermahnen'—Uh. *yúdhyati;* Ber. *judzę;* W. *jubeo;* Boi. ὑσμῖνι. Cf. Lesk. Abl. 298.

jùdra 'Wirbelwind'—B. II, 1, 355; W. *jubeo;* Boi. ὑσμῖνι. Cf. Lesk. Abl. 298.

judù, judė́ti 'sich erregen, zittern; rührig sein, fleissig arbeiten; zanken, schelten'—Uh. *yúdhyati;* B. II, 3, 171.187; W. *jubeo;* Boi. ὑσμῖνι. Cf. Lesk. Abl. 298.

jùdu 'ihr beide'—Uh. *yuvám;* F. *jūs;* B. II, 2, 385.412.427; Boi. 1. δύω (note).

judùs 'zanksüchtig'—Ber. *judzę.* Cf. Lesk. Abl. 298.

jukà 'Blutsuppe' (bes. von Gänseblut)—Ber. *jucha.* Cf. Brückner SlFw. 88.

jundù, jùsti 'in zitternde Bewegung, in Aufruhr geraten'—Uh. *yúdhyati;* B. I, 270.536. II, 1, 442. 3, 397; W. *jubeo;* Boi. ὑσμῖνι. Cf. Lesk. Abl. 298.

jùngas (B. **júngas**) 'Ochsenjoch am Pfluge; Gelenk einer Kette; Gewölbe eines Gemäuers; Verbindungsbügel am Dreschflegel'—Uh. *yugám;* K. *Joch;* F. *juk;* B. I, 623. 793; Ber. *igo;* W. *jugum;* Boi. ζυγόν.

jùngiu, jùngti (B. **júngiu, júnkti**) '(Ochsen) ins Joch spannen'—Uh. *yuktás, yugám, yunákti;* F. *juk;* B. I, 623. II, 3, 275.279.285.382.395.397; Ber. *igo;* W. *jungo, jugum;* Boi. ζεύγνῡμι.

jùnkstu, jùnkti (B. **júnkstu, júnkti**) 'gewohnt werden' (Kur. "doch nur tadelnd von schlechten Gewohnheiten besonders bei Tieren"; Ness. also 'versuchen')—Uh. *úcyati;* F. *biūhts;* B. I, 382.391.940. II, 3, 285.286; (W. *uxor*); Boi. ἔκηλος. Cf. Lesk. Abl. 299.

juntù, jùsti 'fühlen, merken, gewahr werden, (Szyr. also) wachen'—F. *gaumjan;* W. *vātēs.* Cf. Lesk. Abl. 299.

jùpa 'Frauenkittel mit Ärmeln; der Talar der Geistlichen'—Ber. *jupa.* Cf. Brückner SlFw. 88.

jùpanczė 'filzener Regenmantel; Filzsohle'—Ber. *japùndže.* Cf. Ness. 43[b], Brückner SlFw. 88.

júra 'Meer'; **Júra** Name eines Nebenflusses der Memel (des Niemen)—Boi. αὐρ- (Ntr. p. 1099). See next; Ness. 43[b]; Bezz. LF. 119; Lesk. Nom. 227; Sommer 193.

júrės plu. tant. 'Meer, Ostsee'—Uh. *vā́r;* F. *uraz;* W. *ūrīna;* Boi. οὐρέω (& Ntr.). Cf. Lesk. Nom. 227, 439; Sommer 191 ff.

jũs nom. plu. to **tù** 'ihr, Sie' (cf. Kur. Gram. 1305)—Uh. *yuṣmá-;* F. *jūs;* B. I, 114.261. II, 2, 380.385.411.427; Boi. ὑμεῖς.

jūsàsis 'der Eurige'—B. II, 2, 405.406. Cf. Kur. Gram. 983.

jùsti inf.—see *jundù* 'ich gerate in zitternde Bewegung', or *juntù* 'ich fühle'.

jūsũjis 'der Eurige'—B. II, 1, 196. 2, 405.406. Cf. Kur. Gram. 983, Lesk. Nom. 341.

júszė 'schlechte Suppe'; Kur. (around Tilsit and among the fishermen of Kurisches Haff) 'Fischsuppe, Fischbrühe'; Ness. "eine Art Schrotmehlsuppe, von Sauerteig mit Wasser durchgerührt und gekocht"—Uh. *yū́ṣ;* B. I, 785.793; Ber. *jucha;* W. 2. *jūs;* Boi. ζύμη. Cf. Ness. 44[a]; Kur. s. v.; Kur. DLWb. s. v. Fischbrühe; Brückner SlFw. 88.

jũ 'desto'; **jũ . . . jũ** 'je . . . desto' (e.g. **jũ daugiaũs jũ geriaũs** 'je mehr, desto besser')—B. II, 2, 365.714.

jũkas 'Scherz, Spott, Gelächter'—(F. *jiuleis*); B. I, 279; W. *jocus* (thrice); (Boi. ἐψιά (twice)). Cf. Lesk. Abl. 379.

jůkũju, jůkũti 'Scherz treiben'—B. II, 1, 436.444; W. *jocus.*

jũsiu (old form **jũsmi**), **jũsti** 'gürten'—Uh. *yámati;* B. I, 793. II, 3, 98.338; Ber. *-jašǫ;* W. *jungo;* Boi. ζώννυμι. Cf. Wied. 177. 9; Lesk. Abl. 379.

jůsmũ 'Gurt, Hosenband'—Uh. *yámati;* B. I, 752. II, 1, 238; Ber. *-jašǫ.*

jũsta 'Gürtel' (cf. Ness. 40[a]); **dangaũs jũsta** 'Himmelsgürtel, Regenbogen'—Uh. *yámati;* B. I, 156. II, 1,

416; Ber. *-jašǫ;* W. *jungo;* Boi. ζώννυμι. Cf. Lesk. Abl. 379.

jūstau, jūstyti 'gürten'—B. II, 3, 214.

K

-k impera. end.—see *-ki.*

kabẽ 'Haken'—B. II, 1, 222; Boi. κόμβος. Cf. Lesk. Abl. 330, Lesk. Nom. 272.

kabinas id.—B. II, 1, 260. Cf. Lesk. Nom. 399.

kabinù, kabìnti 'hängen, aufhängen'; **kẽmą kabìnti** 'auf der Reise ein Dorf berühren'—Ber. *kobĭ.* Cf. Ness. 169[a], Lesk. Abl. 330.

kablỹs 'Haken, Mistgabel, Türangel' — Boi. κόμβος. Cf. Lesk. Abl. 330.

kabù, kabė́ti 'hangen' — Ber. *kobĭ;* (W. *scamnum*). Cf. Lesk. Abl. 330.

kaczárga 'Ofenkrücke, Feuerhaken' — Ber. *kočerga.* Cf. Brückner SlFw. 88.

kadà 'wann'—Uh. *kadā;* F. *hvan;* B. II, 2, 733; Ber. 9. *kŭda* (s. v. *kŭto*); W. *quando, quis.*

kadagỹs 'Wacholder'—Ber. *kaďǫ;* Boi. κέδρος.

kagenu, kagenti 'schnattern' (von der Gans)—Ber. *kačka.*

kaĩ, kaĩp, kaĩpo (kaipõ) 'wie?, wie, als'—F. *hvaiwa;* B. I, 597. II, 2, 349.369; Ber. *kŭto* (end); W. *nempe, quippe;* Boi. πόθεν.

kaĩkaras 'Horde, Haufe'—(W. *cīvis*). Cf. Geitler LS. 89.

káilis 'Fell' (bes. von kleinen Tieren)—Uh. *celam.*

kaimas 'Dorf'—see *kẽmas.*

kaĩmenė 'Herde' — F. *haims;* (W. *cīvis*); (Boi. κοινός). Cf. Lesk. Abl. 274.

kaimýnas 'Bewohner desselben Dorfes, Nachbar', **kaimýna** 'Nachbarin'; **kaimýna** 'Nachbarschaft' — F. *haims, ahmeins;* B. I, 191. II, 1, 246.273.278; (W. *cīvis*). Cf. Lesk. Abl. 274, Lesk. Nom. 410.

kainė 'Wert, Preis'—F. *arhvazna;* B. I, 178 (*kaina*(?)). II, 1, 262; Ber. *cěna;* Boi. ποινή. Cf. Lesk. Nom. 375.

kaĩp, kaĩpo 'wie'—see *kaĩ*.

kaipstu, kaipti 'hinsiechen, kränkeln'; **nukaipo** pret. 3rd pers. sing. 'siechte hin'—(Ber. *cěpǫ* 1). Cf. Geitler LS. 89; Bezz. LF. 119; Lesk. Abl. 292.

kairẽ 'linke Hand' (cf. Kur. s. v.)—Boi. σκαι[ϝ]ός.

kaiszaũ, kaiszýti 'mehrfach umherstecken'—Ber. *češǫ*. Cf. Lesk. Abl. 274.

kaiszti 'glätten, reiben, schaben'; **apkaiszti** 'abreiben'; **nukáiszti** 'abschaben, glatt machen'—Ber. *česta, češǫ;* W. *caesariēs* (& Ntr.). Cf. Geitler LS. 77, 98; Bezz. LF. 119; Kur. s. v. *káiszau;* Lesk. Abl. 292.

káisztuvas 'Glättinstrument der Böttcher'—Ber. *česta*. Cf. Bezz. LF. 119.

kaĩtinu, kaĩtinti 'erhitzen, heizen; (von der Sonne) brennen, stechen'—Uh. *cétati;* F. *heitō*. Cf. [Lesk. Abl. 292].

kaitrà 'Feuerglut, Hitze'—Uh. *cétati;* F. *heitō;* W. *caelum*. Cf. Lesk. Abl. 292.

kaitrùs 'Hitze gebend' (z. B. gut heizendes Holz)—Uh. *cétati;* F. *heitō;* W. *caelum*.

kaitulỹs 'Schweiss'—Uh. *cétati;* F. *heitō;* W. *caelum*.

kakarýkū, kakarykũ 'kikeriki'. Nachbildung des Hahnenschreies.—Ber. *kukurěkajǫ*.

kãkinu, kãkinti 'hingelangen lassen, hinbefördern' — Boi. πέμπω.

kãklas 'Hals'—Uh. *kākalaka-;* B. II, 1, 129; Ber. *kolo;* W. *collum;* Boi. κύκλος.

kaklãvynỹs 'Halsband'—B. I, 339. II, 3, 240. See prec. & Lesk. Abl. 288.

kaladà 'Block, Klotz' (Kur. "in den die Gefangenen im Gefängnis gelegt werden"; Ness. 175[a] "auf dem die Holzhacker das Holz spalten") — Ber. *kolda*. Cf. Brückner SlFw. 88.

kalavìjas 'Schwert; Eisbrecher an einer Brücke' — Uh. *karavālas*.

kalbà 'Rede, Sprache, Aussprache, Gerücht'—(F. *hōlōn*); Ber. *kolkolŭ*, (*golsŭ*); W. 1. *calo;* Boi. καλέω, σκύλαξ. Cf. Lesk. Abl. 375.

kal̃besis 'Rede, Spruch'—B. II, 1, 525.636.

kal̃besnis 'Gerede, Geplapper'—B. II, 1, 289 (for § 327, b, γ read § 327, b, δ).

kal̃bestis 'Spruch, Rede'—B. II, 1, 439. Cf. Lesk. Nom. 579.

kalbù, kalbė́ti 'reden, sprechen' — (F. *hōlōn*); (Ber. *klabosŭ*). Cf. Lesk. Abl. 375.

káldinu, káldinti 'schmieden oder hämmern lassen; gefangen nehmen lassen, fesseln'—(Ber. *kladivo*).

kaldū̃nai plu. 'Weichselzopf'—Ber. *koltun*. Cf. Brückner SlFw. 88.

kãlė 'Hündin'; auch Schimpfwort auf Weiber — B. II, 1, 277; Boi. σκύλαξ. Cf. Sommer 64-65.

kalėdà 'Kalende, Getreidelieferung an Geistliche und Schullehrer'—Ber. *kolęda*. Cf. Brückner SlFw. 88-89.

kalė̃dos plu. 'Weihnachtsfest'—Ber. *kolęda*. Cf. Brückner SlFw. 88-89.

kalybas 'Hund mit einem weissen Halsring'—W. *callidus;* Boi. κηλίς.

kalkunas masc. 'kalkutischer Hahn, Truthahn'; **kalkuna** fem. 'Truthenne'—Ber. *kan* 1.

kálnas 'Berg, Höhe, Damm'—(Uh. *çilā́*); F. *hallus;* B. I, 143.368.572; Ber. *čelo*, (*kolsŭ*), (*kolnĭcĭ*); W. *celsus, collis;* Boi. κολωνός. Cf. Lesk. Abl. 330.

kalnė̃nas 'Bergbewohner'—B. II, 1, 308. Cf. Lesk. Nom. 388; Kur. DLWb. s. v. Bergbewohner, Bergvolk (on Kurschat's *-ėna-* notice Kur. Gram. 289 & last sentence of § in Leskien).

kálpa 'Schlittenpolster; Querholz am Schlitten, das die Kufen verbindet' — (Ber. *čalŭ, klapĭtĭ*). Cf. Lesk. Abl. 331.

kalpõkas 'oberer Teil eines Filzhutes' (im Gegensatz zur Krempe)—Ber. *kalpák*. Cf. Brückner SlFw. 89.

káltas pret. pass. part. of **kalù**, q. v., 'geschmiedet, geschlagen'—Ber. *kolto.*
káltas 'Meissel'—Ber. *kolto, (kolię).* See *kalù.*
kal̃tas 'schuldig, verpflichtet'—F. *skulan;* (W. *scelus*). Cf. Lesk. Abl. 375.
kaltė̃ 'Schuld, Vergehen' — F. *skulan;* (W. *scelus*). Cf. Lesk. Abl. 375.
kalù, kálti 'schlagen, schmieden, hämmern'—B. I, 479. II, 3, 195 (read 'schlage' for 'schlachte').377-8; Ber. *kolę;* W. 1. *calx, clādēs;* Boi. κλαδαρός, κολετρᾶν, εὔ-κολος. Cf. Lesk. Abl. 375.
kalùpkė 'schlechtes Haus, elende baufällige Hütte'—Ber. *chalupa.* Cf. Brückner SlFw. 89.
kalvà 'kleine Anhöhe, kleiner Hügel'—F. *hallus;* B. II, 1, 208.280; Boi. κολωνός. Cf. Lesk. Abl. 330.
kamãnė 'Erdbiene, Hummel' (Kur.); 'wilde Biene, Waldbiene, Feldbiene' (Ness. 176[a, b])—Ber. *čĭmelĭ, komarŭ.* Cf. Lesk. Abl. 331, Lesk. Nom. 388.
kãmanos plu. 'lederner Zaum' — K. *hemmen;* Ber. *čĭma, chomǫtŭ, komŭ* 1; Boi. κημός. Cf. Lesk. Nom. 387.
kamañtai plu. 'Kummetgeschirr'—K. *Kummet;* Ber. *chomǫtŭ.* Cf. Brückner SlFw. 89.
kamarà 'Kammer; Kammerkollegium, Regierung' — W. *camera.* Cf. Brückner SlFw. 89.
kamè 'wo?'—B. II, 2, 707.
kamẽnas 'Stammende, das dickere Ende eines gefällten Baumes'—Ber. *kŭmy.* Cf. Geitler LS. 64.
kamìnė 'Feldbiene'—Ber. *čĭmelĭ, komarŭ.* Cf. Lesk. Abl. 331, Lesk. Nom. 388.
kamoju, kamoti 'quälen, vexieren'—*kamùju.*
kam̃pas 'Ecke, Winkel; Gegend, Landstrich; Zipfel am Rock; Schnitt Brot; Erk̃er am Hause; eine kleine mit Gesträuch bewachsene Insel, bes. an der Mündung der Flüsse (Ness. 176[b])'—Uh. *kámpate;* F. *hamfs;* B. I, 357.513.582-3; Ber. *kępa, (kętŭ);* W. *campus;* Boi. καμπή, κανθός (twice).

kamszà 'Damm, Auffahrt, erhöhter Weg (Ness. 177[a]); Stopfung, etwa beim Eisgange in einem Strome, der Volksmenge auf dem Markte, in der Kirche etc. (Kur.); Vielesser (Kur.); unnütze Last, Ballast, um nur den Kasten vollzustopfen (MLG. I, 69)' — (W. *premo*). Cf. Lesk. Abl. 331.

kamůju, kamůti 'zusammenpressen, stopfen' (?). Ber., W., Boi., Prell. apparently after Zupitza Germanische Gutturale 108. But Geitler LS. 89, s. v. kanoti, has (*kamoju, kamoti*) 'quälen, vexieren'; and Lalis 140 has (*kamůju, kamůti*) 'to vex, torment, harass, weary, fatigue, excess'. Cf. also Lett. *kamût* 'plagen, quälen'. —Ber. *čĭma, komŭ* 1; (W. *premo*); Boi., Prell. κημός.

kamůlỹs 'Knäuel'—Ber. *komŭ* 1; Boi. (Ntr.) κῶμυς. Cf. Kur. 165[a]; Schleicher LSpr. II, 59, 69, 278.

kanakados 'manchmal', **kanakëk** 'einige', **kanakëli** id., **kanakur** 'mancher Orten'—(W. *cunque*). Cf. Geitler LS. 89; BB. III, 56; IF. II, 210; Geitler LD. 47-48.

kanãpė 'Hanfpflanze', plu. **kanãpės** 'Hanf' — Uh. *çaṇás;* K. *Hanf;* Ber. *konopa;* W. *cannabis;* Boi. κάνναβις. Cf. Brückner SlFw. 89.

kañczus, kanczùkas 'Peitsche, Karbatsche'—Ber. *kamdžíja.* Cf. Brückner SlFw. 89.

kandìs 'Motte, Milbe'—(W. *cossus*). See *kándu* & Lesk. Abl. 375, Lesk. Nom. 236.

kañdis 'Biss'; (Ness. 177[a] also:) "der Beisser, spez. die Motte, Milbe; eine Pferdekrankheit, der Haarwurm" —Ber. *čęstĭ.* Cf. Lesk. Abl. 375, Lesk. Nom. 289.

kándu, kąsti 'beissen'—Uh. *kandaras;* (F. *hnasqus, handugs*); B. I, 420. II, 1, 543; Ber. *čęstĭ, kǫsŭ* 1; (W. *cossus, tondeo*); Boi. κνώδων, (κοντός), (τένδω). Cf. Lesk. Abl. 375.

kandùs 'bissig' (auch von Menschen)—(F. *handugs*); B. II, 1, 492; (Boi. κοντός). Cf. Lesk. Abl. 375.

kanýnkė 'Kaninchen' — K. *Kaninchen.* Cf. Ness. 177[b], Prell. deutsch. Best. in den lett. Spr. 60.

kankà 'Qual, Leiden' — Uh. *kāṅkṣati;* K. *Hunger;* F. *hūhrus;* B. I, 406.576. II, 1, 634; Boi. κάγκανος, (κακός). Cf. Lesk. Abl. 363, Lesk. Nom. 208.

kañkalas 'Glocke, Schelle; ein vom Baume herabhangender Eis- oder Schneezapfen'—Uh. *kalakalas;* F. *hana;* B. II, 1, 128(twice).153; Ber. *kolkolŭ, kǫkolĭ;* Boi. καλέω. Cf. Brückner SlFw. 24, 89; Lesk. Nom. 472.

kankalìjos plu. 'Glockenblumen, Acklei'—Ber. *kǫkolĭ.* Cf. Bezz. LF. 120, Sommer 24.

kankalìkai plu. id.—B. II, 1, 669.673. Cf. Bezz. LF. 120.

kañklės plu. 'die litauische Zither' ("ein sehr einfach konstruiertes gitarrenartiges Instrument, das jetzt ganz aus dem Gebrauche verschwunden ist" Ness. 178[a])— Uh. *kaṅkaṇas;* F. *hana;* W. *cano.* Cf. Brückner SlFw. 24, 89 (note); Lesk. Nom. 472, 498; Sommer 173.

kankù, kàkti 'gelangen, genügen, hinreichen; (beim Waten im Wasser) Grund finden' — Boi. πέμπω. Cf. Lesk. Abl. 375.

kapà Samogit. 'Schock, 60 Stück'—Ber. *kopa.* Cf. Brückner SlFw. 90.

kãpas 'Grabhügel, Grab'; **kapaĩ** plu. 'Friedhof'—F. *skaban, haubiþ;* Ber. *kopa, kopajǫ;* Boi. σκάπτω. Cf. Lesk. Nom. 175.

kãpė 'Weibermütze, Kappe'—Ber. *kapa.* Cf. Prell. deutsch. Best. in den lett. Spr. 61.

kãpinu, kãpinti 'mit Grenzhügeln umgeben'—see *apkãpinu.*

kaplỹs 'Hacke, Karst, Eisaxt, abgenutzte Axt'—Ber. *kopajǫ;* W. *scapulae;* Boi. κάπηλος, 1. κῆπος, σκάπτω. Cf. Lesk. Nom. 458.

kapõczus 'Totengräber'—Ber. *kopajǫ.* Cf. Brückner SlFw. 90.

kapóju, kapóti 'hauen, hacken (z. B. Holz); (mit dem Schnabel) picken'—(F. *hamfs*); B. I, 582; Ber. *kopajǫ;* W. *scapulae, (capio);* Boi. κάπηλος, 1. κῆπος, κόπτω, σκάπτω.

kapõnė 'Hackmesser, Hacke; Hackbrett, Mulde'—K. *Hippe* 1; Boi. κόπτω. Cf. Lesk. Nom. 390.

karãbas 'Tüte'—Ber. *korbĭji.* Cf. Brückner SlFw. 90.

karaĩ plu. 'Steinpocken; rötlich blaue Flecken am Körper beim Typhus'—Ber. *korĭ.*

karalìkas 'Kaninchen; Zaunkönig'. Cf. 2nd § of Berneker's article.—Ber. *korlĭ.* Cf. Brückner SlFw. 90.

karãlius 'König'; Ness. 179ᵃ also: "in der Windmühle der grosse senkrechte Pfeiler, auf dem die Mühle ruht und um den sie gedreht wird"—(K. *Kaiser*); Ber. *korlĭ.* Cf. Brückner SlFw. 90.

kãras 'Streit, Kampf, Krieg; (Samog. also) Armee'—K. *Heer;* F. *harjis;* B. II, 1, 188.218.260; Ber. *-korŭ;* (W. *carino*); Boi. κοίρανος. Cf. Lesk. Abl. 331; Lesk. Nom. 168, 271.

karáuju, karáuti 'kämpfen, kriegen'—Ber. *-korŭ.*

karavõjas 'Fladen'—see *karvõjas.*

karbãczus, karbõczus 'Karbatsche, Peitsche (mit geflochtenem und lederbezogenem Stock; die Schnur ist von Lederstreifen geflochten)'—Ber. *kòrbāč.* Cf. Brückner SlFw. 90.

karbas 'Korb'—Ber. *korbĭji.* Cf. Prell. deutsch. Best. in den lett.' Spr. 61.

karbija "ein dichter, korbartiger Kasten, ein Kober mit freiem Deckel, der auf den Unterkasten aufgeschoben wird, von Weidenreisern oder breiten Baststreifen dauerhaft geflochten" (Ness. 180ᵃ)—Ber. *korbĭji.*

karbõczus 'Peitsche'—see *karbãczus.*

kar̃czai plu. 'Mähne'—(W. *corium*).

karczamà, karczemà 'Schenke, Bierhaus, Wirtshaus'—Ber. *kŭrčĭma.* Cf. Ness. 180ᵃ, Brückner SlFw. 90.

kárdas 'Degen, Schwert'—Ber. *korda.* Cf. Brückner SlFw. 90, 202-3.

karė 'Kampf, Krieg'—B. II, 1, 218.260; Boi. κοίρανος. Cf. Lesk. Nom. 271, Sommer 59.

karélkis 'Schmuckkügelchen, Perle, Koralle'—Ber. *korala.*

Cf. Brückner SlFw. 90, Prell. deutsch. Best. in den lett. Spr. 61.

-kargýti—see *sukargýti* 'verknüpfen'.

karias 'Heer'; plu. 'Krieger'—F. *harjis;* B. II, 1, 188. 2, 129; (Ber. *-korŭ*); (W. *carino*); Boi. κοίρανος. Cf. Lesk. Nom. 309; Sommer 236, 244.

kariù, kárti 'hängen' (bes. am Galgen)—(W. *cardo, cēra, corium*); Boi. κρεμάννυμι. Cf. Lesk. Abl. 373.

kárka 'Oberarm (Szyr.); Schweinefuss von Klaue bis Knie, Vorderfuss des Schweines mit Schulter'—Ber. *korkŭ* (twice). Cf. Lesk. Nom. 214.

kárkė 'Pantoffel'—Ber. *korek.* Cf. Brückner SlFw. 14.

karkiù, kar̃kti 'quarren, schnarren, schreien, krächzen, gackeln'—Ber. *korkoŕǫ;* W. *querquēdula;* Boi. κέρκαξ.

kar̃klas 'Wald- oder Sumpfweide'—Ber. *korkula.*

karnà 'Lindenbast' (woraus die litauischen Sandalen gemacht werden)—Uh. *cárma;* Ber. *kora;* W. *corium;* Boi. κείρω.

karoblius, karoblis 'Schiff, Arche'—Ber. *korabĭ.*

karõsas 'Karausche'—K. *Karausche;* Ber. *karaś.* Cf. Brückner SlFw. 91.

kárpa 'Karpfen'—K. *Karpfen;* Ber. *korpŭ;* W. *carpa;* Boi. κυπρῖνος. Cf. Brückner SlFw. 91.

kárpa 'Warze; Brustwarze'—Ber. *korpavŭ.* Cf. Lesk. Abl. 332.

karpaũ, karpýti 'schneiden, scheren'—Ber. *čŕrpǫ;* W. *carpo;* Boi. 1. καρπός. See *kerpù* & Lesk. Abl. 332.

karstù, kar̃sti 'bitter werden'—B. II, 3, 370. See *kartùs* & Lesk. Abl. 332.

karszė 'hohes Alter, Altersschwäche'—Ber. *kŭrsŭ.* Cf. Lesk. Abl. 375, Lesk. Nom. 272.

karszinu, karszinti 'aufhalten, hinhalten, verzögern'—Ber. *kŭrsŭ.*

karszìs 'Blei, Brassen, Brachsen' (Fisch)—Uh. *kṛsṇás;* Ber. *čirnŭ.* Cf. Lesk. Nom. 236.

kársziu, kárszti 'sich in hohem Alter befinden, altern'—Uh.

kṛçás; Ber. *kŭrsŭ;* W. *cracentes.* Cf. Lesk. Abl. 375.

karsziù, kar̃szti 'kämmen, kämmeln (von der Wolle, auch vom Abkämmen oder Riffeln der Flachsköpfe); (Kur.: als Scherzwort auch) schnell gehen; (Pferde) striegeln; durchhecheln, durchbläuen'—Uh. *kaṣati;* (F. *us-skarjan*); B. II, 1, 416; Ber. *korsta;* W. *carro, curro,* (*squarrōsus*). Cf. Lesk. Abl. 375.

kársztas 'heiss, schwül'—(F. *hauri*); Ber. *krasa, kuŕę;* W. *carbo;* Boi. κέραμος, (καίω). Cf. Lesk. Abl. 332.

kar̃sztis 'Hitze, Schwüle; Brand, Entzündung an einem Gliede; Fieberhitze'—W. *carbo.* Cf. Lesk. Abl. 332.

kartà 'Lage, Schicht, Reihe; Grad der Geschlechtsfolge; Linie, Zweig einer Familie'—Ber. *kortŭ.* Cf. Lesk. Abl. 332.

kar̃tas 'Mal'; **vẽns kar̃t vẽns** 'einmal eins'; **kar̃tais** adv. inst. plu. 'manchmal, zuweilen, zuzeiten'—Uh. *kŕtvas;* B. II, 2, 66(twice).67.719; Ber. *kortŭ.* Cf. Kur. s. vv.; Kur. Gram. 1407-8; Wied. 70, 160; Lesk. Abl. 332; Lesk. Nom. 531.

kartẽsnis 'bitterer'—B. II, 1, 561. See *kartùs* & *-ẽsnis.*

kártis 'Stange; Heubaum (der oben auf ein Fuder Heu gebunden wird, damit während des Fahrens das Heu nicht herabfällt)'—(W. *pertica* (twice)). Cf. Lesk. Nom. 236.

kartumỹnai plu. 'bittre Dinge, Bitterkeiten'—B. II, 1, 278. Cf. Lesk. Nom. 410.

kartùs 'bitter, barsch, ranzig'—Uh. *kaṭúṣ;* K. *hart;* (F. *hardus*); B. II, 1, 176. 2, 682; Ber. *kortŭkŭ;* W. *caro,* (*cancer*), ((Ntr.) *cāseus*); Boi. κείρω, (κράτος (note)). Cf. Lesk. Abl. 332, Lesk. Nom. 252.

karúsas, karúszis 'Karausche' — [K. *Karausche*]; Ber. *karaś.* Cf. Brückner SlFw. 91.

kárvė 'Kuh'—Uh. *çŕṅgam* (read lit. for aksl.); B. I, 454. II, 1, 208; Ber. *korva;* W. *cervus;* Boi. κεραός, (κεκρύφαλος). Cf. Lesk. Nom. 349.

karvẽlė, karvùžė, karvelùžė, karvužẽlė, karvytẽlė, karvytužẽlė dimin. to prec. 'Kuh'—B. II, 1, 674. Cf. Kur. Gram. 361.

karvõjas, karavõjas 'Fladen, Beestfladen, Osterfladen'—Ber. *korvajĭ*. Cf. Brückner SlFw. 91.

kárvpalaikė 'schlechte Kuh'—B. II, 1, 99. Cf. Kur. s. v. palaĩkis.

kàs 'wer, was'; **kàs** indeclinable in adv. combination with a substantive 'jeder, jede', e.g. **kàs dẽną** 'jeden Tag, täglich'—Uh. *kás;* K. *wer;* F. *hvas;* B. I, 587.620. II, 2, 348.349.357.375; Ber. *kŭto;* W. *quis;* Boi. *πόθεν*. Cf. Schleicher LSpr. I, 89; Kur. Gram. 880; Wied. 120. On *kàs* as 'jeder' see *kasmẽts.*

kasà 'Haarflechte, Zopf; (Ness. 184[a] also) Schweinemilz'—K. *Haar* 2; B. I, 784; Ber. *kosa* 1; (W. *carro*); (Boi. *κόμη*). Cf. Brückner SlFw. 91, Lesk. Nom. 208.

kasaũ, kasýti 'kratzen, krauen, striegeln' — Uh. *kaṣati,* (*kásati*); B. I, 572. II, 3, 268.327; Ber. *češǫ;* (W. *carro*); Boi. *κεσκέον, ξαίνω*.

kasinù, kasìnti 'kratzen, jucken' (cf. Schleicher LSpr. II, 279)—(W. *carro*).

kasmẽts, kasmẽtą adv. 'alljährlich'—B. II, 1, 35. 2, 679. See *kàs* & Kur. s. v.

ką́snis m. & f. 'Bissen; (Szyr.) Mehlklösse, mit denen das Federvieh gemästet wird'—B. II, 1, 289 (twice); Ber. *kǫsŭ* 1 (for Abl. 93 read Leskien Abl. 113 = 375). See *kándu* & Lesk. Abl. 375.

kasù, kàsti 'graben'—Uh. *kaṣati,* (*kásati*); Ber. *češǫ;* (W. *carro, cossus*); Boi. *κεσκέον*. Cf. Lesk. Abl. 375.

kasulas 'Jägerspiess'—W. *corulus.* Cf. Geitler LS. 65.

kasvãkaras, kasvãkarą adv. 'allabendlich'—B. II, 2, 352-3. 679. See under *kàs.*

-kaszẽti—see *nukaszẽti* 'entkräftet werden'.

kãtas 'Kater; Anker'—Ber. *kotŭ* 2 (twice). Cf. Brückner SlFw. 91.

katẽ 'Katze'—K. *Katze;* Ber. *kotŭ* 2; W. *cattus.* Cf. Wied. s. v.; Brückner SlFw. 92; Lesk. Nom. 272.

kãtilas 'Kessel'—F. *katils;* Ber. *kotĭlŭ;* W. *catīnus;* Boi. κοτύλη. Cf. Brückner SlFw. 92, Prell. deutsch. Best. in den lett. Spr. 26.

katilinu, katilinti 'plappern, plaudern' — (Uh. *kātkṛtas*); Boi. κωτίλος. Cf. Ness. 185[b].

kãtinas 'Kater; Anker'—K. *Katze;* Ber. *kotŭ* 2 (twice). Cf. Brückner SlFw. 92, l. 1; Lesk. Nom. 405.

katràs, fem. **katrà,** 'welcher von beiden, welcher'—Uh. *katarás;* F. *hvaþar;* B. II, 1, 326; Ber. 6. *kotorŭ* (s. v. *kŭto*); W. *quis, ubi,* 1. *uter;* Boi. πότερος. Cf. Wied. 120, Kur. Gram. 882.

katrul̃ 'in welcher Richtung? wohin?'—B. I, 449.852.

katvycza 'Anker'—Ber. *kotŭ* 2. Cf. Brückner SlFw. 91.

kaugė 'Heuhaufen'—B. I, 331. II, 1, 507. Cf. Geitler LS. 90, Lesk. Abl. 300-301.

káuju, káuti 'schlagen, schmieden; kämpfen, streiten'—Uh. *kavalas;* K. *hauen;* F. *hawi;* B. I, 331.576. II, 3, 378; Ber. *kovą;* W. 1. *cūdo, caudex,* (*plaudo*); Boi. κυδάζω, (κεάζω). Cf. Lesk. Abl. 300-301.

kaukalė Art Wasservogel auf dem Kurischen Haff und der Ostsee —Uh. *kokilás;* Ber. *kukają;* Boi. καύαξ.

kaukarà 'Hügel, Anhöhe'—Uh. *kucas;* K. *hoch;* F. *hauhs;* Ber. *kuča;* W. *cumulus;* Boi. κύπη. Cf. Lesk. Abl. 301.

kaũkas 'Beule, Geschwür'—Uh. *kucas;* K. *hoch;* F. *hauhs;* Ber. *kuča.* Cf. Lesk. Abl. 301, Lesk. Nom. 194.

kaũkas 'Kobold, Gnom, zwerghafter Geist; Zwerg; ungetauft gestorbenes Kind'—F. *hugs;* Ber. *kuka,* (*mora*). Cf. Lesk. Nom. 194. On myths etc. see Geitler LS. 90, Bezz. LF. 63 f.

kaukiù, kaũkti 'heulen (von Hunden und Wölfen); wehklagen (von Menschen)' — Uh. *kókas;* Ber. *kukają, kyčą;* W. *caurio, cucubio;* Boi. καύαξ. Cf. Lesk. Abl. 301.

kaũksmas 'Geheul'—B. II, 1, 252.632. Cf. Lesk. Nom. 423.

káulas 'Knochen; Stein einer Kirsche oder Pflaume'—Uh. *kulyam;* F. *us-hulōn;* B. II, 1, 363; Ber. *kovylĭ;* W. *caulis;* Boi. καυλός. Cf. Lesk. Nom. 194.

kaũlyju, kaũlyti 'unaufhörlich bitten, zu erhalten bemüht sein; zanken, streiten'. Kur. s. v.: "der Begriff von Zanken und Streiten bei Ness. scheint irrtümlich zu sein." But notice, in addition to Ness. 188[b], also Geitler LS. 65, 90.—Ber. *kulikŭ.* Cf. Brückner SlFw. 92, 204.

kaũpas 'aufgeschütteter Haufe, Anhäufung'—Uh. *kûpas;* K. *Haufen;* F. *hups, haubiþ;* B. I, 384; Ber. *kupŭ;* W. *cūpa, cumulus, cubitum;* Boi. κύπη. Cf. Lesk. Abl. 301, Lesk. Nom. 194.

kaũpinas 'gehäuft'—B. II, 1, 272. Cf. Ness. 210[b], Lesk. Nom. 400.

kaupiù, kaũpti 'häufeln'—Ber. *kupŭ.* Cf. Lesk. Abl. 301, Bezz. LF. 122.

kauptùkas 'Häufler, Zusammenscharrer' (vom Schnabel)—B. II, 1, 492. Cf. Lesk. Nom. 516-517.

kaũras (Mielcke **kaurà**) 'Teppich, Vorhang'—Ber. *kover.* Cf. Kur. s. v.; Ness. 188[b]; Brückner SlFw. 92.

káuszas 'grosser Schöpflöffel, Schöpfgefäss aus einem Stücke Holz ausgehöhlt; hölzernes Trinkgeschirr'—Uh. *kóṣas;* (F. *huzd*); Ber. *kovš;* (W. *cūlus*). Cf. Ness. 189[a], Lesk. Nom. 194.

kavóju, kavóti 'bewahren, aufbewahren; pflegen, warten; nähren, mästen'—Uh. *kavíṣ;* F. *skauns;* B. I, 573; Ber. *chovaję;* (W. *caveo*). Cf. Brückner SlFw. 92.

każamẽkas 'Gerber, Kürschner'—Ber. *koža.* Cf. Brückner SlFw. 92.

kedė́ju, kedė́ti 'zerbersten'; **żẽmė iszkedė́jo** 'die Erde ist zerborsten'—B. I, 605.691; Boi. σκεδάννῡμι. Cf. Lesk. Abl. 362.

kedenù, kedénti 'zupfen, Wolle krempeln' — Ber. *kǫdělĭ.* Cf. Lesk. Abl. 362.

kẽk 'wie viel'; **kẽk . . . tẽk** 'wie viel . . . so viel'—B. II, 1, 482. Cf. Kur. s. v.; Kur. Gram. 1041.

kekẽ 'Traube'—Ber. *čečeŕǫ; W. cicer;* Boi. κριός.

kẽkszė 'Hure'—(Ber. *kochajǫ*); (W. *cōmis*); (Boi. κάσᾱς). Cf. Geitler LS. 65; Sommer 133; Brückner SlFw. 100 (note); Prell. deutsch. Best. in den lett. Spr. 38; MLG. I, 239 f.

kekùtis 'Weidenzeisig, Hänfling'—Uh. *cákoras;* Ber. *čečetŭ.*

kẽlė 'Bachstelze' — (W. *cillo*); Boi. κίλλουρος. Cf. Lesk. Nom. 275.

kelì, fem. **kẽlios** 'wie viele; einige'—Ber. 4. *koli* (s.v. *kŭto*). Cf. Kur. Gram. 1019, 1041.

kẽlias 'Weg, Strasse'—(W. *callis*); Boi. κέλευθος, ἀκόλουθος. Cf. Lesk. Abl. 330; Lesk. Nom. 309; Sommer 228, 237, 242, 243.

keliáuju, keliáuti 'wandern, reisen' — (W. *callis*); Boi. κέλευθος. Cf. Sommer 243.

keliñtas, fem. **kelintà**; **kelintàsis**, fem. **kelintóji** 'der, die wievielte'—B. II, 2, 63. Cf. Kur. s. v.; Kur. Gram. 1032; Bezz. LF. 123.

kelỹs 'Knie; Knoten eines Halmes; Knie am Kahn (die Rippe, an welche die Boden- und Seitenplanken angenagelt werden)'—Ber. *kolěno;* W. 1. *calx, colo, poples, scelus;* Boi. κῶλον, πέλω. Cf. Lesk. Nom. 299, Sommer 260.

kelìszkas 'Gläschen'—Ber. *kalešĭ.* Cf. Brückner SlFw. 92, Bezz. LF. 123.

keliù, kélti 'heben; tragen; übertragen, (mit einem Kahn über Wasser) befördern; begehen (z. B. Mord); veranstalten; bereiten, ausrichten (z. B. Gastmahl, Hochzeit, Ernteschmaus); (ein Tor) öffnen; aufstehen machen, erwecken, (von einem Toten) auferwecken; sich heben, aufstehen; anrechnen, für etwas halten'—Uh. *kaláyati, kūṭam;* F. *hallus;* B. I, 121.572. II, 3, 122.368; Ber. *čelo,* (*kolsŭ*); W. *celsus,* (*celer*); Boi. κολωνός. Cf. Lesk. Abl. 330.

kélmas 'Baumstumpf, Stubben; ein tölpischer, ungeschickter Mensch; (Mielcke also) Bienenstock'—(Uh. *kárṇas*); Ber. *čılnŭ, kolmolŭ;* Boi. σκαλμός. Cf. Lesk. Nom. 422, Bezz. LF. 123, Bezz. BGLS. 294.

kelnas (?) 'Kahn'—Ber. *čılnŭ.*

keltis 'Geschlecht'—Ber. *čelověkŭ, čeladĭ.* See *kiltìs.*

kẽmas, kaimas 'Dorf, Gehöft'—(Uh. 1. *ketas, çīmas*); K. *Heim;* F. *haims;* B. I, 191. II, 1, 246; (W. *cīvis*); Boi. κώμη, (κοινός), (κῶμος). Cf. Lesk. Abl. 274, Lesk. Nom. 422.

kemerai plu. 'Alpkraut, Wasserdost'—Uh. *camarikas;* Ber. *čemerĭ;* Boi. κάμαρος.

kemszù, kim̃szti 'stopfen'; **kim̃sztas** pret. pass. part. 'gestopft'—B. I, 415. II, 1, 413; Ber. *čęstŭ, komŭ* 1; W. *cumera;* Boi. κημός, (Ntr.) κῶμυς. Cf. Lesk. Abl. 331.

kenczù, kę̃sti (kentė́ti) 'leiden, dulden, ertragen, gern haben; (with *nè*) hassen'; **pakenczù, pakę̃sti** 'erleiden, sich gedulden'; **pakeñtęs** perf. act. part. 'erlitten habend'—(Uh. *bā́dhate*); B. I, 405.589.724. II, 1, 543. 567. 3, 444.492; (Ber. *kǫtajǫ*); Boi. πένθος. Cf. Lesk. Abl. 331.

kéngė 'Wandhaken; Klinke, Krampe an der Tür; (Mielcke) Überwurf an der Tür'—B. I, 694. Cf. Ness. 193[b]; Kur. s. v.; Lesk. Nom. 265.

kenkiù (usually 3rd pers. sing. **keñkia**), **keñkti** 'weh tun, schaden, fehlen'—Uh. *kā́ṅkṣati;* F. *hūhrus;* B. I, 576. 581. II, 1, 385; (W. *cunctor*); Boi. κάγκανος, (κακός). Cf. Lesk. Abl. 363.

kenklẽ 'Kniekehle'; Ness. 193[b]: "vielleicht auch die Wade (Memel)"—Ber. *kolěno;* W. 1. *calx,* [*colo, poples, scelus*]; Boi. κῶλον.

kentìmas 'das Leiden, Dulden'—B. I, 724. See *kenczù* & Lesk. Nom. 429-430.

kepù, kèpti trans. & intr. 'backen, braten; stark frieren'—Uh. *pácati;* B. I, 873.875 (& Ntr. 1096). II, 3, 121;

W. *coquo;* Boi. ἄρτος (& note), πέπων, (καπυρός). Cf. Lesk. Abl. 368.

kepùrė 'Hut; der Hut auf dem Butterfasse (cf. Ness. 195^a)' —Ber. *čepĭcĭ;* Boi. σκέπας. Cf. Geitler LS. 65; Lesk. Nom. 450; Sommer 201-202, 207.

kepurẽlė 'Hütchen'—B. II, 1, 370.672. Cf. Ness. 195^a.

kepurė̃tas 'mit Hut versehen'—B. II, 1, 406. Cf. Lesk. Nom. 562.

keras 'Zauber'—B. II, 1, 524; Boi. τέρας. Cf. Lesk. Nom. 162.

kẽras 'hoher, alter, verwitterter Baumstumpf; Staude'—Ber. *korenĭ,* (*černŭ* 2); (W. *cornus*); (Boi. 2. κράνος). Cf. Geitler LS. 65, Lesk. Nom. 162.

ker̃dżus, sker̃dżus 'Hirt' (Ness. 195^a 'ein gemieteter Viehhirt, Lohnhirt') — Uh. *çárdhas;* K. *Herde, Hirt;* F. *hairda;* B. I, 546; Ber. *čerda;* W. *creo;* Boi. κόρθυς. Cf. Lesk. Nom. 325.

kerė̃ju, kerė̃ti 'in Stauden wachsen; Wurzeln fassen'; **įsikerė̃ti** 'sich ausbreiten, vermehren, einnisten'—B. II, 3, 217; Ber. *korenĭ.* Cf. Kur. s. v. & Geitler LS. 86, 90.

-ker̃gti—see *priker̃gti* 'anbinden'.

keriù, kerė̃ti 'jemand durch bösen Blick oder durch Worte bezaubern, verrufen, in der Gesundheit schädigen'—Uh. (Ntr.) *kr̥ṇóti;* B. I, 468; Ber. *čara* 3, (*čĭrtŭ*); W. *caragus;* Boi. τέρας. Cf. Lesk. Abl. 331.

kermõszus Samog. 'Jahrmarkt, Kirmes'—Ber. *kermuš.* Cf. Brückner SlFw. 92.

kermùszė 'wilder Knoblauch'—Uh. *kramukas;* K. *Rams;* B. I, 583; Ber. *čermŭša;* Boi. κρόμ(μ)υον.

kernóju, kernóti 'verleumden' — see *iszkernóju* & Geitler LD. 48.

kerpù, kir̃pti 'mit der Schere schneiden, scheren' — Uh. *kr̥pāṇas;* K. *Herbst;* B. I, 570; Ber. *čerpŭ, čĭrpǫ,* (*kŭrpa*); W. *carpo;* Boi. 1. καρπός. Cf. Lesk. Abl. 331-332.

kérszas 'schwarz und weiss gefleckt' (z. B. von Rindern,

Gänsen)—Uh. *kṛṣṇás;* B. II, 1, 255; Ber. *čĭrnŭ;* (Boi. *πρῖνος*). Cf. Lesk. Nom. 161, Bezz. LF. 123.

kérszė 'bunte Kuh'—Uh. *kṛṣṇás;* Ber. *čĭrnŭ.*

kerszìngas 'zornvoll, rachsüchtig'—W. *carbo.* Cf. Lesk. Abl. 332.

kérszis 'schwarzbunter Ochs'—Ber. *čĭrnŭ.* Cf. Lesk. Nom. 302.

kePsztas 'Zorn, Grimm, Rachedurst'—W. *carbo.* Cf. Lesk. Abl. 332.

kerszùlis 'Holztaube, Ringeltaube'—Ber. *čĭrnŭ.* Cf. Lesk. Nom. 491.

kerszùs 'zornvoll, rachsüchtig'—Ber. *krasa;* W. *carbo.* Cf. Ness. 195[b], Lesk. Abl. 332.

kertesis 'Hieb'—B. II, 1, 265.525; Ber. *lemešĭ.* Cf. Geitler LS. 90, Lesk. Nom. 593.

kertù, kiPsti 'scharf hauen, heftig schlagen' (z. B. mit dem Schwert, der Axt, Sense, Peitsche, Hand) — Uh. *kṛntáti;* (F. *hardus*); B. I, 120.448.472.541.571.582. II, 1, 373.431.567. 2, 66. 3, 119.287.431.445.492 (twice); Ber. *čĭrtǫ, kortŭ;* W. *caro, cēna,* (*certo*); Boi. *κείρω* (note). Cf. Lesk. Abl. 332.

kertùkas 'Spitzmaus' — Ber. *čĭrtǫ.* Cf. Geitler LS. 65, Brückner SlFw. 92.

kertùs id.—Ber. *čĭrtǫ,* (*krŭtŭ*). Cf. Geitler LS. 65; Brückner SlFw. 92; Lesk. Nom. 240 (read Brückner S. 92 for . . . 95).

kẽtas 'hart, fest; kernig, kerngesund; hartnäckig' — Ber. *čitŭ.* Cf. Lesk. Nom. 185.

kẽtėju, kẽtėti 'allmählich hart werden, sich verhärten'—B. II, 3, 217.

kẽturesdeszimt, kẽturesdeszimts 'vierzig'—B. II, 1, 95. 2, 22.37.38. Cf. Schleicher LSpr. I, 62; Kur. Gram. 1001, 1013; Wied. 156.

kẽturesdeszimtas 'vierzigster'—B. II, 2, 61. Cf. Schleicher LSpr. I, 63; Kur. Gram. 1001, 1026; Wied. 157.

kẽturesdeszimts 'vierzig'—see *kẽturesdeszimt.*

keturì, fem. **kẽturios** 'vier'—Uh. *catvā́ras;* F. **fidūr-, fidwōr;* B. I, 124.424.492.587. II, 2, 14; Ber. *četyre;* W. *quattuor;* Boi. τέσσαρες. Cf. Kur. Gram. 1007, Wied. 156.

keturiãdeszimtas 'vierzigster'—B. II, 2, 61. Cf. Schleicher LSpr. I, 63.

keturiólika 'vierzehn'—see *keturì* & K. *elf;* [F. *ain-lif*]; B. II, 2, 26.27; [Ber. *-lěkŭ*]; [W. *linquo*]. Cf. Wied. 156.

keturkójis 'Vierfuss'—B. II, 2, 15.

ketùrlinkas 'vierfach'—B. II, 2, 71. Cf. Wied. 160.

ketvérgis 'vierjährig' (von Tieren, nicht von Menschen)—B. II, 1, 513; Ber. *četyre.*

ketverì, fem. **kẽtverios** 'vier' — Uh. *catvarám, catvā́ras;* F. *fidwōr;* B. I, 295. II, 1, 163. 2, 77; Ber. *četyre;* W. *quattuor;* Boi. ὀτρύνω, τέσσαρες. Cf. Kur. Gram. 1033, Wied. 158.

ketvirtainis 'Viertel'—B. II, 2, 73. Cf. Lesk. Nom. 416.

ketvir̃tas 'vierter'—Uh. *caturthás;* B. I, 260.261.339.455. 472.492. II, 1, 391. 2, 15.54 (twice); Ber. *četyre;* W. *quartus* (s.v. *quattuor*); Boi. τέσσαρες. Cf. Wied. 157. 4.

kė̃żu (apparently found only in cmpd. part.'s)—see *apkė̃żęs* 'im Wachstum zurückgeblieben'.

-ki, -k 2nd pers. sing. impera. end.—Ber. *-ka.* Cf. Wied. 176. 3.

kiaũlė 'Schwein'; (Ness. 188* also) eine Pilzenart—Boi. σῦς, (πτελᾶς). Cf. Lesk. Nom. 279.

kiáunė 'Marder'—Ber. *kuna* 1. Cf. Lesk. Nom. 279, Sommer 166.

kiáuras 'durchlöchert, leck, entzwei; (Mielcke also) wüst (von Feldern)'—B. I, 210.275; (Ber. *červĭjĭ, kŭrnŭ*); Boi. σκῦρος, (σωλήν). Cf. Lesk. Abl. 301, Lesk. Nom. 195.

kiáurmedis 'Holunderbaum'—(Ber. *červĭjĭ*). See prec. & *mẽdis.*

kiáuszė, kiáuszia 'Schädel' — Uh. *kóṣas;* (F. *gud-hūs,* *huzd*); (Ber. *čaša*); (W. *cūlus*). Cf. Lesk. Nom. 279, Sommer 139.

kiaũszis 'Ei'. (Ness. 189[a] also) 'Eierschale; Hirnschale'—Uh. *kóṣas;* (W. *cūlus*). Cf. Lesk. Nom. 279.

kiaũtas 'Hülse, Schale'; plu. **kiautaĩ** 'Hülsen (bes. Spreu)' —Uh. *skunắti;* F. *skauda-raips;* Ber. *kǫtajǫ;* W. *cutis;* Boi. κύτος. Cf. Lesk. Nom. 535.

kibìras 'Eimer'—Ber. *čĭbŭrŭ;* Boi. κόφινος. Cf. Lesk. Abl. 330.

kikìlis 'Fink, Hänfling'—Ber. *čečetŭ*. Cf. Lesk. Nom. 483.

kiknóju, kiknóti 'kichern'—Ber. *chochotǫ;* Boi. καχάζω.

kilbasas 'Bratwurst'—Ber. *kolbasa*. Cf. Brückner SlFw. 93.

kýlė 'Bachstelze'—(W. *cillo*); Boi. κίλλουρος.

kilepas (Szyr.) 'ein ungarischer Streitkolben'—Ber. *kelep* (read lit. *kilepas* for lit. *kelepas*). Cf. Ness. 199[b]; Kur. s. v.; Brückner SlFw. 93.

kylìkas, kylỹkas 'Kelch, Abendmahlskelch' — Ber. *kaležĭ*. Cf. Bezz. BGLS. 77, Brückner SlFw. 93.

kìlnas (B. **kílnas**) 'hoch, erhaben, stattlich'—B. II, 1, 258. Cf. Lesk. Abl. 330, Lesk. Nom. 355.

kilnóju, kilnóti 'hin und her heben'—B. II, 3, 215.312. Cf. Lesk. Abl. 330.

kilnùs 'hoch, erhaben, stattlich'—B. II, 1, 291. Cf. Lesk. Abl. 330, Lesk. Nom. 355.

kìlpa 'Steigbügel; Schlinge (bes. zum Vogelfang)' — K. *Halfter* 1; (Ber. *čalŭ*); (W. *calpar*). Cf. Lesk. Abl. 331.

kìlstu, kìlti 'sich erheben'—see *kylù*.

kiltìs 'Geschlecht, Abstammung' — B. I, 460.605; Ber. *člověkŭ, čeladĭ;* Boi. 2. τέλος. Cf. Geitler LS. 91, Lesk. Abl. 330, Lesk. Nom. 548.

kylù or **kįlù, kìlti** (B. **kílti**); **kìlstu, kìlti** (B. **kílstu, kílti**) 'sich erheben, aufsteigen'—B. I, 389. II, 3, 137.312. 370. See *kelìù* & Lesk. Abl. 330, 386.

kilũju, kilũti 'heben'—B. I, 473. Cf. Lesk. Abl. 330.

kimbù, kìbti 'hangen bleiben, sich einhaken'; **prikimbù,**

prikìbti 'sich einhaken, anhaften'; **sukimbù, sukìbti** 'sich anhängen, zusammenhangen' — (Ber. *čĭbanŭ*); (W. *scamnum*); Boi. κόμβος, κόφινος. Cf. Lesk. Abl. 330.

kimenai, kiminai plu. 'Moos zum Verstopfen der Fugen in den hölzernen Gebäuden'—Ber. *čĭmanŭ*. Cf. Ness. 200[a].

kìminė 'Torfmoos, Sphagnum squarrosum'—Ber. *čĭmanŭ*. Cf. Bezz. LF. 124.

kiminu, kiminti '(die Stimme) heiser, dumpf machen'—Ber. *čĭmelĭ*. Cf. Lesk. Abl. 331.

kimonaĩ plu. 'eine Pflanze, die an Brüchen wächst; (Samog.) weisses Moos'—Ber. *čĭmanŭ*.

kìmstu, kìmti 'heiser werden' — Ber. *čĭmelĭ*. Cf. Lesk. Abl. 331.

kim̃sztas pret. pass. part. of **kemszù**, q. v., 'gestopft'—B. I, 415. II, 1, 413; Ber. *čęstŭ*.

kimsztis 'Stöpsel, Ofenstöpsel'—B. I, 415. Cf. Ness. 193[a], Lesk. Abl. 331.

***kindù, *kìsti**—assumed by Kur. for *sukìdęs* 'zerlumpt', q.v.

kinis 'eingewühltes Schweinelager'—B. I, 716. Cf. Ness. 200[b], Lesk. Nom. 269.

kinkaũ, kinkýti 'anspannen, das Geschirr anlegen' (von Pferden)—Uh. *kañcukas; K. Hengst; W. cingo;* Boi. κάκαλα. Cf. Lesk. Abl. 331.

kirba 'Morast, Sumpf, Untiefe'—Uh. (Ntr.) *karbarás*. Cf. Geitler LS. 91, Geitler LD. 49.

kirė̃ti 'böse werden'; **apkirė̃ti** 'überdrüssig werden'—Ber. *čĭrtŭ*. Cf. Lesk. Abl. 331.

-kyrė̃ti—see *įkyrė̃ti* 'zum Ekel werden'.

kirkiù, kir̃kti 'schreien, kreischen' (bes. von der Bruthenne); 'quarren' (von Kindern)—Ber. *kŭrkajǫ; W. querquēdula;* Boi. κέρκαξ.

kirklỹs 'Kreischer' (Kur. s. v. 'wer immer kreischt, wie eine Bruthenne im Nest'; Ness. 200[b] 'Grille, Heimchen') —B. II, 1, 617. See prec. & Lesk. Nom. 456.

kirmėlė̃ 'Wurm, Made, Raupe'—(K. *Wurm*); B. I, 377.

465.605. II, 1, 370. See *kirmis* & Lesk. Abl. 331, Lesk. Nom. 482.

kirmyjù, kirmýti 'träge schlafen' (Ness. 201[a], Kur., Uh. as same word also 'wurmstichig sein')—(Uh. *çrâmyati*); B. I, 546.

kiřminas 'Wurm; Schlange'—B. II, 1, 272. Cf. Lesk. Abl. 331, Lesk. Nom. 404.

kirmis 'Wurm'—Uh. *kṝmiṣ;* (F. *waurms*); B. I, 377.908. II, 1, 173.253; Ber. *čĭrmĭ;* (W. *curvus, vermis*); (Boi. ἕλμις, κορωνός). Cf. Lesk. Abl. 331, Lesk. Nom. 424, and s. v. *kirmėlė̃.*

kirm̃varpa 'Wurmstich, Wurmfrass' (bes. im Holz)—Ber. *čĭrvĭ.* Cf. Lesk. Abl. 356.

kìrna (B. **kírna**) fem.; **kirnas** (Mielcke & Ness.) masc. 'Strauchband aus Weide, das bei dem Aufsetzen und Abmessen des Klobenholzes um die seitlichen Haltestangen geschlungen und mit den Kloben beschwert wird, um die Stangen aufrecht zu halten'—B. II, 1, 263; (Ber. *černŭ* 2); (W. *cornus*); (Boi. 2. κράνος). Cf. Kur. 185[a]; Ness. 201[a]; Lesk. Nom. 364.

***kìrnas** (Ber. & Boi.) 'Kirschbaum'—see references under *Kirnis.*

Kirnis Name eines Gottes; **kirnis** (W.) 'cerasus'—(Ber. *černŭ* 2); W. *cornus;* Boi. 2. κράνος.

kirnis 'Sumpf, Morast'—(Boi. 2. κράνος). Cf. Geitler LS. 91; Lesk. Nom. 364, 371.

kirnos plu. 'eine morastige, mit Bäumen bewachsene Gegend'—(Boi. 2. κράνος). Cf. Geitler LS. 91, Lesk. Nom. 364.

Kirsna Eigenname eines Flüsschens—Ber. *čĭrnŭ.* Cf. Kur. s. v.; Ness. 201[a].

kiřstas pret. pass. part. of **kertù**, q. v., 'gehauen'—B. I, 624. II, 1, 396.

kiřsteriu (kiřsteliu), kiřsterėti (kiřstelėti) 'einen kleinen Hieb tun'—B. I, 449.852. Cf. Lesk. Abl. 332, 449.

***kirstu, kìrsti**—assumed by Lesk. Abl. 382 for *pakìrsti* 'aus dem Schlafe auffahren', q. v.

kirszlỹs 'Äsche' (Fisch)—Uh. *kṛsṇás;* (K. *Asche* 2); Ber. *čĭrnŭ;* (Boi. πρῖνος).

-kìrti—see *įkìrti* 'sich ekeln'.

kir̃tis 'Hieb, Streich; Hiebwunde'—Ber. *čĭrtǫ*. See *kertù* & Lesk. Abl. 332.

kìrvarpa 'Wurm; Wurmstich (bes. im Holz)'—Ber. *čĭrvĭ*. Cf. Lesk. Nom. 212, Lesk. Abl. 356.

kir̃vis 'Axt'—Uh. *kŕviṣ, cárvati;* Ber. *čĭrvŭ;* W. *caro, curis, scrautum;* Boi. κείρω. Cf. Lesk. Nom. 348.

kiszù, kìszti 'stecken, einstecken, stopfen'—Ber. *čcšǫ*. Cf. Lesk. Abl. 274.

kyta 'Quantität von 20 Handvoll Flachs' (Kur.). Ness. 202^{b} '10 Pfund Flachs'—Ber. *kyta*. Cf. Brückner SlFw. 93.

kìts kìtą 'einander'—B. II, 1, 95. Cf. Kur. Gram. 1398, 1399.

kìtur, kitur̃ 'anderswo'—F. *aljar;* B. II, 2, 735.

kiùrstu, kiùrti (B. **kiúrstu, kiúrti**) 'löcherig werden'—B. I, 274. Cf. Lesk. Abl. 301.

klabù, klabė́ti 'klappern (bes. von den Zähnen), pochen, poltern'—Ber. *klabosŭ, klapajǫ*. Cf. Lesk. Abl. 332.

klagù, klagė́ti 'gackern, glucksen'—F. *hlahjan;* B. II, 3, 291; Ber. *klekŭtǫ;* W. *clango;* Boi. *κλάγξ.

klaidaũ, klaidýti 'irreführen'—Ber. *klěvajǫ*. Cf. Lesk. Abl. 275.

klaidinù, klaidìnti id.—Ber. *klěvajǫ*. Cf. Lesk. Abl. 275.

klaimas 'Scheune, Speicher'; East Lith. **kłaĩmas** 'Scheunentenne' (?)—Ber. *klětĭ*. Cf. Geitler LS. 91, Lesk. Nom. 422.

klajùs 'irreführend' (vom Wege)—Ber. *klětĭ, klěvajǫ*. Cf. Lesk. Abl. 275.

klampà 'Sumpf, Morast, in dem man sinkt'—B. I, 415; Ber. *klęsnǫ*. Cf. Lesk. Abl. 332.

klampỹnė id.—Ber. *klęsnǫ*. Cf. Lesk. Abl. 332.

klampóju, klampóti 'fortwährend einsinkend über einen

Sumpf gehen oder reiten' — Ber. *klęsną*. Cf. Lesk. Abl. 332.

-kláuju, -kláuti—see *pasikláuju* 'ich vertraue auf'.

klaupiũs, klaũptis 'niederknien' — B. I, 202; Ber. *kląpŭ, klusę*. Cf. Lesk. Abl. 299.

klaupka 'Kirchenbank'—B. II, 1, 477. Cf. Lesk. Nom. 505.

klausà 'Gehorsam'—K. *lauschen;* B. I, 785. Cf. Lesk. Abl. 299.

klausaũ, klausýti 'hören, anhören; gehorchen; angehören' —Uh. *çróşati;* K. *lauschen;* F. *hliuma;* B. I, 546.564; W. *clueo;* Boi. κλέος. Cf. Lesk. Abl. 300.

kláusiu, kláusti 'fragen'—F. *hliuma;* B. I, 686. II, 3, 386. See prec. & Lesk. Abl. 299.

klebetoju, klebetoti 'Stricke schlagen'—Ber. *klabosŭ*.

klebõnas 'Pfarrer, Priester'. Ness. 217[b]: "auch das Wasserhuhn, das schwarze Schilfhuhn, ein schwarzer Vogel mit einem weissen Fleck auf dem Kopf, den der Volkswitz wohl mit der Tonsur verglichen haben mag, (am Haff)."—B. I, 853. Cf. Brückner SlFw. 94.

klebù, klebė́ti 'wackeln, klappern' (bes. von den Zähnen)— Ber. *klabosŭ, klapają*. Cf. Lesk. Abl. 332.

klegù, klegė́ti 'laut lachen' — (K. *lachen*); (F. *hlahjan*); Ber. *klekŭtą;* W. *clango;* Boi. *κλάγξ.

kleisziũju, kleisziũti 'mit einwärts gebogenen Füssen eilig laufen'—Ber. *klěsną*. Cf. Lesk. Abl. 275.

klejaĩ plu. 'Leim'—Boi. κόλλα. Cf. Brückner SlFw. 94.

klemszóju, klemszóti 'ungeschickt, plump, bäurisch gehen' —Ber. *klęsną*.

klenkù, klèkti 'zu Stücken zusammenbacken (von Blut usw.), gerinnen'—Ber. *kleka, krěkŭ*. Cf. Lesk. Abl. 368.

klẽpas 'ein Brot (bes. von länglicher Form), Wecken'— K. *Laib;* F. *hlaifs;* Ber. *chlěbŭ;* W. *lībum;* Boi. κλίβανος. Cf. Brückner SlFw. 94.

klė̃tis 'ein kleines Vorratsgebäude auf dem Hofe, welches zugleich das Schlafgemach für die Mädchen (zuweilen auch ein Fremdenzimmer) enthält'—(F. *hlain, hleiþra*); Ber. *klětĭ*. Cf. Brückner SlFw. 94, Lesk. Nom. 235.

klėtkà 'Vogelbauer; Marktbude, Kramladen; Kaufmannsschild; Honigwabe; Streif eines Frauenrocks' — Ber. *klětĭ*. Cf. Brückner SlFw. 94.

klẽvas 'Ahorn'—K. *Lehne* 4; Ber. *klenŭ*.

kliaudà 'körperlicher Fehler, Gebrechen'; **kliáudą padarýti** 'Possen treiben, indem man sich z. B. lahm stellt'—Ber. *kludŭ;* W. *claudus*. Cf. Lesk. Abl. 299.

kliaudau, kliaudyti 'aufhalten, hindern'—Ber. *kluka;* W. *claudus*. Cf. Lesk. Abl. 299.

kliaudžu, kliausti id.—Ber. *klěvają;* W. *claudo, claudus;* Boi. *κλείς*. Cf. Ness. 221[b], Lesk. Abl. 299.

kliautė "alles, woran etwas hangen bleibt, oder wodurch es aufgehalten wird, ein Hindernis, daher ein Pfahl im Wasser, an dem Schiffe sich stossen; auch der Baum, der an den Zollstätten die Flüsse sperrt" (Ness. 221[b]); "ein Fehler, Gebrechen, woran man haken bleibt" (Kur.)—Ber. *kluka*. Cf. Lesk. Abl. 299.

klibù, klibė́ti 'wackeln, wacklig sein (z. B. von einem Zahn, von der Klinge eines Messers), klappern (bes. von den Zähnen)'—B. I, 473. Cf. Lesk. Abl. 332.

-klìgu pret.—see *suklìgu* 'schrie auf'.

klýkauju, klýkauti 'unbändig schreien, kreischen, quietschen'—Ber. *kliknę*. Cf. Lesk. Abl. 291.

klykiù, klỹkti 'schreien, kreischen, jauchzen'—Ber. *kliknę*. Cf. Lesk. Abl. 291.

klimpstù, klim̃pti 'einsinken' (in Schlamm usw.)—B. I, 415; Ber. *klęsnę*. Cf. Lesk. Abl. 332.

klýnas 'Keil, Windlasche, Zipfel; Hodenbruch, Netzbruch, Darmwinde, Darmgicht' — B. II, 1, 263; Ber. *klinŭ*. Cf. Brückner SlFw. 94, Lesk. Nom. 361.

klýnė 'keilförmiger Einsatz in den Hemdeärmeln, Lasche' —Ber. *klinŭ*. See prec.

klýnės plu. 'Kleie'—(Ber. *klińę*). Cf. Prell. deutsch. Best. in den lett. Spr. 43, Brückner SlFw. 94.

klinkù, klìkti 'plötzlich pfeifend aufkreischen'—Ber. *kliknǫ*. Cf. Lesk. Abl. 291.

kliokiù, kliõkti Schallwort, 'den Schall *kliõk* verursachen' (beim Strömen eines Bächleins oder beim Giessen)—Ber. *klukajǫ*.

klýstu, klýsti 'sich verirren, im Irrtum sein; irrereden; schwanken (von einem Baume)'—Ber. *klěvajǫ*. Cf. Lesk. Abl. 275.

klìszas 'schiefbeinig; mit schiefen, nach innen gebogenen Füssen'—Ber. *klěsnǫ*. Cf. Lesk. Abl. 275.

kliszė 'Krebsschere'—Ber. *klěsnǫ*. Cf. Lesk. Nom. 282.

kliũdaũ, kliũdýti 'anhaken machen; hindern'—F. *hlauts;* Ber. *kluka*. See *kliũvù* & Lesk. Abl. 299.

kliũnù, kliúti 'anhaken, hangen bleiben'—see *kliũvù*.

kliústu, kliúti id.—see *kliũvù*.

kliũtė 'etwas, woran man hangen bleibt; Hindernis, Sperrbaum, Sperrpfahl'—Ber. *kluka;* W. *claudo;* Boi. κλείς. See next.

kliũtis id.—Ber. *kluka;* W. *claudo;* Boi. κλείς. See *kliũvù* & Lesk. Abl. 299.

kliũvù (kliũnù, kliústu), kliúti 'anhaken, hangen bleiben'—F. *hlauts;* B. I, 572. II, 3, 137.377; Ber. *klěvajǫ, kluka, (klujǫ)*; W. *claudo, claudus;* Boi. κλείς. Cf. Lesk. Abl. 299.

klivas 'schiefbeinig'—B. II, 1, 204. Cf. Lesk. Nom. 344.

klóju, klóti 'hinbreiten, breit hinlegen, bedecken, zum Dreschen anlegen, ausdielen, betten'—Uh. *kiráti;* F. *af-hlaþan;* B. II, 3, 368.379; Ber. *kladǫ* 1, (*klětĭ*). Cf. Lesk. Abl. 376.

klónas (Lesk., Ber. **klõnas**) 'Bleichplatz hinter der Scheune; (Ness. also) die von dem Wohnhause abgelegen gebauten Wirtschaftsgebäude'—B. II, 1, 259; (Ber. *klońǫ*). Cf. Ness. 220[a]; Kur. 192[b], 194[a]; Schleicher LSpr. II, 282; Geitler LS. 92; Bezz. BGLS. 295; Brückner SlFw. 94; Lesk. Abl. 379; Lesk. Nom. 196-7, 361.

klugù, klugëti 'glucksen' — F. *hlahjan;* W. *clango;* Boi. *κλάγξ.

klukszių̀, klukszëti 'glucken; Aufstossen, Schlucken haben' —Ber. *klŭcają* 1.

klumbas 'auf einem Beine lahm, hinkend' — Boi. κλαμβός, κολοβός. Cf. Lesk. Nom. 190.

klum̃bèrės plu. 'Kartoffeln' — Ber. *krompir.* Cf. Prell. deutsch. Best. in den lett. Spr. 43, 44, 61; MLG. IV, 325.

klumpù, klùpti 'in die Knie fallen, niederknien; stolpern (bes. von Pferden)'; **użklumpù, użklùpti** 'mit einem Überfall überraschen, angreifen' — K. *laufen;* F. *us-hlaupan;* B. I, 260.572; Ber. *klǫpĭ, klusę;* W. *culcita;* Boi. 1. κάλπη, (κόλπος). Cf. Lesk. Abl. 299.

kluonas 'Tenne, Scheuer'—(Ber. *klońǫ*). Cf. Lesk. Nom. 196-7, 361 and the references under *klónas.*

klúpau, klúpoti 'in kniender Stellung verharren, knien'— F. *us-hlaupan;* B. I, 261.572; Ber. *klǫpĭ;* W. *culcita;* Boi. 1. κάλπη. Cf. Lesk. Abl. 299.

klustù, klùsti 'Gehör geben, gehorchen'; **paklustù, paklùsti** 'gehorchen'—Uh. *çróṣati;* K. *lauschen;* F. *hliuma;* B. II, 3, 338; Boi. κλέος. Cf. Lesk. Abl. 299.

kmỹnai plu. 'Kümmel'—Ber. *kuminŭ.* Cf. Brückner SlFw. 95.

knabù, knabëti 'abpellen, schälen' (bes. Kartoffeln)—(Uh. *kambalás*); B. I, 394. Cf. Lesk. Abl. 332.

knápė, plu. **knápės** 'Hanf'—Ber. *konopa.* See *kanãpė.*

knãtas 'Docht, Lunte'—Ber. *knot.* Cf. Brückner SlFw. 95.

knebenù, knebénti 'klauben, abpellen' — (Uh. *kambalás*); B. I, 394; Boi. κνῆν. Cf. Lesk. Abl. 332.

knėbių̀, knẽbti (Kur.; read ë ? Notice last sentence of paragraph in Lesk.) 'leise kneifen'—K. *kneipen.* Cf. Lesk. Abl. 332.

knëdenti (?) 'nieten'—W. *nīdor.* Cf. Zupitza Germanische Gutturale 120, Ulmann-Brasche Deutsch-lettisches Wörterbuch s. v. nieten.

kniáuka 'Miauer, Greiner, knurriger Mensch; (Ness. 222[a]) Katze'—Ber. *kńukajǫ*. Cf. Lesk. Nom. 229.

kniaukiù, kniaũkti 'miauen'—Ber. *kńukajǫ;* Boi. κνυζᾶν.

knibù, knìbti 'mit einer Fingerarbeit beschäftigt sein, klauben, zupfen; die Finger nach etwas ausstrecken'—K. *kneipen;* B. I, 393; Boi. κνῆν. Cf. Lesk. Abl. 332.

knisù, knìsti 'wühlen, graben' (von Schweinen) — Uh. *kiknasas;* F. *hnasqus;* Ber. *gnida;* W. *nīdor;* Boi. κνέωρος, κνίζω. Cf. Lesk. Abl. 275.

kniúpsau, kniúpsoti 'dauernd gebückt dasitzen' — Ber. *kńupǫ*. Cf. Lesk. Abl. 316.

knubu, (inf. **knubti** or **knubėti?**) (?) 'gebückt sein' — F. *dis-hniupan.* Cf. Ness. 223[a]; Kur. s. v.; Lesk. Abl. 316.

knúpoju, knúpoti 'auf dem Angesicht liegen; knien'—Ber. *kńupǫ*.

knúpszczas 'auf dem Angesicht liegend'—Ber. *kńupǫ*. Cf. Lesk. Abl. 316.

kóbotas 'Frauenjacke, Kamisol'—Ber. *kabat.* Cf. Brückner SlFw. 95.

kõcza, kũcza; usually plu. **kõczos, kũczos** 'der heilige Abend vor dem Christfest' — Ber. *kutīja.* Cf. *kũcos* & Kur. 195-196, 207; MLG. III, 505 f.

koczóju, koczóti 'Wäsche rollen, mangeln, glätten' — Ber. *kotǫ.* Cf. Ness. 203[b], Brückner SlFw. 95.

kõdas 'Schopf der Vögel; Flachswickel'—see *kũdas.*

kodẽl 'weshalb, warum?'—B. II, 2, 726.

kodỹlas 'Weihrauch'—Ber. *kaďǫ.* Cf. Brückner SlFw. 95.

kõdis 'Wasserkrug; Braubottich; ein hölzernes Gefäss als Mass'—Ber. *kadĭ.* Cf. Brückner SlFw. 95.

kõks 'qualis'—B. II, 1, 498; Ber. 1. *kakŭ* (s. v. *kũto*).

kõliai, kõl 'wie lange, so lange als, bis'—Ber. 4. *koli* (s. v. *kũto*); W. *quālis.*

-kõlti—see *atsikõlti* 'sich anlehnen'.

kópiu (kópu), kópti 'steigen, klettern'—(Boi. κάμπτῃ). Cf. Lesk. Abl. 376.

kopūstas 'Kohlkopf, bes. Weisskohl'—Ber. *kapusta;* (W. *caput*). Cf. Brückner SlFw. 90.
korà 'Strafe'—Ber. *kara.* Cf. Brückner SlFw. 96.
koralus 'Koralle'—Ber. *korala.* Cf. Ness. 205[b], Brückner SlFw. 96.
koravóju, koravóti 'strafen' — Ber. *kara.* Cf. Brückner SlFw. 96.
korczus 'polnischer Scheffel' (zwei preussische Scheffel)—Ber. *koríčí.* Cf. Brückner SlFw. 96.
korỹs 'Wabe, Wabenhonig'—W. *cēra;* Boi. κηρός. Cf. Lesk. Abl. 373.
koróju, koróti 'strafen'—Ber. *kara.* Cf. Brückner SlFw. 96.
korõnė 'Bestrafung'—Ber. *kara* (read *korõnė* for *karõnė*). Cf. Brückner SlFw. 96.
koserẽ 'Luftröhre'—Ber. *kašlí.* Cf. Lesk. Nom. 444.
kósiu, kósėti 'husten'—Uh. *kåsate;* K. *Husten;* B. I, 167. 608. II, 3, 121; Ber. *kašlí.* Cf. Lesk. Abl. 376.
kosulỹs 'Husten'—Uh. *kåsate;* Ber. *kašlí.* Cf. Lesk. Nom. 486.
kószė 'dünner Brei; (Ness.) Grütze'—Ber. *kaša.* Cf. Ness. 205[b]; Schleicher LSpr. II, 282; Brückner SlFw. 96.
kósziu, kószti 'seihen'—Ber. *kaša;* (W. *cōlo*); (Boi. κόσκινον). Cf. Lesk. Abl. 376.
kosztùvas 'Durchschlag, Seihe'—B. I, 296. II, 1, 449. Cf. Lesk. Abl. 565.
kótas 'Büttel, Henkersknecht; (Ness. 206[a] also) Peiniger, Plagegeist'—Ber. *kat* 1. Cf. Brückner SlFw. 96.
kotavóju, kotavóti 'bütteln, ausprügeln; peinigen' — Ber. *kat* 1. Cf. Brückner SlFw. 96.
kovà 'Kampf, Streit, Schlacht'—K. *hauen;* F. *hawi;* B. I, 338; Ber. *kovọ;* W. 1. *cūdo.* Cf. Lesk. Abl. 301.
kóva, kovà 'Saatkrähe'—Ber. *kavŭka.* Cf. Bezz. LF. 127, Lesk. Nom. 343.
kóvas 'Dohle'—Ber. *kavŭka;* W. *caurio.* Cf. Ness. 206[a], Lesk. Nom. 343.
krãgas "eine meist hölzerne Kanne mit einer Giessröhre,

aus der Bier oder Wasser in die Gläser gefüllt wird, ein Krug" (Ness. 223[a]) — (Boi. κρωσσός). Cf. Prell. deutsch. Best. in den lett. Spr. 4; Wied. s. v.

kraipaũ, kraipýti 'fortgesetzt drehen, wenden; umwenden, umkehren' — B. I, 720; Ber. *krěsŭ, (krěpŭ)*; (Boi. κραιπάλη, κραιπνός). Cf. Lesk. Abl. 276.

kraĩtis 'Brautschatz, Mitgift der Braut in Sachen' (von den Verwandten des Bräutigams vor der Hochzeit in dessen Wohnung abgeführt)—Ber. *krĭnǫ*.

kraivas 'schief'—see *kreĩvas*.

krakis 'Schwarzspecht'—Ber. *krek-, krokajǫ*.

krakiu, krakti 'brausen' (von der See)—Ber. *krokajǫ*.

krãlius 'König'—Ber. *korlĭ*. Cf. Brückner SlFw. 90.

kramai plu. 'Grind'—Ber. *kroma*. Cf. Geitler LS. 92, Lesk. Nom. 175.

kramslẽ 'Knorpel'—see *kremslẽ*.

krankiù, krañkti 'röcheln, krächzen, schnarchen, (bes. von dem Raben) schreien'—Uh. *kṛkavâkuṣ;* B. II, 3, 194; Ber. *kręką;* W. *cornix;* Boi. κραυγή.

krankszczù, krañkszti 'krächzen, sich räuspern, gurgeln, (bes. von Pferden) schnarchen'—B. II, 3, 371; Ber. *kręką*.

krañtas 'steiles, hohes Ufer (eines Flusses, nicht des Haffes oder der See, Ness. 223[b])'—(Ber. *krǫtŭ*). Cf. Lesk. Nom. 532.

krãpinu, krãpinti 'besprengen, bespritzen'—Ber. *kropa*. Cf. Brückner SlFw. 96.

krapmẽlei masc. plu. 'Kraftmehl, Stärke'—Ber. *krochmal*. Cf. Ness. 223[b] & notice Kur. *krãkmėlės* fem. plu.

krãsė 'Stuhl, Thron'—Ber. *krěslo, krosno*. Cf. Lesk. Nom. 271.

krasůs, krastis 'sich auf einen Stuhl setzen'—Ber. *krěslo*. Cf. Ness. 224[a]; Kur. s. v.; Lesk. Nom. 271.

krãtas 'Gitter, Rost, Gitterfenster', plu. **krãtai** 'Gitterwerk' —Ber. *krâta*. Cf. Brückner SlFw. 97.

kraũjas 'Blut'—Uh. *kravíṣ;* K. *roh;* (F. *hraiwa-dūbō*); B.

I, 341.448.570.583; Ber. *kry;* W. *cruor;* Boi. κρέας. Cf. Lesk. Abl. 300.

kráuju, kráuti 'häufen, schichten, packen, laden'—Ber. *kradę, kryję;* W. *crux,* (*cumulus*); Boi. κρύπτω, (κρωβύλος). Cf. Lesk. Abl. 300.

kraukiù, kraũkti 'krächzen' (wie eine Rabe oder Krähe)—Uh. *krúñ;* B. II, 3, 194; Ber. *krukŭ;* W. *cornix.* Cf. Lesk. Abl. 300.

kraukl̃ė 'Meerschnecke'—Uh. *krúñcati.* Cf. Lesk. Nom. 463.

kraukl̃ys 'Krähe'—Uh. *krúñ;* Ber. *krukŭ;* W. *cornix;* Boi. κόραξ, κραυγή. Cf. Lesk. Nom. 456, Lesk. Abl. 300.

kraunà 'Messerschale'—see *kriaunà.*

kraupiù, kraũpti trans. 'aufschrecken, anfahren, schelten' —see *susikraupiù.*

kráustau, kráustyti iter. 'laden, packen, aufpacken, kramen, aufräumen'—Ber. *kryję.* See *kráuju* & Lesk. Abl. 300.

kraũszus, kriaũszus 'steiler Abhang'. Kur.: "steiler Bergabhang"; Ness. 225[a]: "steiles, felsiges Ufer am Fluss, an der See."—Ber. *kruchŭ.* Cf. Lesk. Abl. 300 (twice).

kreczù, krė̃sti 'schütteln, schütten, streuen, düngen' — K. *Räder;* B. II, 3, 287 (note); (W. *cerno*). Cf. Lesk. Abl. 333.

kregżdė̃ 'Schwalbe'—Uh. *khargálā;* B. I, 569. II, 1, 467. Cf. Lesk. Nom. 587.

kreidà 'Kreide, Richtschnur'—Ber. *kréda.*

kreipiù, kreĩpti 'wenden, kehren, drehen'—B. I, 720.783; Ber. *krěsŭ,* (*krěpŭ*); W. *crispus, curvus,* (*scurra*); Boi. 2. κίρκος, κορωνός, (κραιπάλη). Cf. Lesk. Abl. 276.

kreĩvas, kraivas 'krumm, schief, gewunden' — B. I, 340. II, 1, 204.663; Ber. *krivŭ;* W. *circus, curvus, scrīnium;* Boi. 2. κίρκος, κορωνός. Cf. Ness. 224[b], 229[b]; Brückner SlFw. 97 (note); Lesk. Abl. 276; Lesk. Nom. 344.

krekenà, usually plu. **krẽkenos** 'Biestmilch'—B. II, 1, 267. Cf. Lesk. Nom. 383.

krēkinůs, krēkintis 'brünstig sein; die Brunst vollbringen' (von Schweinen)—Ber. *krek-*.
krēklas 'Brust'—B. II, 1, 363. Cf. Bezz. BGLS. 296.
kremblȳs 'Pilz' (Mielcke); 'eine essbare Pilzenart, Pfifferling' (Kur.)—Boi. *κράμβος*.
kremslē̃, kramslē̃ 'Knorpel' (Ness. 225[b] "in der Nase, im Ohr"; Kur. "unfertiger, weicher Knochen, den man nagen kann")—B. II, 1, 373; (Ber. *chręstajǫ*). Cf. Lesk. Abl. 333, Lesk. Nom. 461.
kremtù, krim̃sti (Kur., whence Ber., **krem̃sti** (?)) 'Hartes, Bröckliges fortgesetzt beissen; nagen, kauen; jemand kränken'—(Ber. *chręstajǫ*). Cf. Lesk. Abl. 333.
krënà, usually plu. **krēnos** 'Meerrettich' — K. *Kren;* Ber. *chrěnŭ;* Boi. *κεράϊς*. Cf. Brückner SlFw. 97.
krieno Old Samog. 'pretium pro sponsis' — Uh. *krīṇâti;* Ber. *krĭnǫ;* Boi. *πρίασθαι*. Cf. BB. XII, 78.
krenkù, krèkti 'gerinnen' (von Blut, Milch usw.) — Ber. *krěkŭ*. Cf. Lesk. Abl. 368.
krēsa, usually plu. **krēsos** 'Kresse'—Ber. *kres 2*.
krė́slas 'Stuhl; stattlicher Stuhl; Stuhl ohne Lehne; Fussstuhl; der Rungenstock, das Polster auf der Hinterachse des Wagens, in welchem die Rungen stecken'—Ber. *krěslo;* (W. *crēna*). Cf. Brückner SlFw. 97.
kresnas 'Feuerbrand; (Lesk.) Dürrholz, Reisig' — (Ber. *krešo*). Cf. Lesk. Nom. 361.
krēsnos plu. 'beim Kochen zerfallene Dinge'—B. II, 1, 265. Cf. Lesk. Nom. 368.
kretalas (?) 'Sieb'—K. *Räder*. Cf. Geitler LS. 92; Bezz. LF. 128; Lesk. Nom. 474.
kretù, kretė́ti 'sich hin und her bewegen, sich schütteln, wackeln'—B. II, 1, 479. 3, 287 (note). Cf. Schleicher LSpr. II, 283; Lesk. Abl. 333.
kriauklas 'Rippe'—W. *crux*. Cf. Lesk. Nom. 451, Bezz. LF. 149 (*pakraúklai* plu. 'Zwerchfell').
kriaunà, kraunà 'Heft des Messers, Messerschale, Degengriff'—Ber. *krŭňa*, (*černŭ 2*).

kriauszaũ (?), **kriauszýti** iter. 'stossen, schlagen' — Ber. *kruchŭ.* Cf. MLG. I, 85 (*pakriauszýk*) & Lesk. Abl. 300.

kriáuszė 'Birne, Birnbaum' — Ber. *gruša.* Cf. Brückner SlFw. 97 (& note); Lesk. Nom. 279-80; Sommer 137-8.

kriaũszus 'Abhang'—see *kraũszus.*

krijà (Kur.) "der ringsum innerhalb am Rande eines Siebes auf den Boden, wohl zu dessen Befestigung gelegte Bastring"; **krìjos** (Ness. 227[b]) plu. "ein grosser runder Knäuel von Bast oder Rinde, worauf man das Garn aufwindet, um es darnach zu scheren; auch die grosse Spule der Leinweber"—Ber. *iskrĭ, krajĭ, krojǫ.* Cf. Lesk. Abl. 275.

kriksiu, kriksėti 'quaken'—Boi. κριγή. Cf. Ness. 227[b], IF. XIII, 176.

krikszczonìs 'Getaufter, Christ' — Ber. *krĭstĭjanŭ.* Cf. Brückner SlFw. 97.

krykszczù, krỹkszti 'schreien, kreischen, jauchzen' — Ber. *krikŭ;* W. *crīmen;* Boi. κριγή (read *krỹkszti* for *krỹksti*).

krìksztas 'Taufe; Kreuz auf einem Grabe'; **kriksztaĩ** (cf. Ness. 227[b], Kur. 488[a]) plu. 'Fest der heiligen drei Könige am 6. Januar' — Ber. *krĭstŭ.* Cf. Brückner SlFw. 97.

krìksztyju, krìksztyti 'bekreuzen, taufen' — Ber. *krĭstŭ* (read *krìksztyti* for *krìkszyti*). Cf. Brückner SlFw. 97.

kriksztỹnos plu. 'Tauffeier, Taufschmaus'—B. II, 1, 278. Cf. Brückner SlFw. 97.

krintù, krìsti 'herabfallen (von Regentropfen, Blättern, Früchten usw.); fliessen (von Tränen); fallen, sterben (vom Vieh)' — Uh. *kr̥ntáti;* B. II, 3, 287; W. *cēna.* Cf. Lesk. Abl. 333, Bezz. LF. 129.

krypstù, krỹpti 'sich unwillkürlich drehen, wenden; wanken' — Ber. *krěsŭ;* W. *crispus;* (Boi. κραιπάλη). Cf. Lesk. Abl. 276.

krìslas 'Abfall, Brocken, Splitter, Atom'—F. *swartizl;* B. I, 717. II, 1, 373. Cf. Lesk. Abl. 333.

krislýtis 'Bröckchen'—B. II, 1, 677. Cf. Lesk. Nom. 572.

kritìs f. 'Fall'—B. II, 1, 168.633. Cf. Lesk. Abl. 333.

krýtis f. & m. 'Kescher zum Fischen, Hamen'—Ber. *iskrĭ.* Cf. Lesk. Abl. 275.

kriukiù, kriũkti (Lesk. **kriúkiu, kriúkti**) 'grunzen'—Ber. *krukŭ.* Cf. Ness. 230[b]; Kur. 204[a]; Lesk. Abl. 300.

kriuszà 'Hagel'—see *kruszà.*

kriuszù, kriùszti 'zerschmettern'—see *kruszù.*

krivdà, krividà 'Unrecht, List, Betrug'—Ber. *krivŭ.* Cf. Brückner SlFw. 97.

krìvis 'schiefgewachsener, gebückt gehender Mensch'—Ber. *krivŭ.* Cf. Lesk. Abl. 276.

krỹžius 'Kreuz'—Ber. *križĭ.* Cf. Brückner SlFw. 97.

krokiù (krogiù), krõkti 'röcheln, würgen, krächzen, schnarchen, husten, grunzen, schnaufen' — Uh. *kṛkavâkuṣ;* F. *hruks;* B. I, 151. II, 3, 194; Ber. *kračǫ;* W. *cornix;* Boi. κραυγή.

krõmas 'Kram, Kramladen'; **kromù nèszti** 'als Kram (auf dem Rücken) tragen'—K. *Kram;* Ber. *krama.*

kropà (krûpà) 'Grützkorn; Körnchen von Salz, Brot usw.'; plu. **krõpos** 'Grütze'—Ber. *krupa.* Cf. Wied. 292[b], Brückner SlFw. 97.

krópiu (?), **krópti** 'trügen, betrügen'—(W. *creper*); (Boi. κνέφας (note)). Cf. Geitler LS. 93, Lesk. Abl. 376.

krõsas 'Farbe, Färbestoff, Färbekraut'—Ber. *krasa.* Cf. Brückner SlFw. 97.

krõsyju, krõsyti 'färben, malen'—Ber. *krasa.* Cf. Brückner SlFw. 97.

krósnis "ein von Steinen oder Ziegeln gebauter Ofen in Brach- und Badestuben; bei Memel jeder Ofen" (Ness. 230[b])—Ber. *krasa, krešo;* W. *carbo.* Cf. Lesk. Nom. 370.

krùkė 'Gegrunze; Schweinerüssel'; **kiaũliũ krùkė** (Ness. 230[b] after Mielcke) "der Saugott der Heiden; jetzt ein Schimpfwort auf den Schweinehirten" — Ber. *krukŭ*. Cf. Lesk. Abl. 300, Lesk. Nom. 277.

krùkis 'Krücke' — Ber. *krúka* (read lit. *krùkis* for lit. *krùkas*). Cf. Prell. deutsch. Best. in den lett. Spr. 61.

krúmas 'Strauch, Busch'—(Ber. *grŭmŭ*). Cf. Lesk. Nom. 192.

krumenis (?) 'Kinnbacken, Backenzahn' — B. II, 1, 238. Cf. Bezz. BGLS. 296, Lesk. Nom. 418.

krūmýnas 'grosses, dichtes Gesträuch'—B. II, 1, 278.

-krùpęs—see *nukrùpęs* 'schorfig'.

kruszà, kriuszà 'Hagel; (Ness. 231[b] also) Eisscholle'— Ber. *kruchŭ;* W. *cruor, crūsta.* Cf. Lesk. Abl. 300, Geitler LS. 93.

krusztìnė 'Graupe'—Boi. κρούω. See next.

kruszù, krùszti; kriuszù, kriùszti 'stampfen, zerstossen, zerschmettern'—Ber. *kruchŭ;* (W. *cruor*); Boi. κρούω. Cf. Lesk. Abl. 300.

krūtìs 'Brustwarze, weibliche Brust'—B. II, 1, 172 (note); (Ber. *grǫdĭ*). Cf. Lesk. Nom. 238, Bezz. BGLS. 143 (note).

krutù, krutė́ti 'sich regen, sich bewegen; leben; rührig sein, arbeiten'; **apsikrutù, apsikrutė́ti** 'seine Arbeit tun'—Ber. *krŭtŭ*. Cf. Lesk. Abl. 316.

krūtulioju (krūtuliu), krūtulioti iter. 'sich ein wenig bewegen; weben; leben' — B. I, 449; Ber. *krŭtŭ*. Cf. Lesk. Abl. 316.

krutulis 'Landsturm (i.e. Bewegung, das Sich-regen)'— B. I, 449. Cf. Geitler LS. 93, Lesk. Nom. 486.

krūtuliu, krūtulioti 'sich regen'—see *krūtulioju*.

krutùs 'rührig, beweglich, arbeitsam' — Ber. *krŭtŭ*. Cf. Lesk. Abl. 316.

kruvà, krūvà 'Haufe, Menge'—B. I, 574; Ber. *kryjǫ;* W. *crux*. Cf. Lesk. Abl. 300.

krùvinas 'blutig'—B. I, 111.338. II, 3, 319.323; Ber. *kry;* W. *cruentus, cruor;* Boi. κρέας. Cf. Lesk. Abl. 300.

krùvintas pret. pass. part. of next 'blutig gemacht'—B. I, 408. II, 3, 319.323; W. *cruentus;* Boi. *κρέας*.

krùvinu, krùvinti 'blutig machen'—B. II, 3, 319.323. See *krùvinas* & Lesk. Abl. 300.

krúzas 'Trinkkrug'—Ber. *krugla*. Cf. Brückner SlFw. 98.

krûpà 'Grützkorn'—see *kropà*.

kùbilas 'Kübel, ein grosses (Kur. viereckiges) hölzernes Gefäss, das oben an der Öffnung enger ist als am Boden'—K. *Kübel;* Ber. *kŭbĭlŭ*. Cf. Prell. deutsch. Best. in den lett. Spr. 26; Wied. s. v.; Brückner SlFw. 98.

kùcius 'Knüttel, Prügel'—Ber. *kucŭ*.

kuciũju, kuciũti 'prügeln, schlagen'—Ber. *kucŭ*.

kũcos plu. "ein mit abergläubischen Gebräuchen verbundenes Abendessen in der Weihnacht, welches aus Honigwasser, auf gekochte Erbsen gegossen, bestand" (Kur., Ness. 207[a], Mielcke) — Ber. *kutĭja*. Cf. Brückner SlFw. 98.

kũcza, plu. **kũczos** 'Weihnachtsabend'—see *kõcza*.

kũdas 'mager; elend, verkommen, gering' — Ber. *chudŭ*. Cf. Brückner SlFw. 98.

kũdikis 'Kind, kleines Kind' — Ber. *chudŭ*. Cf. Lesk. Nom. 511.

kudlà 'Haarzotte'—Ber. *kǫdrĭ*. Cf. Brückner SlFw. 98.

kudlótas 'zottig, rauh' — B. II, 1, 406. Cf. Ness. 207[a], Brückner SlFw. 98.

kúgis masc. 1) Ness., Kur., Schleicher "ein grosser Heuhaufen von mehreren Fudern, den man auf der Wiese stehen lässt, um ihn im Winter nach Hause zu schaffen"; 2) Bezz., Schleicher, Kur., Wied. 'grosser Hammer, Possekel'—K. *Haufen, Hocke* 1; B. I, 331. II, 1, 507; Ber. *kyjĭ;* W. 1. *cūdo, cumulus;* Boi. *κύπη*. Cf. Ness. 207[a]; Kur. s. v.; Schleicher LSpr. II, 284; Wied. s. v.; Bezz. LF. 129; Lesk. Abl. 300; Lesk. Nom. 524; Sommer 268; Geitler LD. 50; Trautmann Die altpreussischen Sprachdenkmäler 364.

kuilà (**kūlà**), **kùilas, kuilẽ** 'Hodenbruch'—Ber. *kyla.* Cf. Brückner SlFw. 98.
kuilỹs 'Eber, zahmer Eber'—(Uh. *kolás*) ; K. *Keiler;* Ber. *kyla;* (Boi. πτίλαι). Cf. Lesk. Nom. 299; Sommer 256, 257.
kújis 'Hammer; (Szyr. also) Krücke' — Ber. *kyjĭ.* Cf. Ness. 207[a]; Kur. s. v.; Lesk. Abl. 300; Sommer 268. See *kúgis.*
kūkãlis, usually plu. **kūkãliai** 'Raden, Unkraut im Getreide, Agrostemma githago'—Ber. *kǫkolĭ.* Cf. Brückner SlFw. 98.
kùkarka 'Köchin'—Ber. *kùhina.* Cf. Brückner SlFw. 98.
kùkis 'Misthaken'—Ber. *kuka.* Cf. Lesk. Abl. 301.
kukiu, kukti (u or ū?) 'schreien, heulen'; **sukukiu, sùkukti** 'plötzlich aufschreien, aufheulen, aufbellen' — Ber. *kyčǫ.* Cf. Ness. 207[b], Lesk. Abl. 301.
kùknė 'Küche, Feuerherd' — Ber. *kùhina.* Cf. Brückner SlFw. 98.
kùkorė 'Küche'—Ber. *kùhina.* Cf. Ness. 207[b].
kùkorius 'Koch'—Ber. *kùhina.* Cf. Brückner SlFw. 98.
kukulỹs 'Mehlkloss, Brotlaib; Pechfladen'—Ber. *kuča.* Cf. Geitler LS. 66; Brückner SlFw. 98, 204 ("Kuršat" = Kur. DLWb. s. v. Kloss, q. v.).
kukū́ju, kukū́ti 'Kuckuck rufen; wie ein Kuckuck, wie eine Eule schreien'—Uh. *kokilás;* B. I, 575. II, 1, 46; Ber. *kukava;* W. *cucūlus;* Boi. κόκκυ.
kūlà 'Hodenbruch'—see *kuilà.*
kulbõkas "das krumme Holz am Joch des Pfluges oder auch eines Wagens, in welches der Hals des Ochsen oder des Pferdes gesteckt wird" (Kur.)—Ber. *kulbaka.* Cf. Brückner SlFw. 99.
kūlẽ 'Brand im Getreide' (bes. im Weizen; die Ähren werden schwarz und staubig)—F. *hauri;* Boi. καίω. Cf. Lesk. Nom. 279.
kūlė 'Kugel; Keule, Schlegel'—Ber. *kule.* Cf. Brückner SlFw. 99.

kūlḗju, kūlḗti 'brandig werden' (vom Getreide) — Uh. *kūlayati;* (W. *carbo*); Boi. καίω.

kulìkas 'Sack, Beutel, Geldbeutel'—Ber. *kul;* W. *culleus;* Boi. κολεός. Cf. Brückner SlFw. 99.

kulìs 'lederner Sack oder Schlauch; Hodensack; die letzte Abteilung (Sack) des Fischergarns' — Ber. *kul;* W. *culleus;* Boi. κολεός. Cf. Brückner SlFw. 99, Sommer 63.

kūlỹs 'Bund; Bündel; Bund Stroh, Getreide' — Ber. *kul.* Cf. Geitler LS. 66, Brückner SlFw. 99.

kuliù, kùlti (B. **kuliù, kúlti**) 'schlagen, dreschen'—(Uh. *kuṭhāras*); B. I, 474.479; Ber. *kŭlŭ* 1; W. 1. *calx, clādēs;* Boi. κλαδαρός, κολετρᾶν, (Ntr.) κελεός. Cf. Lesk. Abl. 317.

kulkà 'Kugel'—Ber. *kule.* Cf. Brückner SlFw. 99.

kulkszìs, kulksznìs 'Knöchel am menschlichen Fuss; Sprunggelenk beim Pferde'—Ber. *kŭlka;* W. 1. *calx;* Boi. κολετρᾶν.

kulnìs 'Ferse'—B. II, 1, 172.288; Ber. *kŭlka;* W. 1. *calx, caliga;* Boi. κολετρᾶν (& Ntr.).

kùlszė, kùlszis 'Hüfte'; in plu. also 'Senksteine am Netz'—Ber. *kŭlka* (twice). Cf. Brückner SlFw. 99.

kũmas, kūmà masc. 'Gevatter'; **kūmà** fem. 'Gevatterin'—Ber. *kŭmotrŭ.* Cf. Brückner SlFw. 99.

kumbras 'der krumme Griff am Steuerruder'—Uh. *kūbaras;* Boi. κυβερνᾶν. Cf. MLG. I, 17.

kumbryju, kumbryti 'steuern'—Uh. *kūbaras;* Boi. κυβερνᾶν.

kumbrỹs 'der krumme hölzerne Bügel am Joch des Pfluges, worin der Hals des Ochsen steckt; Kummetgeschirr an den einspännigen Fuhrwerken der Russen und Polen; Knie am Kahn, die Rippe, an welche die Boden- und Seitenplanken angenagelt werden; ein Mensch, der einen langen, krummen Hals hat'—Uh. *kūbaras;* Boi. κυβερνᾶν. Cf. Lesk. Nom. 437.

kùmė 'Stute'—Ber. *komonĭ.* Cf. Ness. 209[b], Lesk. Nom. 277-8.

kumẽlė 'Stute; der Steg auf der Geige'—Ber. *komoń*; W. *caballus* (read in text & index *kumẽlė*). Cf. Ness. 209[b]; Lesk. Nom. 277-8; Sommer 201.

kumelỹs 'Fohlen, bes. ein etwas herangewachsenes Hengstfohlen'—Ber. *komoń*; W. *caballus*. Cf. Kur. DLWb. s. v. Füllen; Lesk. Nom. 277; Sommer 274.

kumelýtis 'ein sehr junges Fohlen'—B. II, 1, 677. Cf. Ness. 209[b], Kur. DLWb. s. v. Füllen.

kùmetis 'Instmann; Gärtner, der zu seinem Lohn auch die Benutzung eines Gartens erhält' (cf. Ness. 209[a-b])—Ber. *kŭmetĭ*. Cf. Brückner SlFw. 99, Trautmann Die altpreussischen Sprachdenkmäler 365.

kum̃pas 'krumm'—Uh. *kámpate, kumpas*; (K. *Hüfte*); F. *hamfs, hups*; B. I, 410; Ber. *kǫp* (p. 600), *kǫpa*; W. *campus*, (*cūpa*); Boi. καμπή.

kum̃pis 'Krummstück, das eingepökelte oder geräucherte Schulterstück des Schweines'—(K. *Hüfte*); F. *hups*; Ber. *kǫp* (p. 600). Cf. Brückner SlFw. 99.

kumpsaũ, kumpsóti 'in krummer Stellung sein; gebückt dastehen, dasitzen'—B. II, 1, 541.

kumpstù, kum̃pti 'sich krümmen, krumm werden' — Uh. *kámpate*; F. *hamfs*; Ber. *kǫpa*; W. *campus*; Boi. καμπή.

kùmstė (B., W., Boi. **kúmstė**) 'Faust'—F. *handus*; B. I, 410.586.875. II, 1, 438; (W. *pugil*); Boi. πέντε (note). Cf. Sommer 98.

kunigáiksztis 'Fürst, Herzog; (Szyr. also) der Mond'—Ber. *kŭnędźĭ*. Cf. Prell. deutsch. Best. in den lett. Spr. 4, LBLV. 337.

kùnigas 'Herr; Pfarrer'—see *kùningas*.

kùnigënė 'Pfarrersfrau'—Ber. *kŭnędźĭ*.

kùningas, kùnigas 'Herr; Priester, Pfarrer'—K. *König*; Ber. *kŭnędźĭ*; W. *genius*. Cf. Prell. deutsch. Best. in den lett. Spr. 3-4, Brückner SlFw. 15.

kuntù (kustù), kùsti; atsikustù, atsikùsti 'sich aufrütteln, sich erholen' — B. II, 3, 405; W. *quatio*. Cf. Lesk. Abl. 317.

kupáuju, kupáuti 'tief atmen (mit Hebung der Brust)'— F. *hiufan.*

kùpczus 'Kaufmann, Handelsmann, Vorkäufer'—K. *kaufen;* Ber. *kupǫ.* Cf. Brückner SlFw. 99.

kupczuvênė 'Kaufmannsfrau; Handelsfrau' — B. II, 1, 278-9.

kùpeta (kupetà) 'kleiner Heu- oder Strohhaufe auf dem Felde'—F. *skuft;* Ber. *kupŭ;* W. *cūpa;* Boi. κύπη. Cf. Lesk. Abl. 301.

kupetẽlis id.—B. II, 1, 671. Cf. Lesk. Nom. 481.

kùpinas 'gehäuft' (bei Hohlmassen)—B. II, 1, 260.264. Cf. Lesk. Abl. 301.

kùpinu, kùpinti 'häufen' (bei Hohlmassen)—Ber. *kupŭ.* Cf. Ness. 211[a], Lesk. Abl. 301.

kupiu, kupti 'auf einen Haufen legen; aufräumen, ordnen' —Ber. *kupŭ.* Cf. Ness. 211[a], Lesk. Abl. 301.

kupolauju, kupolauti (?) 'Johannisfeier begehen' — Ber. *kǫpǫ.* Cf. Brückner SlFw. 99.

kupõlė, plu. **kupõlės** 'Johanniskraut'—Ber. *kǫpǫ.* Cf. Ness. 211[b], Brückner SlFw. 99.

kuprà 'Höcker, Buckel; gekrümmter Rücken'—Uh. *kubjás, kū̆pas;* K. *Haufen, Höcker;* F. *hups;* B. II, 1, 353; Ber. *kuprŭ;* W. *cūpa;* Boi. κύπη. Cf. Lesk. Abl. 301.

kùpstas 'Erdhöcker, kleiner Mooshügel auf der Wiese, Maulwurfshügel' — Uh. *kū̆pas;* K. *Hauste, Hübel, (hoch);* Ber. *kustŭ;* W. *cūpa;* Boi. κύπη. Cf. Lesk. Abl. 301.

kūpū́ju, kūpū́ti 'schwer atmen, keuchen'—Uh. *kúpyati;* F. *hiufan;* Ber. *kypǫ;* W. *vapor;* Boi. καπνός (& Ntr.). Cf. Lesk. Abl. 317, 333.

kur̃ 'wo, wohin'—Uh. *kárhi;* F. *aljar, hēr;* B. I, 938. II, 2, 350.735; Ber. 8. *kŭde* (s. v. *kŭto*); W. *cūr, quirquir.*

kurapkà 'Rebhuhn'—Ber. *kuro-pŭty.* Cf. Brückner SlFw. 100.

kur̃bas 'Korb'—Ber. *korbĭji.* Cf. Brückner SlFw. 14.

kur̃czas 'taub'; **kur̃czas żmogùs** 'tauber Mensch'; **kur̃czas**

kẽmas 'ein Dorf, in dem kein Hundegebell zu hören ist'—(Boi. καροῦσθαι).

kūrenù, kūrénti iter. 'heizen, einheizen'—Ber. *kurǫ;* W. *carbo.* See *kùrti* 'heizen' & Lesk. Abl. 317.

kuriù, kùrti (B. **kúrti**) 'bauen' (z. B. einen Kahn, ein Haus)—Uh. *kr̥nóti;* B. I, 473. II, 3, 168; Ber. *čara* 3. *kŭrĭčĭji;* W. *corpus,* (*cēra*); Boi. πραπίς, (κόσμος (note)). Cf. Lesk. Abl. 317.

kuriù, kùrti 'heizen, einheizen' — Uh. *kūlayati;* F. *hauri;* Ber. *kurǫ* (twice); W. *carbo;* Boi. κέραμος, (καίω). Cf. Lesk. Abl. 317.

kùrka 'Truthenne'—Ber. *kurŭ.* Cf. Brückner SlFw. 100.

kùrkė 'Pantoffel'—Ber. *korek.* Cf. Prell. deutsch. Best. in den lett. Spr. 9.

kur̃kinas 'Truthahn'—Ber. *kurŭ.* Cf. Brückner SlFw. 100.

kurkiù, kur̃kti 'quarren, quaken' (von Fröschen)—Ber. *kŭrkajǫ.*

kurklė 'Froschlaich'—K. *Rogen;* Ber. *krĕkŭ.* Cf. Lesk. Nom. 463.

-kurkoti—see *apkurkoti* 'mit Wassermoos überzogen werden'.

kurkulaĩ plu. 'Froschlaich'—Ber. *krĕkŭ.* Cf. Lesk. Nom. 485.

kùrmis 'Maulwurf'—Uh. *kūrmás;* (Ber. *krŭtŭ*).

kùrpė (B., W., Boi. **kúrpė**) 'Schuh; Hemmschuh; Fuss (als Mass), Zollstock'—B. I, 474.517; Ber. *kŭrpa;* W. *carpisculum;* Boi. κρηπίς. Cf. Brückner SlFw. 100; Bezz. LF. 131; Sommer 220; Trautmann Die altpreussischen Sprachdenkmäler 365.

kur̃pius 'Schuster' — [B. II, 1, 224]. See prec. & Lesk. Nom. 325.

kur̃piuvėnė 'Schustersfrau'—B. II, 1, 274.600. See prec.

kur̃s m. 'welcher, der'; **kurì** f. 'welche, die'—B. II, 2, 348. Cf. Kur. Gram. 898; Wied. 120, 127.

kùrstau, kùrstyti 'fortgesetzt Feuer machen, (Feuer, Zorn) schüren'—Ber. *kurǫ.*

kurta 'kurzer polnischer Rock'—Ber. *kurta.* Cf. Brückner SlFw. 100.

kùrtas 'Windhund, Jagdhund'—Ber. *chŭrtŭ.* Cf. Brückner SlFw. 100.

kùrva 'Buhlerin, Hure'—Ber. *kurŭva.* Cf. Brückner SlFw. 100.

kusaũ, kusýti 'reizen, verführen, zum Bösen reizen'—Ber. *kušę.*

kùsinu, kùsinti 'reizen, verführen; Feuer anschüren'—Ber. *kušę.* Cf. Brückner SlFw. 100.

kuskà 'Tuch, Taschentuch, Umhängetuch'—B. I, 719. Cf. Brückner SlFw. 100.

kustù, kùsti 'sich aufrütteln'—see *kuntù.*

kusu, kusti 'reizen, verführen'—Ber. *kušę.* Cf. Brückner SlFw. 100.

kùszinu, kùszinti 'rühren, in Bewegung setzen, anrühren' —Ber. *kŭsenĭcĭ.* Cf. Lesk. Abl. 302.

kũszỹs, kūžỹs 'pudendum muliebre, die Haare darüber'—Uh. *kukṣiṣ;* W. *cūlus;* Boi. κυσός. Cf. Kur. s. vv.; Ness. 214[a, b]; Lesk. Nom. 238, 294; Geitler LS. 93; Bezz. LF. 131.

kùszlas, kuszlùs 'schwächlich, kümmerlich, schlecht' (von Gewächsen)—B. II, 1, 362; Ber. *kŭšĭnŭ.* Cf. Lesk. Abl. 302, Lesk. Nom. 468.

kuszù, kuszė́ti 'sich regen; arbeiten'—Ber. *kŭsenĭcĭ.* Cf. Lesk. Abl. 302.

kutà 'Quaste, Troddel, Franse'—Ber. *kutas.* Cf. Geitler LS. 66, [Brückner SlFw. 100], Lesk. Abl. 317.

kūtis 'Stall'—Ber. *kǫtajǫ, kǫta;* W. *custōs, cutis;* Boi. κεύθω, κύτος. Cf. Lesk. Nom. 294, Brückner SlFw. 100, Geitler LS. 66.

kutỹs 'Beutel, Geldgürtel'—Ber. *kǫtajǫ;* W. *cunnus, cutis;* Boi. κυσός.

kutrus 'hurtig, rüstig, emsig'—B. II, 1, 385. Cf. Lesk. Abl. 317.

kutu, kutė́ti 'aufrütteln, aufmuntern; (Samog.) kitzeln'—

W. *cēveo, quatio;* Boi. πάσσω. Cf. Geitler LS. 66, Lesk. Abl. 317.

kuviûs, kuvėtis (?) 'sich schämen, sich scheuen'—K. *Hohn;* F. *hauns;* B. II, 1, 257; Ber. *kyvają;* Boi. καυνός, (κακός). Cf. Lesk. Abl. 301.

kūzãbas, kūzãvas 'Tüte von Erlenrinde zum Einsammeln der Erdbeeren; Mühlenkorb, das trichterartige hölzerne Behältnis über dem Mühlsteine zum Einschütten des Getreides; Bienenbeute, die Höhlung in einem Baum, in welcher Waldbienen nisten; Samenkolben bei Wasserpflanzen'—Ber. *kozub.* Cf. Ness. 214[b], Kur. 214, Brückner SlFw. 100.

kūžỹs 'cunnus'—see *kūszỹs.*

kũ, kůmì inst. sing. of **kàs**, q. v., 'womit?'—B. II, 2, 365; Ber. *či.* Cf. Kur. Gram. 869, 880; Wied. 120, 122.

kůczė̃s (kũ-czės) 'zu welcher Zeit, wann, irgend wann'—B. II, 2, 714. Cf. Kur. s. v., Wied. s. v.

kũdas, kõdas 'Schopf der Vögel, Zotte; Flachswickel, der um einen Stock gewickelte Flachs zum Spinnen'—F. *skauts;* Ber. *kądělı̆;* W. *cauda;* (Boi. κώδεια). Cf. Ness. 203[b]; Lesk. Abl. 362-3, 379; Lesk. Nom. 196.

kůdẽlis dimin. to prec., q. v., 'Wickel von Flachs etc.'—Ber. *kądělı̆.* Cf. Lesk. Abl. 363, 379; [Lesk. Nom. 196]; Sommer 274.

kũlas 'Pfahl, Zaunpfahl'—Uh. *kīlas;* Ber. *kolŭ;* W. *cāla;* Boi. σκῶλος. Cf. Brückner SlFw. 98.

kůmì inst. sing. of **kàs**, q. v., 'womit?'—see *kũ.*

kůpà 'Pfandgeld, Lösegeld für gepfändetes Vieh'—W. *capio;* Boi. κάπτω. Cf. Brückner SlFw. 98.

kvaĩlas 'dumm, wüst, duselig' (vor Dummheit oder Trunkenheit)—(Ber. *kvilą*).

kvaĩlinu, kvaĩlinti trans. 'verdummen, dumm machen'; intr. 'dumm umhergehen'—(Ber. *kvilą*).

kvakiù, kvakė́ti 'quaken (zunächst vom Frosch); krächzen, schnarchen, schnattern'—Ber. *kvakają.*

kvankszù, kvánkszti 'keuchen; hohl, röchelnd atmen; aufhusten, auswerfen'—Ber. *kvǫkajǫ*.

kvãpas 'Atem, Hauch, Dunst, Duft, Geruch'—Uh. *kúpyati;* F. *af-hwapjan;* B. I, 171.295.313.339. II, 1, 524; Ber. *kopŭtĭ;* W. *vapor;* Boi. καπνός. Cf. Lesk. Abl. 333.

kvarkiù, kvar̃kti 'quarren, glucken'—Ber. *kvĭrknǫ*.

kvatẽra 'Quartier, Wohnung'—B. I, 854. Cf. Brückner SlFw. 101, Prell. deutsch. Best. in den lett. Spr. 41.

kvëczaĩ (kvëczeĩ) 'Weizen'—plu. of *kvëtỹs*, q. v.

kvëczù, kvẽsti 'einladen, invitare'—Uh. *kétas;* (F. *haitan*); B. I, 313.321.339; Ber. *cěla;* W. *invĭtus;* Boi. 2. κίσσα. Cf. Lesk. Abl. 276.

kvepiù, kvepëti 'duften'—Ber. *kopŭtĭ;* W. *vapor;* Boi. καπνός. See next & Lesk. Abl. 333.

kvėpiù (Schleicher, Lesk., Wied. **kvepiù**), **kvẽpti** 'hauchen'—Uh. *kúpyati;* F. *af-hwapjan;* B. I, 171.295; Ber. *kopŭtĭ, kypǫ;* W. *vapor;* Boi. καπνός (& Ntr.). Cf. Lesk. Abl. 333.

kvëtỹs 'Weizenkorn'; plu. **kvëczaĩ (kvëczeĩ)** 'Weizen'—Uh. *çvindate;* K. *Weizen;* F. *hwaiteis;* Ber. *kvĭtǫ*. Cf. Lesk. Nom. 299.

kvëtkà 'Blüte, Blume (mit dem Strauch), Blumenstrauss'—Ber. *kvĭtǫ*. Cf. Brückner SlFw. 101.

kvykiù, kvỹkti 'quieken'—Ber. *kvičǫ*.

kvỹnai plu. 'Kümmel'—Ber. *kuminŭ*. Cf. Brückner SlFw. 101.

kvõsas 'Alaun'—Ber. *kvasŭ*. Cf. Brückner SlFw. 101.

kvõsyju, kvõsyti 'etwas mit Alaun zubereiten, beizen'—Ber. *kvasŭ*. Cf. [Brückner SlFw. 101].

L

lãbas 'gut'; **labaĩ** adv. 'recht, sehr'—Uh. *lábhate;* W. *rabiēs;* Boi. λάφυρον. Cf. Lesk. Abl. 373.

labókas 'recht gut, ziemlich gut'—B. II, 1, 500.505.658.680. Cf. Kur. Gram. 369, 788; Lesk. Nom. 515.

lagone, dimin. **lagonele,** Old Lith. 'Kuchen'—(Ber. *lagana*). Cf. Bezz. BGLS. 297.

lai dial. opt. or permissive particle = Lith. *te-* — Ber. *li;* W. *volo.* Cf. Ness. 350[b], Kur. Gram. 1160.

láibas 'zart, dünn, schmal, schlank, dürr, hager'—B. II, 1, 389; Ber. *libivŭ, (chlĕbŭ).* Cf. Lesk. Abl. 277.

laibikas, laibikis 'langes, schmales Stück Feld'—B. II, 1, 489. Cf. Ness. 351[a], Lesk. Nom. 510-11.

laidinù, laidìnti 'treiben, laufen lassen' (Pferde, Vieh usw.) —F. *lētan.* Cf. Lesk. Abl. 277.

laidokas 'zügelloser, ausgelassener Mensch'—Ber. *lâjdər.* Cf. Ness. 360[b], Brückner SlFw. 102 (note).

laidū́ju, laidū́ti 'bürgen'—B. II, 3, 220-221. Cf. [Lesk. Abl. 276].

láigau, láigyti 'wild umherlaufen, sich tummeln' (von jungen Pferden, Rindern usw.); **laigo** (Ber. after Daukša; cf. BB. XXV, 75) 3rd pers. pres. 'tanzt'—Uh. *réjati;* F. *laikan;* Ber. *lęgają;* (W. *lūdo*); Boi. 2. ἐλελίζω.

laigõnas 'Schwager, Bruder der Gattin'—B. II, 1, 332; Ber. *ligają;* W. *ligo, (lēvir)*; (Boi. δαήρ (note)).

laĩkas 'bestimmte Zeit (bes. Tageszeit), Frist; (Samog.) Zeit, Zeitverhältnisse, Sitten'—Ber. *-lěkŭ.* Cf. Lesk. Abl. 277.

laikaũ, laikýti 'halten: tenere, putare'; **palaikaũ, palaikýti** 'behalten: nicht fortgeben, nicht verlieren, nicht vergessen'—B. II, 3, 169.250.266.491; Ber. *-lěkŭ.* Cf. Lesk. Abl. 277.

laikè adv. loc. sing. 'zur Zeit'—B. II, 2, 708.

láima, láimė 'Glück; die Göttin des Glücks, Segens, Lebens' —Uh. *rātiș;* Ber. *lěti 2;* W. *latro, (laetus), (volēmum)*; Boi. λάτρον. Cf. Lesk. Nom. 186, 222, 276; Trautmann Die altpreussischen Sprachdenkmäler 367; Sommer 166.

laimiù, laimė́ti 'gewinnen' (Geld, einen Prozess, eine

Schlacht)—Uh. *rātiṣ;* B. II, 3, 192.207; Ber. *lětī 2;* W. *latro,* (*laetus*); Boi. λάτρον.

laimùs 'glücklich, selig, glückbringend, günstig, vorteilhaft, gut gedeihend'—Uh. *rātiṣ;* W. *latro,* (*laetus*); Boi. λάτρον. Cf. Lesk. Nom. 261, Geitler LS. 66.

lainas, leinas 'schlank' (bes. vom menschlichen Körper)—B. II, 1, 258; Ber. *libivŭ, lěnĭcĭ,* (*lěnŭ*); W. *lētum,* (*lēnis*); Boi. λειρός. Cf. Lesk. Abl. 277, Lesk. Nom. 355.

laipinu, laipinti 'steigen lassen'—Ber. *lěpŭ 2.* Cf. Lesk. Abl. 277.

laipta 'Stufe'—B. II, 1, 416. See *lipù* & Lesk. Nom. 542.

láistau, láistyti iter. 'wiederholt giessen'—B. II, 3, 242. See *lēju* & Lesk. Abl. 276.

laisvas 'frei, unabhängig'—B. I, 334.702.717. II, 1, 205; (W. *lūdo, līber*). Cf. Lesk. Abl. 276, Lesk. Nom. 344-5.

laisvė 'Freiheit, Unabhängigkeit'—B. II, 1, 643. Cf. Lesk. Abl. 276.

laĩszkas 'Blatt eines Baumes, eines Buches; Blatt Papier, Schein, Dokument'—(Uh. *leṣṭuṣ*); Ber. *listŭ.* Cf. Lesk. Nom. 504.

laĩvas, laiva 'Boot, Kahn, Schiff'—Ber. *lajba.* Cf. Lesk. Nom. 343, Bezz. LF. 132.

laivóju, laivóti—see *iszlaivóju* 'ich mache Biegungen', & BB. IX, 290 (& note).

laižaũ, laižýti iter. 'lecken (mit der Zunge); stechen, beissen (von der Schlange)'; **laĩžo** 3rd pers. pres. 'leckt'—B. II, 3, 162.169.266; Ber. *ližǫ.* See *lëžiù* & Lesk. Abl. 278.

lãjus South Lith. 'Talg' (zum Lichtziehen)—Ber. *lojĭ.* Cf. Brückner SlFw. 101.

lakinė́ju, lakinė́ti iter. 'ein wenig hin und her fliegen, umherfliegen'—W. *lacertus;* Boi. λάξ. Cf. Lesk. Abl. 363.

lakstaũ, lakstýti iter. 'hin und her hüpfen, springen, flattern, umherflättern, umherfliegen, schweben, umherschweifen, wehen (vom Wind)'—Ber. *lastovića, lelo;* W. *lacertus;* Boi. λάξ. Cf. Lesk. Abl. 363.

lakstus 'flüchtig, stürmisch, schnell'—Ber. *lastovića.* Cf. Lesk. Abl. 363.

laktà 'Hühnerstange; Steg im Vogelbauer'—W. *lacertus,* (*lectus*). Cf. Lesk. Abl. 363; Lesk. Nom. 542; Bezz. LF. 132.

laktũkai, latũkai plu. 'Salat'—Ber. *loktika.* Cf. Brückner SlFw. 101.

lakù, làkti 'leckend fressen, schlürfen' (von Hunden, Katzen usw.)—Ber. *ločǫ;* W. *lambo.* Cf. Lesk. Abl. 375.

lakus 'gefrässig'—Ber. *ločǫ.* Cf. MLG. I, 389.

lalũju, lalũti 'lallen' (bes. von Kindern)—Uh. *lalalla;* Ber. *lala* 1; W. *lallo;* Boi. λάλος.

lámdau, lámdyti 'zähmen, zureiten, zur Arbeit anhalten, an Arbeit gewöhnen' (von Pferden, Ochsen); **aplámdau, aplámdyti** 'Starres geschmeidig machen, Wildes bändigen'—Ber. *lomŭ.* Cf. Lesk. Abl. 334.

laminù, lamìnti 'zähmen, zureiten, zur Arbeit anhalten; (Ness. 348[b]) etwas durch anhaltenden Druck nach und nach hinstrecken, z.B. einen Segelkahn allmählich auf die Seite biegen (vom Winde)'; **aplaminù, aplamìnti** 'geschmeidig machen' (z.B. beim Flachsbrechen die holzigen Teile der Stengel)—Ber. *lomŭ.* Cf. Lesk. Abl. 334.

landinù, landìnti 'kriechen machen, kriechen lassen'—Uh. *linduṣ.* Cf. Lesk. Abl. 334.

landonìs 'Wurm im Finger' (eine schmerzhafte Krankheit) —B. II, 1, 638. Cf. Lesk. Abl. 334, Lesk. Nom. 394.

lándžoju, lándžoti iter. 'umherkriechen, umherschleichen'—Uh. *linduṣ;* B. II, 3, 240. Cf. Lesk. Abl. 334.

lankà 'Tal, Wiese (am Fluss)'—(F. *hamfs*); B. I, 416. II, 1, 153. 3, 215; Ber. *lǫka,* (*kǫpa*); W. *lacertus, lacus,* (*campus*), (*prātum*), (*vallēs*); Boi. λάκκος, (καμπή). Cf. Lesk. Abl. 335, Lesk. Nom. 208, Bezz. BGLS. 298.

lañkas 'Bügel, Bogen, Reifen, Radschiene, Tonnenband, Gewölbe, Mauerbogen usw.'—B. II, 1, 152; Ber. *lǫka*. Cf. Lesk. Abl. 334-5, Lesk. Nom. 168.

lankaũ, lankýti 'besuchen, bei jemand einkehren; (Szyr.) untersuchen, visitieren'—Ber. *lǫčǫ*. Cf. Lesk. Abl. 335.

lankióju, lankióti iter. 'vielfach biegen, ausbiegen, meiden; (im Streit) ausweichen, nachgeben; nachsehen, durch die Finger sehen'—Ber. *lǫčǫ*. Cf. Lesk. Abl. 335.

lankóju, lankóti iter. 'hin und her biegen, etwas Steifes biegsam und geschmeidig zu machen suchen'—B. I, XLVI. 288. II, 1, 436.444. 3, 215.418; Ber. *lǫčǫ*. Cf. Lesk. Abl. 335.

lañksmas 'Biegung (bes. des Weges), Umweg; Abschweifung (in der Rede)'—B. II, 1, 252.632. Cf. Lesk. Abl. 335, Lesk. Nom. 423.

lañktis masc. 'Haspel, Garnwinde'—Boi. ἠλακάτη. Cf. Lesk. Abl. 335, Lesk. Nom. 539.

lankùs 'biegsam, geschmeidig'—Ber. *lǫka*. Cf. Lesk. Abl. 335.

lanstva 'Viehstall'—B. II, 1, 449. Cf. Geitler LS. 94, Lesk. Nom. 564.

lãpas 'Blatt' (einer Pflanze, eines Buches)—Uh. *lopāçás;* K. *Laub;* F. *laufs;* Ber. *lepenŭ;* W. *liber;* Boi. λέπω. Cf. Lesk. Nom. 168.

lapatka 'Schulterblatt'—Ber. *lopata*. Cf. Brückner SlFw. 102.

lapáuju, lapáuti 'weichlich, wollüstig sein'—see *lepáuju*.

lãpė 'Fuchs'—Uh. *lopāçás;* B. II, 1, 474.547; Ber. *lisŭ;* (W. *lūpus*); Boi. (Ntr.) ἀλώπηξ. Cf. Lesk. Nom. 273, Sommer 14, MLG. I, 228.

lapkri(s)tỹs 'Blattfall', Name eines Monats: 'November' (Kur. s.v.; Lesk. Nom. 549; Bezz. LF. 133; Ber.); 'Oktober' (Ness. 349[b]; Kur. DLWb. s.v. October)—Ber. *listŭ*.

lasasza (Szyr.) 'Lachs'—Ber. *lososĭ*. See *lasziszà* & Lesk. Nom. 599, Geitler LS. 67.

lãskana 'Lumpen, Lappen'—Ber. *loskutŭ.*
lastà fem., **lástas** (**lánstas**) masc. "ein aus Brettern zusammengeschlagenes Gänsenest, in welchem die Gans ihre Eier legt und auch brütet" (Kur.)—(W. *lectus*). Cf. Ness. 349[b]; Kur. 221[b]; Lesk. Abl. 334; Lesk. Nom. 531 (read KLD for KDL), 542; Trautmann Die altpreussischen Sprachdenkmäler 369.
lãszas 'Tropfen'—Ber. *lasa.* Cf. Lesk. Abl. 373.
laszasza 'Lachs'—Ber. *lososĭ.* See *lasziszà* & Lalis s.v.
lãszinu, lãszinti trans. 'tröpfeln lassen, tropfen machen, einträufeln, abzapfen, auspressen'—Ber. *lasa.* Cf. Lesk. Abl. 373.
lãszis masc. 'Lachs'—Ber. *lososĭ.* See next.
lasziszà fem. id.—K. *Lachs;* B. II, 1, 546; Ber. *lososĭ.* Cf. Lesk. Nom. 599; Trautmann Die altpreussischen Sprachdenkmäler 368; IF. V, 61; KZ. XLV, 288.
laszù, laszëti 'tröpfeln, tropfenweise herabfallen; lecken (von einem Gefäss)'—Ber. *lasa.* Cf. Lesk. Abl. 373.
latãkas 'zusammengelaufenes Wasser; (Ness. 350[a]) Wasserröhre, Wasserleitung; (Kur. 222) Pfütze'—Ber. *lotokŭ;* W. 1. *latex.* Cf. Brückner SlFw. 102.
lãtras 'liederlicher Mensch, Prasser, Trunkenbold, Schelm, Possenreisser, Taugenichts, Bösewicht, Spitzbube, Mörder'—Ber. *lotar.* Cf. Prell. deutsch. Best. in den lett. Spr. 20, Brückner SlFw. 102.
latũkai 'Salat'—see *laktũkai.*
laũkan adv. 'hinaus, aus dem Hause, ins Freie'—B. II, 2, 743. Cf. Ness. 353[a], Wied. 295.
laũkas 'Feld, Flur, das Freie'—Uh. *lokás;* K. *Loh;* B. I, 202; Ber. *lǫgŭ, luča;* W. *lūcus;* Boi. λευκός. Cf. Lesk. Nom. 194.
laũkas 'mit einer Blesse auf der Stirn (von Rindern und Pferden); kahl'—Uh. *rokás, rócate;* F. *liuhaþ;* B. I, 429.546; Ber. *luča;* W. *lūceo;* Boi. λευκός. Cf. Lesk. Nom. 195; Geitler LS. 67; Bezz. BGLS. 298.

laukè adv. loc. sing. 'draussen'; prep. 'ausserhalb'—B. II, 2, 707.743.929. Cf. Ness. 353*.

laukinykas dial. (Godlewa) 'Landmann; (dial. also) Wolf' —B. II, 1, [487].497. Cf. [Bezz. BGLS. 107]; [LBLV. 289]; [Lesk. Nom. 520-1]; MLG. I, 226, 228.

laukininkas 'Feldbewohner, Landmann'—B. I, 414. II, 1, 486. Cf. Lesk. Nom. 520-1.

laukìnis, fem. **laukìnė** 'zum Feld gehörig'; **laukìnė ántis** 'Feldente'; **laukìnė obelìs** 'wilder Apfelbaum'— [B. II, 1, 273]. See *laũkas* 'Feld' & [Lesk. Nom. 401].

láukiu, láukti 'auf jemand warten, exspectare, sich gedulden'; **suláukiu, suláukti** 'erwarten; nach Warten erreichen, erleben, bekommen'; **susiláukiu, susiláukti** 'erwarten und erhalten, bekommen (z.B. ein Kind), gebären' (e.g. **tókį vaikìną susiláukė** 'sie bekamen solch einen Knaben'; **jì jaũ susiláukė** 'sie hat schon geboren')—Uh. *lókate;* B. I, 289. II, 3, 193-4; Ber. *lučę;* W. *lūceo;* Boi. λεύσσω. Cf. Lesk. Abl. 302.

laupyti (?) żem. 'rauben'; **aplaupyti** 'berauben'—Ber. *lupę.* Cf. Geitler LS. 94, Lesk. Abl. 302.

lausztùvas 'Brechinstrument'—see *laužtùvas.*

láužau, láužyti iter. trans. 'brechen'—Uh. *rujáti;* F. *ga-lūkan;* B. II, 3, 268; (Ber. *lusta*); W. *lūgeo;* Boi. λευγαλέος. Cf. Lesk. Abl. 303.

láužis 'Bruch'; **(akmeniũ) láužis** 'Steinbruch'—W. *lūgeo;* Boi. λευγαλέος. Cf. Lesk. Abl. 303.

láužiu, láužti trans. 'brechen'—B. II, 3, 362(note); (W. *luctor*). Cf. Lesk. Abl. 303.

laužtùvas (lausztùvas) 'Brechinstrument (z.B. Nussknacker), Flachsbreche'; **laužtùvai** plu. 'die Brechhölzer an der Flachsbreche'—B. II, 1, 620. Cf. Lesk. Abl. 303, Lesk. Nom. 565.

lavónas 'Leiche, Leichnam'—B. I, 338; Ber. *luna* 2. See *liáuju* & Lesk. Abl. 302.

lazà 'Stock'—see next.

lazdà, lazà 'Stock, Stab; Hasel'—B. I, 569.719; Ber. *loza;* (W. *larix*); (Boi. δρῦς (note)). Cf. Lesk. Nom. 214.
lażas 'Frondienst, Scharwerk'—(Ber. *lazŭ*). Cf. Lesk. Nom. 175.
lȇbas 'mager'—Ber. *libivŭ.*
lẽdas, dial. **lẽdus** (cf. Bezz. LF. 134) 'Eis'; **ledaĩ** plu. '(grober) Hagel'—Ber. *ledŭ;* Boi. λίθος. Cf. Lesk. Nom. 160.
ledìnis 'Eisscholle'—B. II, 1, 273. Cf. Bezz. LF. 134.
lẽdus 'Eis'—see *lẽdas.*
ledvaĩ adv. Samogit. 'kaum, schwerlich, mit Mühe'—Ber. *jed(ŭ)va.* Cf. Brückner SlFw. 102.
léidżu (léidu) (léidmi), léisti 'lassen; zulassen, erlauben, gestatten; herablassen. senken, auswerfen; herauslassen, zapfen; entlassen, (Holz) flössen; (von Gott) schaffen; landen'—F. *lētan;* B. I, 205.334.438. II, 1, 380. 3, 103.483; W. *lassus,* (*lūdo*); Boi. ληδεῖν. Cf. Lesk. Abl. 276.
leikà Samog. 'Trichter'—Ber. *lějǫ.* Cf. Brückner SlFw. 102.
leilas 'durch Benutzung dünn geworden, abgenützt, schlank' (auch von Menschen)—B. II, 1, 351; Ber. *libivŭ;* W. *lētum;* Boi. λειρός, λοιγός, (λείριον). Cf. Lesk. Abl. 277.
leinas 'schlank'—see *lainas.*
leiterė, leterė 'Wagenleiter; ein kleines Fuder (z.B. Heu)' —Ber. *lôjtra.* Cf. Prell. deutsch. Best. in den lett. Spr. 23.
lȇju, lȇti 'giessen, durch Giessen formen'—Uh. *riṇâti;* F. *af-linnan, leiþu;* B. II, 1, 444.449; Ber. *lějǫ;* W. *lībo* 1, (*lībra*), (*līnum*), (*linqueo*); Boi. λείβω. Cf. Lesk. Abl. 276.
lëká 'elftens'—Ber. *-lěkŭ.* See *lëkas.* Cf. KZ. XLIV, 133.
lëkana 'Rest, Reliquie'—B. II, 1, 268. Cf. Lesk. Nom. 387.
lȇkanas 'übrig geblieben'; **lëkanì daiktaĩ** 'Reliquien'—B. II, 1, 268. Cf. Lesk. Nom. 384.
lȇkas 'übrig bleibend, unpaar'—Uh. *rékas;* F. *leiƕan;* B. II,

1, 150. 2, 27; Ber. *-lěkŭ;* W. *linquo;* Boi. λείπω. Cf. Lesk. Abl. 277, Lesk. Nom. 185.

lëkas 'elfter'; **antras lëkas** 'zwölfter' etc.—B. II, 2, 27.59; [Ber. *-lěkŭ*]; Boi. λείπω. Cf. Ness. 365*; Bezz. BGLS. 184-5; Geitler LD. 11; Lesk. Nom. 185; Wied. 157.

lekiù, lė̃kti 'fliegen'—F. *plahsjan;* B. I, 585. II, 3, 163.169; Ber. *lelǫ;* W. *lacertus, lōcusta;* Boi. λάξ, ληκᾶν. Cf. Lesk. Abl. 363.

lekmenė 'Pfuhl, Pfütze'—W. *lacus.* Cf. Lesk. Nom. 361, 420.

lė̃korius 'Arzt'—Ber. *lěkŭ.* Cf. Brückner SlFw. 102.

lëkù (old form **lëkmì**), **lìkti** 'lassen, übrig lassen'; **palinkt** (q.v.) intr. Old Lith. 'bleibt zurück'—Uh. *riṇákti;* K. *leihen;* F. *leiłvan;* B. I, 190.424.589. II, 1, 430.567. 3, 91.114.118.277.388.396.443; Ber. *-lěkŭ;* W. *linquo;* Boi. λείπω. Cf. Lesk. Abl. 277.

lela 'Ziegenmelker'—Ber. *lelĭkŭ.* Cf. MLG. II, 127; Lesk. Nom. 201. See *lėlis.*

lëlas 'gross'—K. *Glied;* B. II, 1, 351; Boi. λειρός. Cf. Lesk. Abl. 277, Lesk. Nom. 468, Geitler LS. 94.

lėlẽ 'Puppe, Spielpuppe; neugeborenes Kind, Wickelkind'; **akė̃s lėlẽ** 'Augenstern' (in dem man das Spiegelbild sieht)—Uh. *lálati;* Ber. *lela.* Cf. Brückner SlFw. 102, Bezz. LF. 135.

lėlis (?) 'Ziegenmelker, Nachtschwalbe, Caprimulgus europaeus'—Ber. *lelĭkŭ;* W. *lolium.* Cf. Lesk. Nom. 201.

lemiù, lémti 'jemand etwas als Schicksal bestimmen' (bes. von Gott und den Göttern)—Ber. *lomĭ.* Cf. Lesk. Abl. 333.

lemoju, lemoti 'lechzen'—B. II, 3, 478; W. *lemures;* Boi. λαμός.

lëmũ, gen. **lëmeñs** 'Baumstamm ohne Äste; Rumpf, Statur, Wuchs, Taille; Leibstück eines Kleidungsstückes; Schaft eines Leuchters; (Szyr.) Weinrebe'—K. *Glied;* F. *lipus;* B. II, 1, 441; Ber. *lemęzŭ, lěnĭcĭ;* (W. *oblīquus*). Cf. Lesk. Abl. 277.

lenciũgas 'Kette'—Ber. *lano.* Cf. Brückner SlFw. 102.
léndrė 'Schilfrohr'—see *néndrė.*
lendù, l̨sti 'kriechen, schleichen, lauern'—Uh. *linduṣ;* W. 2. *lens, lumbus, (lectus).* Cf. Lesk. Abl. 334.
lengvapẽdis 'Leisetreter, Schmeichler'—W. *acupedius;* Boi. πέζα.
leñgvas, f. **lengvà; lengvùs,** f. **lengvì;** adv. **leñgviai** 'leicht, nicht schwer zu machen; gelinde, langsam, allmählich; schwach (vom Bier, von der Stimme); sanft, langmütig'—Uh. *laghúṣ;* K. *leicht, Lunge;* F. *leihts;* B. I, 615.620. II, 1, 200; Ber. *l̆gŭkŭ;* W. *levis;* Boi. ἐλαχύς. Cf. Lesk. Nom. 344.
Leñkas 'Pole', plu. **Leñkai** 'die Polen'; **Leñkai, Leñkū žẽmė** '(das Land) Polen'—Ber. *lędo.* Cf. Brückner SlFw. 103 (& note).
lénkė 'Vertiefung, kleines Tal, niedrige Stelle im Acker, Wiese in einer Vertiefung'—Ber. *lękǫ.* Cf. Lesk. Abl. 334.
lenkiù, leñkti 'biegen, beugen; ausweichen, meiden; schonen; haspeln'—Uh. *sṛñkā, (lakuṭas);* B. I, 416. II, 1, 432.571. 3, 138.382; Ber. *lękǫ, lyko;* W. *lacertus, (linquier), (3. līmus);* Boi. ἠλακάτη, (Ntr.) λοξός. Cf. Lesk. Abl. 334.
lenktuvė 'Haspel, Garnwinde'—(W. *līcium*); Boi. ἠλακάτη (& note).
leñszis 'Linse'—K. *Linse;* Ber. *lęła;* W. 1. *lens.* Cf. Prell. deutsch. Best. in den lett. Spr. 51.
lentà 'Brett, Planke'—K. *Geländer, Linde;* Ber. *lǫtŭ;* W. *lentus;* Boi. ἐλάτη. Cf. Lesk. Nom. 200.
lẽpa 'Linde'; **lẽpos mė́nů** 'der Monat Juli'—Ber. *lipa;* Boi. ἀλίφαλος. Cf. Lesk. Nom. 221.
lepáuju, lepáuti; žem. **lapáuju, lapáuti** 'fortgesetzt weichlich dahinleben, wollüstig sein; umherschweifen, sich umhertreiben (bes. um Sinnengenüsse zu suchen)'—(Boi. λαπίζω). Cf. [Lesk. Abl. 369]. See *lepùs.*

lẽpinu, lẽpinti (**lẽpįti**) 'verwöhnen, verzärteln' (z.B. ein Kind)—(Boi. λαπίζω). See prec.

lëpiù, lẽpti; palëpiù, palẽpti 'befehlen'; **põ prýsėgą lẽpti** 'mit einem Eid beschwören'—B. II, 1, 543; Boi. λίπτω. Cf. Lesk. Abl. 277.

lëpsnà 'Flamme'—Ber. *lipanŭ,* (*lěpŭ* 1); (W. *limpidus*); Boi. λάμπω. Cf. Lesk. Abl. 277.

lëpszas Samogit. 'besser'—Ber. *lěpŭ* 1. Cf. Brückner SlFw. 103.

lepùs 'weichlich, verzärtelt, genusssüchtig'—W. *lepidus;* Boi. λεπτός, (λαπίζω). Cf. Lesk. Abl. 369.

lẽsas, lẽsas 'mager' (von Menschen, Tieren; auch vom Acker)—(Ber. *lichŭ*); W. *lētum;* Boi. λειρός, (λοῖσθος). Cf. Lesk. Abl. 278.

lesù, lèsti 'mit dem Schnabel aufpicken, Körner auflesen, pickend fressen' (von Vögeln)—K. *lesen;* F. *lisan;* B. I, 784. II, 3, 120.446; (Ber. *lasŭ*). Cf. Lesk. Abl. 363.

lëta 'Sache, Angelegenheit; Nutzen'; **lëtas** (gen. sing.) **vyrs** 'tüchtiger Mann'—Ber. *lětĭ* 2. Cf. Geitler LS. 94, Lesk. Nom. 221.

lẽtas 'einfältig, blöde, langsam, träge, feig, abgenutzt, alt, schlecht, gering'—(F. *un-lēps*); (Ber. *lata*); W. *lēnis.* Cf. Lesk. Nom. 166.

lëtauras 'Pauke'—Ber. *litavra.* Cf. BB. XXI, 118.

letenà 'Tatze (bes. eines Bären); obere Seite des menschlichen Fusses, Fusssohle'—B. II, 1, 267.

leterė 'Wagenleiter'—see *leiterė.*

lėtu, lėtėti (**lëtu, lëtėti**?) 'beunruhigen, reizen, ermüden'—W. *līs;* Boi. ἀλείτης. See *lytù.*

lëtùs 'Regen'—B. II, 1, 444.449; (Ber. *lěto*). See *lytùs* & Ness. 359ᵃ, 364ᵇ; LBLV. 338; Lesk. Abl. 276.

lëtùtis 'leichter Regen'—B. II, 1, 677. Cf. Lesk. Nom. 576.

Lëtuvà 'Litauen'—W. *lītus;* Boi. λειμών.

Lëtùvininkas 'Litauer'—B. II, 1, 487. Cf. Lesk. Nom. 520.

lëvas 'Löwe'—K. *Löwe;* Ber. *lĭvŭ;* W. *leo;* Boi. λέων. Cf. Brückner SlFw. 103.

lëžiù, lẽžti (lẽszti) 'lecken; (von der Schlange) stechen, beissen'—Uh. *léḍhi;* K. *lecken* 1; F. *bi-laigōn;* B. I, 191.290.291.432.551.726. II, 3, 380.397.443.492; Ber. *ližǫ;* W. *lingo,* (*lingua*); Boi. λείχω. Cf. Lesk. Abl. 278.

lëžùvis 'Zunge; Sprache, Dialekt; Zünglein einer Wage; Klöppel einer Glocke; Zäpfchen im Halse; Hemmung oder Klinke am Webestuhl, (Ness. 359[b]:) "das Hölzchen, welches den unteren Webestuhl anhält"—K. *lecken* 1; F. *tuggō;* B. II, 1, 220; Ber. *ęzykŭ;* W. *lingua.* Cf. Lesk. Nom. 354, Bezz. LF. 135[a].

liáudis 'Volk'—Ber. *ľudŭ.* Cf. Lalis 173.

liáuju, liáuti (perfective **paliáuju, paliáuti**) 'aufhören (etwas zu tun)'; reflexive **liáujůs, liáutis** (perfective **pasiliáuju, pasiliáuti**) 'aufhören (zu sein, zu geschehen)'—(Uh. *lunā́ti*); (F. *lēw*); B. I, 209.338; Ber. *lěvǫ, luna* 2; (W. 2. *luo*). Cf. Lesk. Abl. 302.

liaupsẽ 'Lob (bes. Gottes), Lobpreisung, kirchlicher Lobgesang'—Uh. *lúbhyati;* K. *Lob;* Ber. *lubŭ;* W. *libet.*

liáupsinu, liáupsinti 'lobsingen, lobpreisen, loben'; **Dẽvą liáupsinti** 'Gottes Lob singen'—Uh. *lúbhyati;* K. *Lob;* Ber. *lubŭ;* W. *libet.*

liaũras 'Lorbeerbaum'—Ber. *lavr;* W. *laurus.*

lỹcius "die Strecke, die Stelle des Vergehens" (Kur. s.v.); "etwas, was man zur Beglaubigung aufzuweisen hat, ein Zeichen, Unterpfand, corpus delicti" (Ness. 363[a]); **vagìs añt lỹciaus nutvértas** 'ein auf frischer Tat ergriffener Dieb'—Ber. *likŭ* 2. Cf. Brückner SlFw. 103 (& note).

liczbà 'Zahl'—Ber. *likŭ* 3. Cf. Brückner SlFw. 103.

lyczýna 'Larve, Maske'—Ber. *likŭ* 2. Cf. Brückner SlFw. 103.

lyczù, lytẽti 'anrühren'—see *lytù.*

lýdau, lýdyti; táukus lýdyti 'Fett, Schmer schmelzen; Talg bereiten' (bei soeben geschlachteten Tieren)—Ber. *lojĭ*; (W. *lāridum*). Cf. Lesk. Abl. 276.

lydimas Samog. '(durch Vertilgung des Waldes) frisch gewonnener Acker'—Boi. λίστρον.

lýdinu, lýdinti 'Fett schmelzen, Talg bereiten'—Ber. *lojĭ*. See *lýdau* & Lesk. Abl. 276.

lydżù, lydëti 'begleiten, das Geleit geben' (bes. bei der Hochzeit, beim Begräbnis)—B. I, 489. Cf. Lesk. Abl. 276.

lyg prep. dial. 'bis'—(W. *aequus*). Cf. Bezz. LF. 136.

lýg adv. 'gleich'—see *lýgus*.

ligà 'Krankheit'; **ligõs pãtalas** 'Krankenbett'—B. I, 96.582. II, 3, 166; Boi. λοιγός, ἀλίβας. Cf. Lesk. Nom. 218-19.

lýginu, lýginti 'gleich machen, ebnen, glätten; vergleichen' —F. **-leikōn*.

ligonas 'Kranker'—B. II, 1, 281. Cf. Lesk. Nom. 393.

lygumà 'ebene Stelle, ebenes Feld, Ebene'—B. II, 1, 250. 624. Cf. Lesk. Nom. 432.

lýgus, neut. **lýgu**, fem. **lýgi** 'gleich, ähnlich, eben, flach, paar'; adv. **lýgiai, lýg** 'gleich, gleichwie, wie'—Uh. *liṅgam*; K. *gleich*; F. *ga-leiki*, **-leikōn*, (*leik*); (Ber. *likŭ* 2); W. *licet*, (*aequus*). Cf. Lesk. Nom. 254.

lyjù (3rd pers. sing. pres. **lỹja, lỹna**), **lýti** impers. 'regnen' —F. *leipu*; B. I, 103. II, 1, 444. 3, 312; Ber. *lějǫ*; W. *lībo* 1; Boi. λείβω. Cf. Lesk. Abl. 276.

-lika numeral suff. (11-19)—see *dvýlika* 'zwölf'.

lỹkius 'Rest, Überschuss, Überbleibsel'—Ber. *-lěkŭ*. Cf. Lesk. Abl. 277.

lìktas adj. pret. pass. part. of **lëkù**, q.v., 'zurückgelassen, übrig'—Uh. *riktás*; W. *linquo*.

limpù, lìpti 'kleben, kleben bleiben, anhaften'—Uh. *limpáti*; K. *bleiben, leben*; F. *bi-leiban*; B. I, 100.519.624 (*lìbdavau* imperfect 1st pers. sing.). II, 3, 279.288 (note).397.443 (*lìpęs* perf. act. part.).492; Ber. *lĭpǫ*; W. *lippus, lino*; Boi. λίπος. Cf. Lesk. Abl. 277.

lỹna 'es regnet'—see *lyjù*.

lìnas 'Flachsstengel'; plu. **linaĩ** 'Flachs'—Uh. *lĩnas;* K. *Leinen;* F. *lein;* Ber. *lĩnŭ;* W. *lĩnum;* Boi. λίνον.

lýnas 'Schleie' (Fisch)—K. *Schleie;* Ber. *liñĭ;* Boi. λείμαξ (& note). Cf. Brückner SlFw. 103.

lìndau, lìndoti (B. **líndau, lį́ndoti**) 'hineingekrochen sein, stecken'—Uh. *lindųș;* B. II, 3, 168. Cf. Lesk. Abl. 334.

lìndynė 'Schlupfwinkel, Versteck, Loch, Höhle'—W. *lumbus.* Cf. Lesk. Abl. 334.

lìndoju, lìndoti (B. **líndoju, líndoti**) 'hineingekrochen sein, stecken'—Uh. *lindųș;* B. II, 3, 168.

linënà 'Flachsfeld'—B. II, 1, 623. See *lìnas* & Lesk. Nom. 413.

lingau (lingoju), lingoti (Ness. 367[b]) 'schweben, sich wiegen, sich hin und her bewegen; wackelnd gehen; (mit dem Kopfe) nicken, wackeln'; **lingũju, lingũti** (**lingóju, lingóti**) iter. 'sich hin und her, auf und ab bewegen, schaukeln'; **sù gálva lingũti** 'den Kopf neigen und wieder erheben'—Uh. *lágati, lañgas, lãñgũlam;* (F. *waggs*); Ber. *lęgają;* W. *langueo;* Boi. λάγγων. Cf. Lesk. Abl. 334.

-linkai, -link '-wärts' (e.g. **auksztýnlinkai** 'aufwärts', **sziáurlink(ai)** 'nordwärts')—Ber. *lękq.* Cf. Lesk. Abl. 334, Lesk. Nom. 202.

linkiù, linkëti 'sich beugen, sich neigen, sich biegen; sich neigen zu, jemand etwas wünschen, wünschen, wollen' —Ber. *lękq.* See *linkstù* & MLG. I, 377; Schleicher LSpr. II, 287; Ness. 368[a]; Kur. s.v.; Lesk. Abl. 334; Geitler LS. 95.

linkstù, liñkti 'sich (unwillkürlich) biegen, krumm werden, sich niegen'—Uh. *sṛñkā,* (*lakuṭas*); (F. *waggs*); B. I, 416. II, 1, 432.571; Ber. *lękq;* W. *lacertus.* Cf. Lesk. Abl. 334.

linkus 'biegsam, geschmeidig'—B. II, 1, 179. Cf. Lesk. Abl. 334.

lynója, lynóti impers. 'leicht regnen'—B. II, 3, 312. See *lyjù.*

linótas 'voll Flachs'—B. II, 1, 406.664. Cf. Lesk. Nom. 562.

linta 'Zierband'—Ber. *lentiji;* W. *lentus, linteum* (s.v. *līnum*). Cf. Brückner SlFw. 103, Bezz. LF. 137.

lipnùs 'klebrig'—B. I, 100. II, 1, 291; Ber. *lĭpq;* Boi. λίπος. See *lipsznùs* & Lesk. Abl. 277.

lýpstinůs, lýpstintis 'sich anschmeicheln'—Ber. *lĭpq.* Cf. Lesk. Abl. 277.

lipstu, lipti (?) 'brennen'; **lipst** pres. 3rd pers. sing. "er brennt"—Ber. *lipanŭ;* (*lĕpŭ* 1). Cf. Lesk. Abl. 277, 395; Geitler LS. 95.

lipsznùs 'klebrig, anhänglich; freundlich, zuvorkommend, zudringlich'—Uh. *limpáti;* F. *bi-leiban;* W. *lippus;* Boi. λίπος. See *lipnùs* & Lesk. Abl. 277.

lìpsztukas 'Liebstöckel' (Pflanze)—Ber. *lubistok.*

lipti inf.—see *limpù, lìpti* 'kleben'; *lipù, lìpti* 'steigen'; or *lipstu, lipti* (?) 'brennen'.

lipù, lìpti 'steigen, klettern, hinaufkriechen'—B. II, 3, 124. 288 (note); Ber. *lĭpq;* Boi. αἰγίλιψ. Cf. Lesk. Abl. 277.

lipùs 'klebrig, haftend'—B. II, 1, 176; W. *lippus;* Boi. λίπος. See *lipsznùs.*

lýsė 'Gartenbeet'—K. *Gleise, lehren;* F. *lais;* B. I, 785; Ber. *lĕcha;* W. *līra,* (*lītus*); (Boi. λίστρον). Cf. Lesk. Nom. 275.

lýstė 'Ackerbeet'—(W. *lītus*). See prec. & Bezz. LF. 137.

lýstu, lýsti 'mager werden'—Boi. λιαρός, (λοῖσθος). See *lêsas* & Lesk. Abl. 278.

lìsz prep. 'ausser, ohne'; **lìsz tõ** 'ohnedies, ausserdem'—Ber. *lichŭ.* Cf. Brückner SlFw. 103.

lytù (**lyczù**), **lytė́ti** 'anrühren, berühren, antasten'—W. *līs.* See *lėtu* & Lesk. Abl. 278.

lytùs 'Regen'—Uh. *riṇáti;* F. *leipu;* B. II, 1, 444; Ber. *lĕjq,* (*lĕto*); W. *lībo* 1; Boi. ἄλεισον, λείβω. Cf. Lesk. Abl. 276.

liũbyju, liũbyti 'gern geniessen' (bes. vom Essen und Trinken)—Ber. *lubŭ.* Cf. Brückner SlFw. 104.

liubysta 'Liebstöckel' (Pflanze)—Ber. *lubistok*. Cf. Brückner SlFw. 104.

liúbiu, liũbė́ti 'zu tun pflegen'—Ber. *lubŭ*. Cf. Brückner SlFw. 104.

liũdė 'Bleilot'—(Boi. λᾶας).

liũdnas 'traurig, niedergeschlagen'—F. *liuts;* Ber. *ludŭ,* (*lěnŭ*). Cf. Lesk. Abl. 302, Lesk. Nom. 356.

liũdžù, liũdė́ti 'traurig sein, trauern'—F. *liuts*. Cf. Lesk. Abl. 302.

liũgas 'Morast, Pfütze, Mistgrube'—Ber. *luža*.

liũstù, liũsti 'traurig werden, sich ängstigen'—Ber. *ludŭ*. Cf. Lesk. Abl. 302.

liũtas 'Löwe'—K. *Löwe;* Ber. *lutŭ,* (*lĭvŭ*). Cf. Brückner SlFw. 105 (& note).

lìzas dial. 'Nest'—B. I, 719. See next.

lìzdas 'Nest'—Uh. *nīḍám;* K. *Nest;* B. I, 546.569.719; Ber. *gnězdo;* W. *nīdus*.

lìžius 'Lecker; (usually) Zeigefinger'—B. II, 1, 224.610. See *lëžių* & Lesk. Abl. 278.

lóbas 'Baumrinde'—see *lũbas*.

lobas 'Flussbett; Tal'—(Boi. ληνός). Cf. Ness. 371[b]; MLG. IV, 180; Lesk. Nom. 197.

lõbęs perf. part. 'reich'—see *lobstù*.

lõbis 'Besitz, Habe, Reichtum' (bes. von beweglichen Gütern)—Uh. *lábhate, lābhas;* B. I, 521. II, 1, 172. 3, 291; W. *rabiēs,* (*labor*); Boi. λάφῡρον. Cf. Lesk. Abl. 373.

lobstù, lõbti 'reich werden'; **lõbęs** perf. part. 'reich'—B. II, 3, [291].448. Cf. Kur. s.v. *lopstù* & Lesk. Abl. 373.

lóju, lóti 'bellen'—Uh. *rā́yati;* F. **laian;* B. I, 288.448. II, 3, 198; Ber. *laję* 1; W. *lāmentum;* Boi. λαίειν. Cf. Lesk. Abl. 377, Brückner SlFw. 104 (note).

lomà 'Einsenkung, niedrige Stelle im Acker; ausgesengter Platz auf dem Felde, auf der Wiese'—B. I, 152; Ber. *lanŭ,* (*lamaję*); W. *lāma, ulva;* (Boi. ληνός). Cf.

Ness. 372[b]; Lesk. Abl. 334; Lesk. Nom. 216-17; BB. XIX, 168.

lomà 'Ziel, Schicksal'—Ber. *lamajǫ, lomŭ.* Cf. Ness. 372[b]; MLG. I, 65; Geitler LS. 95; Lesk. Abl. 334; Lesk. Nom. 197.

lópa 'Klaue des Hundes, Bären'—Ber. *lapa.*

lõpas 'Flick, Lappen'—K. *Lappen;* Ber. *lapŭtĭ;* W. *lappa;* Boi. λάπαθος. Cf. Lesk. Nom. 180, Prell. deutsch. Best. in den lett. Spr. 30, Geitler LS. 67.

lópau, lõpyti 'flicken'—K. *Lappen;* Ber. *lapŭtĭ.* Cf. Prell. deutsch. Best. in den lett. Spr. 30.

lópeta (lopetà) 'Schaufel (Ness. 372[b], eine flache, hölzerne); Pflugschar'—Ber. *lopata.* Cf. Brückner SlFw. 104, Bezz. BGLS. 299.

lopìkas 'Flicker'—B. II, 1, 490.616. Cf. Lesk. Nom. 510.

lopiszys, lopszỹs 'Hängewiege in Form eines Korbes, aus Bast oder Leinwand gemacht'—Ber. *lapŭtĭ;* W. *liber.* Cf. Ness. 372[b], Lesk. Nom. 598.

lopstù, lõpti (Kur. et alibi) 'reich werden'—see *lobstù.*

lopszỹs 'Hängewiege'—see *lopiszys.*

loskà 'Huld, Gnade, Gunst'—Ber. *laskajǫ.* Cf. Brückner SlFw. 104.

lõskavas 'gnädig, sanftmütig, gewogen'—Ber. *laskajǫ.* Cf. Brückner SlFw. 104.

lóva 'Bett, Bettstelle, hölzernes Bettgestell'—Ber. *lava* 1; (W. *lāma* (& Ntr.)); (Boi. ληνός). Cf. Brückner SlFw. 104, 176.

lubà 'Brett der bretternen Zimmerdecke'; **lùbos** plu. 'bretterne Zimmerdecke'—F. *luftus;* Ber. *lubŭ;* W. *liber.* Cf. Geitler LS. 67; Brückner SlFw. 104; Lesk. Nom. 225.

lūbyjûs, lūbytis 'sich lieben'—Ber. *lubŭ.*

lugnas 'biegsam, geschmeidig'—Uh. *rugṇás;* [K. *Locke*]; F. *ga-lūkan;* B. I, 384. II, 1, 256; W. *luctor;* Boi. λυγίζω. Cf. Lesk. Abl. 317.

lugoti(?) 'bitten'—K. *locken* (read lit. *lugoti* for lit. *lu-*

gsti); (W. *lacio*). Cf. Geitler LS. 95; Geitler LD. 51; K. 8th ed. s.v. locken; Lesk. Abl. 317; IF. V, 311-12.

lukai plu. 'eine Lauchgattung, Eschlauch, Graslauch'—Ber. *lukŭ*. Cf. Brückner SlFw. 105.

lúkiu, lūkëti; lūkëju, lūkëti 'ein wenig warten, hoffen'—Uh. *lókate;* B. II, 3, 204; Ber. *lučǫ*. Cf. Lesk. Abl. 302, 439.

luknė 'gelbe Seerose, Mummel'—Ber. *lŭkno*.

lùksztas (**lúksztas**) 'weiche Schale von Äpfeln, Nüssen, Eiern; Hülse vom Getreide; Schote von Erbsen, Bohnen usw.'—Ber. *luska*. Cf. Ness. 374-5; Kur. s.v.; Geitler LS. 67; Lesk. Nom. 538.

lùksztinu, lùksztinti 'aushülsen, ausschälen, schlauben'—Ber. *luska*.

lulỹs 'fetter, ungeschickter, tölpelhafter Mensch, Einfaltspinsel'—Ber. *lola*. Cf. Ness. 375[b].

lùnkas (B. **lúnkas**), plu. **lùnkai** 'Bast; (Kur. s.v.) feiner Lindenbast; (Ness. 375[b]) der unter der äusseren Rinde liegende Bast von jungen Linden, der zu Stricken gedreht, und auch von den Gärtnern zum Anbinden der Blumen und jungen Bäume gebraucht wird'—B. I, 391. II, 2, 85; Ber. *lyko;* (W. *runco*); (Boi. ῥυκάνη). Cf. Lesk. Nom. 189.

lúpa 'Lippe'; **lúpos** plu. 'Mund'—W. *labium*.

lupinai, lupinos plu. 'Schalen, (bes.) Obstschalen'—K. *Läufel;* B. II, 1, 260; Ber. *lupǫ;* Boi. λέπω. Cf. Lesk. Abl. 302, Lesk. Nom. 399.

lupsnìs fem. 'abgeschälte Tannenrinde' (zum Gebrauch der Gerber)—B. II, 1, 289; Ber. *lupǫ*. Cf. Lesk. Abl. 302.

lupù, lùpti 'schälen, die Haut abziehen, schinden'—Uh. *lumpáti;* K. *Läufel;* F. *laufs;* B. I, 107.454. II, 1, 249; Ber. *lupǫ;* W. *lapit, liber,* (*plūma*); Boi. λέπω, λύπη. Cf. Lesk. Abl. 302.

luska 'Lappen', plu. **luskos** 'zerrissene Kleider, Lumpen'—Ber. *luska*. Cf. Lesk. Nom. 505.

luskis 'Lump'—see *luzgis*.

lúszis, lūszỹs masc.; **lūszis** fem. 'Luchs'—Uh. *rúçan;* K. *Luchs;* B. II, 1, 546; W. *lūceo;* Boi. 2. λύγξ. Cf. Lesk. Nom. 299, 238; Trautmann Die altpreussischen Sprachdenkmäler 372.

lúsztu, lúszti 'brechen'—see *lúžtu.*

lutynas, lutynė 'Pfuhl, Lehmpfütze'—Uh. *lavaṇás;* W. *lutum;* Boi. λῦμα. Cf. Ness. 376ª.

lutingas 'stürmisch'—Boi. λύσσα. See next.

lutis 'Sturm, Unwetter'—Ber. *lutŭ;* Boi. λύσσα. Cf. Brückner SlFw. 105.

luzgis, luskis 'Lump'—Ber. *luska.* Cf. Geitler LS. 95.

lũžis 'Bruch'. Kur. s.v.: "ein Bruch, ein Knick an einem Stock; eine Stelle im Walde, wo der Wind viele Bäume umgebrochen hat". Ness. 376ᵇ (*luszis*): "ein Bruch; eine Stelle, wo z.B. Steine gebrochen werden"—W. *lūgeo;* Boi. λευγαλέος. Cf. Lesk. Abl. 303, Lesk. Nom. 294.

lúžtu, lúžti (lúsztu, lúszti); pret. **lúžau**; intr. 'brechen, entzweigehen'; **mẽdis lúžo** 'der Baum ist gebrochen'; **ãkys lúžt** 'die Augen brechen im Tode'; **szirdìs lúžta** 'das Herz bricht'—Uh. *rujáti;* K. *Loch;* F. *ga-lūkan;* B. II, 3, 128.370; W. *lūgeo,* (*luctor*); Boi. λευγαλέος. Cf. Lesk. Abl. 302-3.

lůbà 'tägliche häusliche Arbeit' (z.B. das Füttern des Viehs, Reinigen der Geräte und Gebäude, Wasserholen, Waschen, Kochen usw.)—W. *labor;* Boi. λώβη. Cf. Ness. 371ᵇ, Lesk. Nom. 232.

lũbas, lóbas 'Baumrinde, die äussere bröckelnde Rinde der Birken und Linden; Beinlade'; **lůbaĩ, lobaĩ** plu. 'Buchdeckel, Bucheinband'—F. *laufs;* Ber. *lubŭ;* W. *liber;* Boi. λέπω. Cf. Ness. 373ᵇ; Kur. 236ª, 238ᵇ; MLG. I, 17; Bezz. LF. 138; Brückner SlFw. 104; Lesk. Nom. 197.

lũmas 'lahm'—W. *lanio;* Boi. νωλεμές. Cf. Prell. deutsch. Best. in den lett. Spr. 36.

lůtas 'Einbaum, Kahn, Fischerboot, Flusskahn, Lastkahn' (cf. Ness. 373-4)—Ber. *laty*. Cf. MLG. I, 228; Lesk. Nom. 197; Brückner SlFw. 105.

M

mãcė 'Feurigkeit, Tapferkeit, Schärfe; (older & Biblical) Macht'—Ber. *moktĭ*. Cf. Brückner SlFw. 105.
macìs 'Schärfe, Strenge (z.B. von einem Getränk, vom Rettich); (ecclesiastical) Macht'—Ber. *moktĭ*. Cf. Brückner SlFw. 105.
magarỹczos plu. 'Leikauf, Vertragstrunk, Vertragsschmaus'—Ber. *mogoryč*. Cf. Brückner SlFw. 105.
magaus, magotis 'Ekel empfinden'—Ber. *moglivŭ*.
magenkà, magerkà 'Mützchen'—Ber. *madžárka*. Cf. Brückner SlFw. 105.
magoju, magoti 'nützen, taugen'; **pamagoju, pamagoti** 'helfen'—Ber. *mogǫ; W. magnus;* Boi. μῆχος (note). Cf. Brückner SlFw. 105 (note), 106.
magona 'Mohn'—Ber. *makŭ*. Cf. Bezz. LF. 138, Sommer 172.
magõszius 'wer leicht Ekel empfindet, beim Essen und Trinken wählerisch ist'—Ber. *moglivŭ*.
mailus 'eine Kleinigkeit, etwas Kleines'—(Ber. *mělŭkŭ*); W. *minus* 'kahlbäuchig'. Cf. Ness. 388*.
maĩnas 'Tausch, Wechsel, Veränderlichkeit, Wechselfall des Schicksals'—Uh. *máyate; K. Meineid; F. ga-mains;* B. I, 185. II, 1, 253.257.408; Ber. *měna;* W. *commūnis;* Boi. ἀμείβω (& Ntr.). Cf. Lesk. Nom. 361.
mainaũ, mainýti 'tauschen, wechseln, verwandeln'—Uh. *máyate;* F. *ga-mains;* Ber. *měna;* W. *commūnis*. Cf. Lesk. Abl. 278.
mainù adv. inst. sing. 'wechselweise'—B. II, 2, 717.
maĩstas 'Nahrung, Nahrungsmittel'—Ber. *město*. Cf. Lesk. Abl. 279.
máisza 'Heunetz'—see *máiszas*.

maĩszalas 'Gemisch, Gemengsel'—B. I, 190; Ber. *měšǫ*. See *maiszaũ* & Kur. DLWb. s.v. Gemisch; Lesk. Abl. 279.

máiszas, máisza 'ein grosser Sack, Getreidesack, Hopfensack; ein aus Schnüren gestricktes Heunetz'—Uh. *meşás;* B. II, 1, 165; Ber. *měchŭ*. Cf. Kur. DLWb. s.v. Sack; Lesk. Nom. 186, 222.

maiszaũ, maiszýti 'mischen, mengen; (Speise) umrühren, (Teig) einmachen; (einen Aufruhr, einen Auflauf) erregen'; **maiszaũs, maiszýtis** 'sich mischen, sich mengen; verwirrt werden, handgemein werden'—Uh. *miçrás;* [K. *mischen*]; B. I, 190.568. II, 3, 267; Ber. *měšǫ;* W. *misceo;* Boi. μίγνῦμι. Cf. Lesk. Abl. 279.

maiszokas 'Säckchen'—B. II, 1, 501. Cf. Lesk. Nom. 513.

maĩsztas, maiszta 'Verwirrung, Aufruhr, Auflauf'—K. *mischen;* B. II, 1, 410.635; Ber. *měšǫ*. Cf. Ness. 405[a]; Lesk. Abl. 279; Lesk. Nom. 534, 542.

maità 'Aas'—F. *ga-maiþs*. Cf. Lesk. Nom. 222.

maĩtėlis, meĩtėlis 'verschnittenes Mastschwein'—(Ber. 2. *mětǫ*). Cf. Ness. 405[b], Lesk. Nom. 466.

-maitinu, -maitinti—see *apmaitinu* 'ich verwunde'.

maitinù, maitìnti 'nähren, ernähren, (Vieh) überwintern'—Ber. *město*. Cf. Lesk. Abl. 279.

maiva 'Sumpf in einer Wiese'—(W. *mītis*).

majerõnai, meirõnai plu. 'Majoran'; **meirõnai laukìni** 'Quendel'—Ber. *majorán*. Cf. Brückner SlFw. 106.

maknỹs 'Stotterer'—B. I, 393. Cf. Lesk. Abl. 335.

makonė 'Pfütze'—Uh. *makarandas;* Ber. *mokrŭ*. Cf. Brückner SlFw. 106.

makstaũ, makstýti iter. 'flechten'—Ber. *mazgarĭ*. Cf. Bezz. LF. 138, Lesk. Abl. 364.

maksznà 'ledernes Futteral, Scheide'—(W. *māla*). Cf. Brückner SlFw. 107.

maldà 'Bitte, Gebet'; **maĩdą dũti** 'beten'—Ber. *modla*. Cf. Lesk. Nom. 208.

maldaũ, maldýti 'fortgesetzt bitten'—Ber. *modla.* Cf. Lesk. Abl. 335.
malinỹs 'Quirlstange'—see *milinỹs.*
málka 'Brennholz'—(Ber. *molka*).
malkanas 'hölzern'—B. II, 1, 268. Cf. Lesk. Nom. 384-5.
mal̃kas 'Schluck, einmaliger Zug beim Trinken'—Ber. *melko, molka.* Cf. Lesk. Nom. 175.
malmũ 'Nierenstein usw.'—see *melmũ.*
malnos plu. 'Hirse, Schwadengrütze, Manna'—Ber. *melnŭ;* W. *milium;* Boi. μελίνη. Cf. Lesk. Abl. 335, Lesk. Nom. 365.
malónė 'Gnade, Gunst'—(Uh. *máyas*); Ber. *milŭ;* W. *mītis,* (*melior*); Boi. μείλιχος.
malù, málti 'mahlen'—Uh. *mlâyati;* K. *mahlen;* F. *malan;* B. II, 3, 123.442; Ber. *melǫ;* W. *molo* (twice); Boi. 1. μύλη, (ἀλέω). Cf. Lesk. Abl. 335.
malūnas 'Mühle'—B. II, 1, 280; Ber. *melǫ.* Cf. Lesk. Nom. 397.
malūnininkas 'Müller'—B. II, 1, 616. Cf. Lesk. Nom. 520.
mal̃vinu, mal̃vinti 'abplagen, zahm machen' (z.B. ein Pferd)—(Ber. *mlava*); Boi. (Ntr.) ἀμαλός.
mãma 'Mama, Mutter'—B. I, 161; Ber. *mama;* W. 2. *mamma;* Boi. μάμμη. See *momà.*
mamìkė 'Mutter, Mütterchen'—Ber. *mama.* Cf. Kur. s.v. mãma.
mamýtė 'liebe traute Mutter, lieb Mütterchen'—B. II, 1, 677; Ber. *mama;* W. 2. *mamma;* Boi. μάμμη.
mamùžė 'Mutter, Mütterchen'—Ber. *mama.* Cf. Kur. s.v. mãma.
mán 'mir'—see *mánei.*
màna indeclinable poss. pron. 'mein'—Uh. *má-.* Cf. Kur. s.v.
mãnas poss. pron. 'mein'—B. II, 2, 403.405.406; W. *meus.* Cf. Kur. s.v.
manàsis poss. pron. 'der Meinige'—B. II, 2, 406. Cf. Kur. Gram. 982.

manaũ, manýti 'verstehen, denken'; **iszmanaũ, iszmanýti** 'verstehen, Einsicht haben'—Uh. *mányate;* B. I, 142.492. II, 3, 162.164.169.249; W. *memini, moneo.* Cf. Lesk. Abl. 336.

mañdagus 'geschickt, fein, treffend, anmutig, höflich, anständig, ehrbar'—W. *mundus.*

mándeliei plu. 'Mandeln (Frucht); (Ness. also) Lymphdrüsen in der Mundhöhle'—[K. *Mandel* 2]; Ber. *migdalŭ.* Cf. Kur. DLWb. s.v. Mandel, die; Ness. 382ᵇ; Prell. deutsch. Best. in den lett. Spr. 21.

mandras 'munter'—B. II, 1, 349.378 (twice); Boi. μανθάνω. See next & Lesk. Nom. 441.

mandrùs 'munter, übermütig, stolz'—Uh. *mandhātā́;* K. *munter;* F. *mundōn;* B. II, 1, 349.385..3, 374; W. *memini;* Boi. μανθάνω. Cf. Lesk. Nom. 441.

manè, manę̃s 1st pers. pron. gen. sing.—F. *meins;* B. II, 2, 416.427. Cf. Wied. 163, 164.

manę̀ 1st pers. pron. acc. sing. 'mich'—B. I, 357. II, 2, 413.427; W. *meus.* Cf. Wied. 163.

mánei, mán 1st pers. pron. dat. sing. 'mir'—Uh. *má-;* B. I, 21. II, 2, 418.427; Ber. *mene.* Cf. Wied. 163.

manę̃s pron. gen. 'meiner'—see *manè.*

mañgalis 'Wäschrolle, Mangel'—Ber. *mângan.* Cf. Prell. deutsch. Best. in den lett. Spr. 20.

mãno indeclinable gen. poss. pron. 'mein'—B. II, 2, 416.427. Cf. Wied. 163.

mañtelis 'Mantel'—Ber. *mantija.* Cf. Brückner SlFw. 15.

mãras 'Tod, Pest'; **maraĩ** plu. 'Pestzeit'—Uh. *maras;* B. II, 1, 152; W. *morbus, morior;* Boi. βροτός. Cf. Brückner SlFw. 106, Lesk. Abl. 336.

mãrės plu. 'Binnensee, Haff, Kurisches Haff; (Samog. also) Meer, Ostsee'—Uh. *maryā́dā;* K. *Meer;* F. *marei;* B. I, 448. II, 1, 222; W. *mare;* Boi. ἀμάρᾶ, χείμαρος. Cf. Bezz. LF. 139, Sommer 59.

márgas 'bunt, buntgestreift, gefleckt, sommersprossig'; **margaĩ** adv. 'bunt, zweifelhaft'—Uh. *markás, mṛgás;*

K. *Marke;* B. I, 376-7; Boi. ἀμορβός, μόρφνος (twice). Cf. Bezz. LF. 139; Geitler LS. 67; Lesk. Abl. 337.

maringas 'mörderisch'—B. II, 1, 509.510. Cf. MLG. III, 271; Lesk. Nom. 526.

markà 'Flachsröste; die Stelle, an der Flachs ins Wasser zum Erweichen eingelegt wird'—Ber. *morky.* Cf. Lesk. Abl. 337.

markaũ, markýti 'Flachs einweichen, rösten'—Uh. *marcáyati;* Ber. *morky, broĭi;* W. *marceo;* Boi. μαραίνω. Cf. Lesk. Abl. 337.

markstaũ, markstýti 'blinzeln, winken'—Ber. *morkŭ.* Cf. Lesk. Abl. 337.

marnas 'eitel, vergänglich'—Ber. *mara.* Cf. Brückner SlFw. 106.

mar̃szas 'das Vergessen'—Uh. *marṣas;* B. I, 432.786. Cf. Lesk. Abl. 337.

márszka 'grosses, dichtes Fischernetz, welches zwei Personen im Wasser ziehen; Netz, worauf in der Bade- und Brachstube Malz getrocknet wird; (Bezz. LF. 139) Handtuch (zum Abtrocknen)'—Ber. *merža.* Cf. MLG. I, 133.

marszkiniaĩ plu. tant. 'jackenartiges Hemd von feinem Leinen; Sonntagskleider, Wäsche, Zeug' (cf. Bezz. LF. 139)—Ber. *merža.* Cf. MLG. I, 133.

márszkonas, márszkonis 'leinen'—B. II, 1, 281.

martì 'Braut, junge Frau; Schwiegertochter, bes. Sohnesfrau, die im Hause der Schwiegereltern wohnt'—(Uh. *máryas*); K. *Marder;* F. *marzus,* (*brūþs*); B. II, 1, 218.219. 2, 124; W. *marītus;* Boi. μεῖραξ, (δάμαρ (note)). Cf. Ness. 384[b].

martuvė́, martvė́ 'Pest'—B. II, 1, 448. See *māras* & Lesk. Abl. 336, Lesk. Nom. 564.

marvà, mervà 'eine Art Bremse, Stechfliege'—Ber. *morvŭ.* Cf. Lesk. Nom. 346.

marva 'Mischmasch'—B. II, 1, 203. Cf. Brückner SlFw. 106, Lesk. Nom. 346, Geitler LS. 67.

-mas pres. pass. part. end., e.g. **vẽžamas** 'gefahren werdend' (*vežù* 'veho')—B. II, 1, 230.232. Cf. Wied. 195.

mastĕgůju, mastĕgůti (?) '(das Schwert) schwingen; unnütz herumfuchteln, gestikulieren'—(Boi. μαίομαι (note)). Cf. Prell. 278; Kur. DLWb. s.v. schwingen; Geitler LS. 96; BB. XXIV, 106; XXVI, 305; IF. XIX, 209. See *mostagůju*.

mąstis 'Erwägung, Nachdenken, Verstand'—F. *ansts;* B. II, 1, 437. Cf. Ness. 385[a]; Lesk. Abl. 336; Lesk. Nom. 551.

maszalaĩ plu. 'Mücken, Fliegen, (Mielcke) Ungeziefer'—Uh. *maçákas.* Cf. Lesk. Nom. 472.

mataũ, matýti 'sehen, schauen'—B. II, 1, 352; (Ber. 1. *mětą*); (W. *metus*); Boi. ματεύω.

matũju, matũti 'messen'—B. I, 172.489; Ber. *měra;* W. *mētior;* Boi. μῆτις. Cf. Prell. deutsch. Best. in den lett. Spr. 18.

mauda 'Sorge, Mühe'—(F. *af-mauiþs*); [Boi. μῦθος]. Cf. Lesk. Nom. 229.

máudau, máudyti trans. 'baden, untertauchen'—Uh. *mū́tram;* (W. *mulier*); Boi. μύδος, μιαίνω, ἀμύμων (note & Ntr.). Cf. Lesk. Abl. 303.

maudžù, maũsti 'schmerzen, sich grämen, sehnlich verlangen'—F. *maudjan;* Boi. μῦθος. Cf. Lesk. Abl. (Ntr.) 450.

máuju, máuti 'aufstreifen, anstreifen (z.B. einen Ring an den Finger)' (Boi. 'excursionner'?)—Uh. *mī́vati;* W. *moveo;* Boi. *ἀμεύομαι. Cf. Lesk. Abl. 303.

maukiù, maũkti 'glatt streifen, gleiten lassen, anstreifen, abstreifen; (MLG. I, 383) saufen; (Ness. 389[b]) betrügen, Unrecht tun'—Uh. *muñcáti;* B. II, 3, 397 (*maũksme*); W. *ēmungo.* Cf. Lesk. Abl. 303.

maumiu, maumti 'meckern, summen, brummen, brüllen'—Ber. *momą.* Cf. Lesk. Abl. 318.

maunùs 'heftig, grausam, streng, übermütig'—(Ber. *lěnŭ*). Cf. Lesk. Nom. 357.

mauróti (?) 'wühlen' (vom Maulwurf; vom Rindvieh, das Kornhaufen auseinanderwirft; vom Bullen, der Erde aufwirft); **iszmauróti** 'etwas auswühlen, mit den Hörnern aufscharren'—(Ber. *morvŭ*); (W. *formīca*). Cf. Geitler LS. 87; Bezz. LF. 140; Lesk. Abl. 303; BB. XXVI, 188.

máustau, máustyti 'baden'—Boi. μύδος. Cf. Lesk. Abl. 303.

mãzgas 1) 'Knoten, Fadenverschlingung'; 2) 'Bündchen, Blumenstrauss usw.'; 3) 'Auge einer Pflanze, Knospe' —K. *Masche;* B. I, 723.789; Ber. *mazgaŕi;* Boi. 1. μόσχος (thrice). Cf. Ness. 387[a], Lesk. Abl. 364.

mazgaũ, mazgýti 'stricken'—Ber. *mazgaŕi.* See prec. & Lesk. Abl. 364.

mazgóju, mazgóti 'waschen, spülen'—Uh. *májjati;* B. I, 723.735.789; W. *mergo.*

mãżas 'klein, gering'; adv. **mażaĩ, màż** 'wenig'—K. *mager;* B. II, 1, 561; (Ber. *mĕzinŭ*); (W. *macer*). Cf. Lesk. Abl. 373.

mażeñs—gen. sing. of **mażũ* 'Kleiner', q.v.

mażùkas 'Kleinerchen'—B. II, 1, 492.

***mażũ** 'Kleiner'; **ìsz mażeñs** 'von klein an, von Kindesbeinen an'—B. II, 1, 308. Cf. Lesk. Abl. 373.

meczus 'Schwert'—Ber. *mečĭ.* Cf. Brückner SlFw. 107.

mẽdis 'Baum; Stück Holz'—Uh. *mádhyas;* Ber. *meďa,* (*grana*); W. *medius,* (*mēta*). Cf. Lesk. Nom. 299.

medùs 'Honig'—Uh. *mádhu;* K. *Met;* (F. *miliþ*); B. I, 104.374.523. II, 1, 181; Ber. *medŭ;* Boi. μέθυ. Cf. Lesk. Abl. 335.

medũtas 'voll Honig, honigreich, mit Honig versüsst'—B. II, 1, 407. Cf. Lesk. Nom. 561.

medvynis Old Lith. 'Weinstock'—B. II, 1, 101. Cf. Bezz. BGLS. 106. Notice also the more modern and usual cmpd. *výnmedis:* Kur. 506[a]; Ness. 80[b], 390[b].

mẽgas 'Schlaf'—Uh. *meghás;* Ber. *migŭ;* W. *mico.* Cf. Lesk. Abl. 278.

mĕgmi 'ich gefalle'—see *mĕgstu.*

mëgmì 'ich schlafe'—see *mëgù, mëgóti.*
mègsti 'knoten, stricken'—inf. of *mezgù,* q.v.
mḗgstu (mḗgmi), mḗgti 'gefallen'—(F. *mḗgs*); W. *macto* 2 (twice); Boi. περιημεκτεῖν. Cf. Lesk. Abl. 371.
mëgù (mëgmì), mëgóti 'schlafen'—Uh. *meghás;* Ber. *migŭ.* See *-mingù* & Lesk. Abl. 278.
-mëgù 'ich schlafe ein'—see *-mingù.*
mėgus 'vergnügungssüchtig, wollüstig, wohlgefällig'—W. *macto* 2. Cf. Lesk. Nom. 249.
méilė 'Liebe'—Uh. *máyas;* Ber. *milŭ;* W. *mītis;* Boi. μείλιχος. Cf. Lesk. Abl. 278.
meilùs 'liebreich, gütig'—Ber. *milŭ.* See prec.
meirõnai 'Majoran'—see *majerõnai.*
meĩtėlis 'verschnittenes Mastschwein'—see *maĩtėlis.*
mekenù, mekénti 'meckern, stammeln'—Uh. *makamakā-yate;* B. I, 393; Ber. *mekajǫ* 1; W. *miccio;* Boi. μηκᾶσθαι. Cf. Lesk. Abl. 335.
meknóju, meknóti id.—Ber. *mekajǫ* 1. See prec.
melãgis 'Lügner'—B. II, 1, 511. See next.
mẽlas, usually plu. melaĩ 'Lüge' (B. 'Sünde'; Boi. 'mensonge, péché')—B. II, 1, 524.541; W. *malus;* Boi. βλάσφημος, μέλε[σ]ος. Cf. Lesk. Abl. 335.
mẽlas 'lieb, teuer, angenehm'—Uh. 2. *máyas;* B. II, 2, 563-4; Ber. *milŭ;* W. *mītis;* Boi. μείλιχος. Cf. Lesk. Abl. 278.
mẽlas (Kur. in brackets mėlas) 'Gips'—(Ber. *mělŭ*). Cf. Brückner SlFw. 107 (s.v. melus).
meldžù, melsti 'bitten, beten'; meldžiûs, melstis 'beten'—Ber. *modla.* Cf. Lesk. Abl. 335.
mẽlės (Kur., Uh., Ber., W.), mẽlės (Schleicher, Lesk., Sommer) plu. 'Hefen'—Uh. *málam;* Ber. *mělŭkŭ;* W. *mulleus.* Cf. Kur. s.v.; Kur. DLWb. s.v. Bodensatz, Hefe; Schleicher LSpr. II, 290; Lesk. Nom. 275; Sommer 157.
mėlyna 'livor'—Ber.. *malina.* Cf. Lesk. Nom. 411 & *mėlynė.*

mẽlynas 'blau, dunkelblau, bleifarbig'—Uh. *malinás;* F. *mēl;* B. I, 424; Ber. *malina;* W. *mulleus;* Boi. μέλᾱς. Cf. Lesk. Abl. 335; Lesk. Nom. 411; Bezz. LF. 141.

mẽlynė 'blauer Fleck oder Striemen am Körper' (Folge eines Schlages)—F. *mēl.* See prec. & Kur. s.v., Ness. 392[b].

mẽlys plu. 'blauer Farbstoff (Kur., Lalis); Färberwaid, Isatis tinctoria (Ness. 392[b])'—F. *mēl;* Boi. μέλᾱς. Cf. Lesk. Abl. 335.

melmũ, malmũ 'Nierenstein, Steinkrankheit; Rückgrat, Kreuz des Körpers'; **mélmens, mélmenys** plu. 'Lenden, das an den Nieren liegende Fleisch'—Uh. *mlā́y-ati;* F. *malma;* B. II, 1, 238.247; (Ber. *molmosŭ*); W. *molo,* (*mon̄le*); Boi. 1. μύλη, (μάννος). Cf. Ness. 392-393; Kur. 241, 249; Lalis s.v.; Bezz. BGLS. 300; Lesk. Abl. 335; Lesk. Nom. 417.

mélžu (Ness., Kur. also **milžu**), **mìlžti** (B. etc. **mílszti**) 'melken; streicheln; (einen Menschen) durch Liebkosungen gewinnen; (ein Tier) bändigen'—Uh. *mr̥játi, mr̥ṣṭás;* K. (cf. 8th ed.) *melken;* F. *miluks;* B. I, 117.445.482.554. II, 1, 571. 3, 99.115.[119].123.398. 445; W. *mulgeo;* Boi. ἀμέλγω. Cf. Ness. 400[b], Lesk. Abl. 335.

memė 'Mama, Mutter'—W. 2. *mamma;* Boi. μάμμη. See *māma* & Ness. 393[a].

menas 'Verständnis, Geschicklichkeit, Meisterschaft'—B. II, 1, 517. 2, 85.93.148. Cf. Ness. 381[a] & Lesk. Abl. 336, Lesk. Nom. 162.

mẽnas 'Mond'—B. II, 1, 526; Boi. μήν. Cf. Bezz. BGLS. 300, LBLV. 301, 338.

méndrė 'Rohr'—B. I, 852. Cf. Sommer 174.

ménesẽlis 'Mondchen, (Kur.) der liebe Mond'—B. II, 1, 376.

mẽnesëna (naktìs) 'mondhelle (Nacht)', **mẽnesëna** 'Mondschein'—B. II, 1, 278. .Cf. Ness. 393[a], Lesk. Nom. 412.

mė́nesis 'Monat, Mond'. On the double meaning cf. Ness. 393[a]; Kur. s.v.; Lesk. Nom. 592; Lalis s.v.—Uh. 1. *mā́s;* K. *Mond;* B. II, 1, 298.427.525.526; Ber. *mě̄sę̄cĭ;* W. *mensis;* Boi. μήν (twice).

meñkas 'gering, unbedeutend, klein, schwach, schlecht'—Uh. *mácate,* (*manā́k*); B. II, 1, 477; W. *māceria,* (1. *minor*); Boi. μανός. Cf. Lesk. Nom. 507.

menkė 'Dorsch, Gadus callarias'—Boi. μαίνη. Cf. Brückner SlFw. 205, Sommer 129.

menkùtis 'winzig'—B. II, 1, 677. See *meñkas* & Lesk. Nom. 576, Kur. DLWb. s.v. winzig.

menta (?) 'Geist, Seele'—Ber. *-mętĭ;* W. *mens.* Cf. Geitler LS. 96, Lesk. Nom. 542.

mentẽ 'Spatel'—Ber. *mętǫ.* Cf. Ness. 393[b]; Kur. s.v.; Kur. DLWb. s.v. Spatel; Lesk. Nom. 266.

meñtė 'Schulterblatt'—Ber. *mętǫ.* Cf. Lesk. Nom. 266.

mentùris masc., **mentùrė** fem. 'Quirl, Rührstock; Ackerwinde, Convolvulus arvensis'—Uh. *mathnā́ti;* B. I, 387.522.716. II, 1, 358. 3, 295; Ber. *mętǫ;* W. *mamphur;* (Boi. μόθος). Cf. Lesk. Nom. 449.

menù, miñti 'gedenken, in Gedächtnis haben, erraten, ermahnen'; **menù, minė́ti** 'gedenken, erwähnen'; Old Lith. **miniù, minė́ti** 'gedenken'—Uh. *mánati, mányate;* F. *munan;* B. I, 342.398.399.492. II, 1, 395.430.441. 568. 3, 134.136.147.170.386.396.418.441; W. *memini, minīscitur;* Boi. μαίνομαι (twice), μέμονα, αὐτόματος. Cf. Ness. 380[b]; Bezz. BGLS. 301; Donalitius 231; Lesk. Abl. 335-6. See *miñtas.*

mėnulis 'Mondchen'—B. II, 1, 676. Cf. Lesk. Nom. 492.

mė́nung Samog. 'Mond'—B. II, 2, 126. Cf. Kur. Gram. 731.

mė́nů 'Mond, Monat'—Uh. 1. *mā́s;* K. *Mond;* F. *mēna;* B. I, 132. [II, 2, 128]; Ber. *mě̄sę̄cĭ;* W. *mensis;* Boi. μήν. Cf. Ness. s.v. Menesis, 393[a]; Kur. s.v.; Lalis s.v.; Lesk. Nom. 592; Wied. 117.

mërà 'Mass, Masshalten, Mässigung, (Szyr.) Mittelmässigkeit'—K. *Mal;* Ber. *měra.* Cf. Brückner SlFw. 107 (& note).

mércas 'März'—Ber. *martiji.* Cf. Brückner SlFw. 199.

mérdžu (mérdmi), mérdėti 'sterben, im Sterben liegen'—B. II, 3, 379; W. *morior;* Boi. *βροτός.* Cf. Kur. Gram. 1199, Lesk. Abl. 336. See *mìrsztu, mir̃ti.*

mergà 'Mädchen, Dienstmädchen, Jungfrau, Magd, Braut'—Uh. *mr̥gás;* W. *marītus;* Boi. *μεῖραξ, ἀμορβός.* Cf. Lesk. Nom. 200.

mergẽlė 'Mädchen' (Kur.: "gilt für feiner als *mergà*"; Ness. 394*: "keineswegs in verächtlichem Sinne")—B. II, 1, 376.

mergelẽlė dimin. 'Mädchen'—B. II, 1, 377 (read S. 376 for S. 367). Cf. Ness. 394*.

mergìkė dimin. 'kleines Mädchen'—B. II, 1, 490. Cf. Kur. s.v. mergà; Kur. DLWb. s.v. Mädchen; Lesk. Nom. 511.

merginà 'starkes, grosses Mädchen' (Kur.: "in manchen Gegenden das was *mergà,* 'Mädchen' ")—B. II, 1, 681. Cf. Lesk. Nom. 404.

mẽryju, mẽryti (Kur. mêr-) 'messen; zielen (z.B. mit der Flinte)'—[K. *Mal*]; Ber. *měra.* Cf. Ness. 394*, Brückner SlFw. 107.

merkiù, mer̃kti 'einweichen, ins Wasser tauchen' (z.B. Flachs, Kleider)—Ber. *morky.* Cf. Lesk. Abl. 337.

mérkiu, mérkti 'die Augenlider schliessen, mit den Augen winken, einem zublinzeln'—Uh. *márīciṣ, markás;* F. *bralv, maurgins;* B. I, 383. II, 3, 241.375; Ber. *morkŭ,* (*brěskŭ* 1); Boi. *ἀμαρύσσω, μόρφνος.* Cf. Lesk. Abl. 337.

mẽrnas 'mässig, gross, gering, masshaltend, (von Getränken) schwach'—[K. *Mal*]; Ber. *měra.* Cf. Brückner SlFw. 107.

mervà 'Bremse'—see *marvà.*

mẽs nom. plu. 'wir'—B. II, 2, 386.389.412.427; W. *meus.* Cf. Kur. Gram. 834 ff.; Wied. 163-4; Geitler LS. 96.

mėsà 'Fleisch' (cf. Ness. 395*, Kur. s.v.)—Uh. 2. *mā̆s;* F.

mimz; B. I, 347.389.783; Ber. *męso;* W. *membrum;* Boi. μηρός. Cf. Wied. s.v., Bezz. LF. 141.

mėsẽdis (Kur. & Lesk. **mës-**) 'Fleischfresser'—B. II, 1, 144; Ber. *medvědĭ.* Cf. Kur. 254*, Lesk. Nom. 297.

mẽstas 'Stadt'—Ber. *město.* Cf. Brückner SlFw. 108.

mèsti 'werfen'—inf. of *metù,* q.v.

mëszczonìs 'Städter, Bürger'—Ber. *město.* Cf. Brückner SlFw. 108.

meszkà 'Bär' (von beiden Geschlechtern gebraucht)—Ber. *medvědĭ.* Cf. Brückner SlFw. 108.

mẽszkinas 'männlicher Bär'—B. II, 1, 601; Ber. *medvědĭ.* Cf. Brückner SlFw. 108.

meszkiũju, meszkiũti 'wie ein Bär gehen, langsam gehen'—Ber. *medvědĭ.* Cf. Brückner SlFw. 108.

mėtà, plu. **mẽtos** 'Minze, Krauseminze, Mentha crispa'—Ber. *męta.* Cf. Brückner SlFw. 108.

mẽtas, plu. **mẽtai** 'Jahreszeit, Jahr, Zeit'—B. I, 530; Ber. *měra;* W. *mētior;* Boi. μῆτις. Cf. Lesk. Nom. 160.

(**száukszto**) **mẽtas** '(Löffel) voll'—Ber. *metǫ* 1. Cf. Ness. 396[b]; Kur. 252, 422; Brückner SlFw. 108 (& note); Lesk. Nom. 160; Trautmann Die altpreussischen Sprachdenkmäler 378.

mêtas 'Pfahl, Zaunpfahl, Stange'—Ber. *město;* W. *mēta.* Cf. Lesk. Abl. 278, Lesk. Nom. 535-6.

mẽtau, mẽtyti iter. 'fortgesetzt werfen, hin und her werfen, (Ness. 397[a] also) prahlen'—B. II, 3, 169; Ber. *mětajǫ.* Cf. Lesk. Abl. 364. See *metù.*

metelnykas dial. 'Gaukler, Seiltänzer'—B. II, 1, 498. Cf. Ness. 396[b], Brückner SlFw. 108.

mẽtmens plu. 'Aufzug des Gewebes'—B. II, 1, 243. Cf. Lesk. Nom. 417, [Lesk. Abl. 364].

metra 'Gespenst, Geist'—W. *metus.*

metù, mèsti 'werfen; (in der Weberei) das Garn aufbringen, scheren'; **pàmetu, pamèsti** 'hinwerfen, wegwerfen, fallen lassen, verlieren'—Uh. *átati;* (K. *meiden*); B. I, 719. II, 3, 136.162.169; Ber. *metǫ* 1; (W. *metella,* *meto, mitto*); (Boi. ἄμοτος, μίτος: "Les mots baltiques . . .", μοτός). Cf. Lesk. Abl. 364.

mezgà 'Strickerin'—B. II, 2, 98. See next.

mezgù, mègsti 'Knoten knüpfen, stricken (bes. Netze)'. Ness. 387* also: "Augen, Knospen bekommen (von Bäumen)". See *mãzgas*.—K. *Masche;* B. I, 723.789. 868; Ber. *mazgaři;* (Boi. 1. μόσχος). Cf. Lesk. Abl. 364.

mëžiu, mëžti; (Kur. also) **mëžiu, mëszti** (?) 'Dünger machen, Dünger bearbeiten, misten, Mist fahren, Mist laden'—Uh. *méhati;* K. *Mist;* F. *maihstus;* (W. *mingo*). Cf. Lesk. Abl. 279, 371.

mėžlaĩ (Kur. **mëszlaĩ**) plu. 'Mist, Mistfuhre, Zeit des Mistfahrens'—K. *Mist.* Cf. Schleicher LSpr. II, 290; Lesk. Abl. 279, 371; Lesk. Nom. 451.

mėžlýnas (Kur. **mëszlynas**) 'Misthaufen, Miststätte'—B. II, 1, 623. Cf. Lesk. Nom. 409.

męžù, mĩžti (mĩszti) 'harnen'—Uh. *méhati;* K. *Mist;* F. *maihstus;* B. II, 3, [118].275.[279].284.285.321.443. 492; Ber. *mižǫ;* W. *mingo;* Boi. ὀμῑχεῖν. Cf. Schleicher LSpr. I, 113. 2, II, 290; Lesk. Abl. 279, 398, 408.

mi Old Lith. 'mir; mich'—B. I, 938.985. II, 2, 383.394. 408.427; Ber. *mene;* W. *meus.* Cf. Kur. Gram. 1150, Wied. 164.

midùs 'Met'—Uh. *mádhu;* K. *Met;* (E. *miliþ*); Ber. *medŭ;* Boi. μέθυ. Cf. Bezz. BGLS. 301; Trautmann Die altpreussischen Sprachdenkmäler 376; Lesk. Abl. 335.

migdala 'Mandelbaum, Mandel'—Ber. *migdalŭ.* Cf. Brückner SlFw. 108.

mìgdaliei plu. 'Mandeln'—Ber. *migdalŭ.* Cf. Kur. DLWb. s.v. Mandel, die.

miglà, myglà 'Nebel'—Uh. *meghás;* K. *Mist;* B. I, 449.573. 583. II, 1, 362; W. *mingo;* Boi. ὀμίχλη. Cf. Kur. DLWb. s.v. Nebel; Schleicher LSpr. II, 290; Wied. s.v.; Lesk. Nom. 454; Sommer 182-3.

miglótas (Kur. **migliū́tas**) 'nebelig, trübe'—B. II, 1, 406. Cf. Ness. 399*, Lesk. Nom. 561.

-mìgti 'einschlafen'—inf. of *-mingù,* q.v.

mikenù, mikénti South Lith. 'meckern, stottern'—B. I, 393. See *mekenù* & Lesk. Abl. 335.

miklùs (Mielcke, Ness. 399* **myklus**) 'zäh (von Holz, das sich nicht spalten lässt); fest, derb, stark, kräftig, rüstig'. Cf. Lalis s.v.—Ber. *mokrŭ* (read 'zäh' after *miklùs* and Leskien Nom. 468 for 469).

mìlas 'das grobe Wollentuch, von Bauern zu Hause gewebt' (das feine Fabriktuch: *gelumbė̃*)—(W. *floccus*); Boi. μαλλός. Cf. Kur. s.v.; MLG. I, 229; Lesk. Nom. 164.

mildė̃snis 'frömmer'—B. II, 1, 553. Cf. Wied. 165.

mildus 'fromm, gottergeben'—B. I, 456. II, 1, 176; Ber. *modla;* W. *mollis.* Cf. Lesk. Abl. 335.

mìlyju, mìlyti 'verfehlen, sich irren'—(W. *malus*); Boi. ἀμβλίσκω, (μέλε[σ]ος). Cf. Brückner SlFw. 108 (& note).

milinỹs, malinỹs "der Stock in der Handmühle, der, oben an der Zimmerdecke befestigt, von der Hand des Mahlenden geführt, den oberen Stein der Handmühle dreht" (Kur.); 'Quirlstange'—Ber. *melnŭ;* W. *molo;* Boi. 1. μύλη. Cf. Lesk. Abl. 335.

mýlista 'Huld, Gnade, Leutseligkeit, Bewirtung'; **jõ mýlista, júsu mýlista** 'Euer Gnaden'—Ber. *milŭ.* Cf. Brückner SlFw. 108 (& note). See *tàmista.*

mýliu, mylė́ti 'lieben, bewirten'—W. *mītis;* Ber. *milŭ.* Cf. Lesk. Abl. 278, 412, 413.

-mìlstu, -mìlti—see *susimìlstu* 'ich erbarme mich'.

mílszti (B.) 'melken'—see *mélžu.*

mìlszti, mìlsztis (?) inf. 'sich zusammenziehen' (vom Gewitter); **jaũ pràded mìlszti(s)** 'das Gewitter fängt an sich zusammenzuziehen'; **jaũ mìlszt** 'der Gewitterregen fängt schon an'—Ber. *melstĭ;* Boi. ἀμολγῷ. Cf. Bezz. LF. 142, Lesk. Abl. 335.

milsztuvẽ 'Melkeimer'—Ber. *molstŭ.* Cf. Lesk. Abl. 335, Lesk. Nom. 566.
mìltai (B., W. **míltai**) plu. tant. 'Mehl'—K. *Mehl;* F. *mulda;* B. I, 475.492. II, 3, 442; Ber. *melę;* W. *molo,* (*maltas*); Boi. I. μύλη. Cf. Lesk. Abl. 335.
mylùs 'lieb, lieblich, liebenswürdig, freundlich; verliebt, buhlerisch'—Ber. *milŭ;* Boi. μείλιχος. Cf. Lesk. Abl. 278, Brückner SlFw. 108.
mìlżtas pret. pass. part. of **mélżu,** q.v., 'gemolken'—Uh. *mr̥ṣṭás;* W. *mulgeo.*
milżu, mìlżti 'melken'—see *mélżu.*
minëti 'gedenken, erwähnen'—see *menù* and *miniù.*
minëtinas 'memorandus'—B. II, 1, 269. See prec.
-mingù (**-mëgù**), **-mìgti** 'einschlafen'—Uh. *meghás;* Ber. *migŭ;* W. *mico.* Cf. Lesk. Abl. 278.
mìniava 'Filzgras; eine mit solchem Gras bewachsene Wiese'—Boi. μνίον. Cf. Lesk. Nom. 349.
minyczkà 'Nonne'—Ber. *monachŭ.* Cf. Kur. s.v. & 259[a]; Kur. Gram. 126; Brückner SlFw. 108-9.
minìkas 'Treter, Flachsbrecher'; **linũ minìkas** 'Flachsbrecher'; **ũdu minìkas** 'Gerber'—B. II, 1, 490. See *minù* & Lesk. Nom. 510.
minỹkas 'Mönch'—Ber. *monachŭ.* Cf. Kur. Gram. 126, Brückner SlFw. 108-9.
miniù, minëti Old Lith. 'gedenken'—see *menù.*
mìnkau, mìnkyti 'kneten'—Uh. *mácate;* K. *mengen;* Ber. *mękŭkŭ;* W. *māceria;* Boi. μάσσω, (I. ἀκτή). Cf. Lesk. Abl. 336.
mìnklas 'Teig'—K. *mengen;* Ber. *mękŭkŭ.* See prec. & Lesk. Nom. 451.
mìnksztas 'weich, locker, mürbe'—Uh. *mácate;* Ber. *mękŭkŭ;* W. *māceria;* Boi. μάσσω. Cf. Lesk. Abl. 336.
mĩntas 'gedacht' pret. pass. part. of **menù, mĩnti,** q.v.—B. I, 342.398. II, 1, 395; Boi. αὐτόματος.
mĩnti 'gedenken'—inf. of *menù,* q.v.
mìnti 'treten'—inf. of *minù,* q.v.

mintù, mìsti 'sich nähren' (cf. Ness. 405[a-b])—Ber. *město.* Cf. Lesk. Abl. 279.

minù, mìnti 'treten'; **linùs mìnti** 'Flachs brechen'—Uh. *carmamnâs;* Ber. *gumĭno;* (W. *mino, mons*); Boi. μάτεισαι, μάσσω, μνίον. Cf. Lesk. Abl. 336.

mìrgu, mirgĕti 'flimmern, bunt vor den Augen sein'—Uh. *markás, mṛgás;* F. *maurgins;* Boi. ἀμορβός, μόρφνος (twice). Cf. Lesk. Abl. 337.

myrius 'Sterben, Tod'—B. II, 1, 224. 225.613.630. 2, 101. Cf. Lesk. Nom. 319.

mirklẽ 'Blinzlerin'—B. II, 1, 221.

mirklỹs 'Blinzler'—B. II, 1, 617. 3, 241; Boi. μόρφνος.

mìrksiu, mirksĕti (F. **mírksiu**) 'blinzeln'—F. *bralv;* Boi. ἀμαρύσσω, μόρφνος. Cf. Lesk. Abl. 337. See *mérkiu.*

mìrksnioju, mìrksnioti (B. **mírk-**) 'blinzeln'—B. II, 3, 215. See next.

mìrksnis 'Blick, Wink'; **akẽs mìrksnis** 'Augenblick'—Boi. ἀμαρύσσω. Cf. Lesk. Abl. 337.

mirkstù, mir̃kti 'eingeweicht werden, nass sein'—Uh. *marcáyati;* Ber. *morky, broĭi;* W. *marceo;* Boi. μαραίνω. Cf. Lesk. Abl. 337.

mìrsztu, mir̃ti (B. **mírsztu**) 'sterben; (dial.) Epilepsie bekommen'—Uh. *márate;* K. *Mord;* F. *maurþr;* B. I, 386.455.473; II, 1, 568. 3, 371 (note).441.492; W. *morior;* Boi. βροτός. Cf. Ness. 402[a], Lesk. Abl. 336.

mirsztù, mir̃szti 'vergessen'—Uh. *mṛṣyate;* (F. *marzjan*); B. I, 472; Boi. ἁμαρτάνω. Cf. Lesk. Abl. 337.

mir̃ti 'sterben'—inf. of *mìrsztu,* q.v.

mirtis 'das Sterben, Tod'—Uh. *mṛtiṣ;* K. *Mord;* F. *maurþr;* B. I, 342.455. II, 1, 430; W. *morior;* Boi. βροτός. Cf. Lesk. Abl. 336, Lesk. Nom. 548.

mìsti 'sich nähren'—inf. of *mintù,* q.v.

mìstras 'Meister, Handwerksmeister'—Ber. *magistrŭ.* Cf. Brückner SlFw. 109.

mischlumas (miszlumas) Old Lith. 'Vermischung, Verwirrung'—W. *misceo;* Boi. μίγνυμι. Cf. Bezz. BGLS. 302.

miszrai adv. 'vermischt'—B. II, 1, 348. Cf. Lesk. Nom. 441.

miszriù adv. 'durcheinander'—Ber. *měšǫ.* Cf. Lesk. Abl. 279, Lesk. Nom. 441.

mỹszti (**mỹžti**) 'harnen'—see *męžù.*

misztù, mìszti 'sich mischen'; pret. **miszaũ; sumisztù, sumìszti** 'sich durcheinander mengen, in Verwirrung geraten'—Uh. *miçrás;* K. *mischen;* B. II, 3, 352.360; Ber. *měšǫ;* W. *misceo;* Boi. μίγνυμι. Cf. Lesk. Abl. 278.

mita "der Garnflügel: ein kleines Brettchen, das mit einer Schnur am Ende des Netzsackes befestigt ist und durch seine Lage auf dem Wasser die Stelle des Netzes anzeigt; ein Stecken zum Netzstricken" (Kur.)—W. *mēta;* (Boi. μίτος: "Les mots baltiques. . ."). Cf. Ness. 406[a], Lesk. Nom. 219.

mỹžalaĩ (Ber., Wied. **myžalaĩ**) plu. tant. 'Harn'—Uh. *méhati;* F. *maihstus;* B. I, 551-2. II, 3, 279; Ber. *mižǫ;* W. *mingo.* Cf. Lesk. Abl. 279, Lesk. Nom. 475.

mìžia 'Pisserin; cunnus (bei Tieren und Menschen)'—B. II, 3, 275. See *męžù* & Lesk. Abl. 279, Lesk. Nom. 322.

mnyczkà 'Nonne'—Ber. *monachŭ.* Cf. Kur. s.v., Brückner SlFw. 109.

mnỹkas 'Mönch'—Ber. *monachŭ.* Cf. Brückner SlFw. 109.

mogilà (Ness. 406[b]: "in alten Urkunden und Verordnungen") 'Kirchhof, Dorfkirchhof'—Ber. *mogyla.* Cf. Brückner SlFw. 109 (& note).

mojas 'Mai'—see *mojus.*

móju, móti 'winken, zuwinken, zunicken, durch Winken ein Zeichen, einen Auftrag geben'—B. II, 1, 545; Ber. *majǫ* I; Boi. μηνύω. Cf. Lesk. Abl. 377.

mojus, mojas 'Mai'—Ber. *majĭ.* Cf. Brückner SlFw. 109.

mojũju, mojũti 'fortgesetzt winken, nicken; schwingen, schwenken; drohen; mit dem Schwanze wedeln' (cf.

Ness. 406[b]; Kur. s.v.; Lalis s.v.)—Ber. *maję* 1. See *móju*.

mõkesnis 'Zahlung, Abgabe'—B. II, 1, 289 (read 327, b, δ for 327, b, γ). Cf. Bezz. LF. 206. See next.

mõkestis id.—B. II, 1, 439. Cf. Lesk. Abl. 377.

mókslas 'Lehre, Lehrstoff, Unterricht, Lernen, Studium, Kenntnis, Wissenschaft, Kirchenlehre'—B. II, 1, 373. See *mókstu*.

mokslùs 'gelehrig, gelehrt'—B. II, 1, 385. See prec.

mókstu, mókti 'erlernen'—(W. *macer*). See next.

móku, mokė́ti 'können, verstehen; vermögend sein, imstande sein; zahlen'—B. I, 546; (W. *macer*); (Boi. μακρός). Cf. Lesk. Abl. 377.

mólinas 'lehmig, voll Lehm, mit Lehm beschmutzt'—B. II, 1, 272.

mólis 'Lehm'—Uh. *málam, mālam;* Ber. *malina,* (*mělŭ*); W. *mulleus.* Cf. Lesk. Abl. 335.

moliū̃gas 'fahl, gelblich' (von Gänsen); **moliūgà žąsìs** 'rotgelbe Gans'—B. II, 1, 511. Cf. Ness. 408[a]; Kur. DLWb. s.v. rothgelb; Lesk. Nom. 526.

momà 'Mama, Mutter'—Uh. *māmas;* K. *Muhme;* B. II, 1, 127; Ber. *mama;* W. 2. *mamma;* Boi. μάμμη.

mõnai plu. 'Gaukelei, Zauberei'—Ber. *manŭ;* (W. *manticulor*); Boi. μάτην. Cf. Brückner SlFw. 109.

mõnyju, mõnyti 'verblenden, zaubern'—Ber. *manŭ.* Cf. Brückner SlFw. 109.

mõras 'Maulbeere'—W. *mōrum;* Boi. μόρον.

morczus 'März'—Ber. *martijĭ.* Cf. Brückner SlFw. 110.

mostagûju, mostagûti (?) 'herumfuchteln, hantieren, gestikulieren'—Ber. *machŭ.* Cf. Bezz. LF. 143; Geitler LS. 96; BB. XXIV, 106; XXVI, 306; Prell. 278; IF. XIX, 209; Boi. 601 (note). See *mastė̃gūju.*

mostìs 'Salbe'—Ber. *mastĭ.* Cf. Brückner SlFw. 110.

mosū̃ju, mosū̃ti 'schwenken, schwingen, ausholen'—Ber. *machŭ;* (Boi. μαίομαι (note)). Cf. IF. XIX, 209.

motė̃ (mótė), gen. sing. **moter̃s**, 'Weib, Ehefrau'—Uh.

mātā; K. *Mutter* 1; B. I, 115.129.131.163.169.342. 424.426.486. II, 1, 333. 2, 127.297; Ber. *mati;* W. *māter;* Boi. μήτηρ. Cf. Donalitius 234; Wied. 111, 112, 114; Lesk. Nom. 433.

moterìszkė 'Frauenzimmer, Weib, Ehefrau'—Ber. *mati.* Cf. Sommer 136.

mótyna 'Mutter'—Uh. *mātā;* K. *Mutter* 1; Ber. *mati;* W. *māter.*

motynė̃lė 'Mütterchen'—B. II, 1, 370. Cf. Ness. 409[b], Wied. s.v.

motnė 'Sack am Fischnetz'—Ber. *matajǫ.* Cf. Brückner SlFw. 110.

mozóju, mozóti (?) 'womit hin und her fechten, wedeln, schwenken'—Ber. *machŭ;* (Boi. μαίομαι (note)). Cf. Kur. s.v.; Prell. 278; IF. XIX, 209.

mūdrùs (B., Lesk. **mudrùs**) 'munter'—B. I, 364. See *mundrùs* & Lesk. Nom. 441, Brückner SlFw. 110.

mùdu 'wir beide'—B. II, 2, 386.412.

mukti (?) inf. 'entfliehen, entwischen'—B. I, 111. II, 1, 430.432; W. *ēmungo.* Cf. Geitler LS. 96, Lesk. Abl. 303.

mùlkis (F., B., Boi. **múlkis**) 'Einfältiger, Tropf'—F. *untila-malsks;* B. I, 474.475. II, 1, 479; Boi. μάλκη, (βλάξ (note)). Cf. Geitler LS. 96, Lesk. Nom. 296.

mulvas 'rötlich, gelblich' (bes. von Gänsen)—B. II, 1, 202; W. *mulleus* (twice); Boi. μελάς. Cf. Lesk. Nom. 345.

mul̃vė 'Schlamm, Morast, Sumpf, Rotstelle im Wege'—Uh. *málam;* B. I, 454; W. *mulleus;* Boi. μέλας. Cf. Ness. 410[a], Lesk. Nom. 349.

mul̃vyju, mul̃vyti 'mit Schlamm und Morast beschmieren, besudeln'—W. *mulleus;* Boi. μέλας.

mulvyju, mulvyti 'abplagen, zahm machen' (z.B. ein Pferd)—Boi. (Ntr.) ἀμαλός. Cf. Ness. 410[a].

mul̃vinas 'mit Schlamm bedeckt, beschmutzt (Kur.); sumpfig, moderig (Ness. 410[a])'—B. II, 1, 664. Cf. Lesk. Nom. 400.

mul̃vinu, mul̃vinti 'mit Schlamm und Morast beschmieren, besudeln'—W. *mulleus;* Boi. μέλᾱς.

mulvinu, mulvinti 'abplagen, zahm machen' (z.B. ein Pferd)—Boi. (Ntr.) ἀμαλός. Cf. Ness. 410ᵃ.

mundrùs 'munter, frisch, mutig'—K. *munter;* B. I, 364; W. *memini.* See *mandrùs* & Lesk. Nom. 441, Brückner SlFw. 110.

mùrdau, mùrdyti 'rütteln (z.B. ein Mass, um es zu füllen), schütteln (z.B. etwas im Wasser), einstopfen, einstampfen, mit den Füssen festtreten (z.B. die Garben in der Scheune), (die Wäsche) tüchtig rütteln, hart waschen, einweichen, eintauchen, besudeln' — Boi. βράσσω. Cf. Ness. 410ᵇ; Kur. s.v.; Lesk. Abl. 303.

murkszlenù, murkszlénti; mùrkszlinu, mùrkszlinti 'mit dem Schall *mùrkszt* Flüssigkeiten behandeln, patschen, sudeln, mit zu wenig Wasser waschen, beschmieren'—Boi. μορύσσω. Cf. Kur. s.v.; IF. XIII, 174, 201.

murmenù, murménti 'murmeln'—see *murmlenù.*

mùrmiu, murmė́ti (B. **múrmiu**) 'murren, brummen, murmeln, knurren'—Uh. *marmaras;* B. II, 1, 47; W. *fremo;* Boi. μορμύρω.

murmlenù, murmlénti; murmenù, murménti 'murmeln, murren'—Uh. *marmaras;* B. I, 453; W. *fremo;* Boi. μορμύρω.

mũsas, usually plu. **mũsaĩ** 'Kahm, Schimmel auf saurer Milch, auf verdorbenem Wein, Bier usw.'—K. *Moos;* B. I, 110. II, 1, 166; W. *muscus;* Boi. μύαξ. Cf. Lesk. Nom. 192.

mũsàsis 'der Unsrige'—B. II, 2, 405.406. Cf. Kur. Gram. 983.

musė̃ 'Fliege, Stubenfliege'—(Uh. *mákṣas*); B. II, 1, 222.283.483; W. *musca;* Boi. μυῖα. Cf. Lesk. Nom. 278; Sommer 14, 150.

musėlė̃ id.—B. II, 1, 370. Cf. Kur. s.v., Lesk. Nom. 482.

musómiris, musiómiris, mùsmiris 'Fliegentöter, Fliegenschwamm, ein roter mit weissen Warzen besetzter giftiger Pilz, Agaricus muscarius; Fliegengift'—B. I, 455. Cf. Lesk. Nom. 286.

mūsūjis 'der Unsrige'—B. II, 1, 34.196. 2, 405.406. Cf. Kur. Gram. 983, Lesk. Nom. 341.

muszù, mùszti 'schlagen'—Uh. (Ntr.) *músalas;* W. *mucro.* Cf. Lesk. Abl. 317.

mùturas 'turbanartig gewundenes Kopftuch der Frauen' (see next)—(Boi. μίτρᾱ). Cf. Ness. 413[a]; Kur. s.v.; Lesk. Nom. 448.

muturis 'ein weissleinenes Tuch, das der Neuvermählten am Tage nach der Hochzeit um den Kopf befestigt wird, so dass der eine Zipfel hinten herabhängt'—(Boi. μίτρᾱ: "Les mots lit. . . ."). Cf. Ness. 413[a]; Kur. s.v.; Lesk. Nom. 448.

muturu, muturti 'den Kopf (ut supra) verbinden'—(Boi. μίτρᾱ: "Les mots lit. . . .").

N

-na, -n postpositive e.g. in **rañkon** 'in der Hand', **rankosnà** 'in die Hände'—B. II, 2, 186.789.790.799.801. Cf. Kur. Gram. 602, 1488.

nagà 'Huf'—Uh. *áṅghriṣ, nakhám;* K. *Nagel;* F. *ga-nagljan;* B. II, 1, 647; W. *unguis;* Boi. ὄνυξ. Cf. Ness. 413[a], Lesk. Nom. 214.

nãgas 'Nagel, Kralle'—Uh. *áṅghriṣ, nakhám;* K. *Nagel;* F. *ga-nagljan;* B. I, 493.596.632. II, 1, 647; W. *unguis;* Boi. ὄνυξ. Cf. Ness. 413[a], Lesk. Nom. 175.

nãginė 'schuhartige Ledersohle, Schnürsohle' (von Bauern getragen)—(Ber. *lapŭtĭ*). Cf. Ness. 413[b]; Lesk. Nom. 403; Schleicher LSpr. II, 292.

nagùtis dimin. 'Fingernagel'—B. II, 1, 439; W. *unguis;* Boi. ὄνυξ. Cf. Lesk. Nom. 577; Sommer 244; Trautmann Die altpreussischen Sprachdenkmäler 382.

naikaũ, naikýti 'tilgen, vergehen machen, vernichten'—(Ber. *gybǫ*). Cf. Lesk. Abl. 279.

naikinù, naikìnti id.—(Ber. *gybǫ*). See prec.
nakczà adv. 'in der Nacht, bei Nacht'—B. II, 2, 714.744.752.
naktìgonė 'Nachthut, nächtliches Hüten' (cf. Ness. 414ᵃ; Kur., Lalis s.v.)—B. I, 151; Ber. *gańajǫ*. See *naktìs* & Lesk. Abl. 326.
naktìgonis 'Nachtschwärmer'; (Lalis s.v.) "night-watcher (one who tends horses at night)"—Ber. *gańajǫ*. See prec. & Kur. DLWb. s.v. Nachtschwärmer; Lesk. Abl. 326.
naktìkova '(Kur.) Nachteule; (Ness. 414ᵃ) Nachtrabe'—Ber. *kavǔka;* W. *cavannus.*
naktimìs, naktim̃s adv. inst. plu. 'nachts'—B. II, 2, 719. 745.752.
naktìs 'Nacht'—Uh. *náktā;* K. *Nacht;* F. *nahts;* B. I, 101. 380.596. II, 1, 426.435. 2, 129.289; W. *nox;* Boi. νύξ (& note). Cf. Lesk. Nom. 552.
nãkvinas 'zur Nacht herbergend'—W. *nox;* Boi. νύξ.
nakvýnė 'Nachtherberge'—B. I, 719; W. *nox;* Boi. νύξ. Cf. Ness. 414ᵃ, Lesk. Nom. 354.
nakvóju, nakvóti 'übernachten'—B. I, 719; W. *nox;* Boi. νύξ. Cf. Ness. 414ᵃ, Lesk. Nom. 354.
nãmas, usually plu. **namaĩ** 'Wohnung, Haus; Hausflur'—W. *domus;* Boi. δόμος (& note). Cf. Ness. 414ᵇ, Lesk. Nom. 175.
namẽ, namẽ, namè adv. loc. sing. 'zu Hause, nach Hause'—B. II, 2, 181.515.707.743. Cf. Wied. 96.
namëjis 'der immer zu Hause Sitzende'—B. II, 1, 196. Cf. Lesk. Nom. 342.
namìnis 'zum Hause gehörig' (e.g. **szũ namìnis** 'Haushund')—B. II, 1, 273.
namõn (namũn) adv. 'nach Hause'—B. II, 2, 743.
namùkas 'Haushocker, Stubenhocker'—B. II, 1, 492-3. Cf. Lesk. Nom. 517.
namũn 'nach Hause'—see *namõn.*
nãras 'Taucher, Taucherente'—Boi. ἀρνευτήρ. Cf. Ness. 415ᵃ; Lesk. Abl. 337; Lesk. Nom. 168.

naraũ, narýti 'einen Knoten oder eine Schlinge machen, einrenken'—(W. *nervus*). Cf. Ness. 415[b], Lesk. Abl. 337.

narỹs '(Boi.) lacet'—(Boi. λάρναξ). Cf. Kur. s.v., Lesk. Abl. 337.

narsa fem. 'Zorn, Mut'—B. II, 1, 542. Cf. Bezz. BGLS. 302, Lalis s.v. See next.

nar̃sas masc. 'Zorn, Grimm; Eifer, Ernst'—B. I, 717.786. II, 1, 542; Boi. νόσος. Cf. Lesk. Abl. 338.

narsinù, narsìnti 'erzürnen'—Boi. νόσος. Cf. Lesk. Abl. 338.

narsùs 'grimmig, mutig'—Boi. νόσος. Cf. Lalis s.v., Lesk. Abl. 338.

nartinù, nartìnti 'erzürnen'—Boi. νόσος. Cf. Lesk. Abl. 338.

narva 'Zelle der Bienenkönigin'—K. *Narbe*. Cf. Lesk. Abl. 337.

nasraĩ, (dial.) **nastraĩ** plu. 'Rachen' (bes. von Raubtieren) —Uh. *nas-, nā̆sā;* K. *Nüster;* B. I, 162.786. II, 1, 354; W. *nāris*. Cf. Geitler LS. 97, Lesk. Nom. 434.

nasztà 'Last, Bürde, Tracht'—Uh. *náçati;* B. II, 1, 416; W. *nanciscor;* Boi. ἐνεγκεῖν. See *neszù* & Lesk. Abl. 364.

naudà 'Nutzen, Ertrag, Habe, Gut'—K. *geniessen;* F. *niutan;* B. I, 202; (W. *nūtrio*). Cf. Lesk. Abl. 304.

naũdyju, naũdyti 'begehren, gern mögen'—F. *niutan;* (W. *nūtrio*). Cf. Lesk. Abl. 304.

naũjas 'neu'; adv. **naujaĩ** 'neu'; **ìsz naũjo** 'von neuem'—Uh. *návyas;* K. *neu;* F. *niujis;* B. I, 263.290.297.341. 344. II, 1, 164; W. *novus;* Boi. νέος.

naujënà 'Neuigkeit, Nachricht; Neuerung; neu angelegter Acker'—B. II, 1, 278. Cf. Lesk. Nom. 414.

naujìkas 'Neuling, Anfänger'—B. II, 1, 489. Cf. Lesk. Nom. 510.

naujynà 'Neuigkeit'—B. II, 1, 278. Cf. Lesk. Nom. 410.

naujõkas 'Neuling, Anfänger in der Wirtschaft'; **Naujõkas** Familienname—B. II, 1, 501 (twice).598. Cf. Lesk. Nom. 513.

Naujokìkė Tochter des *Naujõks*—B. II, 1, 490.603. Cf. Schleicher LSpr. I, 59; Kur. Gram. 365; Lesk. Nom. 512.

Naujokýtis Sohn, **Naujokýtė** Tochter des *Naujõkas*—B. II, 1, 604. Cf. Schleicher LSpr. I, 59; Kur. Gram. 365; Lesk. Nom. 572.

navas Old Lith. 'neu'—Uh. *návas;* F. *niujis;* W. *novus;* Boi. *νέος*. Cf. Brückner SlFw. 111. See *naũjas*.

nè 'nicht'—Uh. *ná;* K. *nein;* F. *ni;* B. I, 115.349.486; W. 1. *nē;* Boi. *νη-*. Cf. Kur. Gram. 459, Bezz. BGLS. 41.

negãlė 'Unwohlsein, Schwäche, Kränklichkeit; (Ness. 238* also) Unvermögen, Unmöglichkeit'—Ber. *golmę* 2. See *galiù*.

negaliù, negalė́ti 'kränklich, unpässlich sein'—see *galiù*.

nègi 'nicht doch'—B. I, 985; W. *negōtium*. See next, *nè*, & *-gi*.

negu id.—Ber. 3. *jeg(ŭ)da* (s.v. *i-*); W. *negōtium*. See prec., *nè*, & *-gu*.

neĩ 1) 'und nicht, auch nicht, nicht einmal'; 2) 'wie, gleich, gleichsam'—Uh. *néd;* F. *nei;* B. I, 184.190. II, 1, 45; W. 1. *nē, nī, enim*. Cf. Wied. s.v.; Kur. Gram. 1423, 1424; Schleicher LSpr. I, 146; Kur. DLWb. s.vv.; Lalis s.vv.; Ness. 418*; BB. XXI, 306.

neigì, neĩgi 'auch nicht einmal; wie(?)'—W. *enim*, (*nihil*). See prec. & *-gi*.

nekadà adv. 'zuweilen'—B. II, 2, 351.

nĕkadà adv. 'niemals'—B. II, 2, 733.

nekàs 'irgend wer, jemand, etwas'—F. *ni;* B. II, 2, 351; W. 1. *nē*. Cf. Wied. 120 C; Ness. 419*.

nĕ̃kas 'niemand, nichts'—B. I, 184.190.191. II, 1, 55. 2, 351.613; W. *nī*. Cf. Wied. 120 C; Ness. 418*.

nekliútas 'Unheil, Schlechtigkeit'—F. *hlauts*. Cf. Schleicher LSpr. II, 293; Lesk. Nom. 538.

nĕkóju, nĕkóti '(Korn) schwingen, (Ness. 419* & Kur. s.v. nėkóju) Getreide in einer Mulde schwingen, um es von Staub und Spreu zu befreien'—Boi. λικμός. Cf. Lalis 203[b].

nekuȓs (fem. **nekurì**) 'ein gewisser, irgend ein'—W. *enim*, 1. *nē*.

néndrė (**léndrė**) 'Rohr, Schilf, Rohrstock, Spazierstock'—Uh. *nadás*, (*naḍás*); F. *nati;* B. I, 852; W. *nassa;* Boi. ἀδίκη, (νάρθηξ). Cf. Lesk. Nom. 439, Sommer 174.

nendrýnas, nendrỹnė 'Haufen Rohr, Rohrteich, Rohrbruch'—B. II, 1, 278.

nenů̂rima 'unruhiger Mensch; wilder, schüchterner Mensch'—B. I, 416. Cf. Ness. 441[b], Lesk. Abl. 339.

nepatis, nepotis, nepů̂tis Old Lith. 'Neffe, Enkel'—Uh. *nápāt;* F. *nipjis;* B. I, 147.278.508; W. 1. *nepōs;* Boi. ἀνεψιός. Cf. Bezz. BGLS. 304.

neptis Old Lith. 'Enkel'—B. I, 508; Boi. ἀνεψιός. Cf. Bezz. BGLS. 304. See prec.

neptis Old Lith. 'Enkelin'—Uh. *naptì;* W. 1. *nepōs.* Cf. Bezz. BGLS. 304. See prec.

nepů̂tis 'Neffe, Enkel'—see *nepatis.*

nerėdù adv. 'unordentlich, ungebührlich, unmässig, unbändig, unangemessen, ausserordentlich'—B. II, 2, 717.

neriù, nérti 1) 'tauchen, untertauchen'; 2) 'einziehen (z.B. in einen Ring, in eine Kette), einschlüpfen (z.B. in die Schuhe, Pantoffeln), einfädeln, einschlingen, sticken, stricken'—K. *Narbe;* B. II, 3, 137; (W. *nervus*); Boi. ἀρνευτήρ, (λάρναξ). Cf. Ness. 415[a], 415[b]; Kur. s.v.; Wied. s.v.; Prell. 260; Lalis s.v.; Donalitius 238; Lesk. Abl. 337, 385; Bezz. BGLS. 304; Bezz. LF. 146; Trautmann Die altpreussischen Sprachdenkmäler 387; MLG. I, 389.

nėsti 'non est'—B. I, 840.

nėszczà 'schwanger' (nur von Menschen)—(Ber. *berd'a*). Cf. Lesk. Abl. 364. See next.

neszù, nèszti 'tragen'—Uh. *açnóti, náçati;* F. *bi-nauhan;* B. I, 146.567. II, 3, 136.398.446; W. *nanciscor;* Boi. ἐνεγκεῖν. Cf. Lesk. Abl. 364.

nèt, neta, nete 'so dass, ausser, als, sondern, wenn nicht'—B. II, 2, 732. Cf. Ness. 421[a]; Bezz. BGLS. 304; Geitler LS. 97.

netìkėlis 'Ungeratener, Taugenichts, Tölpel, Geck'—B. II, 1, 370. See *tinkù* & Lesk. Abl. 287.

nẽżas, plu. **nẽżaĩ** 'Krätze'—W. (Ntr.) *niger;* (Boi. κνέφας). Cf. Lesk. Abl. 280.

ninkù, nìkti 'heftig beginnen, auffahren'; **apninkù, apnìkti** 'anfallen, herfallen, überfallen' (Ness. 422[a]: "von Hunden, Bienen und anderen Tieren, nicht von Menschen gebraucht")—(W. *pernix*); Boi. νεῖκος, νίκη. Cf. Lesk. Abl. 279.

nirstù, nir̃sti 'starrköpfig, erbittert, grimmig, wütig werden'; **įnir̃tęs** perf. act. part. 'ergrimmt'—B. II, 3, 364. Cf. Lesk. Abl. 338.

nyrù (nįrù?), nìrti 'sich schlängeln, ranken'—(W. *nervus*). Cf. Ness. 415[b]; Kur. s.v.; Lesk. Abl. 337, 385.

nýtis 'Weberkamm (Hevelte); einzelner Faden'—F. *nēþla;* W. *neo;* Boi. νῆν. Cf. Geitler LS. 98, 68; Brückner SlFw. 111; Lesk. Nom. 546.

nókstu, nókti 'reifen, reif werden'; **pranókstu, pranókti** 'wetteifern, verfolgen, einholen, übertreffen, zuvortun, erreichen'—(Uh. *náhuṣ*); F. *nēlv;* W. *nanciscor;* Boi. ἐγγύς, (ἐνεγκεῖν (note)). Cf. Kur. s.v.; Bezz. BGLS. 305; Lesk. Abl. 377.

nóras 'Wille, Verlangen, Begierde, Appetit'—(Boi. (Ntr.) νώροπι). Cf. Lesk. Nom. 180.

nóriu, norëti 'wollen, wünschen, begehren'—(W. *neriōsus*); (Boi. (Ntr.) νώροπι). Cf. Lesk. Abl. 377, Bezz. LF. 146.

nósis 'Nase'—Uh. *nâsā;* K. *Nase;* B. I, 170.784. II, 1, 171; W. *nāris;* Boi. ῥινα. Cf. Lesk. Nom. 237.

noterė, nůterė (?) 'Nessel'—K. *Nessel;* W. *nassa.* Cf. Ness. 424[a]; Kur. 280[b]; MLG. I, 18, 134; Lalis 212[b].

novyti (?) 'quälen, verderben, töten'—K. *Not;* F. *nauþs;* (W. *neco*). Cf. Bezz. LF. 146[b]; Geitler LS. 98[a,b];

Juškevič 609[b]; Lalis 212[b]; Trautmann Die altpreussischen Sprachdenkmäler 382.

nù 'von'; **nu-** 'herab'—see *nū̃*.

nù adv. 'nun'—Uh. *nú;* K. *nun;* F. *nu;* B. I, 103.375.487; W. *nunc;* Boi. *νῦ*.

nusìdedu, nusidė́ti 'sich anstellen (Ness. 133[a]); sich vergehen, sündigen'—B. II, 1, 410. See *dedù.*

nudelbiù, nudeĩbti (akìs) '(die Augen) niederschlagen'; perf. act. part.: **nudeĩbęs akìs** 'mit niedergeschlagenen Augen'—see *delbiù.*

nudilbstù, nudiĩbti 'die Augen niederschlagen, glupen'; perf. act. part.: **nudiĩbęs akìs** 'mit niedergeschlagenen Augen'—B. I, 472; Ber. *dĩlbǫ*. See *delbiù* & Lesk. Abl. 323.

nudìrlioti (?) 'die Haut abziehen'—Ber. *dĩrlajǫ*. Cf. *dìrti.*

nudirtas pret. pass. part. 'geschunden'—see *dìrti.*

nudraudus 'tadelnswert'—W. *fraus*. Cf. Ness. 153[b], Lesk. Abl. 294.

nuéngiu, nuéngti 'abschinden; abquälen, abtreiben'—see *éngiu.*

nugarà 'Rücken (eines Tieres, eines Menschen, eines Berges)'—Ber. *gora.* Cf. Lesk. Nom. 447.

nùgi 'nun denn'—F. *nu;* B. I, 103. See *nù* 'nun' & *-gi.*

nukaipo 'er siechte hin'—see *kaipstu.*

nukáiszti 'abschaben'—see *kaiszti.*

nukaszė́ti (?) 'ganz entkräftet werden'—(W. *cracentes*); (Boi. *κακός* (note)). Cf. Bezz. LF. 122.

nukrùpęs 'schorfig'—Ber. *krupa*; (W. *scrōfula*). Cf. Bezz. LF. 129, Lesk. Abl. 300.

nulùzgęs (?) 'Abgerissener, Zerlumpter'—Ber. *luska.* Notice Geitler LS. 98, s.v. nulosgas.

numìrėlis 'Verstorbener, Toter'—B. II, 1, 370. See *mìrsztu* & Schleicher LSpr. II, 294; Wied. s.v.; Lesk. Abl. 336; Lesk. Nom. 464.

nūnaĩ 'nun, jetzt'—B. II, 1, 271. 2, 736.747; Boi. *νῦ*. See *nù* 'nun'.

nupelna 'Verdienst'—see *nùpelna.*
nuplė̃sziu, nuplė̃szti 'abreissen'—see *plė̃sziu.*
nusė́das 'Bodensatz'—B. II, 1, 153. Cf. Ness. 458[b], Lesk. Nom. 166.
nusenkù, nusèkti 'abfliessen, trocken werden'—see *senkù.*
nuskur̃dęs perf. act. part. (Kur. **skurstù, skur̃sti** 'verkümmern, im Wachstum zurückbleiben') 'im Wachstum verkümmert'—Uh. *kṛdhúṣ;* B. I, 453-4.726; W. *curtus;* Boi. σκυρθάλιος. Cf. Brückner SlFw. 133.
nusmerkiù, nusmer̃kti 'umbringen'—see *smerkiù.*
nústu, nústi 'begehren, lüstern sein'—see *panústu* & Wied. s.v.
nusùsęs 'krätzig, räudig'; (Ness. 471[b]) "der einen ausgeschlagenen, grindigen Kopf hat"—B. II, 1, 476; (W. 1. *situs*). See *susù* & Kur. 278[b], 415[b].
nũ, nù prep. 'von, fort von, von . . . herab'; **nu-** pref. 'herab, hinab, bis . . . hin'—Uh. *ánu;* F. *ana;* B. II, 1, 507. 2, 790.799.800.802; W. *an-;* Boi. ἀνά, (νόσφι(ν)). Cf. Kur. s.v.; Kur. Gram. 1453 ff.
nũbraukos plu. 'Flachsabgänge'; "das, was beim Schwingen von dem Flachs abgeht"—Ber. *brŭsnǫ.* See *braukiù* & Kur. s.v., Ness. 344[a], Lesk. Abl. 293.
Lett. **nůdaras** 'Abfall von Bast'—Uh. *daras;* B. II, 1, 149. Read, in Uh. & B., lett. for lit.? Cf. Lesk. Abl. 324, Lesk. Nom. 213.
nůdėmaĩ adv. 'gänzlich, ganz und gar'—B. II, 1, 244. Cf. Lesk. Nom. 428.
nůdėmė 'Vergehen, Verbrechen, Sünde'—B. II, 1, 244. Cf. Lesk. Nom. 281, 425; Sommer 162.
nůdė̃tas 'Vergehen, Verbrechen'—B. II, 1, 410. Cf. Lesk. Nom. 536.
nũgas 'nackt'—Uh. *nagnás;* K. *nackt;* F. *naqadei;* B. I, 155.387.599; W. *nūdus;* Boi. γυμνός. Cf. Lesk. Nom. 198, Brückner SlFw. 111 (& note).
nůgata 'Nacktheit'—B. II, 1, 417. See prec. & Lesk. Nom. 569, Brückner SlFw. 111.

nūgis id.—B. II, 1, 172.642. Cf. Kur. DLWb. s.v. Nacktheit; Geitler LS. 98[b]; Brückner SlFw. 111, 112; Lesk. Nom. 300.

nūglas 'plötzlich, jäh' (bes. vom Tode)—B. II, 1, 362.507. Cf. Brückner SlFw. 112, Lesk. Nom. 468.

nůjėgà 'Vermögen'—see *jėgà.*

nůmà, nūmas 'Zins' (von einem Darlehn)—F. *niman;* W. *numerus* (twice); Boi. νέμω. Cf. Lesk. Abl. 379.

nůmarů 'Fallsucht'—B. II, 1, 308.510. Cf. Lesk. Abl. 336.

nūmas 'Zins'—see *nůmà.*

nůpelna, nupelna 'Verdienst, Lohn'—B. II, 1, 261. See *pel̃nas* & Ness. 283[a], Lesk. Nom. 365.

nůrega 'Scharfsinn'—B. II, 1, 155. Cf. Lesk. Abl. 365.

nůtakanà 'Ablauf (des Wassers)'; **vandū yrà nůtakanój** 'das Wasser fällt'—B. II, 1, 268. Cf. Lesk. Abl. 367.

nůterė 'Nessel'—see *noterė.*

nůżiulsnus 'geneigt, abschüssig'—B. II, 1, 292. Cf. MLG. I, 392; Lesk. Nom. 358.

O

õ 'und, aber'—B. I, 152. II, 2, 165.697; Ber. *a.* Cf. Kur. Gram. 1626-7.

obelìs fem. 'Apfelbaum'—Ber. *ablŭko.* See next.

óbůlas, obůlỹs 'Apfel'—K. *Apfel;* F. *apel;* Ber. *ablŭko;* W. *Abella.*

oksai (ůksai) 'kundschaftende Bienen, die Platz für einen Schwarm suchen'—B. II, 1, 542. See *ŭksauju* & Lesk. Nom. 595; Lalis 396[a]; Geitler LS. 99.

ólektis 'Elle'—see *ŭlektis.*

opszrùs 'Dachs; Fischotter'—B. II, 1, 547. Cf. Ness. 30[a].

opùs 'weichlich, leicht verletzlich, zerbrechlich'—Boi. ἠπεδανός. Cf. Lesk. Nom. 253. Notice Geitler LS. 99[b].

óras 'Luft, Wetter, Himmel, das Freie'—W. *ārea.* Cf. Lesk. Abl. 330.

oszkà 'Ziege; (Samog. also) Rehkuh; Cyprinus cultratus

(Fisch); ein Strafinstrument, Fussblock'—Uh. *ajás;* B. II, 1, 601; Ber. *azino.* See *ožỹs* & Ness. 31[b], Lesk. Nom. 506.

oszkënà 'Ziegenfleisch'—B. II, 1, 278. See prec. & Lesk. Nom. 413.

otis 'Steinbutte'—W. *attilus;* Boi. ἐτελίς.

-ovė suff. (e.g. **bendróvė** 'Genossenschaft')—Ber. *dǫbrava.* Cf. Lesk. Nom. 352.

ovyjůs, ovytis 'sich sehen lassen'—Uh. *āviṣ;* Ber. *avě;* W. *audio.* Cf. Ness. 31[a]; Kur. s.v.; Brückner SlFw. 113; Bezz. LF. 148.

ożënà 'Ziegenbocksfleisch'—Uh. *ajínam.*

ożìnis 'zum Ziegenbock gehörig, Ziegen-'; **ożìnis** (vė̃jas) 'Südostwind'—Uh. *ajínam;* B. II, 1, 272; Ber. *azino.* Cf. Ness. 31[b], Kur. s.v.

ożỹs "der Ziegenbock, im Żem. auch der Rehbock . . .; der Holzbock, ein Insekt . . .; der Wendebock, auf dem sich die Garnwinde dreht; der Holzbock der Brettschneider, worauf das Holz liegt, auch das entsprechende Instrument der Holzhacker; die Schneidebank der Tischler und Zimmerleute" (Ness. 31[a])—Uh. *ajás;* B. I, 568. II, 1, 601; Ber. *azino;* (Boi. αἴξ, δίζα). Cf. Lesk. Nom. 299, 577; Sommer 228, 255.

ożiùkas, ożùkas 'Ziegenböckchen'—B. II, 1, 492. Cf. Lesk. Nom. 518, 520; Trautmann Die altpreussischen Sprachdenkmäler 466.

P

-p (e.g.**vakarõp** 'der Abendzeit zu')—see *-pi.*

pa- pref. (e.g. **pãmotė** 'Stiefmutter')—see *põ.*

pabaigà 'Ende, Schluss, Aufhören, Tod'—B. I, 680; (W. *fīnis*). Cf. Lesk. Abl. 271.

pasibaudau, pasibaudyti 'sich erheben, aufbrechen'—Ber. *buďǫ.* Cf. Bezz. BGLS. 311, Lesk. Abl. 294.

pabirỹs 'was sich streut'—Ber. *bĭrlogŭ.* Cf. Lesk. Abl. 321.

pabúklas 'Wesen, Erscheinung; Gerüst, Werkzeug, Instrument'—B. II, 1, 344. Cf. Bezz. LF. 148, Lesk. Nom. 496.

pabulỹs 'Windel; (Ness. 337[a] also) Hintergeschirr, Schwanzriemen (von Pferden)'—B. II, 1, 112. See *bulìs* & Lesk. Nom. 305.

pabundù, pabùsti 'erwachen'—B. II, 1, 567. See *bundù, bùsti.*

pãdas 'Fuss-, Stiefelsohle; Fuss (einer Sache), Grund'—Uh. *pât;* F. *fōtus;* B. II, 1, [131].157. 2, 733.863; W. *pēs;* [Boi. πούς]. Cf. Lesk. Nom. 168.

padėlỹs 'Hingelegtes; Nestei'; (Ness. 133[b] also) "ein Gegenstand, den ein Zauberer irgendwo hinlegt, um einen Zauber zu vollführen"—B. II, 1, 340.365; Ber. *dělo.*

padingstu, padingti 'gefallen, Gefallen haben'; **padingsta mán** 'es gefällt mir'—(W. *disco* (s.v. *decet*)).

padirgti (?) Old Lith. 'hassen, neiden'—(W. *furvus*). Cf. Bezz. BGLS. 307.

pãdis, usually plu. **pãdžai** 'der Schragen, das Untergestell einer Tonne, eines Backtroges'—Uh. *pât;* B. II, 2, 863; W. *pēs.* Cf. Lesk. Nom. 299; Sommer 244, 256; Trautmann Die altpreussischen Sprachdenkmäler 387.

padroszti (?) 'schnell laufen'—(F. *dragan*); W. *traho;* Boi. τρέχω. Cf. Bezz. LF. 109.

padùrmas (Mielcke) 'heftiger Sturm': (**sù**) **padùrmu** inst. sing. 'mit Sturm, mit Ungestüm'; **padùrmai** adv. 'mit Ungestüm, stürmisch' (Lalis: "immediately after, close at the heels")—B. II, 1, 249; Ber. *durĭ;* Boi. θοῦρος. Cf. Kur. s.vv.; Lesk. Nom. 421.

pãdžai plu. 'Untergestell'—see *pãdis.*

pagadà 'günstiges Wetter, günstiger Wind (Kur.); Wetter (Lalis)'—Ber. *godŭ.* Cf. Brückner SlFw. 82, 113; Ness. 235[b].

pagadas 'Verderben, Verbrechen, Schuld'—B. I, 628; (Ber. *gadŭ*). Cf. Ness. 236[a]; Lesk. Abl. 326.

pagal̃ prep. 'entlang, hinter, neben, nach, gemäss, zufolge'—

B. II, 2, 929. Cf. Kur. Gram. 1459; Bezz. BGLS. 56, 71.

pagálba, pagelba 'Hilfe, Beistand'—B. II, 1, 68.155. Cf. Lalis 228; Lesk. Abl. 325; Lesk. Nom. 200.

pagaunus 'hinterlistig, verfänglich'—B. II, 1, 290.291. Cf. Ness. 242ᵃ.

pagelba 'Hilfe'—see *pagálba.*

pasigendù, pasigèsti 'sich sehnen, verlangen, gelüsten, vermissen'—F. *bi-gitan;* B. II, 3, 292.293.294.382; Ber. *gadajǫ;* W. *prehendo;* Boi. χανδάνω. Cf. Ness. 247ᵇ, Lesk. Abl. 326.

pagėžà 'Rache'—F. *ga-geigan.* Cf. Lesk. Abl. 273, Lesk. Nom. 222.

paglóstau, paglóstyti 'streicheln, schmeicheln'—see *glóstau.*

pagranda (Szyr.) 'Diele, Fussboden'—Ber. *grę̨da.* Cf. Ness. 271ᵇ; Lesk. Abl. 328; Lesk. Nom. 210.

pagrindas, usually plu. **pagrindaĩ** 'Brückenbelag, Bohlenlage im Stalle, Stangenlage auf dem Schober, Gerüst, Strassenpflaster'; (Lalis s.v. pagrindas) "foundation, ground, basis"—Ber. *gręda.* Cf. Kur. s.v.; Ness. 271ᵇ; Kur. DLWb. s.v. Gerüst; Lesk. Abl. 328; Lesk. Nom. 163.

pagrindìs f. 'Dielung'—B. II, 1, 168.633. See prec. & Kur. s.v.; Ness. 271ᵇ; Lesk. Nom. 235.

pagrúdo pret. 3rd pers. sing. in **mán szirdìs pagrúdo** 'mir wurde weich ums Herz'—Ber. *grusti.* See *grúdżu* & Kur. DLWb. s.v. weich; Lesk. Abl. 297.

paĩkas 'schlecht, nichtsnutzig, albern, dumm; (Szyr.) eigensinnig, halsstarrig'—K. *Fehde, (feig)*; F. *faih;* B. I, 188; W. *piget.* Cf. Lesk. Abl. 280; Lesk. Nom. 187; Trautmann Die altpreussischen Sprachdenkmäler 398.

pãilgas 'länglich'—B. II, 1, 285. See *ìlgas.*

pailgotinas id.—B. II, 1, 285. Cf. Lesk. Nom. 408, Geitler LS. 103.

pãiras 'locker, fein gemacht (z.B. vom Acker); bröcklig'—W. *rārus;* Boi. ἀραιός. Cf. Lesk. Abl. 329.

paisaũ, paisýti 'den ausgedroschenen Gerstenkörnern die Grannen mit Flegeln oder mit Pferdetrampeln abschlagen'—Uh. *pináṣṭi, peṣayati;* B. I, 785. II, 3, 251; W. *pinso,* (*pavio*); Boi. πτίσσω, (παίω). Cf. Lesk. Abl. 280.

paĩszas 'Russfleck, Schmutzfleck; (plu.) Russ'—W. *pingo;* Boi. ποικίλος. Cf. Ness. 281[a], Lesk. Abl. 280.

paiszau, paiszyti 'berussen, besudeln'—see *iszpaiszau.* Cf. Ness. 281[a].

pajautà 'Empfindung, Sinn, Gefühl (körperliches)'—W. *vātēs.* Cf. Lesk. Abl. 299, Lesk. Nom. 230.

pajėgà 'Vermögen'—see *jėgà.*

pãkalas 'Sensenkeil', "der Keil von Holz oder Horn, mit dem die Sense an dem Sensenstock befestigt wird"—B. II, 1, 153; Ber. *kolą.* See *kalù* & Ness. 175[b]; Lesk. Nom. 176-7; Trautmann Die altpreussischen Sprachdenkmäler 351.

pakantà 'Geduld'—B. I, 716; (Ber. *kątają*); Boi. πένθος. Cf. Lesk. Abl. 331.

pakarnùs 'demütig'—Ber. *-korŭ.* Cf. Brückner SlFw. 114.

pakenczù, pakęsti 'erleiden'—see *kenczù.*

pakýr 3rd sing. pres. 'wird überdrüssig'—Ber. *čirtŭ.* Cf. Lesk. Abl. 331.

pakìrsti (?) 'aus dem Schlafe auffahren'—W. *cardo;* Boi. κόρδαξ. Cf. Bezz. BGLS. 308; Lesk. Abl. 359, 382.

paklaidà 'Irrtum'; plu. 'Irrtümer, Possen, ineptiae'—Ber. *klěvają.* Cf. Ness. 219[a], Lesk. Abl. 275.

paklaidů 'in die Irre Gehender'—B. II, 1, 308. Cf. Lesk. Nom. 381. See prec.

pasikláuju, pasikláuti 'vertrauen auf'—Ber. *kluka.* Cf. Lesk. Abl. 299.

paklódas 'Bettlaken, Umschlagelaken (worin man Kinder auf dem Rücken trägt), Säetuch; Unterfutter (im

Kleide, unter dem Sattel), Polster; hölzerne Schlittenschiene'—B. II, 1, 472. See next & Lesk. Nom. 586.

paklõdė 'Bettlaken'—B. II, 1, 472; Ber. *kladǫ* 1. See *klóju* & Lesk. Abl. 376, Lesk. Nom. 587.

paklusnùs 'gehorsam, willfährig, gütig'—B. I, 785; W. *clueo;* Boi. κλέος. Cf. Lesk. Abl. 299.

paklustù, paklùsti 'gehorchen'—see *klustù.*

pakõliai 'solange als'—see *patõliai.*

pakorẽ 'Galgen'—(W. *cardo*); Boi. κρεμάννυμι. Cf. Kur. DLWb. s.v. Galgen; Lesk. Abl. 373.

pakraũszus 'Abhang'—Ber. *kruchŭ.* See *kraũszus* & Kur. DLWb. s.v. Abhang; Lesk. Abl. 300.

palaida 'Zügellosigkeit, Hurerei'—(W. *lūdo*). Cf. Lesk. Abl. 277, Lesk. Nom. 223.

paláidas 'los, nicht angebunden, ungezügelt, aufgelöst'—(W. *lūdo*). Cf. Lesk. Abl. 276, Bezz. BGLS. 309.

palaidonas 'zügelloser Mensch'—B. II, 1, 308. Cf. Lesk. Nom. 397.

palaidû 'Ausschweifender, nefarius, Hurer'—B. II, 1, 308. Cf. Lesk. Abl. 276.

pãlaikas 'das Übrige, der Rest'—Uh. *rékas;* K. *leihen;* Ber. *-lěkŭ;* W. *linquo;* Boi. λείπω. Cf. Lesk. Abl. 277.

palaistuvas 'Nichtsnutz, Hurer'—B. II, 1, 449. Cf. Lesk. Nom. 567.

palaũkis 'Kader, Wamme am Halse des Rindes'—Ber. *lŭkajǫ;* Boi. λαυκανίη. Cf. Lesk. Nom. 305; Kur. s.v.; Ness. 276[b].

pãlėgis, palėgỹs 'Bettlägerigkeit (bes. beim Kindbett), lange Krankheit'—Ber. *lĕgajǫ;* W. *lectus;* Boi. λέχος. Cf. Lesk. Nom. 288.

palëpiù, palẽpti 'befehlen'—see *lëpiù.*

paliaubà 'das Aufhören, die Unterbrechung'—B. II, 1, 389. Cf. Lesk. Abl. 302.

paliáuju, paliáuti 'aufhören'—see *liáuju.*

paliavà 'Glasur (bei irdenem Geschirr); glasiertes Zeug

(z.B. eine Schüssel)'—Ber. *lějǫ*. Cf. Kur. s.v.; Ness. 276[b]; Brückner SlFw. 114.

palinkt Old Lith. pres. 3rd pers. sing. 'bleibt zurück'—B. II, 3, 277; Ber. *-lěkŭ*. Cf. *lëkù* & Lesk. Abl. 277, Trautmann Die altpreussischen Sprachdenkmäler 404.

pálszas 'fahl' (bes. von Rindern)—Uh. *palitás;* B. I, 448. II, 1, 474; W. *palleo* (twice); Boi. πελιτνός, (παλάσσω (note)).

palùgnas 'geschmeidig, gefällig, dienstfertig, schmeichlerisch, augendienerisch'—K. *Locke*. Cf. Lesk. Abl. 317, Lesk. Nom. 356.

palúkanos plu. 'Wartegeld, Zinsen'—B. II, 1, 268. See *láukiu* & Ness. 375[a]; Kur. s.v.; Lesk. Abl. 302.

pal̃vas 'gelblich weiss, blassgelb, falb'—Uh. *palitás;* K. *fahl;* B. I, 334.340.520. II, 1, 201; W. *palleo;* Boi. πελιτνός, πελᾱργός. Cf. Brückner SlFw. 115 (& note).

pamaczė 'Hilfe, Beistand, Wirksamkeit'—Ber. *moktĭ*. Cf. Ness. 378[a], Brückner SlFw. 105.

pamagoju, pamagoti 'helfen'—see *magoju*.

pàmetu, pamèsti 'hinwerfen, verlieren'—see *metù*.

pamiñklas 'Andenken, Gedächtnis, Denkmal'—B. II, 1, 342. Cf. Lesk. Abl. 335.

pãminos plu. 'Flachsabgänge' (beim Flachsbrechen)—B. II, 1, 155. Cf. Lesk. Abl. 336.

pamplỹs, fem. **pamplė̃** 'Dickbauch' (Kur. s.v.: "gewöhnlich von Kindern, deren Leib aufgedunsen ist"; Ness. 277[a]: "Schimpfwort auf einen kleinen dickleibigen Kerl")—W. *pampinus*. See next & Lesk. Nom. 456.

pampstù, pam̃pti 'aufdunsen'—W. *pampinus;* (Boi. πέμφιξ). Cf. Lesk. Abl. 338, 306.

pántis masc. 'Strick, Fessel' (bes. zum Binden der Füsse der Rinder oder Pferde); usually plu. **pánczai, pánczei** 'Fesseln'—K. *spinnen;* F. *spinnan;* B. II, 1, 409; (W. *pendeo*); Boi. πένομαι. Cf. Lesk. Abl. 338.

panústu, panústi 'sich gelüsten lassen, sich sehnen nach'—

K. *geniessen;* F. *niutan;* W. *nuo,* (*nūtrio*); Boi. νεύω. Cf. Schleicher LSpr. II, 299; Lesk. Abl. 304; Lalis s.v.

papártis, usually plu. **papárczai, papárczei** 'Farn, Tüpfelfarn'—Uh. *parṇám, párpaṭas;* K. *Farn.* Cf. Kur. s.v.; Ness. 277[b]; Bezz. LF. 150; Geitler LS. 53, 101; Brückner SlFw. 115; Lalis s.v.

pãpas 'Brustwarze, Zitze, Lutschbeutel'—W. *pampinus.* Cf. Bezz. LF. 150, Geitler LS. 68.

(plaukaĩ) papeże (?) '(die Haare) stehen aufrecht'—W. *paciscor.* Cf. Geitler LS. 101, Lesk. Abl. 369.

paplava (?) 'Spülicht'—B. I, 338; W. *pluo.* Cf. Lesk. Abl. 304, Geitler LS. 101.

papurpęs 'aufgedunsen, aufgeblasen, stolz'—Boi. πέρπερος. See *purpiù* & Ness. 298[b]. Notice also Kur. s.v. papũręs & Kur. DLWb. s.v. aufgedunsen.

par- 'nieder-, heim-'—B. II, 2, 929. Cf. Kur. Gram. 456-7.

parangùs '(Kur.) geschmeidig, gelenkig; (Ness. 436[a]) hurtig, eifrig'—Boi. ῥίμφα. Cf. Lesk. Abl. 340.

parpiù, pãrpti 'knarren, schnarren, quarren, summen' ("von dem Tone verschiedener Tiere gebraucht")—W. *pulpo.* Cf. Ness. 278[a], Lesk. Abl. 364.

parplỹs 'knarrender Käfer, Maulwurfsgrille'—B. II, 1, 617; W. *pulpo.* Cf. Lesk. Abl. 364, Ness. 278[a].

parpstù, pãrpti 'aufdunsen'—Boi. πέρπερος. Cf. Lesk. Abl. 364.

pãrpti inf.—see *parpiù* or *parpstù.*

pãrszas 'männliches verschnittenes Schwein'—K. *Ferkel;* B. I, 445.450.517.567.630; W. 1. *porcus.*

parszẽlis 'Ferkel'—F. *barnilō;* B. I, 222. II, 1, 364.366.675. 676; W. 1. *porcus.*

parszënà 'Ferkelfleisch'—B. II, 1, 276.278; W. 1. *porcus.*

parszìnis adj. 'vom Ferkel'—W. 1. *porcus.* Cf. Bezz. LF. 151.

parszùkas, parsziùkas 'Ferkelchen'—B. II, 1, 492.676.

pàs prep. 'zu, bei, an'—Uh. *paçcā;* B. II, 2, 877.889 (twice). 891; W. *post;* Boi. πος. Cf. Kur. Gram. 1460.

pasaitas 'Riemen, Strick, Band'—Boi. ἱμάς. See next & Ness. 278[b], Geitler LS. 101.

pásaitis 'verbindender Riemen' (z.B. am Dreschflegel)—B. I, 186; W. *saeta;* Boi. ἱμάς, (κτηδών (note)). Cf. Kur. s.v.; Lesk. Nom. 540; Geitler LS. 101.

pãsaka 'Erzählung, Fabel, Märchen'—K. *sagen;* (Boi. ἐνοπή). See *sakaũ* & Lesk. Abl. 366.

pasakos (?) 'nach, hinterher'—Uh. *paçcā;* W. *post.* Cf. Lalis 241: *pasak.*

pasė̃das 'das Zusammensitzen von Braut und Bräutigam mit ihrem Gefolge'—B. II, 1, 153. Cf. Lesk. Nom. 166.

pasė́lỹs 'Aussaat, Beisaat; Stück Saatland, vom Eigentümer dem Knechte, Sohne, oder Schwiegersohne zu eigener Bestellung überlassen'—F. *saian.* Cf. Donalitius 254; Ness. 459[b]; Kur. s.v.; Lesk. Nom. 460; Lalis 242.

pa-si-(baudau &c.)—see under *pa-(baudau* &c.).

paskýsti 'sich zerstreuen'—see *skýstu.*

pãskui prep. 'nach (örtlich), hinter'; adv. 'hinterher'—Uh. *paçcā;* B. II, 2, 762.889.890; W. *post* (twice). See next.

paskuĩ adv. 'nachher, später'—Uh. *paçcā;* B. I, 152.938.948. II, 1, 481. 2, 168.733.889.890. See prec. & Kur. Gram. 1461, Lesk. Nom. 340.

paskujas 'letzt' (Ness. 278[b]: "der folgende, der hintere")—B. II, 1, 165. Cf. Lesk. Nom. 340.

paslapczomis adv. inst. plu. 'heimlich'—B. II, 2, 720. Cf. Sommer 99, Lesk. Nom. 545.

paslaptà 'Hinterhalt'—B. II, 1, 410. Cf. Lesk. Abl. 344.

pasmė́lys 'falb, bräunlich, von der Sonne verbrannt'—Boi. μελίη. Cf. Lesk. Nom. 247.

pasmerkti (?) 'verderben, umbringen, verdammen'—W. *marceo.* See *smerkiù* & Bezz. BGLS. 310.

pasmìrdė́lis (B. -mír-) 'Stänker, Garsthammel'—B. II, 1, 370.384. Cf. Ness. 489[b]; Lesk. Abl. 344; Lesk. Nom. 465.

paspìlgęs perf. act. part. 'dünn im Stroh (von Korn), im

Wachstum zurückgeblieben'—Uh. 2. *phalgúṣ;* Boi. φελγύνει. Cf. Bezz. LF. 174; Lesk. Abl. 360, 383.

paspudëti (?) 'sich quälen, sich abmühen'—Boi. σπεύδω. Cf. Bezz. BGLS. 311, Lesk. Abl. 310.

pasrùvo (?) pret. 3rd sing. 'er floss'—B. I, 338. Cf. Lesk. Abl. 310, 393.

pastaras 'der letzte'—W. *post.* Cf. Geitler LS. 102; Bezz. BGLS. 311; Lesk. Nom. 446.

pastóju, pastọti 'werden'—see *stóju.*

pastólas 'Gestell', plu. **pastolaĩ** 'Gerüst der Bauleute'—Uh. *sthālam;* K. *Stuhl;* F. *stōls;* B. I, 169; W. *locus, sto.* Cf. Lesk. Abl. 373; Kur. DLWb. s.v. Gerüst; Ness. 503*; Schleicher LSpr. II, 301; Lalis 247.

pastolis 'Hinterhalt'—B. II, 1, 384. Cf. Ness. 503*, Lesk. Nom. 460.

paszalpà 'Hilfe, Unterstützung, Pflege'—K. *helfen;* F. *hilpan.* Cf. Lesk. Abl. 367.

pãszaras 'Viehfutter' (Ness. 516*: "bes. Rauchfutter der Ochsen, Schafe, Pferde")—(Uh. *çurúdh-*); B. II, 1, 151; (Ber. *chorna, kŭrma* 2); W. *Cerēs;* Boi. κορέννῡμι. Cf. Lesk. Abl. 348.

paszlýti 'schief werden'—see *szlýti.*

paszolỹs 'Frost in der Erde, Nachtfrost'—Uh. *çíçiras;* (W. *caleo*). See *szą̃lù* & Lesk. Abl. 374.

paszveitalaĩ plu. 'Putz, Schmuck'—B. II, 1, 365. Cf. Lesk. Abl. 287; Kur. DLWb. s.v. Putz.

pàt 'précisément'—Boi. ποτέ (s.v. πότε). See *tē̃npàt.*

pãtalas, often plu. **pãtalai** 'Bett, Federbett'—F. *fapa;* B. I, 472; W. *tellūs;* Boi. 1. τηλία. Cf. Lesk. Abl. 349, Bezz. LF. 152.

patì 'Ehefrau; selbst'—see *pàts.*

patìs 'Ehemann; selbst'—see *pàts.*

-patni Old Lith.—B. II, 1, 600. See *weschpatni* 'Herrin'.

patogùs 'anständig, höflich, ehrbar, geschickt, gewandt, passend, gelegen'—B. II, 1, 393; Boi. τάσσω. Cf. Lesk. Nom. 253.

patõliai . . . pakõliai 'solange . . . als'—(Ber. *dalĭ*); W. *tālis*.

pàts, patìs masc. 'Ehemann; selbst'; **patì** fem. 'Ehefrau; sie selbst'—Uh. *pátiṣ;* (K. *selb*); F. *brūþ-faþs* (twice); B. I, 153.513. II, 1, 219; Ber. *gospodĭ;* W. *potis, pte, utpote;* Boi. πόσις. Cf. Kur. Gram. 906; Sommer 221, 222, 223, 349.

paũksztas, paũksztis 'Vogel'—(Uh. *phukas*); K. *Vogel* 1; F. *fugls;* B. I, 446; Boi. παῖς. Cf. LBLV. 341; Lesk. Nom. 540; Donalitius 260.

paũtas 'Ei, Hode'; **paũtai** plu. 'Hoden, Hodensack'—Uh. *pótas;* (F. *audags*); W. *pūbēs,* (*ōvum*); Boi. παῖς. Cf. Lesk. Abl. 306.

pãvadas 'Führer; ein Mittel als Führer zum Zweck; der zweite Mann einer Frau'—B. II, 1, 152. Cf. *vedù* & Ness. 60[a-b].

pavaitinù, pavaitìnti 'welken machen'—W. *viēsco*. Cf. Lesk. Abl. 289.

pavéikslas 'Beispiel, Vorbild, Muster'—Boi. εἰκών. Cf. Lesk. Abl. 289; Lesk. Nom. 453; Bezz. BGLS. 312.

paveikslùs 'musterhaft'—Boi. εἰκών. See prec. & Lesk. Nom. 262.

pavéldu, paveldė́ti 'erben'—see *véldu*.

pavelmi 'ich will'; **pavelt** 'er will'—see *velmi*.

pavérsmis 'Quelle, sumpfiger Ort um eine Quelle, Quellgegend'—B. II, 2, 711.

pavìdalas 'Gestalt, gespenstische Erscheinung'—B. II, 1, 361.366; Boi. εἶδος. Cf. Lesk. Abl. 288.

pavidis fem. 'Neid'—B. II, 1, 168. Cf. Lesk. Nom. 237, [Lesk. Abl. 288].

pavìdulis (Mielcke), **pavýdulis** (Ness.) 'Bild, Ebenbild, Gestalt'; **akẽs pavýdulis** 'Augapfel'—F. *fair-weitl;* B. I, 94. II, 1, 361.370; Boi. εἶδος. Cf. Ness. 77[a]; Lesk. Abl. 288; Trautmann Die altpreussischen Sprachdenkmäler 459.

paviduls 'neidisch'—B. II, 1, 361; Boi. εἶδος. Cf. MLG. I, 390; [Lesk. Abl. 288].

pavýdżu, pavydĕti 'neiden, beneiden'—F. 1. *witan;* B. I, 137. II, 3, 153.157.182.410.411.418; W. *video.* Cf. Lesk. Abl. 288.

pavildĕti 'besitzen'—see *vėldu.*

pavýnas 'schuldig, verpflichtet'—(W. *vitium*). Cf. Brückner SlFw. 117.

pażáras, pażiáras 'feuriger Schein am Himmel; ein Lichtschein, der durch die Wolken bricht; Abendrot; Morgenröte'—B. I, 365; Boi. χαροπός. Cf. Lesk. Abl. 371, Ness. 544*.

pażastìs 'Raum unterm Arm, Achselhöhle'—Uh. *hástas;* B. I, 558; (Ber. *-ducha*); Boi. ἀγοστός (twice).

pażiáras 'Schein am Himmel'—see *pażáras.*

pażìnti 'kennen'—see *pażįstu.*

pażintìs fem. 'Kenntnis'—K. *können;* F. *kunnan;* B. II, 1, 434. Cf. Lesk. Abl. 358.

pażióra 'Widerschein am Himmel'; (Kur.) "ein ferner Lichtschein bei Nacht, entweder von einem fernen Feuer oder vom Tagesanbruch"—(W. *augur*); Boi. χαροπός. Cf. Lesk. Abl. 371.

pażįstu, pażìnti (B. & W. **pażínti**) 'kennen, erkennen'; **pażìntas** (B. **pażíntas**) pret. pass. part. 'gekannt, erkannt'—B. I, 419.422.423. II, 1, 399.434. 3, 369.370. 371 (& note); F. *kunþs;* W. *nōsco, gnārus;* Boi. γιγνώσκω. Cf. Lesk. Abl. 358.

pażulnus 'schräg, abschüssig' (z.B. ein Dach)—Uh. *hvárati;* B. I, 260.558; (Boi. χωλός). Cf. Lesk. Nom. 357.

pėdà 'Fusstapfe (von Menschen und Tieren); Fuss (als Mass); Zollstock'—Uh. *padám;* K. *Fuss;* F. *fōtus;* B. I, 527. II, 1, 159. 3, 163; W. *pēs;* Boi. πέδον, πηδόν, [ἐπι-βδαι].

pĕdas 'Getreidegarbe'—Boi. (Ntr.) πέζα. Cf. Ness. 275*, Lesk. Nom. 165.

pẽdinu, pẽdinti 'langsam gehen, leise treten' (z.B. wie eine Katze)—Boi. πηδόν.

pėdǘju, pėdǘti 'Fusstritte machen'—Boi. πηδόν. Cf. Ness. 275[a].

peikiù, peĩkti 'tadeln, schelten, fluchen'—Uh. *píçunas;* K. *Fehde;* F. *faih;* B. I, 188.583; W. *piget.* Cf. Lesk. Abl. 280.

peĩlis 'Messer'—W. 2. *pīlum.* Cf. Lesk. Nom. 299.

pekus Old Lith. 'Vieh'—Uh. *paçúṣ;* F. *faihu;* B. I, 546. II, 1, 180; W. *pecu;* Boi. πέκος. Cf. Lesk. Nom. 240.

pelaĩ plu. 'Spreu'—Uh. *palâvas;* W. *palea.* See *pelūs.*

pelẽ 'Maus'; **pelẽs tãkas** (Mielcke) 'ein falber Strich über des Pferdes Rücken'; **pelẽs ugnìs** 'leuchtendes, faules Holz'; **pẽlės** plu. 'eine Pferdekrankheit'—Uh. *palitás;* B. I, 448.520. II, 1, 222; W. *palleo;* Boi. πελιτνός. Cf. Ness. 282[a], Lesk. Abl. 338.

pelė̃ju, pelė̃ti 'schimmeln'—see *peliù.*

pelė̃kas 'mausgrau'—B. II, 1, 501.

pelenaĩ plu. 'Asche'—B. II, 1, 266.298. 3, 268; W. *pollen;* Boi. 2. πάλη.

pelendrũsė (?) 'Aschenbrödel'—B. I, 827. See *pelenrūsis.*

pelẽnė 'Feuerherd; Aschbehälter, Aschloch'; (Kur., Ness. 282[b]) "ein grobes Laken über der Laugwanne, in welches die Asche zur Laugbereitung geschüttet wird"; (Lalis) 'Ash Wednesday'—B. II, 1, 298; W. *pollen;* Boi. 2. πάλη. Cf. Trautmann Die altpreussischen Sprachdenkmäler s.v. *pelanne, pelanno.*

pelenrũsis masc.; **pelenrũsė, pelenrūsà** fem. 'Aschenbrödel'—(W. 1. *rūdus*). Cf. Lesk. Abl. 307, Lesk. Nom. 297.

pelė́siai plu. 'Schimmel'—B. II, 1, 545. Cf. Lesk. Nom. 594.

peliù (pelė̃ju), pelė̃ti 'schimmeln'—Boi. πελιτνός. Cf. Ness. 283[a]; Kur. 303; Lesk. Abl. 338.

pélkė 'Torfbruch, Morast, Pfütze'; **pélkės** plu. 'Torf'—W.

palūs (twice); Boi. παλάσσω (& note), πτελέα. Cf. Sommer 144.

pel̃nas 'Verdienst, Lohn'—Uh. *páṇate;* B. II, 1, 261. 3, 313; Boi. πωλεῖν. Cf. Lesk. Nom. 361.

pelnaũ, pelnýti 'verdienen'—B. II, 3, 214; Boi. πωλεῖν. See prec.

pelūs plu. 'Spreu'—Uh. *palâvas;* B. I, 467; W. *palea.* Cf. Lesk. Nom. 240, 241 ff.

pëmũ 'Hirtenknabe, (Lalis 263 also) pastor'—Uh. 2. *pâti;* F. *fōdr;* B. I, 803. II, 1, 239.613.615; (W. *ōpilio, pāsco*); Boi. ποιμήν.

pẽnas 'Futter'—W. *penus.* See *penù.*

pênas 'Milch'—Uh. *phénas,* (*páyas*); (Ber. *dĕva, melko*); W. *bibo,* (*spūma*); Boi. πίνω. Cf. Lesk. Abl. 280.

penkerì 'fünf'—B. II, 2, 77 (twice). Cf. Kur. 304[b]; Kur. Gram. 1033; Wied. 158.

peñketas 'Fünfheit'—B. II, 2, 24. Cf. Kur. Gram. 1040; Bezz. BGLS. 189; Lesk. Nom. 571.

penkì, fem. **peñkios,** 'fünf'—Uh. *páñca;* K. *fünf;* F. *fimf;* B. I, 116.122.348.510.587. II, 2, 14.17; W. *quinque;* Boi. πέντε. Cf. Kur. Gram. 1008.

penkiólika 'fünfzehn'—see prec. & [K. *elf*]; [F. *ain-lif*]; B. II, 2, 26.27; [Ber. *-lĕkŭ*]; [W. *linquo*]. Cf. Wied. 156.

penktadeszimtas 'fünfzigster'—B. II, 2, 36.61. Cf. Bezz. BGLS. 185.

penktainis 'Fünftel'—B. II, 2, 73. Cf. Bezz. BGLS. 313.

peñktas 'fünfter'—Uh. *pañcathás;* K. *fünf;* F. *fimftataihunda;* B. I, 126.587. II, 1, 391. 2, 55; W. *quintus* (s.v. *quinque*); Boi. πέντε. Cf. Wied. 157.5.

pentìnas 'Sporn'—B. II, 2, 742. Cf. Lesk. Nom. 404.

penù, penė́ti 'füttern, mästen'—Uh. *panasás;* B. II, 3, 493; W. *penus.* Cf. Lesk. Abl. 369.

pëpala (?) 'Wachtel'—B. II, 1, 128; W. *pīpilo.* Cf. Lesk. Nom. 476.

peř, per- 'durch, entlang, während, hindurch, über, hinüber, mehr als' etc.—Uh. *pári;* F. **fair-;* B. I, 428. II, 2, 865 ff.; W. *per;* Boi. περί. Cf. Ness. 285*; Kur. Gram. 1462 ff., 448; Trautmann Die altpreussischen Sprachdenkmäler 394.

pẽras 'Brut der Bienen'—F. *frasts;* B. II, 1, 524.546; Boi. πόρις. See *periù.*

perdaũg 'zu viel'—B. II, 2, 792; W. *per;* Boi. περί.

pérdżu, pérsti 'furzen'—Uh. *párdate;* K. *farzen;* B. I, 119.424. II, 1, 568. 3, 445.492; W. *pēdo;* Boi. πέρδομαι. Cf. Lesk. Abl. 338.

pereivà m. & f., **péreivis** m. 'Landstreicher'—B. II, 1, 207; Boi. ποῖος. Cf. [Lesk. Abl. 272].

pergas 'Fischerkahn'; "ein aus einem Stamm gemachter Kahn"—(W. *pergula*). Cf. Bezz. LF. 153 & 166: rundinýs.

periù, perẽti 'brüten'—Uh. *pṛthukas;* F. *frasts;* B. I, 467. 479. II, 1, 168.433 (note). 3, 133.183; W. *pario;* Boi. πόρις. Cf. Lesk. Abl. 369.

periù, peřti trans. 'baden; mit dem Badequast schlagen; schlagen, prügeln'—B. II, 1, 432. 3, 136; (Boi. σπαίρω (note)). Cf. Lesk. Abl. 338.

perkù, piřkti 'kaufen'—W. *pretium.* Cf. Lesk. Abl. 338-9.

Perkúnas 'Donnergott; Donner'—Uh. *parkaṭī* (thrice), (*parjányas*); F. *fairguni* (twice); B. I, 514.611; W. *quercus;* (Boi. σπαίρω (note)). Cf. Trautmann Die altpreussischen Sprachdenkmäler 395.

perleñkis 'Anteil, Gebühr, Aufgabe'—Boi. λαγχάνω. Cf. Trautmann Die altpreussischen Sprachdenkmäler 396.

permẽr adv. 'übermässig, zu viel'—B. II, 2, 726.

pérnai 'im vorigen Jahr'—Uh. *páras, parút;* K. *fern* 2; F. *fairns;* B. II, 1, 270. 2, 747; W. *per;* Boi. πέρυσι(ν).

pérsti 'furzen'—inf. of *pérdżu,* q.v.

perstogė 'das Aufhören'—B. II, 1, 507. Cf. Lesk. Nom. 524.

perstóju, perstóti 'aufhören'—see *stóju.*

peřszti, perszẽti impers. "schmerzen, wie wenn Salz oder

Essig in offene Wunden kommen"—W. (Ntr.) *porrīgo*, (*porca*). Cf. Lesk. Abl. 369.

perszù, pir̃szti 'für jemand freien'—Uh. *pṛccháti;* F. *fraihnan;* B. I, 457.492.508.554. II, 3, 446; W. *posco.* Cf. Lesk. Abl. 339.

pė́sczas, pė́szczas adj. 'zu Fuss befindlich'—Uh. *pā́t;* B. I, 717.786; W. *pēs;* Boi. πηδόν. Cf. Ness. 287*; Kur. 308*; Lesk. Nom. 563.

pė̃skinas 'sandig'—B. II, 1, 272.

pė̃skos plu. 'Sand'—(Boi. πάσκος). Cf. Brückner SlFw. 118.

pëstà fem. 'Stampfe'; (Kur.) "ein Stampffass, ein Ende eines Baumstammes, das aufrecht stehend aber ausgehöhlt zum Graupenstampfen gebraucht wird"; (Ness.) "eine hölzerne Stampfe, aus einem Klotz in Gestalt eines Weinglases gehöhlt, in der man Gerste oder Hafer zu Graupen und Grütze stampft"; **pëstas** masc. 'hölzerne Stampfe, Mörserkeule'—Uh. *pinā́ṣṭi.* Cf. Kur. 310; Kur. DLWb. s.v. Mörser, Mörserkeule, Stampfe-Stampffass; Ness. 287*; Lalis 264; Lesk. Abl. 280; Brückner SlFw. 118; Lesk. Nom. 536.

pëszà 'Russ' (bes. am Kessel); notice also Bezz. BGLS. 314—W. *pingo;* Boi. ποικίλος. Cf. Ness. 287*, Lesk. Abl. 280.

pė́szczas 'zu Fuss befindlich'—see *pė́sczas.*

pësziu, pëszti 'zeichnen, schreiben'—F. *filu-faihs;* B. I, 290.630. II, 3, 194; W. *pingo;* Boi. ποικίλος. Cf. Bezz. LF. 154; Lalis 264; Lesk. Abl. 292; Trautmann Die altpreussischen Sprachdenkmäler 392.

pesztùkas 'Raufer, Raufbold'—B. II, 1, 492.616.

pesztùvės plu. 'Rauferei'—(W. *pugil*). Cf. Lesk. Abl. 365.

peszù, pèszti 'rupfen, raufen'—Uh. *pákṣma;* F. *faihu;* B. II, 3, 120; W. *pecten;* Boi. πέκω. Cf. Lesk. Abl. 365.

petỹs, petìs masc. 'Schulter'—W. *pateo;* Boi. πετάννυμι.

pė̃tūs plu. tant. 'Mittagessen, Mittag, Süden'—Uh. *pitúṣ;*

F. *fōdjan;* B. II, 1, 442-3; W. *pāsco, pīnus;* Boi. πατέομαι.

pêva 'Wiese'—(F. *hawi*); B. II, 1, 207; Boi. πόα. Cf. Lesk. Abl. 280.

-pi, -p (e.g. **sūnaũspi** 'zum Sohne', **vakarõp** 'der Abendzeit zu')—B. I, 95. II, 2, 839.844; W. *prope;* Boi. ἐπί. Cf. Kur. Gram. 1477.

piáuju, piáuti 'schneiden, mähen, ernten, schlachten (z.B. Kälber, Geflügel), beissen (bes. von Hunden)'—W. *pavio, puto;* Boi. παίω. Cf. Lesk. Abl. 305.

piaulaĩ plu. tant. 'faules, im Finstern leuchtendes Holz; Feuerschwamm'—B. I, 210; W. *pūs;* Boi. πύον. See *pūvù* & Lesk. Abl. 305.

piautùvas 'Sichel'—B. II, 1, 162.449. See *piáuju* & Lesk. Abl. 305.

pýbelės plu. 'Fibel'—K. *Fibel.* Cf. Prell. deutsch. Best. in den lett. Spr. 54.

pýdau, pýdyti trans. "eine Kuh zum Milchgeben reizen oder beim Melken abwarten, bis sie Milch gibt, . . . wobei die Melkerin auch öfters singt . . ."—B. I, 487. Cf. Kur. s.v. & Lesk. Abl. 280.

pýkastis masc. 'Bosheit, Zorn'—B. II, 1, 439. See *pykstù* & Lesk. Nom. 580.

pìkis m. 'Pech'—W. *pix;* Boi. πίσσα.

pykstù, pỹkti 'böse werden, zornig werden'—K. *Fehde;* F. *faih;* W. *piget.* See *peikiù* & Lesk. Abl. 280.

piktadẽjas 'Übeltäter'—Ber. *dějĭ.* See prec. & next. Cf. Lesk. Nom. 309.

pìktas 'böse, übel, schlimm, schlecht, leicht erzürnt, boshaft, ärgerlich, wütend, zornig'—Uh. *piçunas;* K. *Fehde;* F. *faih;* B. I, 583. II, 1, 412; W. *piget.* Cf. Lesk. Abl. 280, Lesk. Nom. 557.

piktỹn (**eĩti**) adv. 'böser, schlimmer (werden)'—B. II, 2, 703. See prec. & [Lesk. Nom. 411].

pilìs 'Burg, Schloss'—Uh. *pûr;* B. II, 1, 168.170; (W. *populus*); Boi. πόλις. Cf. Ness. 290[b], Sommer 61.

pìlkas (B. **pílkas**) 'grau'—B. II, 1, 477.505.662; W. *palleo;* Boi. πελιτνός, (παλάσσω (note)). Cf. Lesk. Abl. 338.

pilkùtis adj. 'ein wenig grau'—B. II, 1, 677. See prec. & Lesk. Nom. 576.

pìlnas (B. **pílnas**) 'voll'—Uh. *píparti, pūrṇás;* K. *voll;* F. *fulls;* B. I, 345.423.475. II, 1, 256; W. *plēnus,* (*polleo*); Boi. πίμπλημι. Cf. Lesk. Abl. 359.

pilnatis (?) 'Fülle; Vollmond'—B. II, 1, 438. See prec. & Lesk. Nom. 570.

pìltas (B. **pítas**) pret. pass. part. of **pilù**, q.v., 'geschüttet'—Uh. *pūrtás;* B. II, 1, 399.

piltavas, piltuvas 'Trichter, Schöpfeimer, Pumpe'—B. I, 838. See next & Ness. 290[b], Lesk. Nom. 566.

pilù, pìlti (B. **pílti**) 'giessen, schütten, füllen; prügeln'—Uh. 1. *píparti;* F. *fulls;* B. I, 460.473. II, 1, 435. 3, 170; (W. *palea*); Boi. πίμπλημι, πέλανος, πλέω. Cf. Bezz. LF. 154, Lesk. Abl. 359.

pilus (?) 'voll, reichlich'—B. II, 1, 177. 2, 656; W. *pleo;* Boi. πολύς. Cf. Lesk. Nom. 248.

pil̃vas 'Bauch; (Bezz. BGLS. 314 also) Kropf'—B. II, 1, 208. Cf. Lesk. Abl. 359.

pinklas 'Geflecht' (z.B. Korb, Matte, Haarflechte)—K. *Fahne;* B. II, 1, 344. Cf. Lesk. Abl. 338, Lesk. Nom. 496.

pinù, pìnti 'flechten'—K. *Fahne, spinnen;* F. *fana, spinnan;* B. I, 417. II, 1, 458.571. 3, 137; (W. *neo, pendeo, penitus*); Boi. πένομαι, (νῆν), (πίν(ν)η), (τάπης). Cf. Lesk. Abl. 338.

piovìkas 'Mäher'—B. II, 1, 490. Cf. Lesk. Abl. 305.

pypiù, pȳpti 'piepen, pfeifen'—K. *piepen;* B. II, 1, 46; W. *pīpilo;* Boi. πῖπος. Cf. Prell. deutsch. Best. in den lett. Spr. 51; Brückner SlFw. 16.

pir̃dis m. 'Furz'—B. I, 471.522; Boi. πέρδομαι. See *pérdžu.*

pirkalas 'Ware'—B. II, 3, 241. Cf. Lesk. Nom. 475, [Lesk. Abl. 338].

pirkìkas 'Käufer', **pirkìkė** 'Käuferin'—B. II, 1, 222. See *perkù*.

piȓkti 'kaufen'—inf. of *perkù*, q.v.

pirm̃ prep. 'vor' (zeitlich, selten örtlich)—B. II, 2, 888; W. *prandium*. Cf. Kur. Gram. 1470.

pirmà adv. 'zuerst, vorher'—W. *prandium*. See next.

pìrmas (B. etc. **pírmas**) 'primus'—Uh. *pûrvas;* K. *Fürst;* F. *frauja, fruma;* B. I, 423.474. II, 1, 206.226. 2, 51 (twice); W. *per, prandium;* Boi. πράμος, πρόμος, πρῶτος.

pirmatis (?) 'principatus'—B. II, 1, 438. Cf. Lesk. Nom. 570.

pirmdėlỹs masc., **pirmdėlẽ** fem. 'die zum erstenmal geboren hat' (z.B. **pirmdėlẽ kárvė** 'Kuh, die zum erstenmal gekalbt hat'); 'Erstgeburt' (z.B. **pirmdėlỹs kiaũszis** 'erstgelegtes Ei'). Nur von Tieren, nie von Menschen. —F. *daddjan;* B. I, 424; Ber. *dětę, doję;* W. *fēlo;* Boi. θηλή. Cf. Lesk. Abl. 323, Lesk. Nom. 456.

pirszis (?) 'Brust'—Uh. *párçuṣ;* (F. *fairhvus*); B. I, 465. 566. Cf. Geitler LS. 104[a], l. 6; Brückner SlFw. 118.

pirszlỹs 'Freiwerber, Brautwerber'—Uh. *pṛccháti;* B. II, 1, 617; W. *posco*. See *perszù* & Lesk. Abl. 339.

piȓsztas 'Finger; (Ness. 293[b] also) Zehe, Kralle'—W. *compesco;* Boi. πόρκης. Cf. Lesk. Nom. 537.

piȓszti 'für jemand freien'—inf. of *perszù*, q.v.

pirtìs fem. 'Badehaus, Badestube; Flachsbrechstube'—B. II, 1, 432. Cf. Ness. 286[a]; Kur. s.v.; Sommer 147; Lesk. Abl. 338.

pisù, pìsti 'coire cum femina'—Uh. *pásas;* B. I, 100. II, 3, 125.443; W. *pinso,* (*pēnis* (twice)); Boi. πτίσσω, (πέος). Cf. Lesk. Abl. 359.

pìtas 'rund'—(W. *pĭla*). Cf. Ness. 294[a].

piúklas 'Säge; (Bezz. BGLS. 314[b] also) Sichel'—B. I, 542. II, 1, 344; W. *pavio;* Boi. παίω. Cf. Lesk. Abl. 305.

pỹvas 'Bier'; "das Bier der Bierbrauereien, im Gegensatz zu dem *alùs*, das der Bauer sich selbst bereitet" (Ness.

294*)—Uh. *pívas;* W. *bibo;* Boi. πίνω. Cf. Brückner SlFw. 119.

pyzà 'weibliches Schamglied'—see *pìzė.*

pyzdà id.—Uh. *pīḍáyati;* B. II, 2, 840; (W. *pēnis*); Boi. πιέζω. Cf. Brückner SlFw. 118.

pìzė, pyzà id.—(W. *pēnis*). Cf. Brückner SlFw. 118.

plaitau, plaityti—see *atsiplaitau* 'ich mache mich breit, prahle'.

plàktas pret. pass. part. of **plakù**, q.v., 'geschlagen, gegeisselt'—B. II, 1, 398.

plaktùkas "Klopfwerkzeug, zum Einschlagen von Nägeln und zum Klopfen der Sense gebraucht"—B. II, 1, 492.610. See *plakù* & LBLV. 341.

plaktùvas, plu. **plaktùvai** 'Sensenklopfwerkzeug'—B. II, 1, 620. See next & Lesk. Abl. 370.

plakù, plàkti 'schlagen, peitschen, züchtigen, (die Sense) klopfend schärfen'—K. *Flegel;* F. *flōkan;* B. I, 177. 520.584.631. II, 3, 135.137.171.291.448; W. *plango;* Boi. δίπλαξ, πλήσσω. Cf. Lesk. Abl. 370.

plantù, plàsti 'breiter werden'—Uh. *práthati;* W. *planta;* Boi. πλάτος. Cf. Lesk. Abl. 346.

plasztakà 'flache Hand, Handbreite (als Mass)'—(F. *plaqus*); W. *plancus;* Boi. πλάξ, παλαστή. Cf. Lesk. Nom. 508.

platẽsnis 'breiter'—B. II, 1, 553. Cf. Wied. 165.

platì fem. to **platùs**, q.v., 'breit'—(F. *mawi*); B. II, 1, 213 (thrice).

platùs 'breit'—Uh. *pṛthúṣ, prathuṣ;* K. *Fladen;* (F. *mawi*); B. I, 171.510.716. II, 1, 480; W. *planta;* Boi. πλάτος. Cf. Lesk. Abl. 346.

plaũcziai plu. 'Lunge'—Uh. *klómā;* B. I, 852 (fn.). II, 1, 238; W. *pulmo;* Boi. πλεύμων. Cf. Lesk. Abl. 304.

plaũczkepeniai plu. 'Lunge und Leber (eines geschlachteten Tieres)'—B. II, 1, 59.

plaudżu, plausti 'waschen, reinigen'—Uh. *plávate;* B. II, 3,

378.390; W. *aplūda, pluo;* Boi. πλάδος, πλέω. Cf. Lesk. Abl. 304. See *pláuju* & *plústu.*

pláuju, pláuti 'spülen, waschen'—Uh. *plávate;* F. *flōdus;* B. I, 204.429.508. II, 3, 194.378.412; W. *pluo,* (*plōro*); Boi. πλέω. Cf. Bezz. LF. 156, Lesk. Abl. 304. See *plústu* & *plaudżu.*

plaukaĩ plu. 'Haar'—(W. *plūma* (twice)). Cf. Lesk. Abl. 304.

plaũkinas 'behaart'—B. II, 1, 664. Cf. Lesk. Nom. 400.

plaukìnis 'hären'—B. II, 1, 273.665 (twice). Cf. Kur. DLWb. s.v. hären.

plaukiù, plaũkti 'schwimmen; schiffen'—Uh. *plávate;* W. *pluo.* See *pláuju* & Lesk. Abl. 304.

plaũksmas 'Floss; Waschbank; (Bezz. BGLS. 315) Furt' —B. II, 1, 252. Cf. Lesk. Abl. 305.

plaukũtas 'behaart'—B. II, 1, 407. 3, 206.

plausti 'waschen'—inf. of *plaudżu,* q.v.

plautas 'Steg am Bienenstock'—(W. *plaustrum*). Cf. Lesk. Nom. 535.

plauzdinis masc. 'Bett, Deckbett'—(W. *plūma*). Cf. Ness. 306[b], Trautmann Die altpreussischen Sprachdenkmäler 400.

plebõnas 'Pfarrer'—B. I, 853. Cf. Kur. s.v., Brückner SlFw. 119.

pleczù (Kur. & B. -ė-), **plė̃sti; ìszpleczu, iszplė̃sti** 'breit machen, ausbreiten, ausstrecken' (z.B. Flügel, Segel, Äste, die Arme). Boi. "prendre ses aises, se carrer"(?)—Uh. *práthati;* B. I, 171; W. *planta, plānus;* Boi. πλάτος. Cf. Ness. 305[a], Lesk. Abl. 346.

plėgà "ein Schlag, ein Hieb" (Ness. 306[b]); "die Prügel, körperliche Züchtigung" (Kur.); "stripe, stroke, lash, plague, scourge, calamity, misery" (Lalis)—B. II, 3, 366; W. *plango, plēcto;* Boi. πλήσσω. Cf. Brückner SlFw. 119, Lesk. Nom. 206.

pleikiù, pleĩkti "(Fische) am Bauche aufspalten und dann breitlegen" (Kur.)—Boi. (Ntr.) πλίσσομαι. Cf. Ness. 309[a], Lesk. Abl. 292.

plěkiu, plěkti 'schlagen, prügeln, körperlich züchtigen'—B. II, 3, 366; W. *plango, plēcto;* Boi. πλήσσω. Cf. Lesk. Abl. 370.

plẽkiu, plẽkti (?) id.—W. *plango.* See prec. & Lesk. Abl. 370.

plėnė 'Häutchen'—see *plėvė̃.*

plěsziu, plěszti trans. 'reissen, zausen, zerreissen; rauben; (einen frischen Acker) pflügen; (Getreide) schroten; (Ness. 307[b] also) frohlocken'; **nuplěsziu, nuplěszti** 'abreissen (Haut, Kleider); berauben'—B. I, 565; (W. *plēcto*). Cf. Lesk. Abl. 339.

plėvė̃, plėnė 'Haut, Häutchen, Netzhaut, dünne Haut auf der Milch, feine Haut unter der Eierschale'—Uh. *palâvas;* K. *Fell;* F. *filleins;* B. II, 1, 268; W. *palea* (twice), *pellis;* Boi. ἐπίπλοος, πέ-πλος.

plìkas "kahl, nackt, ohne Haare, ohne Federn, ohne Gras" (Ness. 309[a])—B. II, 1, 222. Cf. Lesk. Nom. 182, Sommer 196.

plìkė 'Glatze; kahle Wiese'—B. II, 1, 222.643.

plincas, plinsas; usually plu. **plincai, plinsai** 'Eierkuchen' —Ber. *mlinŭ.* Cf. Ness. 309[b]; Kur. 320[a]; Bezz. LF. 156[b]; Prell. deutsch. Best. in den lett. Spr. 47; Brückner SlFw. 16; Trautmann Die altpreussischen Sprachdenkmäler 401.

pliopiù, pliõpti 'plätschern, rauschen, schwatzen'—W. *pulpo.* Cf. Lesk. Abl. 305.

plytà 'Ziegel'—(W. *later*); Boi. πλίνθος. Cf. Brückner SlFw. 119.

pliúgas '(ein moderner) Pflug'—K. *Pflug.* Cf. Ness. 310[b]; Kur. DLWb. s.v. Pflug; Prell. deutsch. Best. in den lett. Spr. 51; Brückner SlFw. 120.

plóju, plóti 'breit zusammenschlagen, klatschen'; Kur.: "die Hände breit zusammenschlagen, aber dadurch auch etwas breit formen, breitschlagen, z.B. Käse, Kuchen,

Fladen"; Lalis: "to flatten; to make flat or compressed; to clap; to applaud"—B. II, 2, 70; W. *plānus* (twice), *plaudo* (twice); Boi. *πέλανος*. Cf. Lesk. Abl. 377.

plokas 'Estrich'—(F. *plaqus*); W. *plango;* Boi. *πλήσσω*. Cf. Ness. 310[a], Lesk. Abl. 370.

plõkis masc. 'Streich, Hieb, Rutenstreich, Peitschenhieb'—F. *flōkan;* B. II, 3, 291; W. *plango;* Boi. *πλήσσω*. See *plakù* & cf. Ness. 304[a], Lesk. Abl. 370.

plókszczas 'flach, platt'—B. I, 585. II, 1, 480. 2, 70. 3, 291; W. *plancus;* Boi. *πλάξ*. Cf. Lesk. Abl. 370.

plónas 'dünn, schmal, flach, platt, fein'—K. *Flur;* B. II, 1, 259. 2, 70; W. *plānus;* Boi. *πέλανος*. Cf. Lesk. Abl. 339, 377.

plónė 'Fladen, Kuchen'—W. *plānus,* (*puls*); Boi. *πέλανος*.

plóninu, plóninti 'dünn, fein machen; fein spinnen; platt schlagen'—W. *plānus;* Boi. *πέλανος*.

plõtis masc. 'Breite; (Ness. 305[a] also) ein Stück, ein Rest'—B. II, 1, 172. Cf. Lesk. Abl. 346.

plūdìmas 'das Schwimmen, Flottwerden, Fliessen, Überfliessen; Schnupfen'; **kraũjo plūdìmas** 'Blutfluss' (bes. bei Frauen)—K. *fliessen;* W. *pluo.*

plūdìs fem. 'Schwimmholz am Netz'—Uh. *plávate;* B. II, 1, 467; W. *pluo.* Cf. Lesk. Abl. 304.

pluksna 'Feder'—see next.

plùnksna (B. **plúnksna**), **pluksna** (Szyr.), **plúsna** (Bezz. LF. 157[a]) 'Feder; Schreibfeder, Griffel'—K. *fliegen;* F. *fugls;* B. I, 614. II, 1, 252; (W. *plūma*). Cf. Lesk. Abl. 304.

pluskos plu. 'Haarzotten, Haare'—W. *plūma.* Cf. Geitler LS. 104, Bezz. LF. 157[a].

plúsna 'Feder'—see *plùnksna.*

plústu, (pret.) **plúdau, plústi** 'ins Schwimmen geraten, überfliessen; (Ness. 310[b], wrongly as a separate verb, & Donalitius 267) schwatzen, plappern, einfältiges Zeug reden; (Lalis, also trans.) to scold, chide, objurgate'—Uh. *plávate;* K. *fliessen, Floss* (8th ed.); (F.

flauts) ; B. I, 204.486. II, 3, 378; W. *pluo*, (*plōro*) ; Boi. πλάδος, πλέω. Cf. Lesk. Abl. 304. See *plaudżu* & *pláuju*.

põ prep. with inst. 'unter'; with acc. 'über . . . hin, entlang, durch, (distributive) je'; with gen., dat. 'unter, nach (von der Zeit)'; pa-, pó- pref. (e.g. padarýti 'fertig machen', pãmotė 'Stiefmutter', pópëtis 'Nachmittag') —Uh. *paçcā;* B. II, 2, 75.806-9; W. *abs* (s.v. *ab*) ; Boi. πώγων. Cf. Kur. Gram. 449, 1471-5; Trautmann Die altpreussischen Sprachdenkmäler 401.

pódukra, pódukrė 'Stieftochter'—B. II, 1, 334; Ber. *dŭkti*. Cf. Ness. 149ª.

pógimis masc. 'Natur'—B. I, 415. Cf. Lesk. Abl. 325.

pokim adv. 'vor Augen, in Gegenwart'—B. II, 2, 725.

pomėtis fem. 'Gedächtnis'—Ber. *-męti*. Cf. Brückner SlFw. 120.

põnas 'Herr' (auch als Titel vor Namen)—Ber. *gŭpanŭ*. Cf. Brückner SlFw. 120 & Ness. 294ᵇ; Kur. 323ᵇ, 503ª; Lalis 273.

porýt adv. 'übermorgen'—B. II, 2, 709(note).746.

potám adv. 'darauf, nachher, hernach'—B. II, 2, 725-6. Cf. Kur. s.v.; Kur. Gram. 1472; Brückner SlFw. 121.

povisám adv. 'gänzlich'—B. II, 2, 726. Cf. Wied. 347ª.

pożas 'Falz, Fuge' (um z.B. Balken ineinander zu fügen) —W. *paciscor*. Cf. Ness. 295ᵇ.

pożyju, pożyti 'falzen, fügen'—W. *paciscor*. Cf. Ness. 295ᵇ.

pra- 'vorbei-, durch-'—see *prõ*.

prabangà 'Übermass, Verschwendung'—(Uh. *bahúṣ*). Cf. Lesk. Abl. 320, Lesk. Nom. 209 (read Abl. 320 for Abl. 328).

pradas 'Anfang'—B. II, 2, 734; Ber. *dějǫ*. Cf. Bezz. BGLS. 315.

prãdas 'Vorfutter, Abmachsel des Viehfrasses'—Ber. *dějǫ*.

prãdėm adv. 'ganz und gar; zugleich, gleichzeitig, sogleich,

sofort, immerfort, fortwährend'—B. II, 1, 244. Cf. Ness. 311[b]; Kur. s.v.; Lesk. Nom. 428.
pradżà 'Anfang'—F. *snōrjō;* B. II, 1, 185 (twice).
prasidżungù, prasidżùgti 'froh werden'—see *dżungũs.*
pragýstu, pragýsti 'zu singen, zu krähen anfangen'—B. I, 208. II, 3, 379; Ber. *gaję;* (Boi. διθύραμβος). Cf. Lesk. Abl. 273. See *gėdu.*
pragyvenà 'Lebensunterhalt'—B. II, 1, 267. Cf. Lesk. Nom. 382.
pragobinu, pragobinti 'verschachern'—see *gobinu.*
prãkartas 'Krippe im Stall; (Szyr.) Trog'—Ber. *koryto* (read *-tas* for *-tis*). Cf. Lesk. Nom. 532, [Lesk. Abl. 373].
prakarùs 'maserig' (vom Holz)—Ber. *korĭ.* Cf. Lesk. Nom. 251.
prakepesas ein Kartoffelgericht—B. II, 1, 544. Cf. Geitler LS. 104.
prakiùręs 'durchlöchert'—(Boi. σωλήν). Cf. Lesk. Abl. 301.
pramanýtas part. adj. 'falsch, erdichtet'—(W. *mendax*). See *manaũ* & Ness. 382[a], Kur. 242[a], [Lesk. Abl. 336].
pranókstu, pranókti 'einholen, erreichen'—see *nókstu.*
prantù, pràsti 'gewohnt werden'; **suprantù, supràsti** 'verstehen, merken'—F. *frapi;* (W. *interpres*). Cf. Ness. 313[a,b]; Lesk. Abl. 365.
praparszas (Szyr.) 'Graben'—(W. *porca*). Cf. Lesk. Abl. 364.
praperszis masc. 'Blänke im Eise, eine in Folge schneller Strömung nicht zugefrorene Stelle'—(W. *porca*). Cf. Ness. 312[a], Lesk. Abl. 364.
praskudìmas 'nervöses Ermüden'—Boi. σκυδμαίνω. Cf. Kur. 385[b]. See *skundù.*
prãstas 'gering, schlicht, gerade, einfach, schlecht, gemein, gewöhnlich'—W. *probus.* Cf. Brückner SlFw. 121.
pràsti 'gewohnt werden'—inf. of *prantù,* q.v.
praszaũ, praszýti 'fordern, bitten'—Uh. *prcháti;* F. *fraihnan;* B. I, 146.446.450.492.554. II, 3, 162.169.

266.267; W. *posco;* Boi. *θεο-πρόπος*. Cf. Brückner SlFw. 121.

pratęsà 'Verzug, Aufschub'—W. *prōtēlo*. Cf. Ness. 99ᵃ, Lesk. Abl. 350.

pratrýstu, pratrýsti 'heftigen Durchfall plötzlich bekommen'—Ber. *driskają*. Cf. Lesk. Abl. 287-8.

prausiù, praũsti '(das Gesicht) waschen; (Szyr.) ein Kind in warmem Wasser baden'—Uh. *pruṣṇóti;* B. I, 785. II, 1, 263. Cf. Lesk. Abl. 305.

pravėžà, pravožà 'tiefes Fahrgeleise'—B. II, 1, 153. Cf. Lesk. Abl. 357.

pražanga 'Übertretung, Sünde'—Uh. *jáṅghā;* K. *Gang;* F. *gaggan;* B. II, 1, 150. Cf. Lesk. Abl. 358.

prẽ, prì prep. with gen. 'bei, an, zu'; **pri-, pry-** pref. 'hinzu-, bei-' (e.g. **pribúti** 'dabei sein, beiwohnen', **prýszokis** 'das Hinzuspringen')—F. *frisahts;* B. I, 190. II, 2, 881-883; W. *pri* (s.v. *per*), *prae;* Boi. *πρίν*. Cf. Kur. Gram. 451, 1476.

prẽdas, usually plu. **prẽdai** 'Daraufgabe beim Kauf oder Tausch'; Lalis (sing.): "addition, supplement, appendix"—B. II, 2, 734; (W. *praeda*). Cf. Lesk. Abl. 371.

prëdėlẽ 'Beilage'—B. II, 1, 340.365; Ber. *dělo*. Cf. Kur. DLWb. s.v. Beilage.

prẽgi, prẽg prep. with gen. 'bei, an'—B. II, 2, 881. Cf. Kur. Gram. 1476. See *prẽ*.

prëkãlas, preikãlas (Lesk. **prẽkalas, preĩkalas**) 'Amboss' —Ber. *kolą*. Cf. Lesk. Nom. 176.

prẽlikis fem. 'Zufall, Geschick'—B. II, 1, 168. Cf. Lesk. Nom. 237.

prëpàt vandeñs "tout près de l'eau"—Boi. *ποτέ* (s.v. *πότε*). See *tēnpàt*.

prẽskas 'süss, ungesäuert' (von Speisen)—K. *frisch;* F. *fraiw*. Cf. Ness. 314ᵇ, Brückner SlFw. 122.

prẽsz prep. with acc. 'gegen, wider'—B. II, 2, 881. Cf. Kur. Gram. 1478. See *prẽ*.

prì 'bei, an'; **pri-, pry-** 'hinzu-, bei-'—see *prẽ*.

prýbėga 'Zuflucht'—B. II, 1, 154. See *bė́gu* & Lesk. Abl. 370.
prýblindė 'Abenddämmerung'—F. *blinds;* Ber. *blędǫ*. See *blendžiũs*.
pridvėjas (?) 'dumpfig'—Uh. *dhūnóti;* (Ber. *dujǫ*).
pridvẽsas id.—(Ber. *dujǫ*). Cf. Ness. 159*, Lesk. Abl. 361.
prikeřgti (?) 'anbinden, beifügen, verschränken'—(Ber. *kŭrga* 1). Cf. Geitler LS. 104; Lesk. Abl. 363, 401.
prikimbù, prikìbti 'anhaften'—see *kimbù*.
prìliktas 'zugelassen, (vom Schicksal) beschieden'—B. II, 1, 396. See *lëkù*.
prispeiczù, prispeĩsti 'umringend anklemmen'—see *speiczù*.
prisreigti (?) Old Lith. 'darreichen'—W. 2. *frigo*. Cf. Bezz. BGLS. 318.
pritampù, pritàpti 'antreffen, kennen lernen, erfahren'—see *tampù*.
pritiklus 'geziemend, passend'—B. II, 1, 352. Cf. MLG. I, 391, Lesk. Abl. 287.
privìlstu, privìlti 'betrügen'—(Boi. 3. οὖλος (note)). See *apvìlstu* & Lesk. Abl. 354, Trautmann Die altpreussischen Sprachdenkmäler 409.
prõ prep. with acc. 'vorbei, durch'; **pra-** verb. pref. 'vorbei-, durch-, ver-'—Uh. *prá-;* F. **fra-;* B. I, 147.152.429.507 (& Ntr. XLVII). II, 1, 206. 2, 873-876; W. 1. *prō;* Boi. πρό. Cf. Kur. Gram. 450, 1479.
prójûdis 'schwärzlich'—B. II, 1, 55. Cf. Bezz. LF. 159.
prõpẽrnai adv. 'vor zwei Jahren'—B. I, 147; W. 1. *prō*. See *pérnai*.
prõtas 'Verstand'—F. *fraþi;* (W. *interpres*). Cf. Lesk. Abl. 365.
prusnà, also plu. **prùsnos** 'Maul, die dicken Lippen am Maul (des Rindes)'—Uh. *pruṣṇóti;* B. I, 785. II, 1, 263. Cf. Lesk. Abl. 305.
puczù, pũsti 'wehen, blasen, stürmen, jagen, schnauben (vor Zorn)'—Uh. *pupphusas, phutkaroti;* W. *pustula;* Boi. πύννος, φῦσα. Cf. Lesk. Abl. 306.

púdau, púdyti 'faulen machen, faulen lassen; ein Feld brach liegen lassen'—B. II, 3, 268.374; W. *pūs;* Boi. πύον. See *pūvù* & Lesk. Abl. 305.

pūkas 'Flaumfeder; (Ness. 297[a] also) eine Flocke, z.B. von Asche, Schnee; (Bezz. BGLS. 318) Feder'—Uh. *phukas;* K. *Vogel* 1; B. I, 446. Cf. Brückner SlFw. 123.

puknė 'Blatter'—Boi. φῦσα. Cf. Bezz. BGLS. 318.

pūkszczù, pūkszti 'keuchen, schnaufen'—Uh. *pupphusas;* W. *pustula;* Boi. φῦσα.

pukszlė (Szyr.) 'Beule, Spur eines Schlages'—Boi. φῦσα.

púliai, púlei plu. 'Eiter'—Uh. *pûyati, pûlyam;* K. *faul;* F. *fūls;* B. I, 113. II, 1, 361; W. *pūs;* Boi. πύον. Cf. Lesk. Abl. 305.

pulkaĩs adv. inst. plu. 'haufenweise'—B. II, 2, 720. See next.

pul̃kas 'Haufe, Menge' (bes. von Menschen und Tieren)—K. *Volk;* W. *populus.* Cf. Brückner SlFw. 123.

pum̃puras 'Knospe'—W. *pampinus.*

puntù, pùsti 'schwellen'—Boi. πύννος. See *puczù* & Lesk. Abl. 306.

pūnù, púti 'faulen'—see *pūvù.*

pupà 'Bohne'—Ber. *bobŭ;* (W. *faba*); Boi. κύαμος. Cf. Brückner SlFw. 123.

pupů̃lė 'dicke Knospe' (bes. der Salweide)—W. *pampinus.* Cf. Ness. 298[a], Kur. 336[b] (twice).

pūrai plu. 'Winterweizen'—Uh. *pūras;* B. I, 448. II, 1, 353; Boi. πυρός.

purpiù, pur̃pti 'sich aufblähen' (z.B. ein Frosch)—Boi. πέρπερος. Cf. Lesk. Abl. 364, Bezz. LF. 160.

pur̃vas, plu. **purvaĩ** 'Strassenkot'—B. II, 1, 208; W. *spurcus;* (Boi. παρδακός). Cf. Ness. 299[a]; Kur. s.v.; Lesk. Abl. 317.

pùsdylis mė̃nů 'Mond im letzten Viertel'—Ber. *dolnĭ.* Cf. Kur. s.v., Lesk. Abl. 323.

pùsė 'Hälfte, Seite'—B. II, 2, 207.656.

pusiaũ adv. 'halb, mitten entzwei'—B. II, 2, 207.210.707; (Ber. *med'a*).

pusiautinai adv. 'zur Hälfte'—B. I, 399. II, 1, 285. Cf. Lesk. Nom. 407.

puskainiu adv. 'zum halben Preis'—B. I, 178.588-9.621; Ber. *cěna;* Boi. ποινή. Cf. Lesk. Nom. 375. See *kainė*.

pūslē̃ 'Blase; Harnblase'—Uh. *pupphusas;* W. *pustula;* Boi. φῦσα. Cf. Lesk. Abl. 306.

pusnýnas 'ein vom Winde zusammengejagter Schneehaufen'—Uh. *pupphusas.* See next.

pusnìs fem. id.—Uh. *pupphusas;* B. II, 1, 289. Cf. Lesk. Abl. 306.

pũsti 'wehen, blasen'—inf. of *pucžù,* q.v.

pùsti 'schwellen'—inf. of *puntù,* q.v.

pùsviris 'halb gar'—B. I, 472. Cf. Kur. DLWb. s.v. halbgar; Lesk. Abl. 355.

puszìs fem. 'Fichte'—K. *Fichte;* W. *pugil;* Boi. ἐχε-πευκές, πεύκη.

putà 'Schaumblase, Schaum'; (Ness. 300[b]) "der Schaum, auf den Wellen, am Maule eines tollen Hundes, auf dem Pferde, wenn es stark schwitzt usw."—Uh. *pupphusas;* Boi. φῦσα. Cf. Lesk. Abl. 306.

púti 'faulen'—see *pūnù, pūvù.*

putýtis 'junges Tier, junger Vogel' (Zärtlichkeitsausdruck) —Uh. *putrás;* W. *pūbēs;* Boi. παῖς.

putlùs (Mielcke) 'sich blähend, geschwollen, aufgeblasen, stolz'—B. I, 541. II, 1, 362. Cf. Lesk. Abl. 306.

puvesis 'verfaulte Reste'—B. II, 1, 521.525. Cf. Lesk. Nom. 593. Notice Geitler LS. 105.

pūvù (**pūnù**), **púti** 'faulen'—Uh. *pūyati;* K. *faul;* F. *fūls;* B. I, 113. II, 1, 512.521. 3, 268.301.374; W. *pūs;* Boi. πύον. Cf. Lesk. Abl. 305; Kur. 336[b], 340[a].

pũdas 'Topf'—K. *Fass;* (F. *auhns*); B. I, 156 (& note); W. *patro;* Boi. (Ntr.) πέζα.

pũlu, pùlti (B. **púlti**) 'fallen' (cf. Wied. s.v. & Lalis)— (Uh. *skhálati, sphālayati*); K. *fallen;* B. I, 697.716. II,

3, 188.320; (W. *fallo* 4, *palea* 1); (Boi. σφάλλω). Cf. Lesk. Abl. 305-306.

pűsziůs, pűsztis 'sich schmücken'—Uh. *pā́ças;* F. *fāhan;* W. *paciscor;* Boi. πήγνῡμι. Cf. Lesk. Abl. 379.

pűta 'Zechgelag'—Uh. 1. *pā̊ti, pītás;* B. I, 37.157; W. *bibo* (twice); Boi. ἄμπωτις, πίνω (twice). Cf. Lesk. Nom. 543.

R

radastai (?) 'Rosenstrauch; Dornen, Hecke'—(W. *rosa*). Cf. Bezz. BGLS. 318, BB. XXII, 244.

rãgas 'Horn; Ecke, Spitze (cf. Ness. 426[a])'—B. II, 1, 509; W. *cornu,* (*rigeo*); Boi. 1. ἀρχός, κραγγών.

ragűtas 'gehörnt'—B. II, 1, 407.664.

raĩbas 'bunt, gesprenkelt' (von Vögeln)—B. II, 1, 389. Cf. Lesk. Nom. 591, 428.

raikaũ, raikýti iter. '(Brot) mehrfach in Schnitten schneiden'—Uh. *rikháti;* W. *rīma;* Boi. ἐρείκω. Cf. Lesk. Abl. 281.

raimas 'bunt'—see under *raĩbas*. Cf. B. II, 1, 250.

ráiszas 'lahm'—(Uh. *ríṣyati*); B. II, 1, 151. 3, 283; Boi. ῥοικός. Cf. Lesk. Abl. 281.

raiszaũ, raiszýti iter. 'fortgesetzt binden, fesseln'—Uh. *raçanā́,* (*ríṣyati*); W. *corrigia, rīca.* Cf. Lesk. Abl. 281.

ráiszczoju, ráiszczoti iter. id.—B. II, 3, 241. Cf. Lesk. Abl. 281.

ráisziu, ráiszėti 'lahm gehen, hinken'—(Uh. *ríṣyati*). Cf. Lesk. Abl. 281.

raĩsztis masc. 'Band, Binde, (bes.) die Kopfbinde der litauischen Mädchen'; (Lalis) "band, string; (surgery) bandage, sling"—Uh. *raçanā́;* W. *rīca.* Cf. Ness. 443[a]; Bezz. LF. 162; Lesk. Abl. 281.

raivė 'Streifen'—B. II, 1, 477; (W. *rīma*). Cf. MLG. I, 232; Lesk. Nom. 349.

ráiżau, ráiżyti iter. 'mehrfach ritzen, schneiden'; (Lalis) "to scratch, notch, carve, flog, whip"—Boi. ῥήγνῡμι. Cf. Lesk. Abl. 370.

ráiżaus, ráiżytis 'sich recken'—B. I, 504; W. *rēx*. See *rą́żau(s)* & Lesk. Abl. 365.

rakinù, rakìnti 'schliessen'—Uh. *argalas;* K. *Riegel;* W. *arceo*. See next.

rãktas 'Schlüssel'; (Ness. 427ᵃ also) "Spanner an der Flinte"; (Lalis also) "(mus.) clef"—Uh. *argalas;* K. *Riegel;* W. *arceo;* Boi. ἀρκέω. Cf. Lesk. Abl. 375.

ramas (?) 'Ruhe'—F. *rimis*. Cf. Ness. 441ᵃ, Lesk. Abl. 339. Notice also Bezz. LF. 162: *ràms* 'eine Stütze'; plu. 'Stützen, Pfosten'.

ramaũ, ramýti 'beruhigen, besänftigen'—B. II, 3, 249. Cf. Lesk. Abl. 339.

randù, ràsti 'finden, antreffen'—F. *wratōn;* B. II, 3, 321; Boi. περιρρηδής. Cf. Lesk. Abl. (Ntr.) 450.

rangaũ, rangýti iter. 'krümmen, winden'; (Kur.) "steife Dinge, z.B. ein Ankertau mehrfach krümmen, in Ringe legen"; **rangaũs, rangýtis** "sich krümmen, sich winden, wie ein Wurm, wie ein Hund, der in Angst ist" (Ness. 441ᵇ)—B. II, 3, 289. See *rengiũs* & Lesk. Abl. 340.

rangstus 'eilig, hastig'—Boi. ῥίμφα. Cf. Ness. 436ᵃ, Lesk. Abl. 340.

rankà 'Hand; Arm'—B. II, 1, 153. 2, 285; (Ber. *gŭrstĭ*); W. *vergo*. Cf. Lesk. Abl. 340.

rankìkė 'Händchen'—B. II, 1, 490. Cf. Ness. 428ᵃ.

ranszies Old Lith.—see *rą́żau(s)* 'ich recke (mich)'.

rasà 'Tau' (Feuchtigkeit)—Uh. *rásas;* B. I, 784. II, 1, 159.647; W. *rōs;* Boi. ἀπ-εράω, ἔρση (note).

rą̃stas "ein abgehauenes oder abgesägtes unbeschlagenes Ende eines runden Baumstammes" (Kur.)—B. II, 1, 410; (W. *radius*). Cf. Lesk. Abl. 340.

rãtas 'Rad, (bes.) Wagenrad; Ring, Kreis, Umfang; Spinnrad'—Uh. *ráthas;* K. *Rad;* F. *raþs;* B. I, 153.

156.445.472; W. *rota;* (Boi. ἐπί-ρροθος (note)). Cf. Bezz. BGLS. 13; Bezz. LF. 163; Lalis s.v.

ratẽlis 'Rädchen'—B. II, 1, 364; W. *rota.* See prec.

raudà 'Wehklage'—Uh. *ródas;* (F. *grētan*); B. I, 448.541. II, 1, 150; W. *rudo.* Cf. Lesk. Abl. 307.

raudà 'rote Farbe; rotgefärbtes Garn'—Uh. *róhitas, lohás;* K. *rot;* F. *raups;* B. I, 202; W. *ruber;* Boi. ἐρεύθω. Cf. Lesk. Abl. 306.

raũdas 'rot' (bes. von Pferden)—K. *rot;* F. *raups;* B. I, 197.202.424. II, 1, 166; W. *ruber, rōbīgo;* Boi. ἐρεύθω. Cf. Lesk. Abl. 306.

raudóju (ráudmi), raudóti 'wehklagen, jammern, weinen' (bes. um einen Toten)—Uh. *róditi;* (F. *grētan*); B. I, 209; W. *rudo.* Cf. Lesk. Abl. 307.

raudónas 'rot'—Uh. *róhitas;* K. *rot;* W. *ruber;* Boi. ἐρεύθω. Cf. Lesk. Abl. 306.

raudonìkis eine Pilzart—B. II, 1, 489. Cf. Lesk. Nom. 511.

raũdonůju, raũdonůti 'rot schimmern'—B. II, 3, 220.

raudùkas 'Fuchshengst'—B. II, 1, 492. Cf. Bezz. LF. 163.

ráugėju (ráugmi; Kur. **raugmì,** but cf. Kur. Gram. 1200), **ráugėti;** (Schleicher LSpr. I, 116; Kur. Gram. 1200) **riáugmi, riáugėti** 'rülpsen'—(Uh. *yugám*); B. I, 209; W. *erūgo;* Boi. ἐρεύγομαι. Cf. Lesk. Abl. 307.

raugiù, raũgti id.—B. I, 202; W. *erūgo.* See prec.

ráugmi 'ich rülpse'—see *ráugėju.*

ráuju, ráuti '(eine Pflanze) mit der Wurzel aus der Erde ziehen, jäten'—Uh. *rav-;* F. *riurs;* W. *ruo* 3, (*rūna*), (*rūs*); Boi. ἐρυσί-χθων. Cf. Lesk. Abl. 306.

raũkas 'Falte, Runzel'—K. *rauh, Runzel;* W. *rūga;* Boi. ὀρύσσω, (ῥυσός). See next.

raukiù, raũkti 'runzeln, in Falten ziehen; enger machen, zusammenziehen'—Uh. *rūkṣás;* W. *rūga.* Cf. Lesk. Abl. 307.

raũkszlas 'Falte, Runzel'—Uh. *rūkṣás;* W. *rūga;* Boi. ὀρύσσω. See prec.

raumũ 'Muskelfleisch'—Uh. *romanthas;* B. II, 1, 238; (Ber. *gruda*); W. *rūmen.* Cf. Lesk. Abl. 306.

ráunu, ráuti 'ausreissen, jäten'—B. II, 3, 321 (twice). Cf. Ness. 430[b]. See *ráuju.*

raupaĩ plu. 'Masern, Pocken'—Uh. *rúpyati, ropam;* W. *rumpo.* Cf. Lesk. Abl. 307.

rauplẽ 'Blatter, Pocke'; **raũplės** plu. 'Blatterkrankheit'—Uh. *rúpyati;* W. *rumpo.* Cf. Lesk. Abl. 307.

raũpsas, plu. **raupsaĩ** 'Aussatz'—Uh. *rúpyati;* F. *bi-raubōn;* B. II, 1, 543; W. *rumpo.* Cf. Lesk. Abl. 307.

rausiù, raũsti 'scharren, wühlen'—Uh. *loṣṭás;* (W. 1. *rūdus*). Cf. Lesk. Abl. 308.

raũsvas 'rötlich, rot'—B. I, 789. II, 1, 202.205.538.588; W. *russus;* Boi. ἐρεύθω. Cf. MLG. I, 390; Geitler LS. 106; Lesk. Abl. 306; Lesk. Nom. [345], 346.

rãvalas (Szyr.) 'Jäten'—B. I, 338. Cf. Lesk. Abl. 306.

rãvas 'Strassengraben'; (Lalis) "pit, ditch, trench"—W. *ruo* 3. Cf. Geitler LS. 106, Brückner SlFw. 124.

ravẽju (**raviù**), **ravẽti** 'ausreissen, jäten'—F. *riurs;* B. I, 338; W. *ruo* 3; Boi. ἐρυσί-χθων. Cf. Lesk. Abl. 306. See *ráuju.*

rãžas 'blätterloses, dürres Reis, Stoppel, Halm, Besenstumpf, Zinke'—Boi. ῥαχός. Cf. Lesk. Abl. 365, Lesk. Nom. 176.

rą́žau(s), rą́žyti(s) '(sich) recken'; Old Lith. (cf. Bezz. & Lesk.) **ranszies**—Uh. *ṛ́jyati;* K. *recken;* F. *uf-rakjan;* B. I, 434.549. II, 3, 268.288; W. *rego;* Boi. ὀρέγω. Cf. Bezz. BGLS. 42, 319; Lesk. Abl. 365.

ražis 'Stoppel'—Boi. ῥαχός. Cf. Bezz. LF. 163.

rẽczù, rẽsti 'winden, rollen, wickeln, krümmen'; (Ness. 437[b] also) "Pflanzen an Ranken ziehen, dann überhaupt ziehen, pflegen"—Boi. ῥάμνος. Cf. Lesk. Abl. 281.

rẽdas m., **rẽda** f. 'Ordnung, Anordnung, Zurichtung; Gastmahl; Gebühr; Schmuck, Zierde; Gebrauch, Sitte; der bürgerliche Stand'; **arkliũ rẽdas** 'Pferdegeschirr';

galvõs rẽdas 'Todesstrafe' — F. *ga-rēdaba*. Cf. Brückner SlFw. 125.

règsti 'stricken'—inf. of *rezgù*, q.v.

reĩkia, reikė́ti (reĩkti) impers. 'nötig sein'—(W. *rīma*). Cf. Lesk. Abl. 281.

réiszkiu, réikszti 'offenbaren'—B. I, 868. II, 1, 259. Cf. Lesk. Abl. 281.

réiżiůs, réiżtis 'sich brüsten'—B. I, 504; W. *rēx*. Cf. Lesk. Abl. 365. See *ráižaus*.

rĕju, rė́ti 'brüllen, heftig losschreien, schelten, zanken'—Uh. *rāyati;* B. II, 3, 31.204; W. *rāvus, (reor), (verbum)*; (Boi. 2. εἴρω (note)). Cf. Lesk. Abl. 370.

rĕju, rė́ti '(Holz) schichtweise legen'—F. *rapjō;* B. I, 176; W. *reor, (rārus)*; Boi. ἀριθμός (read *rĕju*). Cf. Lesk. Abl. 371.

rëkẽ 'Brotschnitte'; (Ness. 434[b] also) "eine abgestochene Erdscholle"—W. *rīma;* Boi. ἐρείκω. Cf. Lesk. Abl. 281.

rėkiù, rė̃kti 'brüllen, schreien, weinen'—F. *wrōhs;* W. *racco*. Cf. Lesk. Abl. 340.

rëkiù, rė̃kti '(Brot) schneiden; zum erstenmal pflügen'—Uh. *rikháti;* W. *rīma;* Boi. ἐρείκω. Cf. Lesk. Abl. 281.

rĕklės plu. 'Stangengerüst über dem Ofen zum Holztrocknen'; "Holz- oder Eisenstäbe, die im Schornstein angebracht sind und zum Räuchern vom Fleisch benutzt werden"—W. *ratis, (rārus)*. Cf. Bezz. LF. 163. See *rĕju* 'ich schichte'.

rė̃ksmas 'Geschrei, Gebrüll'—B. II, 1, 252. See *rėkiù*.

remiù, rem̃ti 'stützen'—Uh. *rámate;* F. *rimis;* B. I, 415.416. 428. II, 3, 396. Boi. ἠρέμα. Cf. Lesk. Abl. 339.

rengiůs, reñgtis 'sich biegen, sich krümmen, sich anstrengen, sich anschicken, sich rüsten, sich ankleiden, eilen'—Uh. *vṛṇákti;* F. *wruggō;* B. II, 3, 289; W. *vergo;* Boi. ῥάμνος, ῥίμφα. Cf. Lesk. Abl. 340.

renkù, riñkti 'auflesen, sammeln'—B. II, 3, 136; (Ber. *gŭrstĭ*). Cf. Lesk. Abl. 340.

rentù (restù), rèsti "dünner, undichter werden (von den

Zähnen, vom Getreide auf dem Acker etc.)"—B. II, 3, 296. Cf. Lesk. Abl. 340.

-rénżęs perf. act. part.—see *-ręžti* 'recken'.

-rėpiu, -rėpti—see *aprėpiu* 'ich umfasse, begreife'.

rẽplės plu. 'Zange, Kneifzange'—Uh. *rápas;* W. *rapio;* Boi. ἐρέπτομαι.

rễplinu, rễplinti 'plump hinstellen'—(W. *rāpum*). Cf. Lesk. Abl. 370.

rėplióju, rėplióti 'kriechen (bes. auf allen vieren), schleichen, langsam gehen'—W. *rēpo;* (Boi. *ῥώψ). Cf. Lesk. Abl. 370.

resnas 'fleischig, beleibt, stämmig, untersetzt, fest, stark'—(F. (Ntr.) *ga-wrisqan*); B. II, 1, 264.296; (W. *verrūca*). Cf. Geitler LS. 106, Lalis s.v.

rễsti 'rollen, wickeln'—inf. of *rëczù,* q.v.

restù, rèsti 'dünn werden'—see *rentù.*

resvas 'selten, dünn, spärlich'—B. I, 339. Cf. Geitler LS. 106, s.v. **ráswas.**

rẽtas 'dünn, weitläufig, selten, einzeln stehend'—Uh. *viralas;* W. *rārus;* Boi. ἀραιός. Cf. Lesk. Abl. 340.

rễtis masc. "ein Bastsieb mit grossen Löchern; ein siebartig von Bast geflochtener Korb; ein Netzbeutel" (Ness. 437*)—Uh. *viralas;* W. *rārus;* Boi. ἀραιός.

rëtu, rëtėti intrans. 'rollen' (z.B. von Tränen)—B. II, 3, 125. Cf. Donalitius 279, Lesk. Abl. 281. See *ritù.*

rezgìmas 'Stricken'—B. II, 1, 251.

rẽzgis m. 'Geflecht; Korb; eine ausgeflochtene Trage, Misttrage'—W. *restis.* See next.

rezgù, règsti '(mit grossen Maschen) flechten, stricken; binden, schnüren'—Uh. *rájjuṣ;* B. I, 731.789; W. *restis.* Cf. Lesk. Abl. 340.

rė́żiu, rė́żti; rễżiu, rễżti 'schneiden, ritzen, reissen, kerben' —B. I, 290; Boi. ῥήγνυμι. Cf. Lesk. Abl. 370.

-ręžti (B. **-ręszti**) 'recken'; **iszsiręžti** 'sich ausrecken, sich stemmen'; **iszsirężęs** perf. act. part. 'sich ausgereckt habend'; **įsirężęs** (**įsirénżęs**) 'sich gereckt habend'—

B. I, 504. II, 3, 268.288.446.492; W. *rego;* Boi. ὀρέγω. Cf. Lesk. Abl. 365.

riáugmi, riáugėti 'rülpsen'—see *ráugėju.*

rykauju, rykauti 'schalten, herrschen, regieren'—B. II, 3, 220.

rikys Old Lith. 'König'—Uh. *rắț;* W. *rēx.* Cf. Geitler LS. 106; Lalis s.v.; Trautmann Die altpreussischen Sprachdenkmäler 415.

rykmetȳs dial. 'der frühe Morgen'—B. I, 542. Cf. LBLV. 291.

rýksztė 'Rute'—Boi. ῥοικός (read *rýksztė* for *rýkstė*). Cf. Trautmann Die altpreussischen Sprachdenkmäler 416.

rimastìs fem. 'Ruhe, Rast; (Kur.) Gemütsruhe'—B. II, 1, 439. Cf. Lesk. Abl. 339.

rýmau (rýmoju), rýmoti 'in aufgestützter Stellung verharren, aufgestützt dasitzen oder dastehen'—B. II, 3, 168.200. Cf. Lesk. Abl. 339.

rìmstu, pret. **rimaũ, rìmti** (B. **rim̃ti**) 'ruhig werden, sich beruhigen, Ruhe haben, ruhig sein'—Uh. *rámate;* F. *rimis;* B. I, 415.416. II, 1, 430; Boi. ἠρέμα. Cf. Lesk. Abl. 339.

rimtas 'fest, stämmig, tüchtig'—B. I, 415. See prec. & Geitler LS. 106.

rinda 'Linie, Reihe'—(W. *ordior*). Cf. Geitler LS. 106; Bezz. LF. 164; Brückner SlFw. 125 (note); [Lesk. Abl. 339].

rìnga (B. **rínga**) "wer vor Frost oder aus anderer Ursache immer krumm und zusammengezogen dasitzt, umhergeht, Unlust zur Arbeit verrät" (Kur.)—Uh. *vṛṇákti;* F. *wruggō;* B. II, 3, 289; W. *vergo.* Cf. Lesk. Abl. 340.

ringóju, ringóti 'krümmen, kräuseln'—B. II, 3, 289. See prec.

riñkti 'sammeln'—inf. of *renkù,* q.v.

ristas 'schnell, hurtig'—Boi. ὀρίνω. Cf. Geitler LS. 107.

riszczà adv. 'im Trabe'—Boi. ὀρίνω.

rỹszgalvis 'Kopfbinde, Brautschleier'—B. II, 1, 101.

ryszỹs 'Band, Binde; Bündel; (Lalis also) union, society, relation'—W. *rīca;* Boi. ῥίσκος. See next.

riszù, rìszti 'binden'—Uh. *raçanā́;* F. *wruggō;* B. II, 3, 137. 397; W. *corrigia, rīca;* Boi. ῥίσκος, ῥοικός. Cf. Lesk. Abl. 281.

rýtas 'Morgen'; **rýtai** plu. 'Osten, Morgenland'—(F. *urreisan*).

ritìnis m. 'Rolle (Leinwand, Zeug), Knäuel (Garn), Wickel (Flachs); (Lalis also) round, circle'—Uh. *ráthas;* W. *rota.* See *ritù.*

rytój, rytó 'morgen, am nächsten Tage'—B. II, 2, 708.746.

ritù, rìsti trans. 'rollen, wälzen'—Uh. *ráthas;* F. *raþs;* B. I, 153.472. II, 3, 125.443; W. *rota;* (Boi. ἐπί-ρροθος (note)). Cf. Lesk. Abl. 281.

ritulai plu. tant. 'Schubkarren'—Uh. *ráthas;* W. *rota.* See prec.

rõdas, rõds 'willig, gern'—B. II, 2, 679. Cf. Brückner SlFw. 126.

rokė 'Staubregen'—(F. *rign*); (W. *rigo*). Cf. Ness. 445[b]. See next.

rõkia, rõkti impers. 'in Form eines starken Nebels regnen'—(F. *rign*); (W. *rigo*). Cf. Lesk. Abl. 377.

romùs, romas (Kur. DLWb. s.v. gelassen: **rõmas**) 'mild, ruhig, gelassen, sanftmütig, leutselig'—Uh. *rámas;* F. *rimis;* Boi. ἠρέμα, (ἐρῆμος). Cf. Lesk. Abl. 339.

rópė 'Rübe, (bes.) weisse Rübe; (dial.) Kartoffel; Kniescheibe'—K. *Rübe;* W. *rāpum;* Boi. ῥάπυς. Cf. Ness. 446[b], Lalis s.v.

ropėnà 'Rübenfeld'—B. II, 1, 273.275.276.623; W. *rāpum;* Boi. ῥάπυς.

rubà 'Plünderung, Raub'—F. *raupjan.* Cf. Brückner SlFw. 16-17.

rùdas 'braunrot'—Uh. *róhitas;* K. *rot;* F. *rauþs;* W. *ruber.* Cf. Ness. 447[b], Lesk. Abl. 306.

rūdyjù, rūdýti 'rosten'—Uh. *róhitas;* B. II, 3, 222. Cf. Lesk. Abl. 306.

rudìkė (Lesk. Nom. 511) eine Pilzart; (Ness. 448[a] & Kur.) 'Auerhenne'—B. II, 1, 490.

rūdìs 'Rost'—Uh. *róhitas,* (*loṣṭás*); K. *Rost* 2; W. *ruber, rōbīgo;* Boi. *ἐρεύθω*. Cf. Lesk. Abl. 306.

rudù, rudė́ti 'rosten'—B. I, 522; K. *Rost* 2; W. *ruber*. Cf. Schleicher LSpr. II, 313; Lesk. Abl. 306.

rudũ, gen. **rudeñs** 'Herbst'—Uh. *róhitas;* B. II, 1, 308. See *rùdas*.

rudũkė eine Pilzart (Agaricus deliciosus)—B. II, 1, 501. Cf. Ness. 447[b], Lalis 308[b].

rugënà 'Roggenfeld'—B. II, 1, 278.623.

rugỹs 'Roggenkorn'; **rugiaĩ** plu. 'Roggen'—K. *Roggen;* B. I, 716.

rúgiu, rúgti 'rülpsen'—(Uh. *yugám*); K. (8th ed.) *räuspern;* B. I, 433.581; W. *erūgo, rumex;* Boi. *ἐρεύγομαι*. Cf. Lesk. Abl. 307.

rūgóju, rūgóti 'übelnehmen, grollen, murren'—W. *rugio*. Cf. Brückner SlFw. 128.

rúgstu, rúgti 'sauer werden, gähren'—W. *rumex*. Cf. Lesk. Abl. 307.

rùkszlas 'kleine Falte, Runzel'—Uh. *rūkṣás;* W. *rūga*. Cf. [Lesk. Abl. 307].

rūksznus 'mürrisch'—B. II, 1, 292. See next.

rúksztas 'sauer; (von Menschen) ernst, mürrisch'—Uh. *rūkṣás;* W. *rumex*. Cf. Lesk. Abl. 307.

rūksztỹnė 'Sauerampfer'—W. *rumex*. Cf. Bezz. LF. 166.

rum̃bas 'Narbe am Baum, dicke Narbe von einer Wunde, Schwiele an der Hand; Saum eines Rockes, Einfassung der Hosen, Queder'—K. *Rand;* W. *rubus*. Cf. Ness. 450[a], Bezz. LF. 166, Brückner SlFw. 128, Lesk. Nom. 189.

runkù, rùkti 'runzelig werden, Falten im Gesicht bekommen, verschrumpfen'—Uh. *rūkṣás;* K. *rauh, Runzel;* W. *rūga;* Boi. [*ὀρύσσω*], (*ῥυσός*). Cf. Lesk. Abl. 307.

rũp, rūpė́ti 'kümmern, am Herzen liegen, Sorge machen'; **mán rũp** 'es kümmert mich, mir liegt am Herzen'—Uh. *rúpyati, lumpáti;* F. *laufs;* W. *rumpo;* Boi. λύπη. Cf. Lesk. Abl. 307.

rupas 'rauh, höckerig, holprig'—Uh. *rúpyati;* F. *bi-raubōn;* W. *rumpo.* Cf. Lesk. Abl. 307.

rupė 'Muschel'; **rupės** plu. eine Bauchkrankheit bei Pferden —Uh. *rúpyati.* Cf. Ness. 451ᵃ, Lesk. Abl. 307.

rupesnis 'Sorge'—B. II, 1, 289 (for § 327, b, γ read § 327, b, δ). Cf. Geitler LS. 107. See next.

rũpestis fem. & masc. 'Sorge'—Uh. *rúpyati, lumpáti;* F. *laufs;* [B. II, 1, 439]; W. *rumpo;* Boi. λύπη. See *rũp.*

rūpė́ti 'kümmern'—see *rũp.*

rupus 'rauh, grob'—B. I, 783. Cf. Lesk. Abl. 307.

rūpus 'besorgt'—W. *rumpo.* Cf. Lesk. Abl. 307.

rũsỹs, (Ness. 451ᵇ also) **rúsas** "eine Grube in trockenem Boden, bes. im Sande, in welcher man im Winter Gemüse, Kartoffeln und dergleichen aufbewahrt, und die mit einem Erdhügel überschüttet wird" (Ness.)—(W. 1. *rūdus*). Cf. Lesk. Abl. 307-8.

rusiu, rusėti (?) 'glimmen, schwelen'—W. *russus.* Cf. Geitler LS. 99, 107; Bezz. LF. 166; Lalis 310; Lesk. Abl. 307.

rustas 'bräunlich; lila'—K. *Gold;* B. II, 1, 413; W. *russus.* Cf. Geitler LS. 107, Bezz. LF. 165ᵇ, [Lesk. Abl. 306].

rústas, rūstùs 'unfreundlich, zornig aussehend, mürrisch, grimmig, erzürnt, rachsüchtig, traurig'—Uh. *ruṣṭas, róṣati;* B. I, 209; Boi. Ἐρινύς. Cf. Lesk. Abl. 307.

rùsvas 'bräunlich, rotbraun' (bes. von Pferden)—K. *rot;* B. I, 671.789. II, 1, 202.205.514.538.588; W. *russus;* Boi. ἐρεύθω. Cf. Lesk. Abl. 306.

ruszauju, ruszauti 'geschäftig sein'—Boi. ὄρνυμι. See next.

rusziu, ruszėti id.—B. I, 568; Boi. ὄρνυμι. Cf. Ness. 452ᵃ, Lesk. Abl. 308.

ruszus 'tätig, arbeitsam'—Boi ὄρνυμι. See prec.

rūbti (?) 'aushöhlen'—Boi. ἄρβηλος. Cf. Bezz. LF. 165[a]; BB. XVII, 215 & XXVII, 150.

S

są- 'zusammen, mit'—see *sam-*.

sądara 'Eintracht, Vertrag'—see *sándara*.

sagà "Schleife, oder sonst etwas, womit die Leinwand beim Bleichen auf der Erde festgelegt wird" (Kur.); "button, clasp, buckle" (Lalis)—B. II, 3, 294. Cf. Lesk. Abl. 365. See *segù*.

sagis (gender?) 'Reisekleid der Litauerinnen'—W. *sagum*. Cf. Geitler LS. 107.

saiczu (saitu), **saisti** 'Zeichen deuten, prophezeien'—(Uh. *sâma*); Boi. οἴμη. Cf. Ness. 455[b]; Lesk. Abl. 293; Lalis s.v.

saitai plu. 'Gefängnis'—F. *in-sailjan;* Boi. ἱμάς. Cf. Ness. 455[b]. Notice also Bezz. BGLS. 320; Geitler LS. 107; Bezz. LF. 167; Lesk. Abl. 282; Lesk. Nom. 534; Lalis 311. See *sētas* 'Strick'.

saitas 'Zeichendeuterei'—(Uh. *sâma*); Boi. οἴμη. Cf. Ness. 455[b], Lesk. Abl. 293.

saitu, saisti 'prophezeien'—see *saiczu*.

sakaĩ plu. 'Harz'—B. I, 757. II, 1, 165; W. *sap(p)īnus, sūcus, sūcinum, (sanguis)*; Boi. ὀπός, (Ntr.) ἁπαλός.

sãkalas 'Falke'—Uh. *çakunás;* (W. *cicōnia*). Cf. Brückner SlFw. 129.

sakaũ, sakýti 'sagen'; **įsakaũ, įsakýti** 'sagend einschärfen'—K. *sagen;* (F. *saihvan*); B. I, 601. II, 3, 190.250; W. *inquam;* Boi. ἀσπάζομαι, ἐννέπω. Cf. Lesk. Abl. 366.

sakstis 'Schnalle'—B. II, 1, 437. Cf. Lesk. Nom. 551. See next.

saktìs fem. id.—B. II, 1, 437; (W. *sēgnis*). Cf. Lesk. Abl. 365-6.

salà 'Insel'—W. *insula*.

salava 'Insel' (Lalis: 'cape, promontory')—B. II, 1, 205. 624. Cf. Bezz. BGLS. 320.

saldēsnis 'süsser'—B. II, 1, 561. See *saldùs* & *-ēsnis*.

saldumỹnai plu. 'Süssigkeiten, Zuckerwerk'—B. II, 1, 278.649.

saldùs 'süss'—K. *Salz;* F. *salt;* B. I, 341.533. II, 3, 376; W. *sāl* (twice). Cf. Lesk. Abl. 375.

saluba 'Vereinigung'—Ber. *lubŭ*. Cf. Ness. 374*; Brückner SlFw. 104 (note); Archiv XX, 489; Trautmann Die altpreussischen Sprachdenkmäler 417.

salubas (?) Old Lith. 'Verlöbnis, Ehe'—Ber. *lubŭ*. Cf. Trautmann Die altpreussischen Sprachdenkmäler 418. See prec.

sam-, są- pref. 'zusammen, mit' (e.g. **samdas** 'Miete'; **sążinė** 'Gewissen')—Uh. *sám;* B. II, 1, 165. 2, 896; W. *com-, similis;* Boi. ὁμός.

sámalnės 'Schrotmehl'—F. *malma;* (W. *monīle*). Cf. Bezz. LF. 167. See *malù*.

samiszlei adv. 'ohne Unterschied, vermischt'—B. II, 1, 348. Cf. Bezz. BGLS. 320. See *misztù*.

sámtis masc. 'grosser hölzerner Schöpflöffel, Fischsack, Fischnetz; Maurerkelle'—Uh. *sátas;* W. *sentīna;* Boi. ἄσις, (Ntr.) 2. ἄμη. Cf. Lesk. Abl. 366.

sándara (Lesk. Abl. 361, Lesk. Nom. 209) 'Einwilligung, Eintracht'; **sądara** (Szyr., Kur.) 'Friede, Einigkeit, Bündnis, Vertrag'—Ber. *dorgŭ* 1.

sándaras id.—Ber. *dorgŭ* 1. Cf. Bezz. BGLS. 321, Lesk. Nom. 171. See prec.

sãpnas 'Traum'—Uh. *svápnas;* F. *swibls;* B. I, 340.345. 507.520. II, 1, 260; W. *somnus;* Boi. ὕπνος.

sapnũju, sapnũti 'träumen'—B. II, 3, 220.

sarga 'Wache, Schildwache'—(Uh. *rákṣati*). Cf. Ness. 463*. See next.

sárgas 'Hüter, Wächter'—Uh. *sûrkṣati;* F. *saurga;* B. I, 601; W. *servo*. Cf. Lesk. Abl. 366. See *sérgiu*.

sargyba 'Wache'—B. II, 1, 647. Cf. Lesk. Nom. 591, Lalis 313.

sargyklà 'Warte, Wachthaus, Waldwärterhaus'—B. II, 1, 622.

sargovùžis 'Wächter'—B. II, 1, 204. Cf. Lesk. Nom. 351.

sargùs 'wachsam'—(Uh. *rákṣati*); W. *servo*. Cf. Lesk. Abl. 366.

sar̃tas 'fuchsrot' (von Pferden)—B. II, 1, 413. 2, 104; W. *sorbus*.

są̃s old pres. part. 'seiend'—see *ēsąs*.

sąszlavýnas 'Kehrichthaufen'—see *sząszlavýnas*.

saudus old & dial. 'süss'—(Boi. ἀδελφός). Cf. Bezz. BGLS. 73, 321. See *saldùs*.

saugóju (**sáugoju**), **saugóti** 'in acht nehmen, behüten, bewahren'—(F. *siuks*); Ber. *chovajǫ*. Cf. Lesk. Abl. 319.

saugùs 'behutsam, vorsichtig'—(F. *siuks*); Ber. *chovajǫ*. Cf. Ness. 456*.

sáulė 'Sonne'—Uh. *svàr;* F. *sauil;* B. I, 211.439; W. *sōl;* Boi. ἥλιος.

saulẽlė dimin. 'die liebe Sonne; Amarant'—B. II, 1, 672.

saulùžė dimin. 'die liebe Sonne'—B. II, 1, 511.672.678. Cf. Wied. s.v.

saũsas 'trocken'—Uh. *çoṣas;* B. I, 193.490.746. II, 1, 166.541; W. *sūdus*, (*auster*); Boi. αὖος. Cf. Lesk. Abl. 311.

saũsinu, saũsinti 'trocken machen'—Uh. *çúṣyati;* B. II, 3, 383.

saustù, saũsti 'trocken werden'—B. II, 3, 386.493.

sausumà 'trockne Stelle'—B. II, 1, 250.624.

sausùmas 'Trockensein, Trockenheit'—B. II, 1, 250.

sáv refl. pron. dat.—see *sávei*.

sãvas poss. of the refl. pron.—F. *swēs;* B. I, 120.130.317. II, 2, 396.398.403.404.406.

savàsis poss. pron. 'der Seinige'—B. II, 2, 406. Cf. Kur. Gram. 982.

savę̃ refl. pron. acc.—B. II, 2, 413.427. Cf. Wied. 163.

savè, savęs refl. pron. gen.—B. II, 2, 396.416.427. Cf. Wied. 163, 164.

sávei, sáv refl. pron. dat.—B. II, 2, 418.427. Cf. Wied. 163.

sãvo gen. poss. of the refl. pron.—Uh. *svás;* B. II, 2, 398. 406.416.427; W. *sui;* Boi. ἑ. Cf. Wied. 163.

sążinė 'Gewissen'—B. I, 416. Cf. Lesk. Abl. 358.

sẽbras 'Teilhaber, Gefährte'—Uh. *sabhā́;* F. *sibja;* B. I, 520. (Ntr.) XLVII; W. *Sabīni.* Cf. Brückner SlFw. 129, 130 (note).

sė́du, sė́sti 'sich setzen'—Uh. *sī́dati;* F. *sitan;* B. I, 759. II, 1, 489.568. 3, 123.162.399.432 (read *sė́dęs* for *sė́dū*). 433.434.435.447.490.493; W. *sedeo;* Boi. ἕζομαι. Cf. Lesk. Abl. 340.

sė́džu (old form **sė́dmi**), **sėdė́ti** 'sitzen'—Uh. *sī́dati;* F. *sitan;* B. I, 151.485.486.489.523.718. II, 3, 171.182-3. 188; W. *sedeo, sīdo* (s.v. *sedeo*); Boi. ἕζομαι. Cf. Lesk. Abl. 340.

segù, sègti 'heften, schnallen; (ein Pferd) beschlagen'—Uh. *sájati;* B. II, 3, 294; (W. *sagitta, sēgnis*). Cf. Lesk. Abl. 365.

séilė, usually plu. **séilės** 'Speichel, Geifer'—W. *siler.*

seĩnyju, seĩnyti 'gleichkommen'—Boi. ἵκω.

sė̃jis masc. 'das Aussäen'—W. 1. *sero.* Cf. Kur. DLWb. s.v. Aussaat, Saat; Lesk. Nom. 288. See next.

sė́ju, sė́ti 'säen'—Uh. *sā́yakas;* K. *säen;* F. *saian;* B. I, 132.288.775.(Ntr.)1098. II, 1, 433.442. 3, 197.410; W. 1. *sero;* Boi. ἧθω (note). Cf. Lesk. Abl. 371.

sẽkiu, sẽkti 'die Hand ausstrecken, langen, reichen; schwören'; **atsẽkiu, atsẽkti** 'erreichen; abschwören'—B. I, 572; (W. *īcio*); Boi. ἐνεγκεῖν, ἵκω. Cf. Lesk. Abl. 282.

sėklà 'Same'—K. *Same;* B. I, 541. II, 1, 344; W. 1. *sero;* Boi. ἧθω (note). Cf. Lesk. Abl. 371.

seklùs 'seicht'—Uh. *ásakras;* F. *sigqan;* B. II, 1, 385; W. *siccus.* See *senkù.*

sẽkmas 'siebenter'—Uh. *saptamás;* B. I, 521. II, 1, 225. 2, 56 (twice); W. *septem;* Boi. ἕβδομος.

sekmė 'Gelingen, Erfolg; Absatz (von Waren)'—Uh. *sákma.* Cf. Ness. 461ᵃ. See *sekù* 'ich folge'.

sekmẽ (Szyr.) 'Fabel, Märchen, Erzählung, Sprichwort'—K. *sagen;* W. *inquam;* Boi. ἐννέπω. Cf. MLG. IV, 181; Lesk. Abl. 366. See *seku* 'ich sage'.

sèkti 'folgen'—inf. of *sekù,* q.v.

sèkti 'sich senken'—inf. of *senkù,* q.v.

sekti 'erzählen'—inf. of *seku,* q.v.

-sekti—see *į̇sekti* 'eingraben, einschneiden', *iszsekti* 'sculpere'.

sekù, sèkti 'folgen'; **sekũs, sèktis** 'Erfolg haben, gelingen' —Uh. *sácate;* K. *sehen;* F. *saihvan;* B. I, 117.587. II, 3, 120.399.447; W. *sequor;* Boi. ἕπομαι. Cf. Lesk. Abl. 366.

seku, sekti (?) 'erzählen'—B. II, 3, 121. Cf. KZ. XLV, 288; Lalis 318. See *sakaũ.*

selù, selė́ti 'schleichen, leise auftreten'—Uh. *tsárati;* B. I, 456. II, 2, 793; (Ber. *dvigajǫ*); (W. *salio, selāgo*); Boi. ἅλλομαι (& Ntr.), εἰλίποδας. Cf. Ness. 461ᵇ & Lesk. Abl. 366.

sėmenìnis 'zum Leinsamen gehörig'; **sėmenìnis alẽjus** 'Leinöl'—B. I, 387. See next.

sė̃mens, sė̃menys plu. 'Saat, (bes.) Flachssaat'—K. *Same;* F. *saian;* B. II, 1, 237; W. *sēmen;* Boi. ἧθω (note). Cf. Lesk. Abl. 371 (*sėmũ* sing.; cf. Lalis 318).

semiù, sémti 'schöpfen'—Uh. *sátas;* B. I, 122.358.370; W. *sentīna;* Boi. ἄντλος (& Ntr.), ἄσις, (Ntr.) 2. ἄμη. Cf. Lesk. Abl. 366.

sẽna 'Wand; Grenze, Schranke'—B. II, 1, 263; Uh. *sénā;* Boi. ἱμάς. Cf. Ness. 462ᵃ; Kur. 373 (two words); Lalis 320; Lesk. Nom. 365.

sẽnas 'alt'—Uh. *sánas;* K. *Seneschall;* F. *sineigs;* B. I, 116.344. II, 1, 166; (Ber. *junũ*); W. *senex;* Boi. ἕνος.

senãtvė 'hohes Alter'—B. I, 339. II, 1, 450.

sẽnė 'die Alte'—B. II, 1, 221.600. Cf. Sommer 60. See *sẽnis.*

senė́ju, senė́ti 'alt werden'—B. I, 262. II, 3, 217; W. *senex.* Cf. Ness. 462[b], Lalis 318.

senẽsnis 'älter'—B. I, 345. II, 1, 551.554. See *sẽnas* & *-ẽsnis.*

seniaĩ adv. 'lange, seit langer Zeit, vor langer Zeit'—W. *senex.*

senỹn (**eĩti**) adv. 'älter (werden)'—B. II, 2, 703.

sẽnis 'der Alte, Greis'—W. *senex;* Boi. ἕνις. Cf. Sommer 11, 262.

senỹstė 'hohes Alter'—W. *senex.*

senkù, sèkti (perfective **nusenkù, nusèkti**) 'fallen, sich senken (vom Wasserstande); ablaufen (vom Wasser); versiegen, trocken werden'—Uh. *ásakras;* F. *sigqan;* W. *siccus,* (*sentīna*); Boi. ἄσπετος, ἰάφθη, (εἴβω (note)). Cf. Lesk. Abl. 341.

senmotė 'Altmutter, Grossmutter'—B. II, 1, 82.

senóbė 'Altertum, alte Zeit, Vorzeit'—B. II, 1, 388. Cf. Geitler LS. 107, Lalis 319.

senùtis 'Alterchen; lieber, alter Mensch'—B. II, 1, 677.

septyneri 'sieben'—B. II, 2, 77. Cf. Kur. Gram. 1033, Wied. 158.

septynì 'sieben'—Uh. *saptá;* [K. *sieben*]; F. *sibun;* B. I, 116.507.722. II, 2, 18; W. *septem;* Boi. ἑπτά. Cf. Wied. 156.

septyniádeszimtas 'siebzigster'—B. II, 2, 61. Cf. Wied. 157.

septyniólika 'siebzehn'—see *septynì* & [K. *elf*]; [F. *ainlif*]; B. II, 2, 26.[27]; [Ber. *-lěkŭ*]; [W. *linquo*]. Cf. Wied. 156.

septiñtas 'siebenter'—Uh. *saptáthas;* B. II, 2, 19.56 (thrice); W. *septem.* Cf. Wied. 157. 7.

sérgiu (**sérgu**) (**sérgmi**), **sérgėti** 'wachen, bewachen, behüten'—(Uh. *rákṣati*), *sûrkṣatī;* K. *Sorge;* F. *saurga*

(& note); B. I, 601. II, 3, 136; W. *servo;* (Boi. ἐρχατάω). Cf. Lesk. Abl. 366.

sergù, siřgti 'krank sein, leiden'—Uh. *sûrkṣati;* F. *saurga;* (W. *servo*). Cf. Lesk. Abl. 341.

sėris (Szyr.) (?) 'Faden, Pechdraht'—F. *sarwa;* W. 2. *sero;* Boi. 1. εἴρω.

sẽsė dial. 'Schwester'—B. II, 1, 333. 2, 276.277. See *sesũ* & Kur. Gram. 728, 731.

sesẽlė, seserẽlė dimin. to **sesũ**, q.v., 'Schwesterchen'—B. II, 1, 672.

seserėnai, seserynai masc. plu. 'Schwesterkinder; Kinder zwei Schwestern'—B. II, 1, 604; W. *sobrīnus.* Cf. Ness. 464ª, Lesk. Nom. 389. See *sesũ.*

seserycza 'Schwestertochter, Tochter der Schwester der Mutter'; **seseryczos** plu. (also) 'Töchter zwei Schwestern'—B. II, 1, 604. Cf. Ness. 464ª. See prec.

sesýtė dimin. to **sesũ**, q.v., 'Schwesterchen'—B. II, 1, 672.

sẽsti 'sich setzen'—inf. of *sė́du,* q.v.

sesuñg dial. 'Schwester'—B. II, 2, 126. Cf. Kur. Gram. 731.

sesũ 'Schwester'—Uh. *svásā;* K. *Schwester;* F. *swistar;* B. I, 148.340.426. II, 1, 333. 2, 127; W. *soror;* Boi. ἔορ. Cf. Lesk. Nom. 433.

sẽtas "Strick, mit dem das Hornvieh im Stalle an die Krippe gebunden wird"—Uh. *syáti, sétuṣ;* K. (8th ed.) *Saite;* F. *in-sailjan;* B. I, 191; Boi. ἱμάς. Cf. Ness. 464ª-b; Lesk. Nom. 536. See references under *saitai.*

sẽtas, sė̃tas 'feines Sieb' (bes. aus Pferdehaaren)—Uh. *syáti, sétuṣ;* F. *in-sailjan;* B. II, 1, 410; W. *saeta,* (*sīnum*); Boi. ἤθω. Cf. Ness. 465ª; Kur. 372b, 373b; Kur. DLWb. s.v. Sieb; Lesk. Abl. 282; Lesk. Nom. 536; Brückner SlFw. 130.

sė́ti 'säen'—inf. of *sė́ju,* q.v.

si 'sich' (dat. & acc.)—B. I, 259.938. II, 2, 396.408.427. Cf. Kur. Gram. 1142.

sidābras 'Silber'. Old Lith. **sidrabras** 'Silber'; **sidrabinas,**

sidrabrinas 'silbern' (cf. Bezz. BGLS. 322).—K. *Silber;* F. *silubr;* B. I, 870.

sijóju, sijóti 'sieben, sichten'—(W. *simila*) ; Boi. ἤθω, ἰ-μαλιά, (διαττάω). Cf. Lesk. Abl. 282.

sỹkis masc. 'Hieb; Mal'—B. I, 486.489 (read lit. for it.). 504.573. II, 2, 66.67; (Ber. *kortŭ*) ; W. *seco* (twice). Cf. Lesk. Abl. 341.

sylà 'Kraft'—(F. *saiwala*). Cf. Brückner SlFw. 131.

sìlė 'Trog, Schweinetrog'—W. *sīnum;* Boi. δροίτη, σέλμα. Cf. Bezz. LF. 168.

silis masc. 'Krippe'—W. *sīnum;* Boi. δροίτη, σέλμα. Cf. Ness. 465[b].

sìlpnas (B. **sílpnas**) 'schwach, kraftlos, zart, zerbrechlich, müde, matt, träge'—(F. *slēpan*) ; B. II, 1, 258; (Ber. *cholpŭ*) ; W. *labo.* Cf. Lesk. Abl. 359.

silpnókas 'ziemlich schwach, schwächlich'—B. II, 1, 500. Cf. Lesk. Nom. 515.

sìlpstu, sìlpti (F. & W. **sílp-**) 'schwach werden'—(F. *slēpan*) ; W. *labo.* Cf. Hirt Ablaut 299. See *sìlpnas.*

sirg̃ti 'krank sein'—inf. of *sergù,* q.v.

siúlas 'Faden zum Nähen, Zwirnfaden'—Uh. *sī́vyati;* F. *siujan;* B. II, 1, 364.378.619; W. *suo.* See *siū̃vù.*

siulẽ 'Naht, Saum; (Bezz. BGLS. 322) Lappen, Quaste, Zipfel'—B. II, 1, 364. See prec.

siútas pret. pass. part. of **siū̃vù,** q.v., 'genäht, gestickt'—Uh. *syūtás;* F. *anda-pāhts;* B. I, 491.775. II, 1, 398; W. *suo.*

siuvė̃jas m. 'Näher', **siuvėjà** f. 'Näherin'—B. II, 1, 161. Cf. Lesk. Nom. 331, 337.

siuvìkas 'Näher, Schneider'—B. II, 1, 490.616. Cf. Ness. 471[b].

siū̃vù, siúti 'nähen'—Uh. *sī́vyati;* F. *siujan;* B. I, 114.263. II, 1, 434. 3, 137.321; W. *suo;* Boi. 1. ὑμήν, (κασσύω). Cf. Lesk. Abl. 318.

sývas, usually plu. **sývai** 'Saft; Honigseim'—(F. *saiws*) ; (W. *siat*) ; Boi. αἷμα, αἰονάω. Cf. Lesk. Nom. 343.

skabù, skabė́ti 'schneiden, hauen'—F. *ga-skapjan, skaban;* B. I, 782. II, 3, 121; W. *scabo.* Cf. Ness. 472[a], Lesk. Abl. 341.

skabùs 'schneidend, scharf'—K. *schaben;* F. *ga-skapjan;* B. I, 520.629; W. *scabo.* Cf. Ness. 472[a]. See prec.

skaidyti (?) 'teilen, trennen'—B. II, 3, 487. Cf. Bezz. LF. 168, Lesk. Abl. 282.

skaidrùs 'hell, klar' (bes. von dem Wetter; auch von der Stimme)—Uh. *citrás;* B. I, 177.205.499.666; Ber. *cěďǫ;* W. *caelum,* (*scio*). Cf. Ness. 473[b]; Lesk. Nom. 441; Lesk. Abl. 282.

skaidúlios (?) dial., fem. plu. (Ness. 473[b] skaidulis masc.) 'Flachsfasern, Hanffasern'—Ber. (*cěďǫ*), *cěva.* Cf. Kur. s.v., Lesk. Abl. 282.

skáistas, skaistùs 'hell, klar, glänzend, strahlend, geehrt, berühmt, hehr'—B. I, 666. II, 1, 413; Ber. *cěďǫ, cěsta, čistŭ;* W. *caelum, caesius.* Cf. Lesk. Abl. 282.

skaĩstvaris masc. 'Messing, Glanzkupfer, Glockenmetall, Bronze'—Ber. *čistŭ.*

skaitaũ, skaitýti 'zählen, rechnen, lesen (Schrift), vorlesen, (durch Zaubersprüche) besprechen, beten'—Uh. *chinátti;* F. *skaidan;* B. II, 3, 372; Ber. *cěla, čìtǫ;* W. *scindo.* Cf. Ness. 473[a] f.; Bezz. LF. 70; Lesk. Abl. 282.

skaĩtlius 'Zahl, Anzahl; (Ness. 474[a] also) Rechnung, Rechenschaft'—B. I, 541. Cf. Lesk. Abl. 282.

skalà 'Holzspan, Lichtspan'—Uh. *kalā́;* F. *skilja;* B. I, 141.582; W. *scalpo;* Boi. σκάλλω, (Ntr.) κελέοντες. Cf. Lesk. Abl. 341.

skalbiù, skal̃bti 'prügeln, schlagen, mit dem Waschbleuel schlagen, waschen'—(Boi. κόλαφος). Cf. Lesk. Abl. 375.

skãlyju, skãlyti 'fortgesetzt bellen' (bes. von Jagdhunden) —Boi. σκύλαξ. Cf. Brückner SlFw. 131, Lesk. Abl. 342.

skalìkas 'fortgesetzt bellender Jagdhund'—B. I, 595; Boi. σκύλαξ, (σκύμνος). See prec.

-skantù, -skàsti 'hüpfen'—see *suskantù.*

skaplis masc. 'Hohlaxt' (zum Aushöhlen der Tröge)—W. *scabo*. Cf. Geitler LS. 108; Lesk. Abl. 373; Brückner SlFw. 132.

skapoju, skapoti 'schaben, schnitzen'—F. *skaban;* B. I, 583.584; W. *scabo;* Boi. σκάφη. Cf. Ness. 473[a]; Lesk. Abl. 373; Brückner SlFw. 17.

skãptas 'das krumme Schnitzmesser der Löffelmacher'—F. *skaban;* Ber. *kapĭ;* W. *scabo;* Boi. κόπτω. Cf. Lesk. Abl. 373.

skarà 'abgerissener Fetzen, Lumpen'—K. *scheren*. Cf. Lesk. Abl. 342.

skardau, skardyti 'schroten, stampfen, zerstampfen, kämpfen'—B. II, 3, 268. Cf. Geitler LS. 108; Bezz. LF. 169; Lesk. Abl. 343; Brückner SlFw. 132.

skasti 'hüpfen'—see *skastu*.

-skàsti id.—see *suskantù*.

skastu, skasti 'springen, hüpfen'; **suskastu, suskasti** 'aufspringen, in die Höhe hüpfen, rege werden (z.B. Kind im Mutterleibe), in Bewegung kommen, aufgeregt werden'; **suskatė** pret. 'er hüpfte auf'—B. II, 3, 171; Ber. *kolą;* W. *scateo*. Cf. Ness. 473[b]; Bezz. LF. 169; Lalis 324.

skaudùs 'schmerzlich, schmerzhaft, verdriesslich, unangenehm, gewaltig, heftig, furchtbar, grausam, rauh, hart, steil'—Boi. σκυδμαίνω. Cf. Lesk. Abl. 308.

skaũsta, skaũsti (3rd pers. pres.); **skaudė́ti** 'schmerzen'; **mán galvà skaũsti** 'mir tut der Kopf weh'—(Ber. *kuďą*). Cf. Lesk. Abl. 308.

skëdrà, (Szyr.) **skëda** 'Span, Splitter'—Uh. *chidrás;* K. *Scheit;* F. *skaidan;* B. I, 545.630.716. II, 1, 348; (Ber. *cěďą*); W. *scindo;* Boi. σχίζω, σκεδάννῦμι. Cf. Lesk. Abl. 282.

skêdżu, skêsti 'verdünnen' (z.B. Milch mit Wasser)—B. II, 1, 412; Ber. *cěďą;* Boi. σκεδάννῦμι. Cf. Lesk. Abl. 282. See next.

skêdżu, skêsti 'scheiden, trennen' (bes. eine Ehe)—Uh.

chinátti; K. *scheiden;* F. *skaidan* (read scheide for schneide); B. I, 177. II, 1, 412. 3, 397; (Ber. *cěďǫ*); W. *scindo,* (*scandula*); Boi. σχίζω, σκεδάννῦμι, (κίδαφος), (σχάζω). Cf. Lesk. Abl. 282, Bezz. LF. 170. See prec.

skéldu (**skéldžu**) (**skéldėju**), **skéldėti** 'sich spalten, platzen, bersten' (bes. von Steinen und Felsen)—Uh. *kaṇḍanam;* B. II, 3, 379 (twice); Boi. κελεφός. Cf. Ness. 475[b]; Bezz. LF. 169; Lesk. Abl. 341.

skeliù, skelẽti 'schuldig sein, schulden'—Uh. *skhálati;* K. *Schuld;* F. *skulan;* B. I, 703. II, 3, 137; (W. *scelus*). Cf. Lesk. Abl. 342.

skeliù, skélti trans. 'spalten'—Uh. *kaṇḍanam, kalā́;* F. *skilja,* (*skulan*); B. I, 116.141.454.480.582. II, 1, 444; Ber. *čelustĭ, červo,* (*kolǫ*); W. *scalpo,* (*clādēs*), (*laedo*); Boi. δίκελλα, κωλύω, σκάλλω, σκολύπτειν, σκῶλος. Cf. Lesk. Abl. 341.

skẽmenys plu. "der beim Weben oder Wirken durch Trennung der oberen und unteren Fäden mittels der Hevelten entstehende Raum, durch welchen das Schiffchen mit der Fadenspule hindurch geworfen wird; die beim Scheren des Garns zum Weben bewirkte Scheidung der oberen und unteren Fäden für das Einziehen in Kamm (Hevelten) und Blatt" (Kur. 380[b,a]); "die Scher- oder Webergänge der Leinweber" (Ness. 476[b]); "shed, space through which a shuttle crosses the warp; (sing.) section, division, partition, syllable" (Lalis 326[a])—(Ber. *cěďǫ*). Cf. Lesk. Abl. 282, Lesk. Nom. 418.

skérdžu, skérdėti 'Risse bekommen, aufspringen, platzen, bersten'—K. *Schrunde;* B. II, 3, 268.290.374; Ber. *chrędа,* (*berďa*). Cf. Lesk. Abl. 343.

skeȓdžus 'Hirt'—see *keȓdžus.*

skerelis dimin. 'Heuschrecke'—Boi. σκαίρω. Cf. Ness. 477[a].

skeris žem., masc. id.—Boi. σκαίρω.

skeȓsas adj. 'quer, schielend; (Lalis also) adverse, perverse'—B. I, 581.786; Ber. *čersŭ 2;* (W. *cerrītus*); Boi. ἐγ-κάρσιος, (ἄσπρις (note)).

skė̃sti 1) 'scheiden'; 2) 'verdünnen'—see *skė̃džu*.

skęstù, pret. **skendaũ**, **skę̃sti** 'untersinken, im Ertrinken sein'—Boi. σκινθός. Cf. Lesk. Abl. 366.

skiaudžu, **skiaudėti** 'niesen'—Uh. *kṣáuti*. Cf. Ness. 475*.

skiaurė̃ 'durchlöcherter Kahn als Fischbehälter' (cf. Kur. 380, Ness. 475*)—Boi. σκῦρος. Cf. Lesk. Nom. 280.

skiáutė 'Hahnenkamm; Flick, Stück Zeug; Tausendgüldenkraut, Erythraea centaurium; (Lalis also) harlot, doxy' —Boi. σκῦρος (read *skiáutė* for *skiáuti*). Cf. Lesk. Abl. 308, Lesk. Nom. 280, Bezz. LF. 170.

skȳdas 'Schild'—Boi. 2. ἀσπίς.

skilándis masc. 'Wurstmagen, der mit Fleisch gefüllte geräucherte Schweinemagen'—B. II, 1, 470. Cf. Lesk. Nom. 589.

skiliù, **skìlti** (B. **skílti**) 'Feuer anschlagen'—B. I, 464. Cf. Lesk. Abl. 342; Bezz. LF. 170: *skìlt, praskìlt*.

skìlstis (B. **skílstis**) fem. 'Klauenspalte der Tiere'—B. II, 1, 437. Cf. Ness. 476*, Lesk. Abl. 341.

skìlti inf.—see *skiliù* or *skylù* 1 or *skylù* 2.

skìltis fem. 'abgeschnittene Scheibe (von Kartoffeln usw.); (Lalis also) column of print'—Uh. *kalā́*; F. *skildus*. Cf. Lesk. Abl. 341.

skiltuvaĩ plu. 'Feuerzeug (Stein, Stahl und Schwamm)'—B. II, 1, 449.620 (read *skil-* for *szil-*). Cf. Lesk. Abl. 342.

skylù (**skįlù**), **skìlti** (B. **skílti**) 'in Schulden geraten'—K. *Schuld*; B. II, 3, 137.442; (W. *scelus*). Cf. Lesk. Abl. 342.

skylù (**skįlù**), **skìlti** (B. **skílti**) 'sich spalten, platzen'—K. *Schild* 1; B. I, (Ntr.) XLVII. 480. II, 1, 444; Ber. *červo*; W. *scalpo*. Cf. Lesk. Abl. 341.

skiĩvis masc. 'Magen'—Ber. *červo*.

skinù, **skìnti** 'pflücken; (Bäume) beschneiden; (einen Wald) roden'—Uh. *khánati*; (Boi. κατασκευή). Cf. Lesk. Abl. 359.

skirė̃jas 'Schiedsmann'—B. I, 467. Cf. Lesk. Abl. 342, Lesk. Nom. 331.

skýrimas 'Scheiden, Trennen'—B. II, 1, 251. Cf. Lesk. Abl. 342.

skyris m. & f. 'Unterschied, Verschiedenheit'—B. II, 1, 251. Cf. Ness. 478ª; Bezz. BGLS. 101; Lesk. Nom. 287.

skiriù, skìrti (B. **skírti, skir̃ti**) 'trennen, scheiden, absondern, unterscheiden, wählen'—Uh. *kṛṇâti;* K. *scheren;* B. I, 480.571. II, 3, 160.166.170.177.268. 374.442; Ber. *cěřǫ, černŭ 2; čeṛvo, čirvŭ, kora;* W. *caro, muscerda;* Boi. 1. καρπός, κείρω, σκάλλω. Cf. Lesk. Abl. 342.

skỹrius 'Unterschied, Verschiedenheit'—B. II, 1, 225. See prec.

skir̃pstas 'Schiessbeere, Heckenkirsche'—B. II, 1, 446. Cf. Ness. 478ª; Bezz. LF. 170; Lesk. Nom. 537; Trautmann Die altpreussischen Sprachdenkmäler 429.

skirpstus 'Rotbuche'—B. II, 1, 446; W. *carpinus.*

skýstas 'dünn, dünnflüssig, rein, klar, hell'—B. I, 205.716. II, 1, 412; Ber. *cěďǫ, čistŭ;* W. *scindo, (caelum).* Cf. Lesk. Abl. 282; Ness. 475ᵇ, 479ª.

skýstu, skýsti 'dünn werden, gemengt sein'; **paskýsti** 'sich zerstreuen'—B. II, 3, 397.443; W. *scindo;* Boi. σκεδάννῦμι. Cf. Ness. 475ᵇ, Bezz. LF. 170, Lesk. Abl. 282.

sklaidaũ, sklaidýti 'zerstreuen, ausbreiten, hin und her blättern (in einem Buche)'—(W. *laedo*). Cf. Ness. 481ª, Lesk. Abl. 283.

sklempiù, sklem̃pti 'glatt behauen, beschneiden, polieren'—W. *scalpo;* Boi. σκάλοψ. Cf. Lesk. Abl. 369.

sklẽpas 'Gewölbe, Leichengewölbe'—Ber. *klepǫ.* Cf. Lesk. Abl. 369, Brückner SlFw. 132.

skobas 'sauer'; **skobti** (?) 'sauer werden'—W. *scabo.* Cf. Geitler LS. 109, Lesk. Abl. 377.

skolà 'Schuld'—Uh. *skhálati;* K. *Schuld;* F. *skulan;* (W. *scelus*). Cf. Lesk. Abl. 342.

skopiù, skõpti; (Kur.) **skůpiù, skũpti** 'mit dem Messer aushöhlen'—K. *schaben;* F. *skaban;* Ber. *kapĭ;* W. *scabo.* Cf. Lesk. Abl. 373.

skoptuvas 'Hohlmesser'—Ber. *kapĭ.* Cf. Geitler LS. 109. See prec.

skraidaũ, skraidýti 'hin und her in Bogen fliegen, sich im Kreise tummeln, sich im Kreise umherbewegen, kreisen' —Ber. *kridlo.* Cf. Bezz. BGLS. 323; Donalitius 287; Kur. 382; Lesk. Abl. 283.

skrándas 'alter Pelz'—Ber. *chręda.*

skraudu, skrausti (Szyr.) 'rauh werden'—W. *scrautum.* Cf. Lesk. Abl. 320, 403.

skraudus '(Szyr.) rauh, brüchig; (Geitler LS. 109) reissend, schnell fliessend (von einem Strom)'—W. *scrautum.* See prec.

skrebiu, skrebti 'trocken sein oder werden' (z.B. vom Wege, wenn es friert)—Boi. κάρφος, κράμβος. Cf. Ness. 482ᵃ.

skrebù, skrebė́ti 'rascheln, krabbeln, rasseln, zappeln'—Boi. κρέμβαλα. Cf. Lesk. Abl. 343.

skrëczù, skrė̃sti 'drehen, im Kreise herumdrehen'—W. *curvus;* Boi. 2. κίρκος. Cf. Ness. 483ᵃ; Lalis 328ᵇ; Lesk. Abl. 284. See next.

skrëdżù, skrė̃sti 'fliegen'—B. II, 1, 377; Ber. *kridlo.* Cf. Ness. 482ᵇ, Lesk. Abl. 283. See prec.

skrëjù, skrė̃ti 'fahrend einen Bogen machen, in Bogen fliegen, im Kreise bewegen, zirkeln, tanzen, rund einschneiden'—B. II, 1, 377-8; Ber. *kridlo;* W. *curvus;* Boi. 2. κίρκος, (σφαῖρα). Cf. Lesk. Abl. 283.

skrëlas, skrėlas 'Flederwisch, Flügelende einer Gans mit den darin steckenden Schwungfedern'—Ber. *kridlo.* Cf. Ness. 482ᵃ; Kur. 383ᵇ; Brückner SlFw. 133.

skremblỹs 'kleiner Dickleibiger, Zwerg'—B. II, 3, 289; Ber. *kropŭ.* Cf. Ness. 482ᵃ; Lesk. Nom. 462; Lalis s.v.

skreplenù, skreplénti 'zähen Schleim auswerfen'—Ber. *kropa.*

skreplỹs, plu. **skrepliaĩ** 'Schleimauswurf'—Ber. *kropa;* W. *scrapta.* Cf. Kur. 383, Lalis 328.

skrẽsti 'drehen'—inf. of *skrẽczù,* q.v.

skrẽsti 'fliegen'—inf. of *skrẽdżù,* q.v.

skrydinė́ju, skrydinė́ti 'fliegen, schweben, kreisen (von Vögeln)'—Ber. *kridlo.* Cf. Ness. 482[b]; LBLV. 343; Lesk. Abl. 283.

skrìjos plu. 'der von Bast gefertigte Rand oder die Einfassung eines Siebes'—Ber. *iskrĭ, krajĭ, krojǫ.* Cf. Lesk. Abl. 283.

skrindù, skrìsti 'fliegen, kreisen, schnell laufen'—Ber. *kridlo.* Cf. Lesk. Abl. 283.

skrýtis fem. 'Radfelge'—W. *curvus.* Cf. Lesk. Abl. 283.

skritulỹs 'Kreis, Kniescheibe'—W. *curvus.* Cf. Lesk. Abl. 283.

skroblùs (Ness. & Kur.), **skrȯblas** (Szyr.) 'Hagebuche, Weissbuche'—Ber. *grabrŭ.*

skródżu, skrósti 'aufspalten, ausweiden' (bes. Fische)—(Ber. *kradǫ*). Cf. Lesk. Abl. 377.

skùbinas 'eilig'—B. II, 1, 260. Cf. Lesk. Nom. 398, Lalis s.v.

skubùs, skubrùs 'geschwind, schnell, eilig, flink, fleissig'—Uh. *kṣúbhyati;* K. *schieben;* F. *af-skiuban;* B. I, 867. II, 1, 385; Boi. σκύβαλον. Cf. Lesk. Abl. 318.

skubùtės plu. 'Frühkartoffeln'—B. II, 1, 418.

skudrus 'scharf; flink'—Uh. *skúndate;* (F. *schieten*); B. II, 1, 353; Ber. *kydajǫ;* Boi. σκεῦος (note). Cf. MLG. I, 233; Geitler LS. 109; Lalis s.v.

skujà 'Tannen- oder Fichtennadel, Tannen- oder Fichtenzapfen'—Ber. *chvoja.* Cf. Ness. 479[b].

skujokas 'Kernbeisser' (Vogel)—B. II, 1, 501. Cf. Ness. 479[b].

skumbù, skùbti 'sich beeilen'—Uh. *kṣúbhyati;* K. *schieben;* F. *af-skiuban;* Boi. σκύβαλον, (κτύπος). Cf. Bezz. LF. 171, 172; Lesk. Abl. 318.

skundà 'Anklage'—(Ber. *kuďǫ*). Cf. Lesk. Abl. 308.

skundù, skùsti 'nervös müde werden' (cf. Kur. s.v.)—Boi. σκυδμαίνω. Cf. Lesk. Abl. 308.

skùndżu (B. **skúndżu**), **skų́sti** 'klagen, verklagen'—B. II, 3, 382; Boi. σκυδμαίνω. Cf. Lesk. Abl. 308.

skūrà 'Haut, Fell, Leder, Baumrinde' (cf. Ness. 480[b]; Kur. 386; Kur. DLWb. s.v. Haut)—W. *obscūrus;* Boi. σκῦτος. Cf. Brückner SlFw. 133.

skurstù, skuřsti 'verkümmern, im Wachstum zurückbleiben' —W. *curtus.* See *nuskuřdęs.*

skùsti 'müde werden'—inf. of *skundù,* q.v.

skùsti 'schaben'—inf. of *skutù,* q.v.

skų́sti 'klagen'—inf. of *skùndżu,* q.v.

skùtas 'kleines Stück'—Boi. σκῦρος. Cf. Lesk. Abl. 308.

skutù, skùsti 'schaben, scharren, scheren, rasieren, (Fische) abschuppen'—Uh. *kṣurás;* F. *winþi-skaurō;* W. *novācula, seco;* Boi. σκῦρος, κυδάζω, ξύω. Cf. Bezz. LF. 172[a], Lesk. Abl. 308.

skutùlė 'hölzerne Büchse mit einem Deckel' (cf. Ness. 481[a], Kur. 386)—Boi. (Ntr.) σκυτάλη. Cf. Prell. deutsch. Best. in den lett. Spr. 49.

skùzbezdalis masc., eine Pilzenart—B. I, 719.

skȗpiù, skȗpti 'schneidend höhlen'—see *skopiù.*

skverbiù, skveřbti 'mit einem spitzen Werkzeug bohrend stechen'—(W. *sparus*). Cf. Lesk. Abl. 343.

skvetas (Szyr.) 'Flick, Lappen'—Boi. σκῦρος. Cf. Lesk. Nom. 160.

slankà m. & f. 'Schleicher, Faulenzer'—B. I, 387. Cf. Lesk. Abl. 343.

slãpczas 'heimlich, verborgen'—B. II, 1, 416. Cf. Lesk. Abl. 344.

slaptà adv. inst. sing. 'heimlich'—B. II, 2, 717. Cf. Lesk. Abl. 344.

slaptas 'Versteck'—B. II, 1, 410. Cf. Lesk. Nom. 531.

slaptis 'Geheimnis'—B. II, 1, 432. Cf. Lesk. Nom. 551.

slaptomìs adv. inst. plu. 'heimlich'—B. II, 2, 720. Cf. Lesk. Abl. 344.

slapùkas 'sich gerne Versteckender'—B. II, 1, 492.493. Cf. Lesk. Nom. 516. See *slepiù*.

slẽgiu, slẽgti 'beschweren, drücken'—(W. *labor*). Cf. Lesk. Abl. 370.

slêkas 'Regenwurm'—F. *bi͂dagwa;* B. I, 782. II, 1, 477; W. *līmax, salmo;* Boi. λείμαξ. Cf. Trautmann Die altpreussischen Sprachdenkmäler 431.

slenkù, sliñkti 'schleichen, kriechen' — Uh. *sr̥ṅkā,* (*çr̥ṅkhalā*); K. *Schlinge;* B. I, 387.452.472.608. II, 3, 119. 285.444. Cf. Lesk. Abl. 343.

slepiù, slẽpti 'verbergen, verstecken, verheimlichen'—F. *hlifan;* W. *clepo;* Boi. κλέπτω. Cf. Lesk. Abl. 344.

slesnà, sleznà "oberster Teil des Fussblattes am Gelenk"—Ber. *glezĭnŭ*. Cf. Kur. DLWb. s.v. Fuss; Lesk. Nom. 362.

slėsnas 'niedrig'—F. *fulhsni;* B. II, 1, 265. Cf. MLG. I, 391.

slėsnas, slėsnė (?) 'Fussknöchel'—Ber. *glezĭnŭ*. Cf. Ness. 485[a], Lalis 331, Lesk. Nom. 362.

sleznà "oberster Teil des Fussblattes am Gelenk"—see *slesnà*.

slydinė̃ju, slydinė̃ti iter. 'gleiten, wanken, auf glattem Boden unsicher gehen'—Uh. *srédhati*. Cf. Lesk. Abl. 284.

slidùs 'glatt, blank, schlüpfrig'—Uh. *srédhati;* K. *Schlitten;* F. *fra-slindan;* B. II, 3, 365; (W. *lūbricus* 2); Boi. ὀλισθάνω. Cf. Lesk. Abl. 284.

sliñkti 'schleichen'—inf. of *slenkù*, q.v.

slýstu, slýsti 'gleiten, unwillkürlich gleiten beim Gehen'—Uh. *srédhati;* K. *Schlitten;* F. *fra-slindan;* (W. *lūbricus* 2); Boi. ὀλισθάνω. Cf. Lesk. Abl. 284.

slyvà, slỹvas 'Pflaume'—K. *Schlehe;* W. *līveo*. Cf. Ness. 485-6; Bezz. LF. 172; Kur. 388; Lalis 331.

slopstu, slopti (?) 'schwach werden, ohnmächtig werden'—Uh. *lámbate;* W. *labo*. Cf. Geitler LS. 110; Bezz. LF. 172; Lalis 331[b]; Brückner SlFw. 133; Lesk. Abl. 377.

slubnas žem. 'schwach, matt, krank'—K. *Schleife;* F. *sliupan;* W. *lūbricus.* Cf. Ness. 486[a], Brückner SlFw. 134.

sluñkius 'Schleicher, Faulenzer' (auch als Eigenname gebraucht)—B. I, 454. Cf. Donalitius 288; Kur. s.v.; Wied. s.v.; Lesk. Abl. 343.

smãgenės, smagens plu. 'Gehirn; Knochenmark'; **dantũ smãgenės** 'Zahnfleisch'—B. I, 872. II, 1, 297; (W. *mergo*). Cf. Lesk. Abl. 366, Lesk. Nom. 383.

smaguriáuju, smaguriáuti iter. 'naschen'—F. *smakka.* Cf. [Lesk. Abl. 366].

smagùs 'geschmeidig, handlich, angenehm, bequem, vortrefflich; (Lalis also) cheerful, lively, gay, jolly'—(K. *schmecken*). Cf. Lesk. Abl. 366.

smagus 'schwer zu tragen oder zu ziehen'—(W. *mōlēs*); Boi. μόγος. Cf. Ness. 486-7, Lesk. Abl. 366.

smailùs 'spitz, naschhaft, schmeichlerisch'—(F. *aizasmiþa*); Boi. σμίνθος. Cf. Ness. 487[b], 489[a]; Lesk. Abl. 284.

smakrà 'Kinn'—Uh. *çmáçru;* B. I, 375.437. II, 1, 371.384; (W. *māla*).

smalktẽlis, smarktẽlis dimin. 'Stelle im Walde, wo das Holz dicht steht'—B. I, 450.851. Cf. Ness. 487[a], [Lesk. Abl. 344].

smardas 'Geruch, Gestank'—B. II, 1, 152. Cf. Bezz. BGLS. 323; [Lesk. Abl. 344-5].

smardinù, smardìnti 'stinkend machen'—W. *merda;* (Boi. ἄρδα). See *smìrdžu.*

smardvė (Ness.) 'Gestank'—see *smárvė.*

smarkatà 'Rotz'—Boi. μορύσσω. Cf. Brückner SlFw. 134.

smarktẽlis 'dichte Stelle im Wald'—see *smalktẽlis.*

smarkùs 'streng, grausam, heftig, stark, gewaltig'—Uh. *marcáyati;* W. *marceo.* Cf. Lesk. Abl. 367.

smarsas, smarstvas, smarstė "Fett, mit dem man Speisen abmacht, bes. schlechteres Abmachsel" (Ness. 487[b])—F. *smairþr;* B. II, 1, 543; W. *merda;* Boi. σμύρις. Cf.

Lesk. Abl. 345 (*smarstė* should follow *smàrsas*, and *smárvė* should follow *smàrstas*; as they stand, the meanings are confused).

smarstas 'Gestank'—W. *merda*. Cf. Ness. 489[a]. See *smárvė*.

smarstė, smarstvas 'Fett'—see *smarsas*.

smárvė, smardvė 'Gestank'—F. *smarna;* B. I, 339.718; W. *merda;* Boi. σμύρις. Cf. Ness. 487[b], 489[a]; Lesk. Abl. 345.

smáugiu, smáugti 'würgen, erwürgen'—B. I, 745; Boi. σμίχω. Cf. Lesk. Abl. 320.

smaukiù, smaũkti 'glatt streifen, anstreifen'—Uh. *muñcáti;* W. *ēmungo*. Cf. Lesk. Abl. 309.

smėlis (smėlỹs ?) masc. 'Sand'—Ber. *mělŭ*. Cf. Lesk. Nom. 300.

smelus (-ė- ?) 'aschgrau, falb'—Boi. μελίη. Cf. Lesk. Nom. 247.

smerkiù, smer̃kti 'in Not zu versetzen suchen'; **nusmerkiù, nusmer̃kti** 'umbringen'—Uh. *marcáyati;* W. *marceo*. Cf. Lesk. Abl. 367.

smetona żem. 'Sahne'—Ber. *mętǫ*. Cf. Brückner SlFw. 135.

smìlius (pir̃sztas) 'Zeigefinger, Näscher' — (F. *aiza-smiþa*); Boi. σμίνθος. Cf. Lesk. Abl. 284.

smiltìs fem. 'Sand'—Ber. *mělŭ*. Cf. Lesk. Abl. 344.

smir̃das 'Gestank, Stänker'—(Boi. ἄρδα). See *smìrdžu*.

smirdėlė̃ 'Attich, Zwergholunder'—B. II, 1, 370; W. *merda*. See next.

smìrdžu (B. **smírdžu**), **smirdė́ti** 'stinken'—B. I, 764. II, 3, 155.179.353; W. *merda;* (Boi. ἄρδα). Cf. Lesk. Abl. 344. See next.

smìrstu, smìrsti 'stinkend werden'—F. *smarna;* Boi. σμύρις. See prec.

smunkù, smùkti 'gleitend sinken, rutschen'—Uh. *muñcáti;* K. *schmiegen;* B. I, 775; W. *ēmungo;* Boi. ἀπο-μύσσω, μυχός. Cf. Lesk. Abl. 309.

snaĩgala 'Schneeflocke'—Uh. *snihyati;* W. *ninguit.* Cf. Lesk. Abl. 284, Lesk. Nom. 476.

snaĩgo, snaigýti impers. iter. 'in einzelnen Flocken schneien' —B. I, 190. II, 3, 268. Cf. Lesk. Abl. 284.

snãpas 'Schnabel'—K. *Schnabel.*

snarglỹs 'Rotz'—K. *schnarchen.* Cf. Lesk. Abl. 367.

snaudãlius, snudãlius 'wer bei der Arbeit einschläft, schläfriger Mensch'—W. *nuo;* Boi. νυστάζω. Cf. Lesk. Abl. 309.

snaudulỹs 'unwillkürlicher Schlaf, Schlummer' — Boi. νυστάζω. See next.

snáudžu, snáusti 'unwillkürlich schlafen, schlummern'—W. *nūbēs, nuo;* Boi. νυστάζω. Cf. Lesk. Abl. 309.

sne͂ga 'es schneit'—see *sniñga.*

sne͂gas 'Schnee'—Uh. *snihyati;* K. *Schnee;* F. *snaiws;* B. I, 189.190.191.345.588.621.722; W. *ninguit;* Boi. νίφα, ἀγάννιφος. Cf. Lesk. Abl. 284.

snëgýnas 'Schneehaufe'—B. II, 1, 278.

sne͂gt 'es schneit'—see next.

sniñga (sne͂ga, sne͂gt), snìgti impers. 'schneien'—Uh. *snihyati;* K. *Schnee;* F. *snaiws;* B. I, 179.387. II, 3, 115.118.268.279.397; W. *ninguit;* Boi. νίφα. Cf. Lesk. Abl. 284.

snudà, snùdis 'Schläfer, Träumer'—W. *nuo;* Boi. νυστάζω. Cf. Lesk. Abl. 309.

snudãlius 'schläfriger Mensch'—see *snaudãlius.*

snùdis 'Schläfer'—see *snudà.*

snústu, snústi 'unwillkürlich einschlafen'—W. *nuo.* Cf. Lesk. Abl. 309.

sodinù, sodìnti 'sitzen machen, setzen, pflanzen'—W. *sedeo;* Boi. ἕζομαι. Cf. Lesk. Abl. 341. See *sė́du, sė́džu.*

sódis 'Russ'—see *sū̃dis.*

sosta 'Sitz, Stuhl, Thron'—B. II, 1, 410. Cf. Ness. 458*, Lesk. Nom. 543. See next.

sóstas id.—B. I, 151. II, 1, 410; W. *sedeo;* Boi. ἕζομαι. Cf. Lesk. Abl. 340.

sotas 'Sättigung'—see *sótis*.
sótinu, sótinti 'sättigen'—Uh. *asinvás;* F. *saþs;* W. *satis.* See next.
sótis f., **sotas** m. 'Sättigung, Sattheit'—Uh. *asinvás;* K. *satt;* F. *saþs;* B. I, 169. II, 1, 27.173.409; W. *satis;* Boi. ἄατος, ἄδην.
sotùs 'satt, leicht zu sättigen, sättigend, nahrhaft, reichlich' —Uh. *asinvás;* K. *satt;* F. *saþs;* B. I, 169; W. *satis, satur;* Boi. ἄδην. Cf. Ness. 466[b], Lalis 335. See prec.
spáinė "die Streichung des Windes über dem Wasser, welcher sich durch Schaumstreifen kennzeichnet; daher auch diese Schaumstreifen selbst" (Kur.)—Uh. *phénas;* B. I, 716.725; W. *spūma.*
spalỹs, usually plu. **spãliai** 'Schäben, Abfall des Flachses'—Uh. *phálati;* (Ber. *cěva*); W. *spolium;* Boi. σπάλαξ. Cf. Lesk. Abl. 345.
spandyti (?) 'spannen'—B. I, 373; (W. *pando, pendeo*); Boi. σπάω. Cf. Bezz. BGLS. 324, Lesk. Abl. 345.
spañgûgė 'Moosbeere'—(W. *fungus*). Cf. Ness. 491[b].
spanskus 'eng, drückend'—B. I, 717.719. II, 1, 480. Cf. MLG. I, 391; Archiv XVI, 408.
spárdau, spárdyti iter. 'mit den Füssen stossen, stampfen'—B. II, 3, 269; W. *sperno;* Boi. σπαίρω. Cf. Lesk. Abl. 346. See *spiriù.*
sparginti (?) '(Salz auf eine Flüssigkeit) streuen'—W. *spargo;* Boi. σπαργᾶν. Cf. Geitler LS. 110.
spar̃nas 'Flügel, Flossfeder' usw. (cf. Ness. 491[b], Bezz. LF. 174)—Uh. *parṇám;* F. *sparwa* (note); B. I, 345. II, 1, 261; (W. *perna*); (Boi. πτερόν). Cf. Lesk. Abl. 346.
spartas (?) 'Band'—W. *sporta;* Boi. σπάρτος. Cf. Ness. 491[b], Lesk. Abl. 346.
sparvà 'Viehbremse'—B. II, 1, 208; [F. *sparwa* (note)]. Cf. Ness. 491[b], Lesk. Nom. 347.
spąslas 'Falle, Fallstrick'—B. II, 1, 373. Cf. Lesk. Nom. 453.

spą́stas id.—(W. *pendeo*). Cf. Lesk. Abl. 345.
spaudà 'Presse'—Boi. σπεύδω. Cf. Ness. 492ᵃ. See next.
spáudžu, spáusti 'pressen, drücken, plagen, quälen'—Boi. σπεύδω. Cf. Lesk. Abl. 310.
spaustùvas, spaustùvė 'Presse, Kelter, Buchdruckerei, Nussknacker'—Boi. σπεύδω. Cf. Ness. 492ᵃ. See prec.
spëczù, spę̃sti (Kur. & Kur. DLWb.: **spėčžiù, spę̃sti**) 'schwärmen' (von Bienen)—Boi. σπιδής. Cf. Lesk. Abl. 285.
spę̃czus (Kur. **spę̃čžius**) 'Bienenschwarm'—B. II, 1, 225. See prec.
speiczù, speĩsti 'umringen, umgeben, umstellen'; **prispeiczù, prispeĩsti** 'umringend an etwas anklemmen' (z.B. an eine Mauer); **suspeiczù, suspeĩsti** 'umringend zusammenklemmen'—W. *spissus;* Boi. σπιδής. Cf. Lesk. Abl. 285.
(**żolẽ sù**) **speigleĩs** '(Pflanze mit) Hacheln, Stacheln'—W. 1. *pinna;* Boi. σπίλος. Cf. Lesk. Nom. 462.
spëju, spëti 'Musse, Zeit, Gelegenheit wozu haben; schnell genug sein'—Uh. *sphā́yate;* F. *spēdiza, (fēra)*; B. I, 136.150.204.262.782. II, 1, 433. 3, 102.197.410; W. *spatium.* Cf. Lesk. Abl. 371.
spéndžu, spę́sti 'Fallstricke legen; (Kur. also trans.) mit Fallstricken fangen; (Lalis) plot, conspire'—Uh. *spandate;* (W. *pendeo, sponda*); Boi. σπάω. Cf. Lesk. Abl. 345.
speñgia, speñgti impers. 'gellen, klingen'; **mán aũsys speñgia** 'mir klingen die Ohren'—Boi. σπίνος, (φθέγγομαι). Cf. Lesk. Abl. 284.
spenỹs (Kur. **spėnỹs**) 'Zitze (bei Tieren), Zäpfchen im Halse, Ohrläppchen, (Lalis) pin-shaped protuberance'—Uh. *stánas;* K. *Spanferkel;* Boi. στῆθος. Cf. Ness. 493ᵃ; Lesk. Nom. 300; Trautmann Die altpreussischen Sprachdenkmäler 434.
spėrùs 'schnell, flink'—B. II, 1, 350. Cf. Ness. 493ᵃ; Brückner SlFw. 136; Lesk. Nom. 441.

spęsti 'Fallstricke legen'—inf. of *spéndżu*, q.v.
spėsti 'schwärmen'—inf. of *spėczù*, q.v.
spiáuju (**spiáunu**), **spiáuti** 'speien'—Uh. *ṣṭhīvati;* K. *speien;* F. *speiwan;* B. I, 289.519. II, 3, 320.321; W. *spuo;* Boi. πτύω. Cf. Lesk. Abl. 309.
***spilgstu, spìlgti** 'im Wachstum zurückbleiben'—assumed by Lesk. for *paspìlgęs*, q.v.
spynà 'Schloss, Vorlegeschloss'—W. 1. *pinna.*
spìndżu, spindėti 'glänzen, strahlen' (bes. von der Sonne)—(W. *caulae*); Boi. σπινθήρ. Cf. Lesk. Abl. 345.
spìngis masc. 'Durchhau, Waldstrasse, Grenze'—Boi. φέγγος. Cf. Ness. 493[b], Lesk. Abl. 345.
spìngu, spingėti (?) 'glänzen'—(Uh. *pājas*); Boi. φέγγος. Cf. Schleicher LSpr. II, 67, 317; Bezz. BGLS. 325; Lesk. Abl. 345.
spintù, spìsti 'in Schwärmen ausbrechen' (von Bienen)—B. II, 1, 412; W. *spissus;* Boi. σπιδής. Cf. Lesk. Abl. 285.
(**aviũ**) **spirà** 'Schafmist'—B. I, 454; W. *sporta;* Boi. σπάρτος, σπύραθος. Cf. Ness. 494[a]; Lalis 337; Lesk. Abl. 345.
spiriù, spìrti (B. **spírti**) 'mit dem Fuss stossen, hinten ausschlagen; (Lalis also) urge, press, force'—Uh. *sphuráti;* K. *Sporn;* (F. *sparwa*); B. I, 263.464.472. 716.742; (Ber. *dirajǫ*); W. *sperno;* Boi. σπαίρω, σπύραθος. Cf. Lesk. Abl. 345.
spìsti 'ausschwärmen'—inf. of *spintù*, q.v.
spį́stu, spį́sti 'zu glänzen beginnen'—Boi. σπινθήρ. Cf. Lesk. Abl. 345.
spitėlė 'die Nadel in der Schnalle; (Lalis 337[a]) buckle, clasp'—W. 1. *pinna.* Cf. Ness. 494[b].
spitnà 'Dorn der Schnalle'—B. II, 1, 260.265; W. 1. *pinna;* Boi. σπίλος (twice). Cf. Kur. DLWb. s.v. Dorn; Lesk. Abl. 285.
spitulė 'die Nadel in der Schnalle'—B. II, 1, 260; W. 1. *pinna.* Cf. Ness. 494[b].

spitulỹs 'Stern auf der Stirn eines Tieres'—Boi. σπίλος. Cf. MLG. I, 20; Kur. DLWb. s.v. Stern; Lesk. Abl. 285.

spleczù, splė̃sti; ìszspleczu, iszsplė̃sti 'breiten, breitlegen, ausbreiten' (von Zeugen, Decken, Flügeln, Segeln usw.)—W. *later, plānus.* See *pleczù* & Lesk. Abl. 346.

splendżu, splendėti (?) 'leuchten'—W. *splendeo;* Boi. σπληδός. Cf. Ness. 495[b].

splintù, splìsti (?) 'breit werden'—W. *later.* Cf. Lesk. Abl. 346.

sprãgilas 'Dreschflegel'—(W. *flagrum*).

spragù, spragė̃ti 'prasseln, knistern, platzen'—Uh. *sphūr-jati;* B. I, 481.716; (Ber. *chrę̨stajǫ*); W. *spargo,* (*fla-grum*), (*frāgor*); Boi. σπαργᾶν, σφαραγεῖσθαι. Cf. Lesk. Abl. 346.

sprainas (Mielcke) 'steif, starr, übersichtig' (vom Auge)—Boi. σπείρω.

sprangùs 'würgend, schwer hinabzuschlucken; **sprangì dúna** 'hartes, trockenes Brot'—K. *Sprenkel* 1; (F. *ana-praggan*); Boi. σπάργω. See *springstù.*

spráudau, spráudyti iter. 'etwas gewaltsam in einen engen Zwischenraum drängen'—B. II, 3, 268.378. Cf. Lesk. Abl. 309.

spráudżu, spráusti 'etwas gewaltsam in einen engen Zwischenraum drängen, klemmen'—F. *sprautō;* B. II, 3, 268.378.390. Cf. Lesk. Abl. 309.

spréndżu, spręsti 'mit der Hand spannen, umspannen; (Lalis 337) judge, decide, determine'—B. II, 3, 286. 382. Cf. Lesk. Abl. 346.

sprengu, sprengė̃ti (?) intr. 'würgen'—Boi. σπάργω. Cf. Ness. 496[a]; Bezz. LF. 175; Lesk. Abl. 346.

spriaũnas, spriaunùs 'stattlich, lustig, frisch, munter, keck, rüstig'—Uh. *prapharvī.* Cf. Lesk. Abl. 309, Brückner SlFw. 136.

sprìndis (B. **sprindìs**) masc. 'Spanne'—B. II, 3, 286. Cf. Lesk. Abl. 346.

springstù, spriñgti intr. (Lalis trans.) 'würgen (beim

Schlucken); (Lalis also) eat greedily'—K. *Sprenkel* 1; Boi. 1. ἀσφάραγος, σπάργω. Cf. Lesk. Abl. 346.

spriústu, spriústi (Kur.) 'heftig gleiten'—see *sprústu.*

spróga 'Spalte; Ausweg, Ausflucht; Schössling am Baume; springender Funke, platzendes Stückchen'—B. I, 481; W. *spargo;* Boi. σφρᾱγίς. Cf. Ness. 496*, Lesk. Abl. 346.

sprógstu, sprógti (Kur. **sprókstu, sprókti**) 'bersten, spalten, platzen, ausschlagen, knospen; (Lalis also, vulgar) die, expire'—Uh. *sphûrjati;* B. I, 481; W. *spargo;* Boi. σπαργᾶν. Cf. Lesk. Abl. 346.

-sprùkęs—see *iszsprùkęs* 'entschlüpft'.

sprústu, sprústi (Kur. & F. also **spriústu, spriústi**) 'heftig gleiten, aus einer Klemme entgleiten, entwischen'; **įsprústu, įsprústi** 'gleitend hineinspringen, in eine Klemme gleiten'—F. *sprautō;* B. II, 3, 378. Cf. Lesk. Abl. 309, 388.

-spudḗti—see *paspudḗti* 'sich quälen'.

spudinu, spudinti (?) 'gehen, eilen, sich davon machen, entwischen, davonschleichen'—Boi. σπεύδω. Cf. Geitler LS. 111; Bezz. LF. 175; Lesk. Abl. 310.

spùrgas (B. **spúrgas**) "der Ansatz zum Laube, ein Knoten oder Auge am Baum, Weinstock, Hopfen; der Ansatz zu jungen Federn; ein Knöpfchen am Hemde oder Tuch" (Ness. 495*)—Uh. *sphûrjati;* B. I, 417.473.476. 481; (Ber. *chręstają*); W. *spargo;* Boi. σπαργᾶν, σφαραγεῖσθαι. Cf. Lesk. Nom. 189.

spùrzdu spùrzu (B. **spúr-**), **spurzdḗti spurzḗti** 'flattern, rütteln'—B. I, 719.

sraĩgė, straĩgė 'Schnecke'—(F. *wraiqs*); B. I, 190.330. 610.782; (W. *vergo*); Boi. ῥαιβός. Cf. Lesk. Nom. 276.

sraigis masc. 'Blindschleiche'—Boi. ῥαιβός. Cf. Bezz. LF. 176. See prec.

srautas 'Strom, Fluss'—B. II, 1, 408.527. Cf. Geitler LS. 111; Lesk. Abl. 310; Lalis 342: *strautas.*

sravà 'Fliessen, Bluten; Menstruation'—Uh. *sravas;* B. I, 294.782; II, 1, 150.634. 3, 315; Boi. ῥέω, ῥύπος. Cf. Ness. 496ᵇ, Lesk. Abl. 310.

srãvinu, srãvinti 'fliessen lassen, bluten machen'—B. I, 304. Cf. Ness. 496ᵇ. See prec.

sraviù, sravė́ti 'leise fliessen, sickern' (z.B. Blut, Saft, Bach)—Uh. *srávati;* B. I, 424.722; W. *Rōma;* Boi. ῥέω, ῥύπος. Cf. Lesk. Abl. 310.

srebiù (srėbiù), srẽbti 'schlürfen'—B. I, 289.454.493.511. II, 3, 130.259.261; W. *sorbeo;* Boi. ῥοφεῖν. Cf. Lesk. Abl. 369.

srẽgti (?) "ermüden, quälen, vom Hunger gequält werden" —(W. *frīgeo*). Cf. Geitler LS. 111, Archiv XV, 480.

sriaubiu, sriaubti (Szyr.) 'schlürfen'—W. *sorbeo.* Cf. Lesk. Abl. 310.

sriobiù, sriõbti (sriůbiù, sriůbti) id.—W. *sorbeo.* Cf. Lesk. Abl. 369.

srovẽ, dial. **strovė** (LBLV. 344, Kur. s.v.) 'Strom, Strömung, tiefe Stelle im Strom'—Uh. *srávati;* B. I, 782.786.827. II, 1, 222; W. *Rōma;* Boi. ῥέω. Cf. Lesk. Abl. 310.

srudžu, srusti 'blutig machen'—B. II, 3, 374.390. Cf. Ness. 496ᵇ, Lesk. Abl. 310.

srutà, usually plu. **srũtos** 'Mistjauche; (Lalis also) drainings, slop'—Uh. *srutás;* B. I, 108. II, 1, 395.635; Boi. ῥέω. Cf. Lesk. Abl. 310.

srutỹnė 'Jauchengrube'—B. II, 1, 278. See prec.

***srũvù, srúti** 'fliessen'—assumed by Lesk. for *pasrùvo,* q.v.

stabarai plu. 'trockene Baumäste'—Uh. *stambhas;* F. *stafs.* Cf. Geitler LS. 111.

stãbas 'Schlagfluss'; **stabas** 'Bildsäule, Götzenbild; (Lalis also) post, stake'—Uh. *stambhas;* K. *Stab,* [*Stapel*]; F. *stafs;* B. II, 3, 293; (Ber. *kapĭ*); (Boi. στέφω) (read *stabas* for *stobas*). Cf. Bezz. BGLS. 325; Geitler LS. 111; Lalis 338; Lesk. Abl. 347; Lesk. Nom. 169.

stabaũ, stabýti; (Ness. 499ᵇ) **stebau, stebyti** 'zum Stehen bringen, aufhalten, hemmen'—Uh. *stabhnâti;* F. *stafs;* B. II, 3, 293; (W. *tabula*); Boi. ἀστεμφής. Cf. Lesk. Abl. 347.

stabdaũ, stabdýti id.—Uh. *stabhnâti;* F. *stafs.* See prec.

stãgaras, stegerỹs 'dürrer Pflanzenstengel; Halm, Reis, Strunk'—F. *us-stagg;* B. II, 1, 357; Boi. στάχυς. Cf. Lesk. Abl. 367.

staĩbis masc., plu. **staĩbiai** 'Pfosten; Schienbein, Schenkel' —Uh. *stíbhiṣ;* W. *stīpo, tībia;* Boi. στείβω. Cf. Ness. 499[b]; Kur. 402; Bezz. BGLS. 325[b]; Lesk. Abl. 347.

staibus 'stark, tapfer'—Uh. *stíbhiṣ;* W. *stīpo;* Boi. στείβω. Cf. Ness. 499[b], Lalis 339, Lesk. Abl. 347.

staigà adv. 'hastig, eilend, schnell, plötzlich, jählings'—Uh. *stighnoti;* F. *steigan;* (W. *mustēla, vestīgium*); Boi. στείχω. Cf. Lesk. Abl. 285.

staigaus, staigytis (?) 'eilen'—F. *steigan;* B. I, 571; Boi. στείχω. Cf. Lesk. Abl. 285.

stãklė (Mielcke) 'Lisse (am Leiterwagen)'; **stãklės** plu. 'Webstuhl, Gestell der Leinweber'—B. I, 177. II, 1, 341; W. *sto,* (1. *stagnum*). Cf. Lesk. Abl. 373.

stãlas 'Tisch'—Uh. *sthálam;* F. *stōls;* W. *locus.* Cf. Brückner SlFw. 136.

staĩdas 'Stall'—F. *and-stald.* Cf. Prell. deutsch. Best. in den lett. Spr. 49.

stambas 'Stengel, Strunk (bes. von Kohl)'—Uh. *stambás, stambhas;* K. *Stummel.* Cf. Ness. 497[b], Lesk. Abl. 347.

stam̃bras, stem̃bras, stembrỹs 'Stengel, Halm'—K. *Stummel, Stump;* B. I, 386. II, 1, 355. Cf. Ness. 498[a], Lesk. Abl. 347.

stambùs 'grob' (z.B. Mehl, Brot, Tuch, Mensch)—K. *Stummel;* B. II, 3, 293. Cf. Lesk. Abl. 347.

stàpteliu, stàptelėti; stàpteriu, stàpterėti 'augenblicklich stillstehen, stocken'—Uh. *sthāpayati.* Cf. Lesk. Abl. 347.

staras 'Hamster'—K. *Hamster;* Ber. *chomĕstorŭ.*

stataũ, statýti 'stellen, hinstellen, feststellen, setzen, einsetzen, anstellen, anordnen, verordnen'—B. I, 170.177. 489. II, 1, 397; W. *sto;* Boi. ἵστημι. Cf. Lesk. Abl. 373.

statìnė (Kur.: "nämlich -týnė" — ?) 'grosse hölzerne Wanne; (Lalis) barrel, cask'—Boi. στάμνος. Cf. Lesk. Nom. 403.

statùs 'stehend, aufrecht, steil; unhöflich, derb, trotzig'—B. II, 1, 397; W. *sto.* Cf. Lesk. Abl. 373.

stáunu 'ich stehe'. "Eine nordlittauische Präsensform (bei Memel) für *stóviu* 'stehen'" (Kur.).—Boi. σταυρός. Cf. Ness. 499ᵇ; MLG. I, 65; Schleicher LSpr. I, 114; Kur. Gram. 1186.

stẽbas 'Stab, Stock, Pfeiler, Mast'—F. *stafs;* (W. *tabula*); Boi. ἀστεμφής. Cf. Lesk. Abl. 347.

stebau, stebyti 'aufhalten'—see *stabaũ.*

stebiűs, stebė́tis 'staunen, sich wundern, sich entsetzen'—Uh. *stabhnā́ti;* (W. *tabula*); Boi. ἀστεμφής. Cf. Lesk. Abl. 347.

stėbiűs, stẽbtis 'sich hoch aufrichten, sich auf die Fussspitzen stellen, grosstun, sich stemmen, sich bemühen, ringen, trachten'—Uh. *sthāpayati.* Cf. Lesk. Abl. 347.

stebulỹs 'Radnabe'—(Boi. στέφω). Cf. Ness. 500ᵃ, [Lesk. Abl. 347].

stegė 'Stichling, Stechbüttel'—F. *us-stagg.* Cf. Ness. 500ᵃ.

stegerỹs 'Stengel'—see *stāgaras.*

stẽgiu, stẽgti '(ein Dach) decken'—Uh. *sthágati;* K. *Dach;* B. II, 3, 399.447.493; W. *tego;* Boi. στέγω. Cf. Lesk. Abl. 371.

stẽgius 'Dachdecker'—B. II, 1, 224.

stẽktojis id.—B. I, 573; W. *tego;* Boi. στέγω. Cf. Kur. 404ᵃ, l. 6. See *stẽgiu.*

stelbiù, stel̃bti 'schal werden'—W. *stlembus.* Cf. Lesk. Abl. 369.

stembiù, stem̃bti 'in Stengel schiessen (von Pflanzen); (Lalis 340 also) oppose, resist'—Uh. *stabhnā́ti;* F.

stafs; B. II, 3, 293.382; (W. *tabula*); Boi. ἀστεμφής. Cf. Ness. 498ᵃ, Lesk. Abl. 347.

stem̃bras, stembrỹs 'Stengel'—see *stam̃bras.*

sténgiu, sténgti 'Kraft an etwas setzen, sich anstrengen'; **sténgiûs, sténgtis** 'widerstreben, sich widersetzen, sich sträuben'—Uh. *táṅgati;* F. *stigqan;* B. II, 3, 285 (twice).382. Cf. Lesk. Abl. 347.

stenù, stenė́ti 'ächzen, stöhnen'—Uh. *stánati;* B. I, 726. II, 3, 117.184; W. *tono;* Boi. στένω. Cf. Lesk. Abl. 347.

stẽpinu, stẽpinti 'ausrecken, gross machen; versichern, festsetzen'—Uh. *sthāpayati.* Cf. Ness. 501ᵃ, Bezz. BGLS. 326.

stèrptis (?) 'auf etwas bestehen' in **ùż sãvo teisỹbę stèrptis** 'auf seinem Rechte bestehen'—W. *sterilis.* Cf. Geitler LS. 111, Lesk. Abl. 347.

stýgau, stýgoti 'an einem Orte ruhig verweilen, verharren' —F. *staks;* W. *instīgo.* Cf. Lesk. Abl. 285. See *stingù.*

stìklas 'Glas' (Stoff, Trinkglas)—F. *stikls.* Cf. Brückner SlFw. 137.

styma, stymas 'Schwarm ziehender Fische'—Uh. *styā́yate;* W. *stīpo.* Cf. Ness. 501ᵇ, Prell. deutsch. Best. in den lett. Spr. 49.

stim̃bras 'Schwanzstummel; das dicke Ende der Peitschenschnur; Traubenkamm; Glockenklöppel'—K. *Stummel;* B. I, 386.413. II, 1, 355. Cf. Ness. 501ᵃ, Lesk. Abl. 347.

stimpù, stìpti 'steif werden, erstarren, umkommen, verrecken'—Uh. *stíbhiṣ;* K. *steif;* W. *stīpo;* Boi. στείβω. Cf. Lesk. Abl. 285.

stìngstu, stìngti (B. **stínkstu, stínkti**) 'gerinnen; steif, dick werden'—B. II, 3, 285; W: *stīpo,* (1. *stagnum*); Boi. στείβω. Cf. Lesk. Abl. 347. See *sténgiu.*

stingù, stìgti 'an einem Orte ruhig werden, verweilen'—F. *staks;* B. II, 3, 279; W. *instīgo;* Boi. στίζω. Cf. Lesk. Abl. 285.

stiprinóju, stiprinóti 'stärken, kräftigen'—B. II, 3, 312. See next.

stìprinu, stìprinti id.—B. II, 3, 312. See next.

stiprùs 'stark, kräftig, fest'—Uh. *stibhiṣ;* K. *steif;* W. *stīpo;* Boi. στείβω. Cf. Lesk. Abl. 285.

stìpti 'erstarren, verrecken'—inf. of *stimpù*, q.v.

stỹras 'starr'; **į ką styromìs akimìs žiūrėti** 'jemand mit starren Augen ansehen'—F. *stains;* W. *stīpo;* Boi. στίλη. Cf. Kur. DLWb. s.v. starr. See *styrstù*.

stýrau, stýroti 'steif und lümmelhaft dastehen'—W. *stīpo;* Boi. στίλη. See prec.

styrstù, stỹrti 'steif und starr werden, erstarren'—W. *stīpo;* Boi. στίλη. Cf. Lesk. Abl. 360.

styru, styrėti 'starr, steif sein, erstarren (z.B. vor Schreck, Kälte); (Lalis) to jut out, stick out'—W. *sterilis*. Cf. Ness. 502ª.

stobras 'Säule'—K. *Stab*. Cf. Bezz. BGLS. 326, Lesk. Abl. 347.

stodas Samogit. "eine Herde Vieh, bes. Pferde"—K. *Stute*. Cf. Ness. 502ᵇ, Brückner SlFw. 137.

stógas 'Dach'—Uh. *sthágati;* K. *Dach;* B. I, 152.571.583. 726. II, 1, 154; W. *tego;* Boi. στέγω. See *stėgiu*.

stóju, stóti 'treten, sich stellen, stehen, aufstehen'; **stójůs, stótis** 'sich stellen, auftreten, sich erheben, entstehen, werden, sich zutragen, sich ereignen'; **pastóju, pastóti** 'werden'; **perstóju, perstóti** 'aufhören, abbrechen'—Uh. *sthā-;* F. *standan;* B. I, 164.169.262.489.723. II, 1, 433.442. 3, 100.197.385.409.493; W. *sto* (twice); Boi. ἵστημι, στέαρ. Cf. Ness. 502, 503; Lalis 342; Lesk. Abl. 373.

stokas 'Pfahl, Zaunpfahl'—(W. 1. *stagnum*). Cf. Ness. 503ᵇ, Prell. deutsch. Best. in den lett. Spr. 49.

stomů 'Wuchs, Statur, Körperlänge'; "ein drei bis vier Ellen langes Stück weisser, feiner Leinwand, welches bei Hochzeiten von der Braut dem Freiwerber geschenkt wird" (Kur.); "measure of three ells" (Lalis)

—Uh. *sthâma;* F. *stōma* (read statur for natur); B. II, 1, 238; W. *stāmen;* Boi. στήμων. Cf. Lesk. Abl. 373.

stónas 'Stand, Zustand'—B. I, 164.722. II, 1, 259; W. *dēstino;* Boi. δύστηνος. Cf. Brückner SlFw. 137, Lesk. Nom. 361.

stónė "ein gebrückter Pferdestand im Stalle" (Ness. 504[a]); 'stable, stall' (Lalis)—K. *Stute.* Cf. Brückner SlFw. 137.

stóras 'dick, umfangreich, stark, schwer, grob, schwanger'—Uh. *sthirás;* K. *starr;* F. *and-staurran;* B. I, 204. II, 1, 350; W. *restauro, sterilis.* Cf. Lesk. Nom. 442.

storỹn (**eĩti**) 'dicker (werden)' adv.—B. II, 2, 703. See prec. & [Lesk. Nom. 411].

stovà 'Stelle, Standort'—F. 1. *staua;* W. *restauro;* Boi. σταυρός. Cf. Ness. 502[a], Lesk. Abl. 374.

stovis masc. (Ness. fem.) 'Zustand'—Boi. σταυρός. Cf. Ness. 502[b]; Lalis 342; Lesk. Abl. 374; Lesk. Nom. 348.

stóviu (dial. **stáunu**, q.v.), **stovė́ti** 'stehen'—Uh. *sthā-, sthāvarás;* F. *standan, stōjan;* B. I, 332. II, 3, 252; W. *restauro;* Boi. σταυρός. Cf. Lesk. Abl. 374.

stovus 'stehend' (vom Wasser)—B. II, 1, 204; Boi. σταυρός. Cf. Lesk. Nom. 344; IF. IX, 370.

straĩgė 'Schnecke'—see *sraĩgė.*

strãja 'Streustroh; ein mit Stroh ausgelegter Pferdestall'—W. *sterno.* Cf. Ness. 505[b], Prell. deutsch. Best. in den lett. Spr. 49.

strautas 'Strom'—see *srautas.*

strãzdas 'Drossel'—(Uh. *tardás*); (K. *Drossel* 1); B. I, 727.768.856; Ber. *drozdŭ;* W. *turdus;* Boi. ἀστραλός, στρουθός.

strė̃giu, strė̃gti 'erstarren, zu Eis werden'—(F. *ga-staurknan*); W. *frīgeo, stringo* 2; Boi. ῥῖγος. Cf. Lesk. Abl. 285.

strė̃nos plu. 'Lenden, Kreuz'—(W. *strebula*); Boi. στέρνον.

striùbas 'kurz'—W. *truncus.* Cf. Lesk. Nom. 191.

striùgas (Lalis **striukas**) 'kurz, schwach, knapp'—W. *truncus*.

strovė 'Strömung'—see *srovė̃*.

strũgas (Lalis **striugas**) 'Schneidemesser mit zwei Handgriffen, Schnitzmesser'—F. *striks*. Cf. Brückner SlFw. 138.

strujus 'Greis'—B. I, 686. Cf. Ness. 507ᵃ.

strungas 'gestutzt, mit gekapptem Schwanze'—W. *truncus*. Cf. Ness. 507ᵃ, Lesk. Nom. 190.

stubà, dial. **èstuba** 'Stube, Wohnung, Wohnhaus'—K. *Stube;* Ber. *ìstŭba*. Cf. MLG. I, 47 (note 4); Bezz. LF. 205 (Ntr.); Brückner SlFw. 17; Prell. deutsch. Best. in den lett. Spr. 6.

stúgstu, stúgti (Kur. **stúkstu, stúkti**) 'steif in die Höhe stehen' (z.B. von den Ohren eines Hasen)—K. *Stauche;* W. *restauro;* Boi. *στυγεῖν*. Cf. Lesk. Abl. 318.

stumiù, stùmti 'stossen, schieben'—W. *stuprum;* Boi. *στυφελός*. Cf. Lesk. Abl. 318.

stůlys 'ein vom Winde abgebrochener Baumstumpf'—F. *stōls*. Cf. Ness. 504ᵇ.

sù prep. with inst. 'mit'—Uh. *sám;* B. I, 387. II, 2, 546.547 (note).789.897; W. *com-, similis;* Boi. *ξύν* (& note). Cf. Kur. Gram. 1480.

sūbóju, sūbóti 'sich mit dem Oberkörper wiegen, schaukeln' —(Ber. *chyba*). Cf. Lesk. Abl. 310.

súdau, súdyti 'würzen, salzen'—F. *sūts;* W. *suāvis;* Boi. *ἥδομαι*.

sudìrgstu, sudìrgti 'elend werden, abnehmen, herunterkommen; entzweigehen; schlecht, unangenehm, ungünstig werden; zornig werden'; **sudìrgo** pret. 'es ist schlechtes Wetter geworden'—Ber. *-dorga* 3. Cf. Ness. 143ᵃ, Lesk. Abl. 324.

sudrìbėlis (Scheltwort) 'Zusammengesunkener; (Lalis) clumsy one, heavy person, lubber'—Ber. *drębĭ*. See *drimbù*.

sudrìbęs perf. act. part. 'schlaff in den Gliedern hangend' (von einem Müden)—B. II, 1, 568. 3, 446. See *drimbù*.
sudrykstù, pret. **sudriskaũ, sudrìksti** intr. 'zerreissen; zerlumpt werden'—Ber. *drasają*. Cf. Schleicher LSpr. II, 319; Ness. 155[b]; Donalitius 294; Kur. s.v. driskaũ; Wied. s.v. drykstù; B. II, 3, 360; Lesk. Abl. 325, 382.
sudrugti (?) 'sich gesellen, verbinden, buhlen'; **sudrugo** pret. 3rd sing.—Ber. *drugŭ*. Cf. Bezz. BGLS. 327, Lesk. Abl. 295.
sudrus 'üppig, geil' (vom Wuchs der Pflanzen)—Ber. *-dorvŭ*. Cf. Geitler LS. 112.
sugaubti 'Getreide einführen'—see *gaubiù*.
suginù, sugìnti 'den Kreisel zurückschlagen' (dial.); Ness.: 'das Vieh zusammentreiben'—(W. 2. *fīlum*). See *ginù* & MLG. I, 225; Ness. 256[a]; Lesk. Abl. 326.
sugodau, sugodyti 'erwägen'—see *godau*.
sugraudìnti 'betrübt machen'—see *graudinù*.
sugrąža (Szyr.) 'Rückzug'—B. II, 1, 155. Cf. Lesk. Abl. 328.
sugružinu, sugružinti 'vernichten'—Ber. *gryzą*. Cf. Lesk. Abl. 297.
susigūžiù, susigū̃žti 'sich zusammenkauern' — see *gūžiù, gūžti*.
sujaudìnti 'in Bewegung setzen, rütteln'—Ber. *judzę*. Cf. Lesk. Abl. 298. See *jùdinu*.
sujaũdrinu, sujaũdrinti 'aufhetzen'—see *jaũdrinu*.
sukargýti (?) 'verschränken, verknüpfen, verwickeln'—(Ber. *kŭrga* 1); (W. *corbis*). Cf. MLG. I, 80; Bezz. LF. 121; Lesk. Abl. 363.
sukìdęs perf. act. part. 'zerlumpt, abgerissen'—Boi. σκεδάννῦμι. Cf. Kur. 412 & s.v. kindù; Lesk. Abl. 291.
sukimbù, sukìbti 'sich anhängen'—see *kimbù*.
suklẽkęs 'geronnen'—Ber. *kleka*. Cf. Lesk. Abl. 368.
suklìgu (?) dial. pret. 3rd pers. sing. 'schrie auf' (von der Ente)—Ber. *klekŭlą;* W. *clango;* Boi. *κλάγξ. Cf. Lesk. Abl. 275, 397.

susikraupiù, susikraũpti 'zusammenschauern, sich zusammenkauern' (Ness., vor Kälte)—Ber. *krupa*. Cf. Ness. 231[a], Lesk. Abl. 300.

sukrùs 'gedreht, drehbar, gewandt, lebhaft, beweglich, schnell, fleissig'—B. II, 1, 353. See *sukù*.

sùktinas 'drehbar'—B. II, 1, 269.652. Cf. Lesk. Nom. 405-6. See next.

sukù, sùkti 'drehen, winden, kehren, wenden, würgen, schwindeln, lügen'; **sukũs, sùktis** 'sich drehen, sich wenden, sich herumbewegen; hurtig, behende, fleissig sein'—F. *af-swaggwjan;* B. I, 255. II, 3, 137; W. 2. *sucula*. Cf. Lesk. Abl. 310.

sukukiu, sukukti 'aufheulen'—see *kukiu*.

sulà 'abfliessender Baumsaft, Birkensaft'—Uh. *sunóti, súrā;* F. *bi-sauljan;* B. I, 454.456. II, 1, 363 (& n.); W. *sūcus, (salio), (salīva)*; Boi. ὑετός, 2. ὕλη. Cf. Lesk. Nom. 226.

suláukiu, suláukti 'erwarten; erleben, bekommen'; **susiláukiu, susiláukti** 'erwarten und erhalten'—see *láukiu*.

sulýg prep. with inst. 'in gleicher Ausdehnung mit'; **sulýg stalù** 'so hoch (so lang) wie der Tisch'—B. II, 2, 929.

sùltis (B. **súltis**) fem., usually plu. **sùltys** 'Saft des Obstes' —F. *bi-sauljan;* B. II, 1, 363 (note). Cf. Ness. 469[b].

sulũju, sulũti 'Birkensaft fliessen lassen'; **béržas sulũja** 'die Birke saftet'—F. *bi-sauljan*. See *sulà*.

sumania 'consilium'—B. II, 1, 185. Cf. Lesk. Nom. 313.

sùmdau, sùmdyti 'hetzen'—F. *swumfsl*.

susimìlstu, susimìlti 'sich erbarmen'—Ber. *milŭ*. Cf. Ness. 400[b]; Lesk. Abl. 278, 395.

sumisztù, sumìszti 'sich mischen'—see *misztù*.

sunka 'Saft, Baumsaft'—B. II, 1, 363 (note). Cf. Ness. 469[b].

sunkiù, suñkti 'die letzten Flüssigkeiten von Trebern, Hefen usw. durch Neigen der Gefässe abfliessen lassen, absickern lassen; (Lalis) to strain, to filter'—B. II, 3, 382; W. *sūcus, (sentīna)*.

sūnùs 'Sohn'—Uh. *sūnúṣ;* K. *Sohn;* F. *sunus;* B. I, 109.775. II, 1, 290. 2, 129.291; Boi. υἱύς.
suplės plu. 'Schaukel'—B. II, 1, 620. Cf. MLG. I, 234. See *supù.*
suprantù, supràsti 'verstehen'—see *prantù.*
supù, sùpti 'schwingen, schaukeln, wiegen'—B. II, 3, 137. 162; W. *dissipo,* 2. *sucula;* (Boi. κτύπος (note)). Cf. Lesk. Abl. 318.
súras 'salzig'—K. *sauer;* B. I, 114. II, 1, 351; (W. *rumex*); Boi. ῥυτή.
surbiù, sur̃bti 'saugen, schlürfen'—B. I, 454; W. *sorbeo;* Boi. ῥοφεῖν. See *srebiù.*
surblis masc. 'Saugrohr'—B. II, 1, 620. See prec.
surmà 'Pfeife, Flöte, Schalmei'—W. *susurrus,* (*sūra*); Boi. ὕραξ. Cf. Ness. 471*, Brückner SlFw. 139.
su-si- (gūžiù &c.)—see under *su-*(*gūžiù* &c.).
suskantù, suskàsti (Mielcke) 'aufhüpfen'—B. II, 3, 292; Ber. *kolǫ.* Cf. Lesk. Abl. 375.
suskastu, suskasti id.—see *skastu.*
suskis masc. 'Aussatz, Krätze' (Lalis, 'scabby person, scab')—B. I, 784. II, 1, 476. Cf. Geitler LS. 113. See *susù.*
susna 'Grind'—B. II, 1, 263. Cf. Lesk. Nom. 365, Lalis 357.
suspeiczù, suspeĩsti 'umringend zusammenklemmen'—see *speiczù.*
susù, sùsti 'räudig werden'—Uh. *çúṣyati;* B. I, 110.490. II, 1, 568. 3, 127.448.493. Cf. Kur. s.v., Lesk. Abl. 311. See *nusùsęs, saũsas.*
sutógti 'einig werden mit'—Boi. τάσσω. Cf. Lesk. Nom. 253.
sutrenkiù, sutreñkti 'zerstossen'—see *trenkiù.*
sutrẽszkinu, sutrẽszkinti 'zerprasseln'—see *trẽszkinu.*
sùtveriu, sutvérti 'zusammenfassen, erschaffen'—see *tveriù.*
suvalaũ, suvalýti 'sammeln, ernten'—see *valaũ.*
sū̃dis (sódis), plu. **sū̃džai** (sū̃džei) 'Russ'—Uh. *sādás;* F.

sitan; B. I, 158; W. *sedeo, (suāsum)*; Boi. ἕζομαι. Cf. Lesk. Abl. 379, Brückner SlFw. 135 (& note).

sū̃las 'Bank, Sitz, Stuhl' (cf. Bezz. BGLS. 328, Lalis 352) —(W. *solium, solum*); Boi. σέλμα.

svagiù, svagė́ti 'tönen'—F. *ga-swōgjan;* Boi. ἠχή.

svaiginė́ju, svaiginė́ti 'mit schwindelndem Kopfe umherschwanken, taumeln; (Lalis) to stroll about, ramble about'—B. I, 609. See next.

svaigstù, svaĩgti (Kur. **-k-**) 'Schwindel bekommen, taumeln, schwanken; (Lalis also) to grow mad'—B. I, 609. Cf. Lesk. Abl. 293.

svaĩnė 'Schwester der Frau, Frau des Bruders, Frau des Bruders des Gatten'—B. I, 269. Cf. Kur. DLWb. s.v. Schwägerin.

svãras 'Gewicht, Pfund, Wage'—K. *schwer* (read *sváras* for *svárus*); F. *swērs;* B. I, 316; W. *sērius;* Boi. 1. ἕρμα, ἀείρω. Cf. Ness. 508[a]. See *svarùs.*

svarbùs 'gewichtig'—B. II, 1, 389.

svarùs 'schwer' (von Gewicht)—K. *schwer;* F. *swērs;* B. I, 782; Ber. *chvorŭ, (chvorują)*; W. *sērius;* Boi. 1. ἕρμα. See *sveriù.*

svẽczas, svẽtis 'Gast'—(F. *niþjis*); B. II, 1, 416; W. *sēd, (satelles)*; Boi. ἕταρος. Cf. Ness. 508[b]; Lesk. Nom. 309; Sommer 238 f., 257.

sveriù, svefti 'wägen'—K. *schwer;* F. *swērs;* B. I, 316.782. II, 3, 137; (Ber. *chvorują*); W. *sērius;* Boi. 1. ἕρμα, ἀείρω. Cf. Lesk. Abl. 348.

svẽstas 'Butter'—(W. *sūdo*); (Boi. ἴδος (note)). Cf. Lesk. Abl. 286, Bezz. LF. 180.

-svẽtinu—see *apsisvētinu* 'ich mache mich bekannt'.

svẽtis 'Gast'—see *svẽczas.*

svidù, svidė́ti 'glänzen'—W. *sīdus;* Boi. (Ntr.) ἰνδάλλομαι. See next.

svidùs 'blank, glänzend'—Uh. *çvindate;* W. *sīdus;* Boi. (Ntr.) ἰνδάλλομαι. Cf. Ness. 509[b], Lesk. Abl. 286.

svìldinu, svìldinti 'sengen lassen'—B. II, 3, 376. See *svylù*.

svilmis "der Geruch, den ein glimmender Gegenstand verbreitet"—K. *schwül*. Cf. MLG. I, 20. See next.

svylù (**svị̀lù**), **svìlti** (B. **svílti**) 'sengen, schwelen'—K. *schwül;* F. *wulan,* (*swiltan*); B. II, 3, 376; W. *sōl;* Boi. ἀλέα, σαλά(μ)βη. Cf. Lesk. Abl. 348.

svilus 'glimmend, versengt'—K. *schwül;* F. *wulan,* (*swiltan*); Boi. ἀλέα. Cf. Ness. 509ᵇ. See prec.

svyrù (**svị̀rù**), **svìrti** (B. **svírti**) "nach einer Seite hin das Übergewicht bekommen" (Kur.); "schweben, wanken, schwanken, baumeln, taumeln" (Ness. 510ᵃ)—B. II, 3, 137. See *sveriù*.

svóras 'Gewicht an der Uhr'—K. *schwer;* F. *swērs;* W. *sērius;* Boi. 1. ἕρμα. Cf. Kur. DLWb. s.v. Gewicht. See *sveriù*.

svõtas 'Hochzeitsgast, Brautvater, Gevatter, Brautführer, Vater des Schwiegersohns, weitläufiger Verwandter'—F. *sidus;* W. *sodālis*.

SZ

szaipaũs, szaipýtis iter. 'die Zähne fletschen, das Gesicht verziehen, spottend lächeln'—Uh. *çiprā;* F. *haifsts*. Cf. Lesk. Abl. 286.

szakà 'Ast, Zweig, Zacke, Arm eines Flusses'—Uh. *çā́khā;* F. *hōha;* B. I, 548; (W. *seco*).

szakalỹs 'Splitter'—Uh. *çákalas*.

szaknìs 'Wurzel'—Uh. *çā́khā;* B. II, 1, 288; (Ber. *korenĭ*).

szakniũtas 'voll Wurzeln'—B. II, 1, 407.

szalìs 'Seite, Gegend, Land'—(F. *halbs*); B. II, 1, 389; W. *clīno;* Boi. κλίνω.

szalma 'ein langer Balken'—Boi. ξύλον (note). Cf. Ness. 512ᵃ.

szálmas 'Helm'—K. *Helm* 1; F. *hilms;* W. *cēlo*. Cf. Brückner SlFw. 140.

szalnà 'Reif, Nachtfrost'—Uh. *çíçiras;* F. *smarna;* B. I, 567. II, 1, 263; (W. *caleo*). Cf. Lesk. Abl. 374.

szalnis 'Schimmel' (Pferd)—B. II, 1, 256. Cf. Lesk. Nom. 356.

száltas 'kalt'—Uh. *çíçiras;* (F. *kalds*); B. I, 476.567. II, 1, 173.411; Ber. *choldŭ* (twice), *koldęd'ĭ;* W. (*caleo*), *gelidus;* (Boi. σκέλλω). Cf. Lesk. Abl. 374.

szaltìnis masc. 'Quelle'—B. II, 1, 273; Ber. *koldęd'ĭ.*

szal̃tis masc. 'Kälte, Frost'—Uh. *çíçiras;* B. II, 1, 173.197.

szālù, szálti 'kalt werden, frieren'—Uh. *çíçiras;* (F. *kalds*); B. I, 389; W. (*caleo*), *gelidus;* (Boi. σκέλλω). Cf. Lesk. Abl. 374.

szankinù, szankìnti 'springen machen'; **árklį szankìnti** 'ein Pferd sprengen'; **apszankinù, apszankìnti** (**kumēlę**) '(eine Stute) bespringen lassen'—Uh. *çaknóti;* (W. *cantērius*); Boi. κηκίω. Cf. Lesk. Abl. 374.

szankus 'schnell, behende, beweglich, hitzig'—K. *Hengst;* (W. *cantērius*); Boi. κηκίω. Cf. Lesk. Abl. 374, MLG. I, 390.

szãpalas 'Döbel (Fisch), Cyprinus dobula'—Uh. *çapharas;* Ber. *korpŭ;* W. *carpa;* Boi. κυπρῖνος.

szãpas 'Stroh- oder Heuhalm'; **szãpai** plu. "verstreute Halme" (Kur.), "der Rückstand, den eine Überschwemmung auf den Feldern zurücklässt" (Ness. 513*)—Uh. *çāpas.*

szárka 'Elster'—Uh. *çāriș;* B. I, 340 (note); W. *cornix;* Boi. κόραξ. Cf. Lesk. Nom. 214.

szar̃kas 'Kleidungsstück'; (Ness. 513*) "der tuchene Überrock der Fischer (am Haff)"—(W. *sarcio*); (Boi. ἕρκος). Cf. Brückner SlFw. 140.

szarmà 'Reif, gefrorener Tau'—Uh. *çíçiras;* B. II, 1, 249; (W. *caleo*) (read *szarmà* for *szarnà;* likewise in Zupitza Die germanischen Gutturale 185, to which W. refers—cf. J. Schmidt Zur Geschichte des indogermanischen Vocalismus II, 76, 457). Cf. Lesk. Abl. 348.

szármas 'Aschenlauge'—B. II, 1, 249; Boi. κορέω. Cf. Lesk. Abl. 348.

szarmonys 'Wiesel'—B. II, 1, 240. Cf. Lalis 364, Lesk. Nom. 421.

szarmũ, szermũ 'wilde Katze, Hermelin, Wiesel'—(Uh. *çárma*); K. *Hermelin.* Cf. Ness. 513[b], Kur. 421, Lalis 364, Lesk. Abl. 348.

szárvas, plu. **szarvaĩ** 'Harnisch, Rüstung, Wehr und Waffen; Ausstattung (bes. der Braut); Hausgerät; (plu.) menstrua'—F. *sarwa.* Cf. Ness. 513[b], Lesk. Nom. 343.

szarvas (?) 'grauschwarz' (vom Pferde)—B. II, 1, 200. Cf. MLG. I, 390, Lesk. Nom. 345.

szãszas, plu. **szaszaĩ** 'Ausschlag, Schorf, Grind, Räude'—(Boi. κόκκος). Cf. Lesk. Abl. 349.

sząszlavýnas, sąszlavýnas 'Kehrichthaufen'—B. I, 786. Cf. LBLV. 291, [Lesk. Abl. 311].

száudau, száudyti iter. 'mehrfach schiessen, umherschiessen'—(Uh. *svádhitiș*); F. *schieten;* B. II, 3, 269.376; (W. *sublica*). Cf. Lesk. Abl. 312. See *száuju.*

szaudỹklė 'Weberschiffchen'—B. II, 3, 376.

száudinu, száudinti 'schiessen lassen'—B. II, 3, 376. See next.

száuju, száuti 'schiessen'—(Uh. *svádhitiș*); F. *schieten;* B. I, 566.567. II, 3, 269.376; (W. *cauda, sublica*); Boi. σκεῦος. Cf. Lesk. Abl. 312.

szaukiù, szaũkti 'schreien, rufen, nennen, (ein Brautpaar) aufbieten'—Uh. *çúkas;* Ber. *chukaję;* (W. *cōcio*); Boi. καύχη, (κτύπος). Cf. Ness. 522[a], Lesk. Abl. 312.

száuksztas 'Löffel'—(W. *cinnus*); Boi. κυκᾶν.

szaũnas 'tüchtig, brav, derb, gut, schön, trefflich, schnell, hastig, heftig'—(Boi. σαῦλος). Cf. Lesk. Abl. 312.

szè 'hierher'—B. I, 550; W. *-ce.* Cf. Ness. 520[a], Lalis 364.

szeima, szeimýna 'Gesinde, Hausdienerschaft'—Uh. *çīmas;* K. *Heirat;* F. *heiwa-frauja;* B. I, 790. II, 1, 278; W.

cīvis, (2. *situs*); Boi. κεῖμαι, (κτίζω (note)). Cf. Lesk. Abl. 286.

szeimynykszczas, szeimýnyksztis 'einer vom Gesinde, Dienstbote'—B. II, 1, 503. Cf. Lesk. Nom. 583.

szeĩp 'so; sonst'—W. *nempe*. Cf. Lalis 365.

szeirỹs 'Witwer'—B. II, 1, 353; W. *hērēs*.

szeivà 'Rohrspulchen im Weberschiffchen; (Ness. 517*, VI after Brodowski also) Pfeifenrohr; (Lalis also) quill' —Ber. *cěva*. Cf. Lesk. Nom. 347.

szẽkas 'Grünfutter, frisch gemähtes Gras'—Uh. *çākam*; (F. *hawi*). Cf. Lesk. Nom. 166.

szelbiû̃s, szelbtis (?) 'sich zu helfen suchen'—F. *hilpan*. Cf. Kur. s.v., Lesk. Abl. 369.

szelmũ 'Giebel, Dachfirst; (Lalis also) pediment, frontal'—F. *hiuhma*; B. II, 1, 236; Boi. ξύλον (note). Cf. Geitler LS. 114*, Lalis 365, Lesk. Nom. 418.

szelpiù, szel̃pti 'fördern, helfen, unterstützen, pflegen'—K. *helfen*; F. *hilpan*; (Ber. *cholpŭ*). Cf. Lesk. Abl. 367.

szẽmas 'aschgrau, blaugrau' (von Ochsen, Sand usw.)—Uh. *çyāmás*; B. I, 95.268.289.490. II, 1, 246.662; Boi. Κίμων (& note). Cf. Lesk. Nom. 428.

szę̃nakt adv. 'diese Nacht'—B. II, 2, 683.746.

szẽnas 'Heu'—B. II, 1, 262; (W. *fēnum*); Boi. κοινά, (σχοῖνος), (χιλός).

szeñdėn 'diesen Tag, heute'—B. II, 2, 322.683.745; Ber. *dĭnĭ*.

szėpiû̃s, szẽptis 'die Zähne fletschen, das Gesicht verziehen, spottend lächeln'—Uh. *çiprā*. Cf. Lesk. Abl. 286.

szėrìkas 'Fütterer'—B. II, 1, 490 (twice). Cf. Lesk. Abl. 348.

szerỹs 'Borste'—(W. *crīnis*). Cf. Lesk. Abl. 348.

szeriù, szérti 'füttern'—(Uh. *çáṣpam, çurúdh-*); B. II, 1, 522; (Ber. *chorną, kŭrma* 2); W. *Cerēs*; Boi. κορέννυμι. Cf. Lesk. Abl. 348.

szerksznas 'grauschimmelig'—B. II, 1, 200.256. Cf. Lesk. Abl. 341.

szer̃menys, szer̃mens plu. 'Begräbnismahl, Leichenschmaus' —W. *Cerēs, silicernium;* Boi. κορέννῡμι. Cf. Lesk. Abl. 348.

szermùkszlė, szermùksznė 'Eberesche'—Ber. *čermŭcha;* Boi. κόμαρος (note).

szermũ 'Wiesel'—see *szarmũ.*

szer̃nas 'wilder Eber'—B. II, 1, 263; (W. *scortum*). Cf. Lesk. Abl. 348.

szernùkas dimin. 'Frischling'—(W. *scortum*). See prec.

szeszerì 'sechs'—B. II, 2, 77. Cf. Wied. 158.

szeszì 'sechs'—Uh. *ṣáṭ;* F. *saihs;* B. I, 119 (& Ntr. XLII). 259.564.781.786. II, 2, 14.17; W. *sex;* Boi. ἕξ. Cf. Wied. 156.

szesziólika 'sechzehn'—see prec. & [K. *elf*]; [F. *ain-lif*]; B. II, 2, 26.[27]; [Ber. *-lěkŭ*]; [W. *linquo*]. Cf. Wied. 156.

szẽszios plu. 'Sechswochen, Wochenbett'—B. II, 2, 17; W. *sex;* Boi. ἕξ.

szẽszkas 'Iltis'—Uh. *káças;* B. I, 545.

szesztainis 'sechseckig'—B. II, 2, 73. Cf. Lesk. Nom. 416.

szẽsztas 'sechster'—Uh. *ṣaṣṭhás;* F. *saihs;* B. II, 1, 391. 2, 55; W. *sex;* Boi. ἕξ. Cf. Wied. 157. 6.

szẽszuras 'Schwiegervater'—Uh. *çváçuras;* K. *Schwäher;* F. *swaihra;* B. I, 116.340.546.786; W. *socer;* Boi. ἑκυρός. Cf. Lesk. Nom. 448.

sziáurė 'Norden; Nordwind'—F. *skūra;* B. I, 210.567. II, 1, 354; W. *caurus.*

sziaurỹs 'Nordwind'—F. *skūra;* B. I, 567. II, 1, 354; W. *caurus.* Cf. Lesk. Nom. 263.

szìcze 'hier'—B. I, 849. Cf. Ness. 520[b]. See *szìs.*

szikszǹà 'weiches, gegerbtes Leder; Riemen' — (W. *hedera*); (Boi. κισσός). Cf. Lesk. Nom. 369.

szikù, szìkti 'cacare'—Uh. *çákṛt;* (W. *caco*); Boi. κόπρος, (κακκάω). Cf. Lesk. Abl. 291.

szìlas 'Heide; Heidekraut; (Ness. 518[a], Lalis 367 also) Fichtenwald'—(Boi. κάλαμος).

szil̃tas 'warm'—B. II, 1, 173; W. *caleo*. Cf. Lesk. Abl. 360.
sziltis masc. 'Wärme'—B. II, 1, 173. Cf. Ness. 518[b].
szylù, szìlti (B. szílti) 'warm werden'—B. II, 1, 468; W. *caleo*. Cf. Lesk. Abl. 360.
szilus 'August'—B. II, 1, 468; W. *caleo*.
szį̃met 'dieses Jahr, heuer'—B. II, 2, 322.683.
szim̃tas 'hundert'—Uh. *çatám;* K. *hundert, tausend;* F. *hunda;* B. I, 343.379.397.537.547. II, 2, 41.42.85; W. *centum;* Boi. ἑκατόν.
szimtàsis 'hundertster'—B. II, 2, 62. Cf. Schleicher LSpr. I, 63; Kur. Gram. 1027; Wied. 157.
szimteriópas 'hundertartig, hundertfach'—W. *centum*.
sziõliai 'jetzt'; **iksziõliai** 'bisher, bis jetzt'—(Ber. *dalĩ*).
szipulys 'Splitter, Holzspan, Holzscheit'—Boi. (Ntr.) κίφος (read *szipulys* for *szipylus*). Cf. KZ. XLIV, 58; Lesk. Nom. 487.
szir̃dyjůs, szir̃dytis 'zu Herzen nehmen, zürnen'—B. I, 262. Cf. Ness. 519[b], Lalis 369, Brückner SlFw. 141. See *szirdìs*.
szir̃dis fem. 'Kern im Holz, Mark eines Baumes'—W. *cor;* Boi. καρδίā. Cf. IF. Anzeiger XXI, 98.
szirdìs fem. 'Herz'—Uh. *çraddhā́;* K. *Herz;* F. *hairtō;* B. I, 95.539.541.634. II, 1, 132.141.174; W. *cor;* Boi. καρδίā.
szir̃mas 'grau' (bes. von Pferden) — Uh. *çiçiras;* F. *sniumjan;* B. II, 1, 249.256.662; Boi. κορέω. Cf. Lesk. Abl. 348. See *szirvas*.
szirmókas 'Grauschimmel'—B. II, 1, 501. Cf. Lalis 369, Lesk. Nom. 513. See prec.
szirszlỹs 'Wespe'—B. I, 786. II, 1, 359.364; W. *crābro;* Boi. κέρας (note). Cf. Donalitius 303. See *szirszũ*.
szirszonas id.—B. II, 1, 308. Cf. Ness. 520[a], Lesk. Nom. 397.
szirszonė 'Hornisse'—K. *Hornis;* B. II, 1, 296; W. *crābro*. Cf. Bezz. BGLS. 329.
szirszonis id.—B. II, 1, 308. Cf. Bezz. BGLS. 100.

szirszū̃ 'Wespe'—K. *Hornis;* B. I, 479.567.786. II, 1, 296.359.550; W. *crābro;* Boi. κέρας (note). Cf. Ness. 520ᵃ; Lesk. Abl. 348; Lesk. Nom. 381; Trautmann Die altpreussischen Sprachdenkmäler 427 f.

szirvas 'grau'—B. II, 1, 200.202; Boi. κιρρός, (κιλλός). Cf. Ness. 520ᵃ; Lalis 369; Lesk. Nom. 345; Lesk. Abl. 348. See *szir̃mas.*

szìs, fem. **szì** 'dieser, diese'—K. *hier;* F. *hidrē;* B. I, 96.550. II, 1, 211.219. 2, 322; W. *-ce, cis;* Boi. ἐκεῖ, καινός, (-κις).

szisaĩ 'dieser'—B. II, 2, 346. Cf. Kur. Gram. 980.

szìtas, fem. **szità** 'dieser, diese'—B. II, 2, 322. Cf. Kur. Gram. 986.

sziūbà, szūbà 'kostbares Kleid, Frauenpelzrock'; **sziū̃bas, szū̃bas** 'Kleid, Rock, Pelzrock'—Ber. *jupa.* Cf. Ness. 522ᵃ, Brückner SlFw. 143.

sziùilė 'Schule'—see *sziúlė.*

sziùkszmės plu. 'feine Späne, Geröll, Auskehricht'—(W. *cinnus*); Boi. κυκᾶν. Cf. Lesk. Abl. 318.

sziùksztus 'mit Spreu oder Kleie gemischt'; **sziuksztì dū̃na** 'Brot von ungereinigtem Getreide' — (W. *cinnus*); Boi. κυκᾶν. See Ness. 523ᵃ & prec.

sziúlė, sziùilė 'Schule'—German loan-word. Cf. Brückner SlFw. 18, Prell. deutsch. Best. in den lett. Spr. 35.

sziūlõkas 'Schüler'—B. II, 1, 501.

sziùrės plu. 'Schachtelhalm'—(Boi. σωλήν (& note)). Cf. Lesk. Nom. 278; Ness. 524ᵇ; Lalis 369; Sommer 63.

szývas 'weiss, grau' (von Pferden)—Uh. *çyāvás;* F. *hiwi;* B. II, 1, 201.662; (W. *caelum*); Boi. Κίμων. Cf. Ness. 520ᵇ; Lalis 369; Brückner SlFw. 142; Lesk. Nom. 345.

szývis masc. 'Weissschimmel, Grauschimmel'—F. *hiwi.* See prec.

szyvókas 'Grauschimmel'—B. II, 1, 501. See *szývas* & Lesk. Nom. 513.

szlaĩtas 'Bergabhang; Mitglied'—Uh. *çráyati;* K. *lehnen* 1; F. *hlain;* B. I, 188.425.490.550. II, 1, 410; Ber. *klońę;*

W. *clīno;* Boi. κλίνω (read *szlaĩtas* for *slaĩtas*). Cf. Lesk. Abl. 286, Lesk. Nom. 534.

szlaĩtis id.—Ber. *klońǫ*. See prec. & Kur. DLWb. s.v. Bergseite; Lesk. Abl. 286; Lesk. Nom. 540.

szlãjos, szlãjės plu. 'Schlitten'—Ber. *klońǫ*. Cf. Sommer 21, 39; Lesk. Abl. 286.

szlajùs 'schräg, schief'—Ber. *klońǫ*. Cf. Lesk. Abl. 286.

szlampù, szlàpti 'nass werden'—Boi. κλέπας. Cf. Lesk. Abl. 374.

szlãpias 'feucht, nass'—B. I, 516; Ber. *chlapajǫ;* Boi. κλέπας. See prec.

szlapókas 'feucht, klamm'—B. II, 1, 500. Cf. Ness. 526[a], Lesk. Nom. 515.

szlaunìs 'Hüfte, Oberschenkel'; **szlaũnys** plu. "die Arme an Wocken, Wagen und andern Gestellen, in denen Räder hängen und sich bewegen"—Uh. *çróṇiṣ;* F. *ana-būsns;* B. I, 202.567. II, 1, 287 (twice); W. *clūnis;* Boi. κλόνις. Cf. Ness. 526[b]; Bezz. LF. 183; Lalis 370.

szleĩvas 'schiefbeinig, krummbeinig'—Uh. *çráyati;* F. *hlain;* B. I, 490. II, 1, 204.207.590.663; Ber. *klońǫ;* W. *clīno, clīvus;* Boi. κλίνω. Cf. Kur. DLWb. s.v. -beinig; Lesk. Abl. 286; Lesk. Nom. 344; LBLV. 140, 345. Read *szleĩvas* for *szleĩvis* in B. I, 490; Ber. *klońǫ;* Lesk. Abl. 286.

szlëjù, szlë̃ti trans. 'anlehnen'—Uh. *çráyati;* K. *lehnen* 1; F. *hlain;* Ber. *klońǫ;* W. *clīno;* Boi. κλίνω. Cf. Lesk. Abl. 286.

szliaužiu, szliaužti 'kriechen, schleichen'—Ber. *lyža*. Cf. Lalis 370, Lesk. Abl. 311.

szlìję̨s perf. act. part. 'sich geneigt habend, schief'—B. I, 257; Ber. *klońǫ;* W. *clīno;* Boi. κλίνω. See *szlýti* & Kur. 433; Bezz. LF. 183[b], l. 12; Lesk. Abl. 286.

szlitė Old Lith. 'Leiter'—Ber. *klětĭ, klońǫ;* W. *clīno;* Boi. κλίνω. Cf. Bezz. BGLS. 330, Lesk. Abl. 286.

szlìtė 'Garbenhocke'; "zehn Paar zusammengestellter Garben auf dem Felde"—B. I, 487; Ber. *klěti*. Cf. Ness. 527ᵃ, Lesk. Abl. 286. See *szlitìs*.

szlýti (?) 'sich neigen'; **paszlýti** 'schief werden, langsam zur Seite fallen, straucheln'—K. *lehnen* 1; B. I, 102. 487.490; Ber. *kloňǫ*. Cf. Kur. DLWb. s.v. straucheln; Bezz. LF. 183ᵇ, ll. 5 & 8; Lesk. Abl. 286, 397.

szlitìs 'Garbenhocke'—B. I, 487. II, 1, 429; Ber. *klěti*, *kloňǫ*. Cf. Lesk. Abl. 286. See *szlìtė*.

szliũżės plu. 'Schlittschuhe'—Ber. *lyža*. Cf. Ness. 528ᵇ; Kur. 433; Lalis 371; Lesk. Abl. 311; Lesk. Nom. 279.

szlìvas (so read *szlìvis* in both Lesk. Abl. & Ber.; *szlìvis* is a noun) 'schiefbeinig'—B. II, 1, 204.207; Ber. *kloňǫ*. See *szleĩvas* & Lesk. Abl. 286; Kur. DLWb. s.v. -beinig; Lesk. Nom. 344.

szlovẽ 'Ehre, Ruhm, Herrlichkeit, Pracht'—F. *hliuma;* B. II, 1, 154; W. *clueo;* Boi. κλε[ϝ]ω. Cf. Brückner SlFw. 142, Lesk. Nom. 281.

szlúbas 'Trauung'—Ber. *ľubŭ*. Cf. Brückner SlFw. 142.

szlùbas 'hinkend, lahm'—(W. *calamitas*); (Boi. κολοβός (note)).

szlũju, szlũti 'fegen, wischen'—F. *hlūtrs;* W. *cluo;* Boi. κλύζω. Cf. Lesk. Abl. 311.

szlũta 'Besen, Ofenwisch, Fliegenwedel'—F. *hlūtrs;* W. *cluo;* Boi. κλύζω. See prec. & Ness. 527ᵃ.

szlůtgiřnė 'Flederwisch'—B. II, 1, 101.

szmánta 'Sahne'—Ber. *mętǫ*. Cf. Prell. deutsch. Best. in den lett. Spr. 55.

szmulas 'ohne Hörner'—Boi. κεμάς. Cf. Geitler LS. 115.

szmulis m., f. **-ė** 'Ochse, Kuh ohne Hörner'—Boi. κεμάς. Cf. Ness. 529ᵃ.

sznibżdù, sznibżdẽti 'zischen, gischen, zischeln, flüstern'—B. I, 393. Cf. Ness. 529ᵇ, Lesk. Abl. 349.

szóku, szókti 'springen, tanzen'—F. *skēwjan;* B. I, 546.554. 567.689; (Ber. *izokŭ*); W. *cacula*, (*cantērius*); Boi. κηκίω, κίκυς. Cf. Lesk. Abl. 374.

szónas 'Seite' (bes. des Körpers)—(Boi. σανίς).

sztái 'sieh hier'—B. II, 2, 322. Cf. Wied. p. 77.

szũbà, szũbas 'Kleid, Rock'—see *sziũbà*.

szúdas 'Exkrement, unflätiges Zeug'—Uh. *çũdrás;* Boi. κυθνόν.

szúdinas 'mit Exkrement besudelt'—B. II, 1, 664.

szùkė 'Lücke, Scharte, Scherbe; irdnes Gefäss'—Uh. *çváñcate*. Cf. Donalitius 305, Lesk. Abl. 318.

szùkos plu. 'Kamm'—Uh. *çváñcate*. Cf. Lesk. Abl. 318.

szùlas 'Daube, Ständer, Türpfosten'—Boi. ξύλον (note). Cf. Ness. 523[b], Brückner SlFw. 143.

szulnas 'stattlich, herrlich, vortrefflich'; (Lalis) "brave, gallant, daring, dauntless, honest, upright"—(Boi. σαῦλος). Cf. Lesk. Nom. 356.

szuñg dial. 'Hund'—B. II, 2, 126. Cf. Kur. Gram. 731.

szunis id.—Boi. κύων. See *szũ* & Ness. 523[b], Kur. 441[a].

szuntù, szùsti intr. 'schmoren, brühen, faulen'—(F. *hunsl, sauþs*); B. I, 790. II, 1, 355; (W. *cāseus*). Cf. Lesk. Abl. 312.

szupù, szùpti 'faulen' (von Holz)—(Boi. σαπρός). Cf. Ness. 524[a], Lesk. Abl. 318.

szurksztus 'scharf, rauh, hart, grob' (z.B. Flachs, Zeug)—(W. *crīnis*); Boi. κόρση (note). Cf. Ness. 524[a], Brückner SlFw. 143.

szuszinu, szuszinti "mit zischendem Geräusch durch die Luft fahren (wie der Blitz)"—Uh. *çvásiti;* W. *queror*. Cf. Ness. 524[b].

szũ, gen. **szuñs** 'Hund'—Uh. *çvā́;* K. *Hund;* F. *hunds;* B. I, 103.296.312(note).338.546. II, 1, 171.296. 2, 126. 295; W. *canis;* Boi. κύων.

szûlỹs 'Galopp; (Lalis) jump, hop, skip'; **szûliaĩs** adv. inst. plu. 'im Galopp'—Uh. *çalabhás;* B. I, 154. II, 2, 720; W. *celer*. Cf. Lesk. Abl. 380.

szvaisà 'Licht, Lichtschein'; **szvaisùs** 'licht, hell'—B. II, 1, 542. Cf. Ness. 532[b], Lesk. Abl. 287.

szvaitaũ, szvaitýti 'hell machen, beleuchten; schwingen, fechten'—Uh. *çvétate;* K. *weiss;* F. *hveits;* B. I, 190. II, 3, 267.269; W. 1. *vitrum.* Cf. Lesk. Abl. 287.

szvankszczù, szvañkszti 'keuchen; hohl, röchelnd atmen'—Ber. *kvǫkajǫ.*

szvánkus 'anständig, fein, artig, höflich'—W. *pontifex;* Boi. κομψός.

szvãrinu, szvãrinti 'reinigen'—Boi. κορέω.

szvarùs 'sauber, rein, nett'—Boi. κορέω, κύρω (note).

szvëczù, szvė̃sti 'leuchten'—Uh. *çvétate.* Cf. Lesk. Abl. 287. See *apszvëczù.*

szveiczù, szveĩsti 'glänzend machen, putzen, reinigen, schmücken'—Uh. *çvétate;* B. II, 1, 413 (read *sz-*). Cf. Lesk. Abl. 287.

szvelnùs 'weich, sanft, mild'—(W. *colostra*). Cf. Lesk. Abl. 349.

szveñdrai plu. 'Typha latifolia' (eine Schilfart)—B. I, 122.320.338.535.707. II, 1, 378; W. *combrētum.* Cf. Lesk. Nom. 436.

szveñtas 'heilig'—Uh. *máhiṣvantam, çvāntás;* F. *hunsl;* B. I, 336.390.567. II, 1, 411. 3, 323; W. *pontifex.*

szvêntinu, szvêntinti 'heiligen, weihen'—B. II, 3, 323.

szvësà 'Licht, Lichtschein, Sonnenlicht; (Lalis also) enlightenment'; **szvësùs** 'licht, hell'—B. II, 1, 542. Cf. Lesk. Abl. 287.

szvidus (?) 'blank, glänzend'—Uh. *çvíndate;* F. *hveits.* Cf. Ness. 533[a]. See *svidùs.*

szvilpỹnė 'Rohrpfeife'—B. II, 1, 621. See next.

szvilpiù, szvil̃pti 'pfeifen, zwitschern, zischen, summen'—Boi. σάλπιγξ. Cf. Lesk. Abl. 349.

szvìnas 'Blei'—(Boi. κύανος). Cf. Brückner SlFw. 144.

szvintù, szvìsti 'hell werden, aufleuchten, anbrechen (vom Tage)'—Uh. *çvétate;* F. *hveits;* B. II, 3, 279. Cf. Lesk. Abl. 286.

szvìrksztu, szvìrkszti (B. **szvírkszti**) 'pfeifen, sausen'—B. I, 341 (note); W. *cornix.* Cf. Ness. 533[b], Lesk. Abl. 349.

szvitkus 'glänzend, blinkend'—B. II, 1, 477. Cf. Ness. 533[b], Lesk. Nom. 507.

szvitrinė́ju, szvitrinė́ti 'schimmern, flimmern'—B. II, 1, 349; W. 1. *vitrum*. Cf. MLG. I, 70; Geitler LS. 115[b]; Lesk. Abl. 287. See next.

szvytrū́ju, szvytrū́ti; szvitrū́ju, szvitrū́ti 'blinken, flimmern; blinken lassen, schwingen; (Lalis gives only:) to brandish, to wave'—Uh. *çvitrás;* B. I, 295. 541. II, 1, 349; W. 1. *vitrum*. Cf. Lesk. Abl. 287.

szvitù, szvitė́ti 'hell sein, glänzen, flimmern'—Uh. *çvétate;* B. I, 338.541. Cf. Lesk. Abl. 286. See prec.

T

tà 'diese'—see *tàs*.

tadà 'dann, alsdann'—Uh. *tadā́;* B. II, 2, 733.

taĩ neut. to **tàs**, q.v.; conj. 'so'; adv. 'so, also, deshalb, da, dann'—Boi. το-.

táikus 'ebenmässig gefügt, geordnet, gut eingepasst, gleichmässig; (Lalis also) peaceful, peaceable, agreeing, living in concord, quiet, mild, gentle'—F. *þeihs*. Cf. MLG. I, 391; Lesk. Nom. 263; Lesk. Abl. 287.

taĩp 'so, also, auf diese Weise; ja'—B. II, 2, 369.692; W. *quippe*. See *teĩp*.

tãkas 'Fusssteig; Tenne; Lauf des Flusses, Wassergang; durchlöcherter Strich am Oberärmel des Weiberhemdes' —B. I, 146. II, 1, 150. Cf. Bezz. BGLS. 331; MLG. I, 283; Lesk. Nom. 169. See *tekù*.

talkà "die zusammengebetenen Leute bei den grösseren Landwirtschaftlichen Verrichtungen, die nach beendigter Arbeit (besonders nach der Ernte) durch eine Mahlzeit belohnt werden" (Donalitius 307; cf. also Ness. 88[a], Kur. 447, MLG. I, 284, Geitler LS. 115, Lalis 377)—B. II, 1, 153. Cf. Lesk. Abl. 349.

talõkas 'erwachsen, mannbar; (Kur. also) gross, lümmelhaft'—W. *tālea;* Boi. τᾶλις. Cf. Lesk. Nom. 514.

talpà "der ausreichende Raum zur Unterbringung von Personen und Sachen"—Uh. *tálpas;* W. *talpa.* See *telpù.*
talpnus 'fassend, umfangreich'—B. I, 686. Cf. MLG. I, 391. See *telpù.*
tàmista, tam̃sta (**tãvo mýlista,** q.v.) Russ.-Lith. (höfliche Anrede) 'deine Gnade; (Lalis) you, mister, sir'—B. II, 1, 41; Ber. *milŭ.* Cf. Kur. DLWb. s.v. Gnade, Brückner SlFw. 108.
tampaũ, tampýti iter. 'ausrecken, ausdehnen, spannen, breit machen; (Lalis) to pull, tug, haul, tear'—B. I, 404. Cf. Lesk. Abl. 350.
tampù, tàpti 'werden'; **pritampù, pritàpti** 'antreffen, kennen lernen, erfahren'—(W. *porticus*); Boi. τόπος. Cf. Ness. 88[a,b]; Lesk. Abl. 375.
tamsà 'Dunkelheit, Finsternis'—Uh. *támas;* K. *dämmern;* B. I, 537. II, 1, 517.542; W. *tenebrae.* See *témstu.*
tam̃sta 'deine Gnade'—see *tàmista.*
tamsùs 'dunkel, finster; (Lalis also) ignorant'—Uh. *támas;* B. II, 1, 179.542; W. *tenebrae.* See *témstu.*
tãnas 'Geschwulst, Wassersucht, Gliedwasser'—W. *tendo;* Boi. τείνω. Cf. MLG. I, 286; Lesk. Abl. 350.
tánkus 'dicht, fest, häufig'—Uh. *tanákti;* K. *dicht;* F. *þāhō, þeihan, þeihvō;* B. I, 526.546.579. II, 1, 178. Cf. Lesk. Nom. 253.
tapalas 'Pappel'—W. *pōpulus.* Cf. Brückner SlFw. 144.
tàpti 'werden'—inf. of *tampù,* q.v.
tarnáitė 'Dienerin'—B. II, 1, 601.674.
tar̃nas 'Diener, Aufwärter, Ministrant (bei der Messe)'—B. II, 1, 261; (W. *Jūturna*); Boi. τόρνος.
tarnáuju, tarnáuti 'dienen'—B. II, 3, 220.
tarpà 'Gedeihen, Wachstum'—Uh. *tŕ̥pyati;* F. *þaurban;* B. I, 512; Boi. τέρπω. Cf. Lesk. Abl. 367.
tárpas 'Zwischenraum, Zwischenzeit'; **tamè (tam̃) tárpe** 'unterdessen'—B. II, 2, 708. Cf. Lesk. Nom. 169.
tarpstù, tar̃pti 'gedeihen, zunehmen, genesen'—Uh. *tŕ̥pyati;* F. *þaurban, þrafstjan;* Boi. τέρπω. Cf. Lesk. Abl. 367.

tàs masc., **taĩ** neut., **tà** fem. 'dieser, -es, -e; der, das, die' —Uh. *tá-;* F. *þata;* B. I, 21.148.163.178.344.387.523. 930. II, 2, 313.357.375.377; W. *ista;* Boi. το-. Cf. Wied. 122, 131.

tasaĩ 'dieser'—B. II, 2, 346.

tąsaũ, tąsýti 'zerren, recken, dehnen, umherzerren'—Uh. *taṁsáyati;* F. *at-þinsan;* B. II, 3, 253.268; W. *prōtēlo.* Cf. Lesk. Abl. 350.

tąsùs 'dehnbar, streckbar, hämmerbar, elastisch'—B. I, 783. Cf. Lesk. Abl. 350.

taszaũ, taszýti 'Bauholz behauen, zimmern'—Uh. *tákṣati;* K. *Deichsel* 2; B. I, 540.562.568.790; W. *texo;* Boi. τέκτων. Cf. Lesk. Abl. 367.

taszką acc. sing. (**taszkas** or **taszka**, masc. or fem.?) 'Verhau, Schanze'—B. II, 1, 477. Cf. Geitler LD. 65, Lesk. Nom. 504.

tataĩ 'gerade das, dasselbe'—B. II, 2, 346.

táukas 'Fettstückchen'; **taukaĩ** plu. 'Fett, Schmer, Schmiere, Mark in den Knochen'—Uh. *tavīti;* B. II, 2, 49; W. *tūcētum, tumeo;* Boi. ταῦς, τύλος. Cf. Lesk. Abl. 313.

tauras, tauris 'Auerochs'—Uh. *sthávíras;* F. *stiur;* B. I, 174 (note); W. *taurus;* Boi. ταῦρος. Cf. Bezz. BGLS. 331; MLG. I, 294; Lalis 381; Lesk. Nom. 435; Trautmann Die altpreussischen Sprachdenkmäler 446.

tautà 'Land, Volk, Nation'; **Tautà** (Pruss.-Lith.) 'Oberland, Deutschland'—K. *deutsch;* F. *þiuda;* B. I, 197. 530. II, 1, 410; W. *tumeo;* Boi. Τευταμίδης. Cf. MLG. I, 294; Lalis 381; Lesk. Nom. 543; Trautmann Die altpreussischen Sprachdenkmäler 446.

táv 'dir'—see *távei.*

tãvas poss. pron. 'dein'—Uh. *tvás;* F. *þeins;* B. I, 120.130. 317. II, 2, 383.403.404.406; W. *tū;* Boi. σύ.

tavàsis poss. pron. 'der Deinige'—B. II, 2, 406. Cf. Kur. Gram. 982.

tavę acc. sing. 'dich'—B. II, 2, 383.413.427. Cf. Wied. 163.

tavè, tavę̃s 2nd pers. pron. gen. sing.—Uh. *tvás;* F. *þeins;* B. II, 2, 416.427. Cf. Wied. 163, 164.

távei, táv 2nd pers. pron. dat. sing. 'dir'—B. II, 2, 418.427. Cf. Wied. 163.

tãvo indeclinable gen. poss. pron. 'dein'—B. II, 2, 416.427. Cf. Wied. 163.

tè 'da! nimm!'—F. *du-þē;* B. II, 2, 314.346; Boi. τῆ.

teĩp 'so, also, auf diese Weise; ja'—B. II, 2, 364.709; W. *nempe.* Cf. Bezz. BGLS. 332. See *taĩp.*

tẽk 'so viel'—B. II, 1, 482. Cf. Kur. s.v.; Kur. Gram. 1041.

tekė̃las 'drehbarer Schleifstein'—B. II, 1, 370.610.

tẽkinas 'laufend, im Lauf'—B. II, 1, 260. 3, 323. Cf. Lesk. Abl. 367.

tẽkinu, tẽkinti 'laufen lassen, auf einem drehbaren Schleifstein schleifen, drechseln'—B. II, 3, 323. See *tekù.*

tèkti 'hinreichen'—inf. of *tenkù,* q.v.

tekù, tekė́ti 'laufen, fliessen, leck sein, aufgehen (von der Sonne), heiraten (vom Weib)'—Uh. *tákti;* F. *þius;* B. I, 146.488.575. II, 1, 423-4. 3, 120; (Boi. θής (note)). Cf. Lesk. Abl. 367.

telpù, tiĨpti 'hineingehen, Raum worin haben, hineinpassen' —Uh. *tálpas;* B. I, 516.686.(Ntr.) 1093; W. *talpa.* Cf. Lesk. Abl. 350.

telžu; telžti 'beharnen'—Boi. σταλάσσω. Cf. Geitler LS. 116; MLG. I, 301; Lesk. Abl. 367. Notice also Lalis 377[b]: *telžiu, telžti* 'to flog, to whip'.

tė̃myju, tė̃myti 'merken, genau betrachten, sich einprägen'; **tė̃myjůs, tė̃mytis** 'sich kennen lernen, sich etwas genau merken, im Gedächtnis behalten'—(W. *timeo*); Boi. τημελεῖν. Cf. Brückner SlFw. 145.

tempiù, tem̃pti 'spannen, durch Ziehen dehnen; (Lalis also) to pull, haul, drag, lug'—B. I, 366.404; W. *antemna, templum;* Boi. τάπης. Cf. Lesk. Abl. 350.

temptýva 'Bogensehne'—W. *templum;* Boi. τάπης. Cf. MLG. I, 301; Lesk. Nom. 353. See prec.

témstu, témti 'verfinstern, dunkel werden'; **jaũ témsta** 'es wird schon dunkel'—Uh. *támas;* K. *dämmern;* B. I, 178; W. *tenebrae.* Cf. Lesk. Abl. 350.

tenkù, tèkti 'zukommen, zufallen, zuteil werden, erhalten, genug haben, sich hinerstrecken, hinreichen, mit etwas ausreichen'—Uh. *tanákti;* K. *gedeihen;* F. *þeihan, þeihs;* B. I, 125.382.404.526.546.579.(Ntr.)1094; (W. *porticus, tempus* (s.v. *templum*)); Boi. τόπος. Cf. Lesk. Abl. 369.

tēnpàt 'eben dort'—F. *brūþ-faþs;* W. *utpote* (s.v. *pte*); Boi. ποτέ (s.v. πότε). Cf. Kur. s.v., Kur. Gram. 1425.

tenuȓ 'dort, dahin'—B. II, 2, 735. Cf. Ness. 93[b].

tenvas 'dünn, zart'—Uh. *tanúṣ;* F. *uf-þanjan;* B. I, 340.416. 521. II, 1, 200; W. *tendo, tenuis;* Boi. ταν-. Cf. Geitler LS. 116; MLG. I, 303; Lesk. Abl. 350.

tersziù, teȓszti 'beschmutzen, abfärben, Wiesen verschlämmen'—Boi. τάργανον. Cf. MLG. I, 306; Lesk. Abl. 351.

tësà adv. 'in Wahrheit, zwar, freilich'—B. II, 2, 717.

tęsiù, tę̃sti 'ziehen, dehnen, recken'—Uh. *taṁsáyati;* K. *gedunsen;* F. *at-þinsan;* B. I, 371.783. II, 1, 371. 3, 253.338.389-90.445; W. *prōtēlo, (portisculus).* Cf. Lesk. Abl. 350.

teszmũ 'Euter'—B. II, 1, 238.607. Cf. Lesk. Abl. 351.

tetà 'Tante'—B. II, 1, 127; W. *tata;* Boi. τέττα.

tetervas m. 'Birkhahn', **teterva** f. 'Birkhuhn'—Uh. *tittiras;* W. *tetrinnio;* Boi. τέτραξ. Cf. MLG. I, 310; Lesk. Nom. 347.

tẽtervinas m. 'Birkhahn, (Mielcke) Auerhahn'; **tetervina** f. 'Birkhuhn'—Uh. *tittiras;* B. II, 1, 273; W. *tetrinnio;* Boi. τέτραξ. Cf. Schleicher LSpr. II, 328; Lesk. Nom. 405.

tẽtis 'Vater, Väterchen'—Uh. *tatás;* F. *atta;* B. II, 1, 127; W. *tata;* Boi. τέττα.

tėtýtis dimin. 'Väterchen'—W. *tata;* Boi. τέττα. See prec.

ti Old Lith. 'dir, dich'—B. I, 259.938. II, 2, 383.394.408. 427. Cf. Wied. 164.

tikyba, tikỹbė 'Glaube, Zuversicht, Hoffnung, Treue, Religion'—B. II, 1, 390.636. Cf. MLG. I, 313; Lalis 385; Lesk. Nom. 591; [Lesk. Abl. 287].

tìknagas 'Feuerstein'—see *tìtnagas*.

tìkras 'passend, recht, wirklich, echt, eigentlich, sicher, zuverlässig, rechtschaffen, tüchtig, lauter, wahrhaftig, geschickt, eigen'—F. *þeihan;* B. II, 1, 352. Cf. Lesk. Abl. 287.

tìkslas 'Belieben; (Lalis) purpose, object, scope, aim, end' —B. II, 1, 373. Cf. Lesk. Abl. 287, Lalis 385.

tìkti 'taugen'—inf. of *tinkù,* q.v.

tìlė, plu. **tìlės** 'Bodenbretter im Kahn'—Uh. *talam;* K. *Diele;* B. I, 458.472.473. II, 1, 380; W. *tabula, tellūs;* Boi. I. τηλία. Cf. Ness. 105*, Lesk. Abl. 349, Sommer 63.

tiĩpti 'hineinpassen'—inf. of *telpù,* q.v.

tìltas 'Brücke'—Uh. *taṭas, (tīrthám)*; W. *tellūs.* Cf. Lesk. Abl. 349.

tylù, tìlti 'still werden, verstummen'—W. *locus.* Cf. Lesk. Abl. 360.

tilvìkas 'Brachhuhn, Schnepfe'—Uh. *ṭiṭṭibhas;* Boi. τιτυβίζω. Cf. MLG. I, 315; Lalis 386; Lesk. Nom. 512.

Tilžė̃nas 'Tilsiter'—B. II, 1, 308.

tìmpa 'Sehne' (des Körpers, bes. am Fuss)—W. *templum;* Boi. τάπης (twice). Cf. Lesk. Abl. 350.

timpsaũ, timpsóti 'ausgestreckt und träge liegen'—W. *templum.* Cf. Lesk. Abl. 350.

timpstù, tim̃pti 'sich dehnen, recken'—B. I, 404; Boi. τάπης. Cf. Lesk. Abl. 350.

tìmsras (B. **tímsras**), **timsrus** 'dunkelrot, schweissfüchsig' —Uh. *tamisram;* B. I, 410.417.419.423.672. II, 1, 385; W. *tenebrae.* Cf. MLG. I, 317; Lesk. Abl. 350.

-tinas end. of verb. adjs. (e.g. **bútinas** 'seiend, bleibend, wesentlich')—B. II, 1, 269. Cf. Lesk. Nom. 405-6.

tìngiu, tingḗti 'träge, unlustig, faul sein; faul werden; zaudern'—(W. *taedet*). See next.

tingùs 'träge, faul'—B. II, 1, 493; (W. *taedet*). Cf. Lesk. Abl. 360.

tiñklas 'Netz, Fischernetz; Spinngewebe'—K. *dehnen, Dohne, [Donner]*; W. *tendo*, 1. *tenus;* Boi. ἀτενής, τείνω. Cf. Bezz. LF. 188, Lesk. Abl. 350.

tinkù, tìkti 'taugen, passen, genügen, gefallen'—F. *þeihan, þeihs.* Cf. Lesk. Abl. 287.

tìnti 'schwellen'—inf. of *tį́stu*, q.v.

tyras, usually plu. **tyrai** 'ödes Land, Wüste, Heide, Steppe, mit Gras überwachsener Morast'—W. *tābeo;* Boi. τῖλος. Cf. MLG. I, 319; Geitler LS. 117; Lalis 386; Lesk. Nom. 165.

týras, tỹrė 'Brei, (bes.) Kinderbrei'—Boi. τῖλος.

tirpstù, tiȓpti 'einschlafen, erstarren, gefühllos werden'—B. I, 472.520. II, 3, 445; W. *torpeo;* Boi. στέρφος. Cf. Lesk. Abl. 351.

tirsztù, tiȓszti 'dickflüssig, trübe werden; gerinnen'; **tiȓsztas** 'trübe, dickflüssig; dicht (von Wolken, Regen, Bevölkerung usw.)'—Boi. τάργανον. Cf. MLG. I, 321; Bezz. LF. 189; Lesk. Abl. 351.

tį̃sis (?) masc. 'Fischzug'—B. I, 416. Cf. Lesk. Abl. 350 & Ness. 99* (whence Kur. & Lesk.; but see Nesselmann MLG. I, 322: 'Fischzeug'—probably a misprint).

tį́stu, pret. **tinaũ, tìnti** 'schwellen, an der Wassersucht leiden; schwer atmen'—B. II, 3, 441; W. *tendo;* Boi. τείνω. Cf. Lesk. Abl. 350.

tįstù, tį̃sti 'sich dehnen, recken; dehnbar, schmiedbar sein'—B. I, 416; W. *prōtēlo.* See *tęsiù.*

tytaras 'Truthahn'—Uh. *tittiras;* W. *tetrinnio;* Boi. τέτραξ. Cf. Ness. 107*.

tìtnagas, dial. (B.) **tìknagas** 'Kiesel, Feuerstein'—(Uh. *títhiṣ*); B. I, 542; W. *titio;* Boi. τιτώ.

-togti—see *sutógti* 'einig werden mit'.

tõks 'talis'—B. II, 1, 498.

toksaĩ id.—B. II, 2, 346. Cf. Kur. Gram. 980.

tõl 'bis dahin, solange'—W. *tālis.*

tolẽrius 'Teller'—B. I, 875. Cf. MLG. I, 325; Brückner SlFw. 146.

tolì adv. 'weit, fern'—(Ber. *daľi*); W. *tālis*. Cf. Lesk. Abl. 349.

tólimas 'fern, entfernt'—B. II, 1, 251. 2, 701.

tolỹn adv. 'fort, vorwärts, weiter, in die Ferne'—B. II, 2, 703.

tólinu, tólinti 'entfernen'—(Ber. *daľi*).

tõlis masc. 'Weite, Entfernung, Abstand'—B. II, 1, 251. Cf. MLG. I, 326; Lesk. Nom. 301; [Lesk. Abl. 349].

tólo gen. in **ìsz tólo, isztólo** 'von fern'—B. II, 2, 725. Cf. Kur. 460, Lesk. Abl. 349.

tolùs 'fern, entfernt'—(Ber. *daľi*); W. *tālis*. Cf. Lesk. Abl. 349.

tometùkas 'einer von jenem Jahre'—B. II, 1, 34. Cf. Lesk. Nom. 517.

torẽlius 'Teller'—B. I, 875. Cf. Brückner SlFw. 146.

traidinù, traidìnti 'zum Durchfall bringen, Durchfall erregen'—Ber. *driskają*. Cf. Lesk. Abl. 288.

trakas 'alberner Mensch'—B. II, 3, 290; Boi. ἀτρεκής. Cf. MLG. I, 327; Lesk. Abl. 352.

trakus 'albern, toll, wütend'—B. I, 472. II, 3, 290. Cf. Lalis 388, Lesk. Nom. 250. See prec.

trandẽ, trandìs fem. 'Motte, Made, Holzwurm'—B. II, 1, 168. 3, 289; W. *tarmes*. See *tréndu*.

trañksmas 'Gedränge, Lärm, Getöse, Getümmel' — K. *dringen;* F. *þreihan;* W. *truncus*. Cf. Lesk. Abl. 352.

trankùs 'holperig, stössig' (vom Wege)—Ber. *drąkŭ;* W. *truncus*. Cf. Lesk. Abl. 352.

trą́sza fem. sing. 'Moder; Dünger, Kuhmist; (Lalis) fatness of soil, fertility'—Boi. τάργανον. Cf. MLG. I, 329; Lesk. Nom. 209; [Lesk. Abl. 352].

trąszai masc. plu. 'verstocktes, verfaultes Getreide oder Stroh; allerlei Moderndes, Verdorbenes'—Boi. τάργανον. Cf. Geitler LS. 117; MLG. I, 329; Lesk. Nom. 169; [Lesk. Abl. 352].

traszkù, traszkḗti 'rasseln, krachen, poltern, klappern'—K. *dreschen;* (F. *þriskan*). Cf. Lesk. Abl. 351, 367.

trẽczas 'dritter'—Uh. *tṛtī́yas;* F. *þridja;* B. II, 1, 391. 2, 12.53; W. *tertius* (s.v. *trēs*). Cf. Wied. 157. 3.

treczõkas 'Dreier, Dreigroschenstück, Silbergroschen; Drittstange am Wagen'—B. II, 1, 501. Cf. MLG. I, 332; Lesk. Nom. 513.

trḗda 'Durchfall'—Ber. *driskajǫ*. Cf. MLG. I, 332. See next.

trẽdżu, trẽsti 'Durchfall haben'—Ber. *driskajǫ;* W. *foria.* Cf. Lesk. Abl. 288.

treigỹs 'dreijährig' (von Tieren, nicht von Menschen)—B. II, 1, 513. Cf. Lesk. Nom. 524.

trẽjetas 'Dreiheit, drei zusammengehörige Stücke'—B. II, 2, 24. Cf. Lesk. Nom. 571.

trejì, fem. **trẽjos** 'drei, je drei, zu dreien'—Uh. *trayás;* B. II, 1, 163.168. 2, 77. Cf. Kur. Gram. 1033, Wied. 158. 3.

trejópas 'dreierlei'—B. II, 2, 234. Cf. Kur. Gram. 1036, Wied. 159.

trẽjos 'drei'—fem. of *trejì*, q.v.

trẽkszti 'pressen'—inf. of *trẽszkiu*, q.v.

tréndu (tréndżu), trendḗti 'von Motten, Würmern zerfressen werden'—Uh. *tṛṇátti, tradás;* B. I, 452. II, 3, 277.289.377.382; W. *tarmes,* (*tardus*); Boi. τείρω. Cf. Lesk. Abl. 367.

trenkiù, treñkti 'schütteln, dröhnend stossen, schmettern, heftig schlagen'; **sutrenkiù, sutreñkti** 'zerstossen'—K. *dringen;* F. *þreihan;* B. I, 142. II, 3, 135; Ber. *drǫkŭ;* W. *truncus,* (*torqueo*). Cf. Lesk. Abl. 352.

trenkù, triñkti 'waschen, baden' (Behaartes, z.B. Schafe, den Kopf)—Ber. *drǫkŭ*. Cf. Lesk. Abl. 352.

trepenu, trepenti 'to tread noisily, to trample'—Boi. τραπεῖν. Cf. Lalis 389.

trepsiu, trepsėti 'to tread noisily, to trample; (Lesk.) strampeln'—Boi. τραπεῖν. Cf. Lalis 389, Lesk. Abl. 352.

trepstu, trepti 'mit den Füssen scharren, stampfen, zappeln, poltern'—W. *trepidus;* Boi. τραπεῖν. Cf. MLG. I, 334; Lesk. Abl. 352.

trẽszkinu, trẽszkinti 'prasseln machen; (Lalis) to crack, rend, break, cause to crackle'; **sutrẽszkinu, sutrẽszkinti** (so read F.'s *sutrèszinti?* Or is there a *treszinti* 'zerprasseln' beside *trẽszkinti* id. as *treszinti* 'faulen lassen' beside *treszkinti* id.? For the last three words of the proportion see MLG. I, 335) 'zerprasseln, mit Prasseln zerbrechen'—(F. *priskan*). Cf. Lesk. Abl. 351.

trẽszkiu, trẽkszti; trẽszkiu, trẽkszti 'quetschen, pressen'—F. *priskan.* Cf. Ness. 114[a]; Kur. 463[b]; Lalis 389[a]; Lesk. Abl. 288.

treszkù, treszkė́ti 'prasseln, knistern, knacken, schnattern, plappern'—B. II, 3, 360. Cf. Lesk. Abl. 351, 367.

tręsztù, trę́szti (Kur. **trèszti**) 'trocken faulen, morsch werden, stocken, verwesen'—Boi. τάργανον. Cf. MLG. I, 336; Lesk. Abl. 352; Lesk. Nom. 169. Notice also Lalis 389: *tręsziu, tręszti* 'to manure, to fertilize'.

trìdė, tryda 'Durchfall'—Ber. *driskają;* W. *foria.* Cf. Lesk. Abl. 287-8, Lalis 389.

trìgubas 'dreifach'—B. II, 2, 71; Ber. *gŭbežĭ;* (Boi. κυφός). Cf. Lesk. Nom. 191, [Lesk. Abl. 297-8].

trijũ gen. of **trỹs**, q.v., 'trium'—B. I, 100. Cf. Wied. 156. 3.

trikójis 'Dreifüssler, Dreifuss'—B. II, 2, 11; Boi. τρεῖς.

trìkti 'fehlgehen'—inf. of *trinkù,* q.v.

trýlika 'dreizehn'—K. *elf;* [F. *ain-lif*]; B. I, 103.495. II, 2, 26.27; [Ber. *-lěkŭ*]; W. *trēs,* [*linquo*]; Boi. τρεῖς. See *trỹs* & Kur. Gram. 1010, Wied. 156.

trýliktas 'dreizehnter'—B. II, 2, 59. Cf. Wied. 157.

trìlinkas 'dreifach, dreigedoppelt'—B. II, 2, 71.

trimù, trìmti 'zittern' (vor Frost, Angst, Scham)—Uh. *taralás;* F. *þramstei;* B. I, 434; W. *tremo;* Boi. τρέμω. Cf. MLG. I, 338; Lesk. Abl. 351.

trìnka 'Haublock'—Ber. *drąkŭ;* W. *truncus.* Cf. Lesk. Abl. 352.

trìnkis, trinkỹs masc. 'Stoss, Schlag, Anstoss'; **perkúno trìnkis** 'Donnerschlag'—F. *þreihan;* W. *truncus.* Cf. Geitler LS. 117; Bezz. LF. 190; MLG. I, 339; Lesk. Abl. 352.

triñkti 'waschen'—inf of *trenkù,* q.v.

trìnku (**trìnkiu**), **trinkė́ti** 'fortgesetzt klopfen, poltern, dröhnen' (z.B. vom Wagen beim Fahren über Steine oder gefrorene Erde)—Ber. *drǫkŭ.* Cf. Lesk. Abl. 352.

trinkù, trìkti 'fehlgehen, nicht zustande kommen, in Unordnung kommen, sich irren (beim Reden, Zählen usw.)' —B. I, 472. II, 3, 290; Boi. ἀτρεκής. Cf. Lesk. Abl. 352.

trinù, trìnti 'reiben, feilen, sägen, (Kleider) waschen'; **szeivàs trìnti** 'die Weberspulchen mit Garn füllen'—Uh. *turás;* F. *þriskan,* (*þreihan*); W. *tero;* Boi. τείρω. Cf. Lesk. Abl. 352.

trynùczei plu. 'Drillinge'—B. II, 2, 78. Cf. MLG. I, 340.

trypiù, trỹpti 'stampfen, treten'; **isztrypiù, isztrỹpti** '(Korn) austrampeln'—Boi. τραπεῖν. Cf. Lesk. Abl. 352.

tripsė́ti (?) 'auftreten'—Boi. τραπεῖν. Cf. Lesk. Abl. 352.

trirą̃žis 'dreizinkig, dreizackig'—Boi. ῥᾱχός. Cf. Lesk. Abl. 365.

trỹs 'drei'. Other forms also indexed separately.—Uh. *tráyas;* K. *drei;* F. *þreis;* B. I, 100.424.521. II, 2, 11; W. *trēs;* Boi. τρεῖς. Cf. Wied. 156. 3.

trìsdeszimt 'dreissig'—B. II, 1, 95. 2, 37. Cf. Wied. 156.

trìsdeszimtas 'dreissigster'—B. II, 2, 61. Cf. Wied. 157.

trìsdeszimts 'dreissig'—B. II, 2, 22.37.38. Cf. Wied. 156; MLG. I, 341.

trisè loc. of **trỹs** 'drei', q.v.—F. *þreis;* B. II, 2, 11. Cf. Wied. 156. 3.

trìsros 'dreimal'—B. I, 939. Cf. LBLV. 291, 342; [Brückner SlFw. 127].

-trýstu, -trýsti—see *pratrýstu* 'ich bekomme den Durchfall'.

trisziu, triszti (MLG. I, 342 **tr̨isziu, tr̨iszti**) 'düngen'; **triszimas** 'Düngung'; **trisztas** 'gedüngt'. Szyr.—Boi. τάργανον. Cf. Ness. 116*, Lesk. Abl. 352.

triszu, triszéti 'zittern, schaudern'—Uh. *trásati;* F. *þrasabalþei;* B. I, 457. 568. II, 3, 351 (twice).352; W. *terreo;* Boi. τρέω. Cf. Ness. 116*, Lesk. Abl. 360.

tritainis masc. 'Drittel'—B. II, 2, 12.73. Cf. MLG. I, 342; Lesk. Nom. 416.

triùszkinu, triùszkinti "zermalmen (bes. von hohlen, rohrartigen Dingen, welche beim Zermalmen hohl und dumpf schallen)" (Kur.); "to break, crack, smash, crush" (Lalis)—Boi. τέρυς.

trobà 'Gebäude, Haus, Wohnung'—K. *Dorf;* F. *þaurp;* B. I, 175.439.507. II, 1, 154; W. *trabs;* Boi. τέραμνον. Cf. Lesk. Nom. 218.

trõtyju, trõtyti 'an Leib und Leben schädigen, quälen, verderben, verwahrlosen'—F. *þrōþjan.* Cf. Brückner SlFw. 147.

trũkis masc. 'Zug (z.B. Fischzug); Riss, Bruch, Spalte'—Boi. τρύχω. Cf. Ness. 118*, Lesk. Abl. 312.

trúkstu, trúkti intr. 'reissen, entzweigehen, bersten'; (Lalis also) 'to lack, to be wanting, to be deficient'—Boi. τρύχω. Cf. Lesk. Abl. 312.

truniù, trunëti 'faulen, modern'—F. *þrūts-fill;* Boi. τέρυς, τιτρώσκω. Cf. Kur. 466, Lalis 392, Lesk. Abl. 318.

trupù, trupëti 'in Brocken zerfallen, zerbröckeln'—Boi. τρῡπᾶν, (θρύπτω (note)). Cf. Lesk. Abl. 295, 313.

trupùs 'bröckelig'—Boi. τρῡπᾶν, (θρύπτω (note)). See prec.

truputỹs 'Brocken'—B. II, 1, 418. See prec.

truszìs 'Schilf; Schachtelhalm'—Boi. θρύον. Cf. Bezz. LF. 190, Lesk. Nom. 238.

truszkù, truszkëti 'knistern, prasseln'—Boi. τέρυς.

tù 'du'. Other 2nd pers. pron. forms separately indexed.—Uh. *tú;* F. *þu;* B. I, 105.529. II, 2, 410.427; W. *tū;* Boi. σύ.

tugu 'σύγε'—Ber. *-go.* See *-gu.*

túkstantis masc. 'tausend'—Uh. *tavâs;* K. *tausend;* F. *þūsundi;* B. I, XLII (Ntr.). II, 2, 47.49; W. *tumeo.* Cf. Kur. Gram. 1015; Wied. 156; Brückner SlFw. 147.

tūkstantȳ̃sis 'tausendster'—B. II, 2, 62. Cf. Wied. 157.

túlas 'so mancher'—Uh. *tūlam;* B. I, 114.434. II, 1, 363; W. *tumeo, (tum)*; Boi. τύλος.

tùlkas 'Dolmetscher'—K. *Dolmetsch;* W. *loquor.* Cf. Brückner SlFw. 148.

tunkù, tùkti 'fett werden' (von Masttieren)—Uh. *tavīti;* F. *þwastiþa;* W. *tumeo;* Boi. ταΐς, τύλος. Cf. Lesk. Abl. 313.

tuntais adv. 'haufenweise, scharenweise'—Boi. τύντλος. Cf. Ness. 109[b], Lesk. Nom. 538.

tuntas 'Gefolge, Menge'—Boi. τύντλος. Cf. Ness. 109[b]; Geitler LS. 118; Lalis 392; Lesk. Nom. 538.

tupiù, tupė̃ti 'hocken, kauern, (von den Vögeln) sitzen'—K. *Ducht;* F. *þiufs;* B. II, 1, 155; Boi. ἐντυπάς. Cf. Lesk. Abl. 313.

tūpiù, tũpti 'sich niederkauern, sich hinhocken, sich niedersetzen'; **tūpiū̃s, tũptis** id.—K. *Ducht;* F. *þiufs;* Boi. ἐντυπάς. See prec.

tur̃gus 'Markt', **turgãvietė** 'Marktplatz'—B. II, 1, 91. Cf. Brückner SlFw. 148, Lesk. Nom. 241.

turiù, turė̃ti 'haben, besitzen, halten; müssen; Junge werfen (von Tieren)'—B. II, 3, 192; (Ber. *imamĭ*); W. *pariēs.* Cf. Lesk. Abl. 318.

turklẽlis masc. 'Turteltaube, Lachtaube'—B. I, 541. Cf. Ness. 110[a], Lalis 393.

tursas (?) 'der Hintere'—Boi. στόρθυγξ. Cf. Ness. 111[a], Lesk. Nom. 189.

tursaũ, tursóti 'mit ausgestrecktem Hinterteil dastehen oder kauern'—(W. *tergum*).

tursomegis (?) masc. 'Schlaf auf dem Bauche'—(W. *tergum*). Cf. Ness. 111[a], Lesk. Nom. 189.

tūtlȳ̃s 'Wiedehopf'—W. *tussis;* Boi. τυτώ.

tūtū́ju, tūtū́ti 'tuten'—W. *tussis;* Boi. τυτώ.

tūzgenù, tūzgénti 'an die Tür klopfen'—(Uh. *tujáti*); W. *stuprum;* Boi. ἀτύζω.

túzgiu, tūzgė́ti 'dumpf dröhnend klappern, klopfen'—(Uh. *tujáti*); W. *stuprum;* Boi. ἀτύζω.

tūžbà 'Kummer, Angst, Gram, Sorge, Betrübnis'—Boi. ἀτύζω. Cf. Brückner SlFw. 148.

tūžyju, tūžyti 'ängstigen, quälen, bange machen; sich ängstigen'; **tūžyjůs, tūžytis** 'sich grämen, sich ängstigen'—(Uh. *tujáti*); Boi. ἀτύζω. Cf. Brückner SlFw. 148.

tů̃, tůmì inst. sing. of **tàs,** q.v., 'mit dem, damit'; **tů̃, tůjaũ, tůjaũs** adv. 'gleich, sofort'—B. II, 2, 365; (Ber. *abĭje*). Cf. Wied. 122. See *jaũ*.

tů̃czės 'zu der Zeit, damals'—B. II, 2, 714.

tůjaũ 'sofort'—see *tů̃*.

tůmì 'mit dem'—see *tů̃*.

tvainýtis (?) 'buhlen, sich unkeuschen Gelüsten hingeben' —Boi. σαίνω. Cf. Geitler LS. 118; MLG. I, 75; Lesk. Abl. 353.

tvãnas 'Überschwemmung, Flut'—Uh. *tavīti;* F. *þwahan;* W. *tōlēs;* Boi. σαίνω, ταΰς, τύντλος. Cf. Lesk. Abl. 353.

tvankùs 'schwül'—Uh. *tvanakti;* Boi. σάττω. Cf. Lesk. Abl. 353.

tvanùs 'leicht anschwellend' (von einem Fluss)—F. *þwahan;* Boi. σαίνω. Cf. Lesk. Abl. 353.

tvarklas (?) 'Hirt'—B. II, 1, 345. Cf. Bezz. BGLS. 333, Lesk. Abl. 353, Lesk. Nom. 502.

tvártas 'Einzäunung, Verschlag, Hürde; (Lalis) stable'—Uh. *toraṇam;* B. II, 1, 408; W. *pariēs;* Boi. σορός. See *tveriù*.

tvenkiù, tveñkti '(z.B. einen Fluss) anschwellen, anstauen machen; dämmen'—Uh. *tvanakti;* W. *pānus*. Cf. Lesk. Abl. 353.

tveriù, tvérti 'fassen, greifen, einfassen, umfassen, einzäunen; halten, ausdauern; machen, schaffen'; **sùtveriu, sutvérti** 'zusammenfassen, erschaffen, schöpfen'—Uh.

toraṇam; B. I, 260.310.339. II, 1, 168; (Ber. *imamĭ*); W. *pariēs,* (*torus*), (*turris*); Boi. σαργάνη, σειρᾶ, σορός, (σωρός), τάρπη, τύραννος. Cf. Ness. 122ᵃ; Lalis 394, 359; Lesk. Abl. 353; Brückner SlFw. 148.

tvinkstù, tviñkti 'anschwellen, schwären, trächtig sein, eutern'—Uh. *tvanakti;* W. *pānus;* Boi. σάττω. Cf. Lesk. Abl. 353.

tvìnti 'anschwellen'—inf. of *tvį́stu,* q.v.

tvìrtas (B. **tvírtas**) 'fest, beständig, standhaft'—B. I, 260. 261.482. II, 1, 472; W. *pariēs.* Cf. Lesk. Abl. 353, Brückner SlFw. 148.

tvìrtinu, tvìrtinti (B. **tvírt-**) 'festmachen, befestigen, bestätigen'—B. II, 3, 323.

tviskù, tviskė́ti 'leuchten, flackern, stark blitzen'; **tvìska** 'es blitzt'—Uh. *tviṣáti;* B. II, 3, 352; Boi. σείω. Cf. Lesk. Abl. 353.

tvį́stu, tvìnti (B. **tvínti**) 'anschwellen, steigen' (vom Wasser)—Uh. *tavīti;* F. *þwahan;* B. I, 321. II, 3, 318; W. *tōlēs;* Boi. σαίνω, ταῦς, τύντλος. Cf. Lesk. Abl. 353.

tvóju, tvóti 'tüchtig prügeln, schlagen'—Uh. *títaü-;* Boi. διαττάω. Cf. Geitler LS. 118, Lalis 394, Lesk. Abl. 378.

tvorà 'Zaun'—B. II, 1, 154.168; W. *pariēs.* Cf. Lesk. Abl. 353.

U

údra 'Fischotter'—Uh. *udrás;* K. *Otter* 1; B. I, 522. II, 1, 347; W. *lutra, unda;* Boi. ὕδρος.

ū̃drū̃ju, ū̃drū̃ti; ū̃drója, ū̃dróti 'eutern, trächtig sein'—Uh. *ū́dhar;* K. *Euter;* B. I, 114; W. *ūber;* Boi. οὖθαρ. Cf. Lalis 395, Prell. deutsch. Best. in den lett. Spr. 34.

ugnãvietė 'Feuerstätte, Feuerherd'—B. II, 1, 91.

ugnìs fem. 'Feuer'—Uh. *agníṣ;* B. I, 146.387. II, 1, 287. 2, 93; W. *ignis.*

úkana 'bewölkter Himmel (Kur.); trübes, regnerisches Wetter (Ness.); cloudiness, gloom, gloominess, obscurity (Lalis)'—B. II, 1, 268.

úkanas 'trübe, bewölkt'—B. II, 1, 268; W. *umbra, (aquilus)*. See next.

úkas 'caligo'—W. *umbra*. Cf. Lalis 395, Lesk. Abl. 314.

úkis masc. 'Bauernhof' (Lalis 'farm; farming, husbandry, agriculture')—Uh. *ókas;* Boi. ἴκηλος.

ūkstaũs, ūkstýtis (Lesk. **úkstaus, úkstytis**) 'sich trüben, sich mit Wolken beziehen'; **dangùs ũkstos** 'der Himmel bezieht sich'—W. *umbra*. Cf. Kur. s.v.; Kur. DLWb. s.v. trüben; Lesk. Abl. 314.

ulbũju, ulbũti; ulbauju, ulbaũti 'rufen, singen, krahlen, winseln'—W. *ulula;* Boi. ὀλολύζω. Cf. Ness. 34ᵃ.

ulũju, ulũti; ulóju, ulóti; ululóju, ululóti 'schreien, rufen, jauchzen, heulen'; **ulula bañgos** 'es rauschen die Wellen'—Uh. *ululìș;* B. II, 1, 46. 3, 178.198.204; W. *ulula;* Boi. ὀλολύζω. Cf. Ness. 34ᵃ, Brückner SlFw. 149.

undũ (?) Samogit. 'Wasser'—B. I, 107; W. *unda;* Boi. ὕδωρ. Cf. Ness. 34ᵃ; BB. XXIII, 296. See *vandũ*.

ùngau 'ich wimmerte'—see *ùnkstu*.

ungnis Old Lith. 'Feuer'—W. *ignis*. See Bezz. BGLS. 42 & *ugnìs*.

ungurỹs 'Aal'—Uh. *áhiș; (K. Aal)*; B. I, 387; W. *anguis,* (Ntr.) *ancorago;* Boi. ἔγχελυς, ἴμβηρις.

unksna (?) 'Schatten'—W. *umbra*. Cf. Ness. 34ᵇ, Lesk. Abl. 314.

ùnkstu, pret. **ùngau, ùnkti; ùnkstau, ùnkstyti** 'wimmern' (wie ein Hund)—Boi. ἀγανακτέω. Cf. Ness. 34ᵇ, Kur. 475. Notice also Geitler LS. 103, *paungstoti* 'unter den Bart brummen'; Bezz. LF. 192, *paùnkstauti* 'in den Bart brummen, sich mit ganz feiner Stimme vernehmen lassen'; Lalis 395, *ungszti* 'to snarl, to growl'.

upáitė 'Flüsschen, Bach'—B. II, 1, 677. Cf. Kur. DLWb. s.v. Flüsschen; Ness. 34ᵇ.

ùpė 'Fluss, Strom'—Uh. *ápas;* (F. *alva*); B. I, 146. II, 1, 222; W. *amnis* (read "Strom" for "Wasser"), (*vafer*); Boi. ὀπός (read 'cours d'eau' for 'eau').

upẽlis 'Flüsschen, Bach'—B. II, 1, 671.

urbinu, urbinti 'mit dem Pfriemen ein Loch machen'—Boi. ἄρβηλος. Cf. Geitler LS. 88[a]; Bezz. LF. 192; BB. XVII, 215 & XXVII, 150.

urnoju, urnoti 'wickeln'—see *apurnoju*.

ùrva, urvas 'Höhle des Wildes'—Uh. *ūrvám;* B. II, 1, 208; W. *urvum;* Boi. οὐροί. Cf. Ness. 35[b], Lalis 397.

-usi fem. perf. act. part. suff.—B. II, 1, 217.564; F. *bērusjōs*. Cf. Wied. 151.

usnìs 'Distel, Brennessel, Hagedorn' (cf. Kur. 476, Bezz. LF. 192)—Uh. *úṣas;* B. I, 106; W. *ūro;* Boi. ὕνη.

uszės plu. dial. 'Wochenbett'—B. II, 2, 17.55; W. *sex;* Boi. ἕξ. Cf. Ness. 35[b]; Wied. 156; Lesk. Nom. 283; Trautmann Die altpreussischen Sprachdenkmäler 454.

usz- (klumpù &c.)—see under *už-* (*klumpù* &c.).

ùż prep. 'hinter, für, anstatt, wegen, um; (after comp.) als'; **ùż-** pref. 'hinter-, zu-, ver-'—B. II, 2, 764.846.849.850. 851.904-906. Cf. Kur. Gram. 1484-5.

uż- 'auf, hinauf'—B. II, 2, 735.764.847.904-906. Cf. Kur. Gram. 454.

użsiburyti (?) 'sich ereifern, erzürnen, zornig sein'—Ber. *burę*. Cf. BB. XXVI, 188; Sommer 181 (note).

użdà 'Beilage'—B. II, 2, 734. Cf. Ness. 134[a]; Kur. s.v.; Lesk. Nom. 233.

ùżdaras 'Abmachsel, Gewürz'—B. II, 3, 269. Cf. Lesk. Abl. 361.

użdas 'impensa'—B. II, 2, 734.735. Cf. Ness. 134[a]; Kur. s.v.; Lalis 398; Lesk. Nom. 199.

ùżdoris masc. 'verschliessbarer Raum; Kammer, Stall, Hürde' —B. I, 152. Cf. Lesk. Abl. 361.

użsigaũbti 'verhüllen'—see *gaubiù*.

użgaudl(i)oju, użgaudl(i)oti 'necken'—see *-gaudl(i)oju*.

użgrëjù, użgrẽti "beim Fischen mit dem Netz auf etwas stossen, es ins Netz bekommen"—see *grëjù*.

ùżklodas 'Bettdecke' ("meistens von grober Leinwand, die über das aufgemachte Bett gebreitet wird")—Ber. *kladę* I. See *klóju*.

užklumpù, užklùpti 'überraschen, angreifen'—see *klumpù.*

ùžmarka "wer mit halbgeschlossenen Augen oder ein Auge zugekniffen etwas ansieht" (Kur.); "der die Gewohnheit hat, ein Auge zuzumachen" (Ness. 394[b])—Ber. *morkŭ.* See *mérkiu.*

ùžmova 'alles, was aufgestreift wird; (Lalis) sheath, case, casing'; **rañkū ùžmova** 'Muff'; **galvõs ùžmova** 'Kapuze, Kappe'—W. *moveo.* See *máuju.*

ùžsakas 'Aufgebot'—Boi. ἐνέπω. Cf. Lalis 403, Lesk. Abl. 366. See *sakaũ.*

užtemis masc. 'Verfinsterung' (der Sonne, des Mondes)—B. I, 417. See Ness. 89[a] & *témstu.*

užtęsas 'Leichentuch'—B. II, 3, 253; W. *prōtēlo.* Cf. Lesk. Abl. 350.

užů-, užu- 'hinter, für'—B. II, 2, 846.847.849.

užũgana 'breites Ackerbeet; breiter Rücken zum Sommergetreide; (Bezz.) die zuletzt gezogene, etwas tiefere Furche; (Lalis) pasture, pasturage, common'—B. II, 2, 846. Cf. Ness. 32[b]; Bezz. LF. 193; Lalis 406; Lesk. Nom. 387.

ùžvadas 'Verteidiger, Rechtsbeistand, Advokat, Vertreter, Ersatz' (Lalis only 'substitute')—F. *wadi.* Cf. Ness. 61[a]; MLG. I, 236; Lalis 406; Lesk. Abl. 368. See next.

užvadũju, užvadũti 'vertreten, ersetzen'—see *vadũju.*

ùžvakar adv. 'vorgestern'—B. II, 2, 726.746.

úžvalkas, úžvalkalas 'Bettüberzug; (Ness. 63[b] *užvalkas* also) Hülle, Decke; (Lalis *užvalkalas* also) clothes, dress, garment'—Uh. *valkás;* B. I, 450. II, 1, 152. Cf. Lesk. Nom. 173, Lesk. Abl. 355. See *velkù.*

užvaža, ùžvažas 'Auffahrt, der Weg auf eine Anhöhe'—B. I, 489. II, 1, 149. Cf. Ness. 75[a], Lesk. Abl. 357.

úžveizdas 'Aufseher, Haushälter, Schaffner, Inspektor, Verwalter'—B. II, 1, 155. Cf. Lesk. Abl. 288.

ùžveriu, užvérti 'schliessen'—see *verìù.*

Ů

ŭdas 'Mücke, Moskito'—B. I, 337.

ůdegà 'Schwanz, Schweif, Schleppe; Zipfel des Kopftuchs; Stiel des Apfels, der Birne; ein Unkraut unter dem Flachs'—B. II, 1, 511; (F. *fauhō*). Cf. Bezz. LF. 193, Lesk. Abl. 380.

ůdẽgis, fem. **-ė** 'geschwänzt; Fuchs'; **ůdẽgė** 'Komet'—(F. *fauhō*).

ůdìmas verb. noun 'das Riechen'—W. *odor;* Boi. ὀδμή. See next.

ŭdżu, ŭsti 'riechen, durch den Geruch wahrnehmen'—B. I, 154.487. II, 3, 175.448; Ber. *adajǫ;* W. *odor;* Boi. ὀδμή. Cf. Lesk. Abl. 380.

ŭga 'Beere, Kirsche'—F. *akran;* B. I, 158.204.599; Ber. *agoda;* (W. *ūva*); (Boi. ὄā).

ŭgis masc. "Wachstum; einjähriger Schössling, Reis, Spross am Baum; Glied eines Stengels oder Halmes zwischen zwei Knoten"—F. *akran;* (Ber. *jagla*). Cf. Ness. 32ᵃ, Lesk. Abl. 314.

ū̃glis masc. id.; (Mielcke also) 'Gewächs'—(Ber. *jagla*); (W. *ūva*); Boi. ὄβρια. Cf. Ness. 32ᵇ, Lesk. Abl. 314.

ůglus 'Gewächs, Pflanze'—(Ber. *jagla*). Cf. Ness. 32ᵇ.

ůksai 'kundschaftende Bienen'—see *oksai.*

ŭksauju, ŭksauti 'ansehen, ausspionieren'—B. I, 153.157.487; W. *oculus.* Cf. Geitler LS. 87, 99 (s.v. oksas); Bezz. LF. 193. See *oksai.*

ůlẽ 'Höhle' (Ness. 32ᵇ, Lesk. Nom. 281 = *ůlà* 'Fels')—W. *alvus.*

ŭlektis, ólektis 'Elle'—Uh. *aratniș, lakuțas;* K. *Elle;* F. *aleina;* B. I, 153.157.424; W. *lacertus;* Boi. λάξ. Cf. Bezz. BGLS. 306.

-ůnis—Ber. *gŭrtanĭ.* Cf. Lesk. Nom. 394.

ŭsis masc. 'Esche'—K. *Esche;* B. I, 154.772. II, 1, 483; Ber. *asenĭ;* W. *ornus;* Boi. ἀχερωίς, ὀξύā.

ůslē 'Nasenloch'; plu. **ůslės** 'Nase'—B. II, 1, 373. Cf. Schleicher LSpr. II, 334; Lalis 396.

ůslỹs 'Schnüffler, Späher, Akziseeinnehmer'—B. II, 1, 373.

ůstas m., **ůsta** f. 'Hafen, Flussmündung, das Tief'—Uh. *ās;* B. I, 156.204.491. II, 1, 404; W. *ōs, ōstium;* Boi. *παρήϊον.* Cf. Ness. 30[b], Geitler LS. 99[b], Lalis 396.

ũsti 'riechen'—inf. of *ũdžu,* q.v.

ũszvis 'Schwiegervater, Vater der Frau'; **ũszvė** 'Schwiegermutter, Mutter der Frau'—W. *uxor.*

V

vãbalas, vabůlas 'Käfer'—K. *Wiebel;* B. II, 1, 363.366 (twice); (W. *vappo*). Cf. Ness. 44[a], Lesk. Abl. 494.

vadinù, vadìnti 'rufen, nennen, holen lassen, bitten, einladen, locken'—Uh. *vádati;* Boi. *αὐδή.*

vadũju, vadũti '(ein Pfand) einlösen; erlösen, befreien; vertreten, ersetzen'; **użvadũju, użvadũti** 'helfen, für jemand eintreten, vertreten, ersetzen'—Uh. *vadhū̇ṣ;* K. *wett;* F. *wadi;* W. *vas;* Boi. *ἄ(ϝ)εθλον.* Cf. Ness. 45[a]; Kur. 481; MLG. I, 236; Lalis 406, 407. See *ùżvadas.*

vadżóju, vadżóti 'führen, leiten, umherführen; zur Frau haben'—B. II, 3, 240. Cf. Lesk. Abl. 368.

vagilis (?), **vagilius** 'Dieb'—B. II, 1, 368. Cf. Lesk. Nom. 483, Lalis 408.

vágis masc. 'Zapfen, Pflock, Keil; krummer, hölzerner Nagel'—K. *Weck;* B. I, 326.614; W. *vōmer;* Boi. *ὀφνίς.* Cf. Ness. 45-6; Schleicher LSpr. II, 334; Lalis 408.

vagìs, gen. **-ẽs** masc. 'Dieb, Räuber'—W. *vagor,* (*vafer*). See next.

vagiù, võgti 'stehlen'—W. *vagor;* (Boi. *ἄγνυμι* (note)). Cf. Lesk. Abl. 374.

vaidalas 'Erscheinung, Trugbild'—B. II, 1, 366; Boi. *εἶδος.* Cf. Lesk. Nom. 473, Bezz. LF. 194.

vaidas 'Gesicht, Phantasiebild, Erscheinung'—B. II, 1, 155.

Cf. Ness. 76[b]; Lesk. Nom. 186; Lalis 408; Lesk. Abl. 288.

vaĩdvilkis 'Ränkestifter'—B. II, 1, 146. Cf. Lesk. Abl. 354.

vaĩkas 'Knabe, Junge, Sohn'; **vaikaĩ** plu. 'Kinder'—Ber. *čelověkŭ.* Cf. Lesk. Nom. 187.

vaikesas 'Bursche, Junge, Knecht'—B. II, 1, 544. Cf. Geitler LS. 119; Bezz. LF. 194[a]; Lalis 408[b]; Lesk. Nom. 594.

vaikestis 'junges Kind'—see *vaikisztis.*

vaikìnas "Junge, Bursche; grosser unfeiner Knabe" (Kur.); "kleiner Junge, junger Bursche" (Ness.); "lad, boy, young fellow, chap" (Lalis)—B. II, 1, 272.601.681. Cf. Lesk. Nom. 405.

vaikisztis, vaikestis 'junges Kind'; **vaĩkesczei** plu. 'junge Kinder'—B. II, 1, 671.672.677. Cf. Ness. 56[a]; Kur. 482[b]; Archiv XIII, 317; Lesk. Nom. 582-3.

vaĩkpalaikis 'schlechter Junge'—B. II, 1, 99. Cf. [Lesk. Abl. 277].

vaina 'Fehler, Gebrechen'—B. II, 1, 263.635. Cf. Bezz. BGLS. 336. See *vainóju.*

vainìkas 'Kranz, Brautkranz, Krone; Jungfrauschaft'—B. II, 1, 494. Cf. Ness. 57[a]; Bezz. LF. 194; Lalis 409; Lesk. Nom. 511; Lesk. Abl. 288.

vainóju, vainóti 'schmähen, schelten, schimpfen, bereden'; refl. (Lalis) 'to scold each other, to quarrel, wrangle, brawl, altercate'—W. *vēnor, vindex,* (*vitium*).

-vaitinu—see *pavaitinù* 'ich mache welken'.

vaĩvaras, vaivarys, vaĩveris masc. "das Männchen vom Iltis, Marder, Eichhorn, Reh und anderen Tieren"; **vaiverẽ, voverẽ** 'Eichhorn'—B. I, 838. II, 1, 128; W. *viverra;* Boi. (Ntr.) αἰέλουρος, (σκίουρος). Cf. Lesk. Nom. 267, Trautmann Die altpreussischen Sprachdenkmäler 460.

vaizdaĩ plu. 'Brautschau'—B. II, 1, 155. Cf. Lesk. Nom. 186, Lesk. Abl. 288.

vajóju, vajóti iter. 'mehrfach nachjagen, verfolgen'—W. *vēnor.* See *vejù* 'ich verfolge'.

vãkar adv. 'gestern'—B. II, 2, 683.746.

vakaraĩs adv. inst. plu. 'abends'—B. II, 2, 719.745. Cf. Kur. s.v. *vãkaras.*

vãkaras 'Abend'; **vakaraĩ** plu. 'die Abendgegend, Westen, westliche Länder'; **vakarũ vė́jas** 'Westwind'—B. I, 303. 838. II, 1, 625; W. *vesper;* Boi. ἑσπερος.

vakarè adv. loc. sing. 'abends'—B. II, 2, 708.745. Cf. Kur. s.v. *vãkaras.*

vakarìnis, fem. **-ė** 'abendlich, Abend-, westlich'; **vakarìnė** (**žvaigzdẽ**) 'Abendstern'—B. II, 1, 271.

vãlas, usually plu. **valaĩ** 'Schweifhaare des Pferdes'—Uh. *vâlas;* W. *adūlo.* Cf. Lesk. Abl. 354.

valaũ, valýti 'reinigen, fortschaffen, zusammenbringen, ernten; (Lalis only) to clean, cleanse, purge, purify, scour'; **iszvalaũ, iszvalýti** 'reinigen, fortschaffen (bes. Mist aus dem Stall)'; **įvalaũ, įvalýti** 'einbringen, einernten'; **suvalaũ, suvalýti** 'zusammenbringen, sammeln, ernten; (Lalis also) to clear, clear away, take away, remove'—W. *lōrum*; Boi. εἴλω. Cf. Lesk. Abl. 354.

valdaũ, valdýti 'walten, lenken, regieren, herrschen, besitzen' —K. *walten;* F. *waldan;* W. *valeo.* Cf. Lesk. Abl. 354.

valdõvas 'Herrscher, Regent'—K. *walten.* Cf. Ness. 48[a], Lalis 410. See prec.

vãlė 'Wille, Erlaubnis, Macht'—Uh. *vṛṇâti;* W. *valeo.* Cf. Brückner SlFw. 150; [Lesk. Nom. 312]; Sommer 53, 54, 55.

vãlinas (Mielcke) 'Wall'—W. 2. *vallus.* Cf. Lesk. Nom. 405.

válkioju, válkioti iter. 'umherschleppen, schleifen, ziehen'— B. II, 3, 240. Cf. Lesk. Abl. 355.

vaĩksmas 'Zug'; (**žuviũ**) **vaĩksmas** 'Fischzug'—B. II, 1, 252. Cf. Lesk. Abl. 355.

valtis masc. 'Garn, Fischernetz'—Uh. *vaṭas;* W. *volvo;* Boi. εὔληρα. Cf. Ness. 49[b].

váltis fem. 'Haferrispe, Haferspelte'—W. *volvo;* Boi. λάσιος. Cf. Ness. 49[b]; Kur. 487; Lesk. Nom. 552; Trautmann Die altpreussischen Sprachdenkmäler 465.

váltis fem. "ein Kahn mit flachem Boden, wie er auf den Flüssen und auf dem Haff gebraucht wird" (Ness. 49[b], Kur. 487); "boat, yawl, skiff, wherry, scull, canoe" (Lalis 411)—W. *volvo.* Cf. Lesk. Nom. 552, Lesk. Abl. 354.

vãnagas 'Habicht, Raubvogel'—F. *ahaks;* B. II, 1, 506.511. Cf. Ness. 50[a], Bezz. LF. 194.

vandũ, gen. **-eñs** masc. 'Wasser'—Uh. *udakám;* F. *watō, wintrus;* B. I, 107.330.541. II, 1, 310.579. 3, 281; W. *unda;* Boi. ὕδωρ.

vapsà 'Bremse, (bes.) Pferdebremse; (Lalis) wasp'—K. *Wespe;* B. I, 337.789.868. II, 1, 539; W. *vespa.*

varaũ, varýti 'treiben, jagen, fördern'; **varaũs, varýtis** 'sich treiben, rudern'—Uh. *vārάyati.* Cf. Bezz. LF. 195.

var̃das 'Name, (bes.) Vorname; (gram.) Substantivum'—Uh. *vratám;* K. *Wort;* F. *waurd;* B. I, 535; W. *verbum;* Boi. 2. εἴρω. Cf. Lesk. Abl. 356.

várganas 'ärmlich'—B. II, 1, 268. Cf. Lesk. Nom. 385.

var̃gas 'Not, Elend, Trübsal'; **vargaĩ** plu. 'Unglück, Unglücksfälle'—K. *rächen;* F. *wraks;* W. *urgeo;* (Boi. ἔργω).

vargstù, var̃gti (Kur. **warkstù, war̃kti**) 'Not leiden, im Elend sein, elend werden'—K. *rächen;* W. *urgeo.*

varlė̃ 'Frosch; (Lalis also) gore, gusset'—(W. *rāna*); Boi. ῥόδον. Cf. Sommer 178.

várna 'Krähe'; **var̃nas** 'Rabe'—B. I, 991 (twice). II, 1, 256. Cf. Ness. 54[a], Bezz. LF. 195.

varnùkas, varniùkas 'junger Rabe, junge Krähe'—B. II, 1, 492.

várpa 'Ähre'—W. *repens;* Boi. ῥαπίς. Cf. Lesk. Abl. 356.

varpaũ, varpýti 'durchlöchern, aushöhlen'—(Ber. *čĭrvĭ*). Cf. Ness. 54[a], Lesk. Abl. 356.

varpstis 'Spule, Spindel, dünne Stange, Schaft'; **varpstė̃**

'bewegliche Achse; Welle, um die sich etwas dreht; Spule, Spindel, Schaft'; **veȓpstė** 'Spindel' — Uh. *várpas;* F. *wairpan;* B. I, 141; W. *verbēna,* (*sarcio*); Boi. ῥάπτω. Cf. Ness. 68ᵃ; Lesk. Nom. 539; Lesk. Abl. 356; Lalis 413; Bezz. BGLS. 337; Bezz. LF. 195.

varsà 'Flocke von Wolle oder Haaren; (Lalis) lock, hair, nap'—(W. *birrus*); Boi. βερβέριον. Cf. Ness. 54ᵇ; Lalis 413; Brückner SlFw. 151.

vaȓsmas 'Pfluggewende'—B. II, 1, 252. See next.

varsnà f., **varsnas, varsnis** m. "Pfluggewende, eine Strecke auf dem Acker, nach deren Bestreichung mit dem Pfluge man umwendet, die Länge der Furchen und Rücken"; 'Meile; ein Stück Acker'; **varsnà rãszto** 'Abschnitt, Paragraph'—B. II, 1, 265.289. Cf. Ness. 69ᵃ, Lesk. Abl. 357. See next.

vaȓstas 'Pfluggewende; (Lalis also) a short distance, verst' —Uh. *vr̥ttás;* B. II, 1, 410; W. *verto.* Cf. Ness. 69ᵇ; Lalis 413; Lesk. Abl. 357; Brückner SlFw. 151. See prec.

vaȓtai plu. tant. 'Tor, Tür'—Uh. *vr̥tás;* B. I, 316. II, 1, 410; W. *aperio;* Boi. ἔρυσθαι (note 4). Cf. Lesk. Abl. 356.

vartaũ, vartýti iter. 'fortgesetzt wenden, hin und her wenden, umwenden, umwerfen'—Uh. *vártate, vartáyati;* F. *fra-wardjan;* B. I, 137.439.521. II, 3, 169.245.251.266. 267; W. *verto.* Cf. Lesk. Abl. 357.

varus 'kochbar; (Lalis) easily boiled, digestible'—B. II, 1, 154. Cf. Ness. 67ᵃ, Lesk. Abl. 356.

várżas 'ein aus Weidenreisern geflochtener Korb zum Fischfang, bes. zum Aalfang; Reuse'—(W. *urceus*). Cf. Lesk. Abl. 357, Brückner SlFw. 151.

vasarà 'Sommer'—Uh. *vasantás;* B. I, 306.493.838. II, 1, 160.347.625; W. *vēr;* Boi. 2. ἔαρ, (ὀπώρā).

vasarýmetis 'Sommerzeit'—B. II, 1, 21.

vasarìnis 'dem Sommer angehörig, sommerlich'—B. II, 1, 270.625; Boi. 2. ἔαρ.

vą̃szas 'Haken; (Lalis also) angle'—B. II, 1, 150; (W. *ancus*); (Boi. 1. ὄγκος).
vãszkas 'Wachs'—Uh. *vāgurā́*; K. *Wachs*; W. *vēlum*.
vasztà 'Fuhre'—see *vażtà*.
vãżis, vażys masc. 'kleiner, leichter, einspänniger, schmalgleisiger, brettener, vorn hoch in die Höhe gekrümmter Schlitten, in dem nur eine Person sitzen kann (Ness., Kur.); (Lalis) sledge, sled, sleigh'—F. *waghen*. Cf. Lesk. Abl. 357.
vażtà (B. **vasztà**) 'Fuhre, Fuder, Wagenlast; öffentliches Fuhrwerk, Mietswagen; (Lalis) coach, carriage'—B. II, 1, 410.635. Cf. Ness. 74[a], Lalis 414, Lesk. Abl. 357.
vė́daras 'Eingeweide, Magen; Wurstmagen; (Lalis) black pudding, blood pudding'—Uh. *udáram*; B. II, 1, 330; W. *vensīca*.
vedìkas 'Führer'—(K. *Enterich*).
vėdinù, vėdìnti 'lüften, kühlen, der Luft aussetzen; (Getreide) abfegen, umstechen'—B. II, 3, 378.
vedlỹs 'Bräutigam (von der Verlobung bis zur Hochzeit)'—B. II, 1, 617. Cf. Ness. 59[b], Lalis 415, Lesk. Abl. 368.
vedù, vèsti 'leiten, führen; heiraten (vom Mann; vom Weib nur, wenn es im Hause bleibt); Kinder haben; Junge bekommen'—Uh. *vadhū́ṣ*; F. *ga-wadjōn*; B. I, 124.210. 326.541. II, 3, 119.136.398.446; (W. *vas, uxor*); Boi. ἕδνον. Cf. Lesk. Abl. 368.
vèdu dial. dual 'wir beide'—Uh. *vayám*; F. *wit*; B. I, 931. II, 2, 11.380(note).383.412.427.455; Boi. 1. δύω (note). Cf. Kur. Gram. 854 a, Wied. 164.
véidas 'Angesicht; Wange; Aussehen, Schein, Gestalt; Erscheinung'—Uh. *vétti*, 1. *védas*, 2. *vḗdas*; F. 2. *witan*; B. I, 293.522. II, 1, 155.518.524; W. *video*; Boi. εἶδος. Cf. Lesk. Abl. 288.
veidmainỹs 'Heuchler, Gleisner, Scheinheiliger'—(Ber. *likū̃ 2*). See prec. & *mainaũ*.
veikiù, veĩkti 'tun, machen, verrichten, anfangen'; **apveikiù, apveĩkti** 'bezwingen'—Uh. *vīciṣ*; F. 1.

weihan; B. I, 576. II, 3, 282.443; W. *vinco;* Boi. εἴκω (note). Cf. Lesk. Abl. 289.

veikùs 'schnell, flink, bereitwillig, fleissig'—Uh. *vīciṣ.* Cf. Lesk. Abl. 289.

veisiù, veĩsti 'fortpflanzen'—B. I, 785. Cf. Lesk. Abl. 289. See next.

veislė̃ 'Brut, Gattung, Art, Zucht, Geschlecht, Familie'—B. I, 785; (W. *vīlis*); (Boi. ἴλη). See prec.

veislùs 'fruchtbar'—B. I, 785. Cf. Lalis 415. See *veisiù.*

véizdmi (véizdu, véizdżu), veizdė́ti 'sehen, hinblicken, suchen'; **veizdi, veizd** Old Lith. impera. 'sieh'—Uh. *vétti;* F. 2. *witan;* B. I, 206.522.624.659.718. II, 1, 155; W. *video;* Boi. οἶδα. Cf. Bezz. BGLS. 116, 222; Lesk. Abl. 288.

vė̃jas (vė̃jes: cf. Wied. 97, Sommer 230-231) 'Wind'—Uh. *vâti;* K. *wehen;* F. *waian;* B. I, 132.337. II, 1, 158. 224; W. *ventus;* Boi. ἄημι.

vejù, výti 'nachjagen, verfolgen'; **výtas** pret. pass. part. 'verfolgt'—Uh. *véti,* 2. *vītás;* B. I, 288; W. *vēnor;* Boi. ἵεμαι. Cf. Lesk. Abl. 288.

vejù, výti 'winden, drehen, wickeln'; **výtas** pret. pass. part. 'gewunden'—Uh. *váyati, vyáyati,* 1. *vītás;* K. *Weide* 1; F. *baurgs-waddjus;* B. I, 103.130.262.337. II, 1, 398. 434.443. 3, 136.408 (note); W. *vieo;* Boi. ἦτριον, ἴτυς (twice), ὑφή, (Ntr.) ἰδνόομαι. Cf. Lesk. Abl. 288.

vėkà 'Kraft, Stärke'—Uh. *vīciṣ;* F. *waihjō;* B. I, 326; W. *vinco, vix.* Cf. Schleicher LSpr. II, 337; Lesk. Abl. 289.

vėlà 'Draht'—B. II, 1, 365. Cf. Lesk. Abl. 288.

velbliũdas 'Kamel'—see *verbliũdas.*

véldu (veldė̃ju), veldė́ti 'regieren, besitzen, an sich bringen, in Besitz nehmen'; **pavéldu (paveldė̃ju), paveldė́ti** 'erben, erblich besitzen, innehaben'; **pavildė́ti** 'besitzen'—K. *walten;* B. I, 481. Cf. Ness. 47[b], 48[a]; Kur. 300; Bezz. BGLS. 312; Lesk. Abl. 354.

vėlýbas adj. 'spät, von später Art' (e.g. **vėlýbos ropùtės** 'Spätkartoffeln')—B. II, 1, 389.587.

vẽlyju, vẽlyti 'wünschen, gönnen, anraten'—Uh. *vṛṇā́ti;* F. *wiljan;* W. 2. *volo;* Boi. ἔλδομαι. Cf. Brückner SlFw. 152. See *velmi.*

veliù, vélti '(Tuch) walken; (Haare, Fäden etc. ineinander) verwirren, verschlingen; (Tatsachen durch Lügen) verdrehen'—Uh. *vā́lati;* F. *af-walwjan;* B. I, 151.481. II, 3, 265.379; W. *volvo;* Boi. εἴλω, εὔληρα. Cf. Lesk. Abl. 353.

velkẽtas, usually plu. **velkẽtai** 'Zochschleife, Pflugschleife, zwei im spitzen Winkel zusammengefügte Holzscheite zum Hinausbringen des Pfluges auf das Feld'—B. II, 1, 414. Cf. Ness. 63[a]; Kur. DLWb. s.v. Schleife; Lesk. Abl. 354. See next.

velkù, vil̃kti 'ziehen, schleppen, schleifen'—Uh. *valkás;* K. *Wolf* 1; F. *wulfs;* B. I, 450.609. II, 1, 217. 3, 136; W. 1. *sulcus* (twice), *lūpus,* (*ulcus*); Boi. ἄλοξ, ἕλκω. Cf. Lesk. Abl. 354.

velmi Old Lith. 'ich wünsche, ich will'; **pavelmi** 'ich will, ich erlaube'; **pavelt** 3rd pers. sing. 'er will'—F. *wiljan;* B. I, 121. II, 3, 90; W. 2. *volo;* Boi. ἔλδομαι. See *vẽlyju* & Bezz. BGLS. 198, 199, 200, 312, 338.

velniavà 'Teufelsnest; (Lalis) devilry, deviltry, devilish trick'—B. II, 1, 205.624. Cf. Lesk. Nom. 350.

veltuĩ adv. Samog. 'unnütz, vergebens, umsonst'—Uh. *vṛthā́.* Cf. Lesk. Abl. 354, Lalis 417, Ness. 64[a].

vėmalaĩ plu. 'Ausgespienes, Vomiertes'—B. I, 342; W. *vomo;* Boi. ἐμέω (& Ntr.). See next.

vemiù, vémti 'speien, sich erbrechen'—Uh. *vámiti;* F. *wamm;* B. I, 122.178. II, 3, 386.442.493; W. *vomo;* Boi. ἐμέω. Cf. Lesk. Abl. 355.

vėmũ 'Erbrechen'—B. II, 1, 308. Cf. Bezz. LF. 196.

vẽnas m., **vënà** f. 'ein, eine'; plu. **vënì, vẽnos** 'lauter'—Uh. *ena-;* K. *ein* 1; F. *ains;* B. I, 940.944. II, 2, 7. 332;

(Ber. *inŭ*); W. *ūnus;* Boi. οἰνός. Cf. Kur. Gram. 1003, Wied. 156. 1.

vënatis 'Einheit'—B. II, 1, 438. Cf. Lesk. Nom. 570.

vënatras 'einer von beiden'—B. II, 1, 326; Boi. ἕτερος. Cf. Lesk. Nom. 568.

vënerì, fem. **vȇnerios** 'ein, eine'—B. II, 2, 77. Cf. Wied. 158. 1.

véngiu, véngti 'meiden, ausweichen, unterlassen, keine Lust haben, etwas ungern tun'; **iszvéngiu, iszvéngti** 'vermeiden, entfliehen, entrinnen'—Uh. *vañjulas;* F. *waihsta;* W. *vagor.* Cf. Lesk. Abl. 355.

vëniñtelis, fem. **-lė** adj. 'einzeln, einsam, einfach, einzig, ganz allein'—B. II, 2, 63. Cf. Lesk. Nom. 585.

vȇninu, vȇninti 'einigen'—B. II, 3, 323. Cf. Ness. 65.

vȇnlinkas 'einfach, einzeln'—B. II, 2, 71. Cf. Lesk. Abl. 334.

vënókas, fem. **vënokà** adj. 'einerlei'—B. II, 1, 498. Cf. Wied. 159, Lesk. Nom. 514.

vënólika 'elf'—see *vënũlika.*

vënulei adv. 'obiter'—B. II, 1, 364.377. Cf. Bezz. BGLS. 338.

vënuntas adj. 'einzig, allein'—B. II, 2, 63. Cf. Ness. 64[b], Lesk. Nom. 585.

vënuntelis 'einsam'—B. II, 2, 63. Cf. Bezz. BGLS. 339, Lesk. Nom. 585.

vënũlika (vënólika) 'elf'—K. *elf;* F. *ain-lif;* B. II, 2, 5. 26.27; [Ber. *-lěkŭ*]; W. *linquo.* See *vȇnas* & Kur. Gram. 1010, Wied. 156. 11-19, [Lesk. Abl. 277].

vënũliktas 'elfter'—B. II, 2, 59. Cf. Wied. 157. 11-19.

verbà 'Weidenrute, Birkenrute, Reis, Gerte, Palmzweig'—Boi. ῥάμνος. Cf. Brückner SlFw. 152. See *viȓbas.*

verbliũdas (verblũdas), velbliũdas (velblũdas) 'Kamel' —B. I, 450.851. Cf. Ness. 66[b]; Bezz. BGLS. 338; Brückner SlFw. 152.

verczù (old **vertù**), **veȓsti** 'wenden, kehren, umwenden, umkehren, verwandeln, umwerfen; nötigen, zwingen;

(Lalis also) to translate, to turn into another language'; verczũs, veȓstis 'sich drehen, sich wenden, sich umkehren, sich verwandeln; Handel treiben; (Lalis also) to gush, to spurt, to rush'—Uh. *vártate;* F. *wairþan* (read *verčiù* for *versziù*), (*bugjan*); B. I, 316.439; II, 1, 433.442. 3, 385.388.398; W. *verto;* Boi. *ῥατάνη. Cf. Ness. 68-69, Lalis 418, Lesk. Abl. 357.

vérdu, vìrti (B. **vírti**) 'kochen, sieden' trans. and intr.; 'wallen, sprudeln, quellen'—K. *warm;* (F. *warmjan*); B. I, 151.472.613. II, 1, 154. 3, 379; W. *ūrīna,* (*formus*); Boi. οὐρέω, (θερμός (note)). Cf. Lesk. Abl. 355-6.

vérgas 'Leibeigener, Sklave'—(W. *verna, urgeo*). Cf. Lesk. Nom. 161.

vergyba 'Sklaverei, Leibeigenschaft, Dienstbarkeit'—B. II, 1, 388. Cf. Ness. 67*, Lesk. Nom. 591.

verginė id.—(W. *verna*). Cf. Ness. 67*.

vẽryju, vẽryti 'glauben, trauen'—B. II, 2, 550. Cf. Brückner SlFw. 152.

veriù, vérti 'auf- oder zutun, öffnen oder schliessen; einfädeln'; **àtveriu, atvérti** 'öffnen, aufmachen'; **ùžveriu, užvérti** 'schliessen, zumachen'—Uh. *vṛṇóti;* F. *warjan,* (*wairdus*), (*ga-lūkan*); B. I, 264.316.323.338.439. II, 1, 571. 3, 137.193.263; W. *aperio* (& Ntr.); Boi. ἐρύσθαι (note 4). Cf. Lesk. Abl. 356.

veȓpalas, usually plu. **verpalaĩ** 'Gespinst, Garn'—W. *verbēna.* See next.

verpiù, veȓpti trans. 'spinnen'—Uh. *várpas;* K. *Werft* 1; F. *wairpan;* B. I, 141. II, 3, 398; W. *verbēna,* (*sarcio*); Boi. ῥάμνος, ῥάπτω. Cf. Lesk. Abl. 356.

veȓpstė 'Spindel'—see *varpstis.*

versmẽ 'Quelle'—B. II, 3, 132; W. *ūrīna*; Boi. οὐρέω, (Ntr.) ἄρδω. Cf. Lesk. Abl. 356.

veȓsti 'wenden, kehren'—inf. of *verczù,* q.v.

veȓszis masc. 'Kalb'—Uh. *vṛ́ṣā;* B. I, 786; W. *verrēs;* Boi. ἔρση, οὐρέω.

veȓtas 'wert, würdig, billig'—Uh. *vaṇík;* K. *Wert;* F. *wairþs.* Cf. Prell. deutsch. Best. in den lett. Spr. 36, Brückner SlFw. 153.

vertù 'ich wende, kehre'—old pres. of *verczù,* q.v.

veržỹs, viržỹs 'dicker, bastener Strick; Wagenseil, Ackerstrick'—F. *wruggō;* B. I, 471; Boi. ἐρχατάω. Cf. Ness. 71[a], Lesk. Nom. 285, Lesk. Abl. 357.

veržiù, veȓžti 'schnüren, einengen, pressen, drängen'—K. *würgen;* F. *wargiþa, (wrikan)*; B. I, 316.452.454.567. II, 3, 137.398; (Ber. *berďa*); W. *vergo, vermina, (verna), (urgeo)*; Boi. ἐρχατάω, (ἔργω). Cf. Lesk. Abl. 357.

wesmenui (dat.) Old Lith. 'dem Führer'—B. II, 1, 243. Cf. Bezz. BGLS. 338.

vèsti 'führen, heiraten'—inf. of *vedù,* q.v.

vė̃stu, vė̃sti 'sich abkühlen, luftig werden'; **pavė̃sti** 'sich erkälten'—Boi. ἄσθμα. Cf. Bezz. LF. 197[b], Lesk. Abl. 372.

vėsùs 'kühl, luftig, schattig, Schatten gebend (von Bäumen)'—Boi. ἄσθμα. See prec.

vësziù, vëszė̃ti 'zu Gast gehen, zu Gast sein, weilen; (Lalis also) to participate in a feast'—Uh. *víṭ;* F. 2. *weihs;* B. I, 557. II, 3, 192; W. *vīcus.* Cf. Lesk. Abl. 289.

vė̃szkelis masc. 'Landstrasse'—Uh. *víṭ.* See prec. & Lesk. Nom. 185.

vësznė̃, vësznì 'Gastin'—B. II, 1, 215.550; (Ber. *gospodī*). Cf. Schleicher LSpr. II, 98, 338; Wied. 79; Sommer 221; Lesk. Abl. 289.

vė̃szpatis, vė̃szpats, gen. -ës masc. 'Herr, regierender Herr, Heȓrgott'—Uh. *víṭ, viçpátiṣ;* F. *gawi,* 2. *weihs;* B. I, 153. II, 1, 86; Ber. *gospodī* (twice); W. *potis, vīcus;* Boi. οἶκος, πόσις. Cf. Lesk. Nom. 308.

weschpatni (vëszpatni) Old Lith. 'Herrin, Hausherrin'—

B. II, 1, 215(& note).283.550.600; Boi. πότνια. See prec. & Sommer 221.

vèsztas 'gefahren'—see *vèžtas.*

vëtà 'Platz, Ort, Stelle, Beschäftigung'—(Boi. (Ntr.) οἶκος). Cf. Lesk. Nom. 222.

vëtau, vëtyti '(Getreide) worfeln'—Uh. *vāti;* F. *dis-winþjan;* B. I, 1098 (Ntr.). II, 3, 214; W. *vannus* (twice); Boi. ἄημι, αἰνω.

vėtỹklė 'Worfschaufel, Futterschwinge' — Uh. *vāti;* F. *dis-winþjan;* Boi. αἰνω. Cf. Kur. DLWb. s.v. Schaufel, Worfschaufel, Wurfschaufel.

vëtra 'Sturmwind, Sturm, Unwetter, Gewitter'—B. I, 991. II, 1, 344.379; W. *ventus.* See *vějas.*

vétuszas 'alt, bejahrt'—Uh. *vatsarás;* (F. *fairns*); B. I, 785. II, 1, 544; W. *vetus* (twice); Boi. ἔτος. Cf. Lesk. Nom. 599, Ness. 73*.

vežas (?) 'Abweg'—B. II, 1, 153. Cf. Ness. 73*, Lesk. Nom. 166.

vežą̃s m., **vežantì** f. pres. act. part. of **vežù,** q.v., 'vehens'—F. *hulundi;* B. II, 1, 211.216.458.459. 2, 106.124. 287.299.

vėžẽ 'Wagen- oder Schlittengeleise, Spur'—F. *wigs;* B. I, 489; W. *veho;* Boi. ὄχος. Cf. Lesk. Abl. 357.

vežìmas 'das Fahren; Fuhrwerk, (bes.) Wagen; Fuder'—F. *waghen;* B. II, 1, 251 (note); W. *veho;* Boi. ὄχος. Cf. Bezz. LF. 197, Lesk. Nom. 429-30.

vèžtas (B. **vèsztas**) pret. pass. part. of **vežù,** q.v., 'gefahren'—B. II, 1, 397.

vežù, vèžti (B. **vèszti**) trans. 'fahren, vehere; ziehen (von Pferden)'—Uh. *váhati;* F. *ga-wigan;* B. I, 129.293. 294.549.568. II, 1, 433.568. 3, 119.398.445.492; W. *veho;* Boi. ὄχος. Cf. Lesk. Abl. 357.

vỹburiu, vỹburti; vỹburioju, vỹburioti 'schwingen, (mit dem Schwanze) wedeln. fuchsschwänzen'—F. *weipan;* W. *vibro.*

výdra 'Sturm'—B. II, 1, 379; W. *ventus*. Cf. Lesk. Nom. 438.

vidras id.—B. II, 1, 379; W. *ventus*. Cf. Bezz. BGLS. 338.

viduĩ adv. 'im Innern, drinnen'—B. II, 2, 707. Cf. Lesk. Nom. 340.

vidur̃ys 'Mitte; das Innere'; **viduriaĩ** plu. 'Eingeweide'—B. II, 1, 358; W. *dīvido*.

vidùs 'Mitte, Inneres, Inwendiges'—Uh. *vidhúṣ*, (*vídhyati*); B. II, 1, 181.330 (note); W. *dīvido, vensīca*.

-výdżu, -vydė́ti—see *pavýdżu* 'ich neide'.

vikrùs 'munter, behende, rührig'—Uh. *vīcíṣ*; K. *Weigand*; F. 1. *weihan*; B. I, 98. II, 1, 349; W. *vinco*. Cf. Lesk. Abl. 289.

vykstù, vỹkti 'sich irgendwohin begeben, anlangen, eintreffen; zutreffen, wahr werden; (Lalis also) to succeed'—W. *vinco*. Cf. Lesk. Abl. 289.

vìlbinu, vìlbinti "locken, anlocken, besonders hinterlistig, betrüglich; äffen, vexieren, zergen, zum besten haben" —Boi. ἐλεφαίρομαι. Cf. Ness. 79*, Wied. s.v.

-vildė́ti—see *pavildė́ti* 'besitzen'.

vìlgau, vìlgyti 'anfeuchten, befeuchtend glätten' (bes. Brot vor dem Einschieben in den Ofen)—Uh. *vṛjanī́* 'Wolke' (s.v. *vṛjánam*); W. *welk*; Boi. ἠλύγη. Cf. Lesk. Abl. 354.

vilióju, vilióti 'verlocken, verführen, betrügen, täuschen'—Uh. *véllati*. See next.

vỹlius 'List, Betrug, Täuschung, Verführung'—Uh. *véllati*; B. II, 1, 225; (W. *vīlis*). Cf. Lesk. Abl. 354.

vil̃kas m. 'Wolf'; **vìlkė** f. 'Wölfin'—Uh. *vṛ́kas*; K. *Wolf* 1; F. *wulfs*; B. I, 104.115.138.146.152.207.255.293.455.486.596.723. II, 1, 165.221.600. 2, 129.134.168.283; W. *lŭpus*; Boi. λύκος. Cf. Ness. 79, Lalis 422, Lesk. Nom. 282.

vilkiù, vilkė́ti 'sich kleiden, bekleidet sein, gekleidet gehen, (Kleider) angezogen tragen'—B. I, 472. Cf. Lesk. Abl. 354.

vil̃kti 'schleppen'—inf. of *velkù*, q.v.

vilkùtis masc. 'junger Wolf'—B. II, 1, 677. Cf. Lalis 423, Lesk. Nom. 576. See *vil̃kas*.

vìlna (B. **vílna**) 'Wollfaser, Wollhärchen; Wolle'; **vìlnos** plu. 'Wolle'—Uh. *ūrṇā;* K. *Wolle;* F. *wulla;* B. I, 293.317.475. II, 1, 257; W. *lāna;* Boi. λῆνος, 2. οὖλος. Cf. Lesk. Abl. 353, Brückner SlFw. 153.

vilnìs fem. 'Welle, Woge'—Uh. *ūrmíṣ;* K. *Welle;* F. *wulan;* B. I, 315.382. II, 1, 288. 3, 320; W. *volvo;* Boi. εἰλύω. Cf. Bezz. BGLS. 339, Lesk. Abl. 353.

vilnõnis, vilnõnas adj. 'wollen'; **vilnõnas** masc. 'der Wollene (i.e. Rock); (Lalis) woolen cloth, woolen'—B. II, 1, 281. Cf. Ness. 79[b], Donalitius 324, Brückner SlFw. 153. See *vìlna*.

vilpiszỹs 'wilde Katze'—Uh. *vṛ́kas, vṛkī́ṣ;* F. *wulfs;* W. *lūpus, volpēs;* Boi. λύκος. Cf. Ness. 80[a], Lalis 423.

vìlstu, vìlti 'betrügen'—see *apvìlstu, privìlstu*.

viltis fem. (Ness. also masc.) 'Hoffnung, Vertrauen'—W. 2. *volo;* Boi. ἔλδομαι. Cf. Ness. 80[a], Lalis 423. See next.

vilûs, viltis 'hoffen, erwarten, vertrauen'—B. II, 1, 442; W. 2. *volo;* Boi. ἔλδομαι. Cf. Ness. 80[a], Lesk. Abl. 354.

vìmdau, vìmdyti (W., Boi. **vím-**) 'erbrechen machen, Ekel erregen'—W. *vomo;* Boi. ἐμέω. See *vemiù* & Lesk. Abl. 355.

vỹnas 'Wein; (dial. also) Branntwein'—B. II, 1, 262; W. *vīnum*. Cf. LBLV. 347, Brückner SlFw. 153.

vìngis (B. **víngis**) masc. 'Bogen, Krümmung, Abweichung' —Uh. *vañjulas;* F. *waihsta;* B. I, 364; (Ber. *lǫka*); W. *vagor*. Cf. Lesk. Abl. 355.

vìngiûju, vìngiûti (W. **víngûti**) 'Bogen, Umwege machen; sich schlängeln; Bogenlinien zeichnen'—W. *vagor*. See prec.

-vynỹs 'Band'—see *kaklavynỹs*.

vìras 'Finne im Schweinefleisch'—B. I, 467; W. *varus;* Boi. ῥόμος.

výras 'Mann, Ehemann'—Uh. *vīrás;* F. *wair;* B. I, 101.298. 445. II, 1, 353; W. *vir;* Boi. *ἴς*.

vir̃balas 'hölzerner Stab, Leitersprosse, hölzerner Nagel, dünnes Stäbchen, Stricknadel, Schreibgriffel, Sensenpflock, hölzerner Stöpsel; (Lalis also) prong, tine; grade, degree'—W. *verbēna;* Boi. *ῥάμνος*. See next.

vir̃bas 'Reis, Gerte, Rute, Zweig'—(F. *wairpan, tains*); B. I, 472; W. *verbēna, urbs;* Boi. *ῥάβδος, ῥάμνος*. See *verbà*.

virbìnis masc. 'Schlinge'—W. *verbēna;* Boi. *ῥάμνος*. Cf. Ness. 82ᵃ. See prec.

virė̃jas 'Koch'—B. I, 473.

vìrinu, vìrinti 'kochen lassen'—B. I, 473. Cf. Lesk. Abl. 355.

vyrmoterìnis 'Mann und Frau betreffend, ehelich'—B. II, 1, 59.100. Cf. Ness. 82ᵃ.

vìrpiu, virpė̃ti 'zitterig sein, beben, wanken' (vor Angst, Schwäche, Alter); (Lalis) 'to vibrate, oscillate, quiver, tremble'—B. I, 141; W. *repens;* Boi. *ῥάπτω*. Cf. Lesk. Abl. 356.

virpu, virpti 'zittern, beben, wanken'—Boi. *ῥάπτω*. Cf. Ness. 82ᵃ. See prec.

virpulỹs 'Zittern der Glieder' (als Schwäche oder Krankheit); (Lalis) 'vibration, trembling, tremor'—W. *repens*. Cf. Ness. 82ᵇ, Lalis 421, Lesk. Abl. 356. Notice also Geitler LS. 121: *wirpulei* plu. 'dickgewordene Suppe, Gallerte'.

virstù, vir̃sti 'umfallen, stürzen; sich in etwas verwandeln, zu etwas werden'—B. I, 455.471.717. II, 1, 431.442. 567. 3, 370.398.445; W. *verto*. Cf. Lesk. Abl. 357.

virszùs 'das obere Ende, Spitze, Oberfläche, das Äussere; (Lalis also) loft, upper floor; cover, lid, top'—Uh. *várṣma;* B. I, 337.773.786. II, 1, 181.498; W. *verrūca;* Boi. *ἀείρω*, 2. *ἕρμα* (& note). Cf. Lesk. Nom. 239.

vìrti 'kochen'—inf. of *vérdu*, q.v.

virtìnis masc. 'Schlinge'—Boi. ἀείρω, ἀρτάω. Cf. Ness. 69[b], Lesk. Abl. 356.
virvė̃ 'Strick, Seil; (Ness. also) Krampf'—Uh. *varatrā́;* F. *waurms;* B. I, 338.425; W. *urvum;* Boi. ἀείρω, (ἦτριον (note)). Cf. Lesk. Abl. 356.
vir̃žis masc. 'Heidekraut'—Boi. ἐρείκη. Cf. Ness. 83[a], Lesk. Nom. 285.
viržỹs 'Strick'—see *veržỹs.*
viržiu, viržė́ti (**vìržiu, viržė̃ti**?) 'mit Stricken binden'—Boi. ἐρχατάω. Cf. Ness. 71[a], Lesk. Abl. 357. See *veržiù.*
visadà adv. 'immer, stets'—B. II, 2, 733. See next.
vìsas, f. **visà** 'ganz'; plu. **visì**, f. **vìsos** 'alle'—Uh. *víçvas;* B. II, 1, 200.
visgù, visgė̃ti 'sich bewegen, zittern, schlottern'—Uh. 1. *véṣati.* Cf. Lesk. Abl. 292.
vislùs 'fruchtbar'—B. II, 1, 385. Cf. Ness. 76[a], Lalis 426. See *veislùs.*
výstas 'Schnürbrust, Frauenweste, Brustbekleidung ohne Ärmel'—B. II, 3, 364; W. *virga.* See next.
výstau, výstyti '(ein Kind) wickeln'—Uh. *veṣṭate;* B. II, 3, 364; W. *virga.* Cf. Lesk. Abl. 288.
výstyklas 'Windelband, Windel'; **vystyklaĩ** plu. 'Windel'—B. II, 1, 344.
výstu, pret. **výdau, výsti** 'gewahr werden, erblicken'—B. II, 3, 397. Cf. Lesk. Abl. 288.
výstu, pret. **výtau, výsti** 'welken' — (Uh. 3. *jināti, vyā́thate*); W. *viēsco*; (Boi. δειελός). Cf. Lesk. Abl. 289.
visumèt adv. 'allzeit, stets'—B. II, 2, 714.
visur̃, vìsur adv. 'überall'—B. II, 2, 735.
vỹszna, vỹsznė 'Kirsche, Kirschbaum'—K. 8th ed. *Weichsel;* W. *viscum;* Boi. ἰξός. Cf. Ness. 84[b], Brückner SlFw. 153.
výti 'verfolgen'; **výtas** 'verfolgt'—see 1. *vejù.*
výti 'winden'; **výtas** 'gewunden'—see 2. *vejù.*

výtinu, výtinti 'welken machen'—W. *viēsco*. See 2. *výstu*.

výtis fem. 'Weidengerte, Tonnenband'—Uh. *vetasás;* F. *baurgs-waddjus;* B. I, 103. II, 1, 434; W. *vieo, vītis;* Boi. ἴτυς. Cf. Ness. 78[b], Lalis 427, Lesk. Abl. 288.

vyzdỹs 'Augapfel'—W. *video*. Cf. Lesk. Abl. 288.

vyżà 'Bastschuh'; "der litauische Originalschuh, eine aus je zwei Finger breiten Streifen von Lindenbast geflochtene Sohle, welche mit schmalen Bändern unterhalb des Knöchels an dem mit leinenen Lappen und Binden umwickelten Fusse befestigt wird" (Ness. 85[a])—B. II, 1, 507. Cf. Lesk. Nom. 600.

vógrauju, vógrauti 'krahlen' (von kleinen Kindern); (Lalis) 'to grumble, growl, snarl'—W. *vāgio;* Boi. ἠχή, περι-άγνυται.

võgti 'stehlen'—inf. of *vagiù*, q.v.

vójęs 'leidend'—Boi. ἄτη. Cf. MLG. I, 73; Lesk. Abl. 378.

võlas 'Walze; Welle'—B. I, 151. Cf. MLG. I, 21; Bezz. BGLS. 337[a]; Kur. 511; Lesk. Nom. 179; Lesk. Abl. 354. See next.

vólas, usually plu. **vólai** "das Lagerholz, die Unterlagen, auf welche die Zimmerleute die zu behauenden Hölzer legen; auch allg. eine Unterlage, die das darauf zu legende vor der Berührung mit dem Fussboden sichert" (Ness. 86[a])—Boi. εἴλω. Cf. Lesk. Abl. 354, Brückner SlFw. 154. See prec.

võlas 'Wall; (Lalis) mound of earth, bulwark, rampart'; **võlai** plu. "die wallartigen, langen Reihen, in welche auf den Wiesen das Heu zusammengeharkt wird" (Ness. 86[a])—see Brückner SlFw. 154.

volyklà 'Stelle, wo man sich herumgewälzt hat; eine zerwälzte Stelle; Schweinebucht'—B. II, 1, 622. Cf. Lesk. Nom. 500.

vorà 'lange Reihe (von sich hintereinander bewegenden Gegenständen, z.B. Wagen, Gänsen); (Lalis) Indian file, single file'—Uh. *āvaliṣ*, (1. *vāras*); Boi. ἀείρω. Cf. Lesk. Abl. 356, Lesk. Nom. 217.

vóras 'Spinne'—Boi. *ἀείρω, ἦτριον.* Cf. Lesk. Abl. 356, Lesk. Nom. 179.

võs adv. 'kaum, ungern'; **võs ne võs** 'mit genauer Not'—Ber. *jed(ŭ)va* (twice).

votìs 'bösartiges, offenes Geschwür'—(Uh. *ávātas*); F. *wunds;* Boi. *ἄτη* (& note), *ὠτειλή.* Cf. Lesk. Abl. 378.

voverẽ 'Eichhorn'—see *vaĩvaras.*

vóžiu, vóžti 'stülpen, den Deckel schliessen, den Deckel öffnen'—W. *vāgīna.* Cf. Lesk. Abl. 378.

Z

Lett. **zeri** plu. 'Glutsteine'—Ber. *kuřǫ* (read le. for lit.).

zokãnas 'Gesetz (bes. das mosaische); Ordensregel (der Mönche)'—Ber. *konŭ.* Cf. Brückner SlFw. 156.

Ż

žãgaras 'dürrer Ast'; **žagaraĩ** plu. 'Gestrüpp, Reisig'—K. *Kegel* 1, *Kufe* 1. Cf. Lesk. Nom. 446.

žaginỹs 'Pfahl, Pfosten'; **žaginiaĩ** plu. 'Palisaden; (dial.) Gerüst von Pfählen und Stangen, auf welches die Erbsen zum Trocknen aufgehängt werden'—K. *Kegel* 1, *Kufe* 1.

žãgrė 'Gabelholz, Gabelstange am Pfluge; Pflug'. Lalis 'plowshare; (wooden) plow'.—K. *Kufe* 1. Cf. Ness. 538[a].

žáidžu, žáisti 'spielen (e.g. **añt smuĩko žáisti** 'auf der Violine spielen'); den Beischlaf vollziehen; schwirren (von der Schwalbe)'—(F.(Ntr.) *gailjan*); W. *haedus;* (Boi. *κίθαρις*). Cf. Lesk. Abl. 293.

žáislas 'Spiel, Spielzeug'—B. II, 1, 373.619. Cf. Lesk. Abl. 293.

žaizdà 'Wunde, Schaden'—Uh. *héḍati;* F. *us-gaisjan;* B. I, 691.723. II, 3, 377. See *žeidžù.*

žãlas 'rot, rotbraun' (von Rindern)—Boi. *χαλκός* (read *žãlas* for *zãlas*).

żãles 'grün'—see *żãlias.*

żalesa "früh im Jahr spriessendes Gras, auf welches die jungen Gänse getrieben werden"—B. II, 1, 544. Cf. Kur. 515, Lesk. Nom. 594 (twice).

żalesas 'Grünspan'—B. II, 1, 544. Cf. Ness. 541ᵃ, Lesk. Nom. 594.

żalgà 'Stange'—K. *Galgen* (read *żalgà* for *zalga*); F. *galga.* Cf. Ness. 538ᵇ, Lalis 429, Lesk. Nom. 215.

żàlgas id.—F. *galga.* See prec. & Lesk. Nom. 176.

żãlias, żãles 'grün; roh, ungekocht; (Lalis also) immature, unripe'—Uh. *háriṣ;* K. *gelb;* F. *gulþ;* B. I, 429.552; W. *flāvus.* Cf. Ness. 541ᵃ, Lesk. Abl. 357.

żaliū̃kė eine Pilzart—B. II, 1, 501. Cf. Lesk. Nom. 516.

żalsvas 'grünlich'—B. II, 1, 202. Cf. Geitler LS. 122, Lalis 429, Lesk. Nom. 346.

żaltỹs, żaltis masc. 'Schlange' (Kur., "und zwar die ungiftige"; Ness., "bes. die grosse Bruchschlange mit bläulich weissen Schildern, die den Kühen die Milch aussaugt"; Lalis, "adder, viper, serpent")—B. I, 719. Cf. Sommer 249, Lesk. Nom. 552.

żàlvas 'grünlich'—B. II, 1, 201. Cf. Bezz. LF. 202, Lesk. Nom. 345. See *żelvas.*

żam̃bas 'Balkenkante; (Lalis) edge, brim; (wooden) plow'—Uh. *jámbhas;* W. *gemma;* Boi. γόμφος. Cf. Ness. 538ᵇ, Lalis 429, Lesk. Abl. 368.

żándas 'Kinnbacke, Kiefer'—Uh. *hánuṣ;* F. *kinnus;* W. *gena;* Boi. γένυς. Cf. Lesk. Abl. 358, Lesk. Nom. 170.

żãras 'Reihe, Ordnung beim Gehen; (Lalis) course, way, round, turn'—(W. *forus*); Boi. χορός. Cf. Ness. 539ᵃ, Brückner SlFw. 157, Lesk. Nom. 170.

żardas 'Stangengerüst auf dem Felde zum Getreidetrocknen; Holzwerk, worauf man die Erbsen und Wicken zum Trocknen aufhängt; (Lalis) a frame for drying corn or flaxseed; Scheiterhaufen'—F. *gairda;* Ber. *gordŭ.* Cf. Ness. 539ᵃ; Lalis 429; Trautmann Die altpreussischen Sprachdenkmäler 418; Brückner SlFw. 157.

żar̃dininkas 'Instmann; Aufseher über einen grossen Rossgarten; Gärtner, der zu seinem Lohn auch die Benutzung eines Gartens erhält; (Lalis also) owner of a small piece of ground'—Ber. *gordŭ.*

żar̃dis masc. 'Garten, Rossgarten, grosser umzäunter Weideplatz; (Lalis) fence, enclosure'—Uh. *gṛhás;* F. *gairda,* (*gards*); Ber. *gordŭ;* W. *cohors;* Boi. χόρτος.

żargaũs, żargýtis iter. 'die Beine auseinanderspreizen'—B. II, 3, 267-8. Cf. Lesk. Abl. 358.

żarýjos plu. 'glühende Kohlen; Feuernelken'—B. I, 547. 566; (W. *augur*); Boi. χαροπός. Cf. Sommer 24, Lesk. Abl. 371, Lesk. Nom. 317.

żárna 'Darm, (bes.) Dünndarm'; **żárnos** plu. 'Därme, (bes.) die dünnen Gedärme'—Uh. *híras;* K. *Garn;* B. I, 552. II, 1, 261; W. *haruspex, hernia;* Boi. χορδή.

żarstaũ, żarstýti 'mehrfach scharren'—W. *ēr;* Boi. χαράσσω. See *żeriù.*

żartas, żer̃tas 'Spass, Scherz, Kurzweil'—F. *gairnei;* (W. *horior*); Prell. χαίρω. Cf. Ness. 539[a], 544[b]; Kur. 516[b]; Brückner SlFw. 157.

żą́sinas 'Gänserich'—B. II, 1, 601. Cf. Lesk. Nom. 405.

żąsìs 'Gans'—Uh. *haṁsás;* K. *Gans;* B. I, 345.783. II, 1, 171.526(note). 2, 246; Ber. *gąsĭ;* W. *anser;* Boi. χήν.

żąsýtis 'junges Gänschen'—B. II, 1, 671. Cf. Lesk. Nom. 572.

żaudus 'ärgerlich, reizbar, empfindlich'—(W. *boa*); (Boi. βουβών (note)). Cf. Geitler LS. 122.

żáunė (**żiáunė**) 'Bissen Brot'—B. I, 291.

żavėti 'zaubern'—see *żaviu.*

żavinù, żavìnti 'umbringen'—Uh. *juhóti;* (W. *fūnus* 4). Cf. Lesk. Abl. 314.

żaviu, żavėti 'zaubern'—Uh. *hávate;* B. I, 557-8. II, 3, 150; (W. *avē*). Cf. Geitler LS. 122[b]; Archiv XVI, 421; Lalis 430; IF. XIII, 117.

żaživóju, żaživóti dial. '(Tabak) schnupfen'—B. I, 849. Cf. LBLV. 291, 347.

żėbiù, żė̃bti "langsam, wenig, mit langen Zähnen essen oder fressen"—Uh. *jámbhate.* Cf. Ness. 540[a], Lesk. Abl. 372.

żẽdas 'Blüte; die monatliche Reinigung der Frauen; Ring, Fingerring'; **żėdaĩ** plu. 'monatliche Reinigung'; **baltì żėdaĩ** 'weisse Blüten, (i.e.) der weisse Fluss der Frauen'—F. *keinan* (read *żẽdas* for *zẽdas*); Prell. νεογιλλός. Cf. Ness. 546[a], 540[a]; Kur. 521; Lalis 433; Lesk. Abl. 290; Lesk. Nom. 185.

żėdżu, żė̃sti 'formen, bilden (z.B. aus Ton, Wachs); bauen; einbilden, phantasieren'—B. II, 3, 194; W. *fingo;* Boi. τεῖχος. Cf. Ness. 540[b]; Lalis 433; Lesk. Abl. 290; Trautmann Die altpreussichen Sprachdenkmäler 423.

żėdżus 'Bildner, Töpfer'—B. II, 1, 224. Cf. Ness. 540[b], Lesk. Nom. 323.

żeidżù, żeĩsti 'verwunden, verletzen, beleidigen'—Uh. *hẽḍati;* F. *us-gaisjan;* (W. *foedus*). Cf. Lesk. Abl. 290.

żeliù, żélti 'grünen, wachsen'—Uh. *háriṣ;* F. *gulþ;* B. I, 178; W. *fel, flāvus;* Boi. χλωρός. Cf. Lesk. Abl. 357.

żelmũ 'Schössling, junges Grün, junge Pflanze'—Boi. χλεμυρός. See prec.

żelvas 'grünlich'—B. I, 324.334. II, 1, 201; W. *helvus;* Boi. χλόη, χόλος. Cf. Lesk. Nom. 345, Lalis 430. See *żeliù.*

żelvỹs 'grünender Stamm'—F. *gulþ.* Cf. Ness. 541[b], Lesk. Abl. 357.

żėmà 'Winter'—Uh. *himás;* B. I, 170.178.343.548.568; W. *hiems;* Boi. χεῖμα.

żẽmas 'niedrig'—W. *humus;* Boi. χαμαί.

żémbu, żémbėti 'keimen'—Uh. *jambúṣ;* W. *gemma.* Cf. Lesk. Abl. 368.

żẽmė 'Erde, Land, Boden, Acker'—Uh. *kṣás;* F. *guma;* B.

I, 137.142.551.562.792. II, 1, 135.221.222. 2, 99; W. *humus;* Boi. χαμαί.

żemỹn 'abwärts'—see *żemyniui*.

Żemýna die Erdgöttin der heidnischen Litauer—B. II, 1, 278. Cf. Ness. 543ᵃ.

żemyniui, żemỹn adv. 'nach unten zu, abwärts, herab, hinab, nieder'—B. II, 2, 703.742. Cf. Ness. 542ᵇ, Bezz. BGLS. 342, Lesk. Nom. 411.

żemiū́tas 'voll Erde, mit Erde beschmutzt'—B. II, 1, 407. 664.

żëmkiñtis adj. 'den Winter über aushaltend'; **żëmkiñtis óbûlas** 'Winterapfel'—B. I, 405.589.716; Boi. πένθος. Cf. Lesk. Abl. 331.

żengiù, żeñgti 'schreiten, gehen; Schritt gehen (von Pferden); auf einen Berg steigen'—Uh. *jáṅghā;* K. *Gang;* F. *gaggan;* B. I, 349.555-6.577. II, 3, 122; Boi. κοχώνη. Cf. Lesk. Abl. 358.

żénklas, żinklas 'Zeichen, Wunderzeichen, Buchzeichen, Zettel, Quittung, Bescheinigung, Legitimation, Pass, Bild, Statue'—Uh. *jñātás;* B. I, 541. II, 1, 341.344. 3, 170.303; W. *nōsco;* Boi. γέγωνα, γιγνώσκω. Cf. Ness. 543ᵇ; Kur. 519, 523; Lesk. Abl. 358.

żenklus 'kenntlich'—B. II, 1, 385. Cf. Ness. 554ᵃ, Lesk. Nom. 263.

żéntas 'Schwiegersohn; Schwager'—Uh. *jāmātā;* F. *kuni;* B. I, 119.178.364.405(note).566. II, 1, 335; W. *gener;* Boi. γαμβρός.

żentė 'Schwägerin'—see *jentė*.

żergiù, żeȓgti 'die Beine spreizen, zum Schritt das Bein vorspreizen, seitwärts schreiten, langsam und mit grossen Schritten gehen, langsam gehen, stolzieren, auf ein Pferd aufsteigen'—(Boi. χορός). Cf. Lesk. Abl. 358.

żėriù, żėrḗti 'strahlen, glänzen, glühen, schimmern'—(W. *augur, consīdero*); Boi. χαροπός (twice), ὠχρός, (λεύσσω); B. II, 2, 817. Cf. Lesk. Abl. 371.

žeriù, žer̃ti 'scharren, kratzen, schüren'—K. *kehren* 2; F. *us-skarjan;* W. *ēr,* (*hirūdo*); Boi. χαράσσω. Cf. Lesk. Abl. 358.

žer̃tas 'Scherz'—see *žartas*.

žẽsti 'formen'—inf. of *žiedžiù*, q.v.

žiáunė 'Bissen Brot'—see *žáunė*.

žýdu (**žýdžu, žýdmi**), **žydė́ti** 'blühen'—F. *keinan;* (Boi. νεογιλλός); Prell. νεογιλλός. Cf. Ness. 546ᵃ, Lesk. Abl. 290.

žìlas 'grau' (bes. von Haaren)—(W. *galbus*); Boi. γλαυκός. Cf. Lesk. Abl. 357.

žylù (**žilstù**), **žìlti** 'grau werden'—W. *flāvus*. Cf. Ness. 546ᵃ, Lesk. Abl. 357.

žilvìtis masc. 'Grauweide, Korbweide'—W. *vieo, vītis;* Boi. ἴτυς. See 2. *vejù*.

žinaũ, žinóti 'wissen, kennen'—Uh. *jñātás;* K. *können;* F. *kunnan;* B. I, 388.413.416.548. II, 3, 168.298.303.312; W. *nōsco;* Boi. γιγνώσκω. Cf. Lesk. Abl. 358.

žìndu (B. **žíndu**), **žį́sti** '(an der Brust) saugen' (von Kindern und Tieren)—Boi. νεογιλλός. Cf. Lesk. Abl. 358.

žindùkas 'Lutschbeutel; (Lalis also) suckling'—B. II, 1, 493.610. Cf. Ness. 548ᵃ, Lalis 434, Lesk. Nom. 516.

žinė 'Kunde'—see *žinià*.

žinginis masc. 'Klappkraut, Sumpfschlangenkraut'—Boi. γιγγίς. Cf. Ness. 548ᵇ, Lalis 434.

žingslis masc. 'Schritt'—B. II, 1, 384. Cf. Lesk. Nom. 460.

žiñgsnis (Kur., Uh., F., B., **žiñksnis**) masc. 'Schritt, Tritt; Stufe, Staffel; Vergleichungsgrad der Adjektiva'—Uh. *jáṁhas;* F. *gaggan;* B. II, 1, 289. Cf. Ness. 548ᵇ, Lesk. Abl. 358, Lesk. Nom. 373.

žinià, žinė 'Kunde, Kenntnis, Nachricht, Wissenschaft'—F. *af-gudei* (s.v. *af-gups*), *bandi;* B. II, 1, 185. Cf. Ness. 547ᵃ; Schleicher LSpr. II, 341; Wied. s.v.; Sommer 55; Lesk. Abl. 358.

žinklas 'Zeichen'—see *ženklas*.

žiñksnis 'Schritt'—see *žiñgsnis.*

žinóti 'wissen'—inf. of *žinaũ,* q.v.

žinóvas 'Kenner, Wissender'—B. II, 1, 204. Cf. Geitler LS. 122, Lesk. Nom. 351.

-žìnti 'kennen'—see *-žį́stu.*

žióju, žióti; žiójůs, žiótis 'den Mund aufsperren, gähnen'—K. *gähnen;* F. *ga-geigan;* B. I, 280(note).568.857. II, 1, 435. 3, 162.198.493; W. *hio* (twice); Boi. χιράς. Cf. Lalis 435, Lesk. Abl. 378.

žióra 'Widerschein am Himmel'—Boi. χαροπός. See *pažióra.*

žioróju, žioróti 'strahlen, glühen, brennen'—Boi. χαροπός. Cf. Lesk. Abl. 371.

žiotìs fem. 'Riss, Kluft, Öffnung'; (Lalis 435) **žiotys** plu. 'mouth, jaws; gulf, abyss'—B. II, 1, 435. Cf. Ness. 550[a], Lesk. Abl. 378.

žìrgas 'Ross'—(Boi. χορός). Cf. Lesk. Abl. 358.

žìrklės (B. **žírklės**) plu. 'Schere'—F. *gilþa;* B. I, 454.552. II, 1, 341; (Ber. *bĭrkŭ*); W. *furca;* Boi. σχαλίς. Cf. Lesk. Nom. 498, Sommer 178.

žìrnis (B. **žírnis**) masc. 'Erbse'—Uh. *jīrṇás, (ghárṣati), (mudgás);* F. *kaurn;* B. I, 418.474.568. II, 1, 257; (Ber. *gorchŭ*); W. *grānum;* Boi. γίγαρτον.

žį́sti 'saugen'—inf. of *žìndu,* q.v.

-žį́stu, -žìnti—see *pažį́stu* 'ich kenne'.

-žýstu, -žýsti 'aufblühen'—F. *keinan;* Prell. νεογιλλός. Cf. Lesk. Abl. 290.

žiupõnas (župõnas) Samog. 'Frauenjoppe; (Ness.) das Unterkleid der Polen; (Lalis) raiment'—Ber. *jupa.* Cf. Ness. 550[b]; Lalis 435; Brückner SlFw. 158.

žiūriù, žiūrė́ti 'sehen, schauen, hinsehen, ansehen'—(W. *augur*). Cf. Lesk. Abl. 319.

žlaũktai (žliaũktai) masc. plu. (Lalis, sing. **žliauktas** 'swill, medley, refuse'); **žlaũktys (žliaũktys)** fem. plu. 'Treber'—W. *flocces.* Cf. Kur. 526[a]; Lalis 435; Lesk. Abl. 314; Lesk. Nom. 553, 601 (Ntr.).

żlėjà 'Dämmerung'—K. *glühen;* F. *glaggwō;* B. I, 150; (W. *flamma, galbus*); Boi. χλιδή, (γελάω).

żliaũktai, żliaũktys 'Treber'—see *żlaũktai.*

żmogẽlis 'Menschlein'—B. II, 1, 376. Cf. Schleicher LSpr. I, 56.

żmogżúda masc. 'Mörder'—B. II, 1, 472. Cf. Lesk. Nom. 587.

żmũ (Old Lith.), **żmogùs** (sing. only) 'Mensch'; **żmonà** 'Weib'; **żmónės** plu. 'Menschen, Leute'—Uh. *kṣás;* F. *guma,* (1. *manna*); B. I, 152.387. II, 1, 222.295. 511.598; W. *homo,* (*augur*); Boi. χαμαί. Cf. Ness. 553[a]; Kur. Gram. 593, 694; Bezz. BGLS. 30, 121; Sommer 160, 161; Lesk. Nom. 370, 375, 381.

żolẽ 'Gras, Kraut, Pflanze'; **żõlės** plu. 'Kräuter, Arznei'—Uh. *háriṣ;* B. I, 158; W. *flāvus.* Cf. Bezz. LF. 203, Lesk. Abl. 357.

żolýnas 'Grasstaude, Platz voll Grasstauden, Rasenplatz; (Lalis also) flower garden, flower'—B. II, 1, 623. Cf. Lesk. Nom. 409.

żudaũ, żudýti 'ums Leben bringen, töten; (Bezz.) martern, quälen; (Lalis) to destroy, waste, lose'—(W. *fūnus* 4). Cf. Bezz. LF. 203, Lesk. Abl. 314.

żuk- 'Fisch-' (e.g. **żukmistras** 'Fischmeister; ein Beamter, der die Fischerei auf dem Haffe beaufsichtigt'; **żuksparnis** 'Fischaar')—Uh. *kṣú;* B. I, 104.565.580. II, 1, 483; Boi. ἰχθῦς. Cf. Ness. 552[a]; Bezz. BGLS. 330[b]; Lesk. Nom. 317, 505; Trautmann Die altpreussischen Sprachdenkmäler 441. See *żuvìs.*

żupõnas 'Frauenjoppe'—see *żiupõnas.*

żūstu, żūti 'fischen'—B. II, 3, 370. Cf. Lesk. Abl. 314.

żuvìmas 'das Umkommen; (Lalis) vanishing, perishing, loss'—(W. *fūnus* 4). Read *żuvìmas* for W.'s *żumìmus* & for Prell.'s (s.v. χέω, whence W.) & Kur.'s (s.v. *żūvù,* whence apparently Prell.) *żumìmas* ? Cf. Ness. 552[b] (*prażuvimas*), Lalis 438, Lesk. Abl. 314.

żuvìs fem. 'Fisch'—Uh. *kṣú;* B. I, 565.794. II, 1, 137.141. 171. 2, 293; Boi. ἰχθῦς. Cf. Lesk. Abl. 314.

żũvù, żúti 'umkommen'—Uh. *juhóti;* (W. *avē, fundo, fūnus* 4). Cf. Lesk. Abl. 314.

żvaigżdė̃, żvaigzdė̃, żvaizdė̃ 'Stern'—Ber. *gvězda,* (*gvižd̆žǫ*). Cf. Sommer 116, 117.

żvaĩras 'schielend, mit schielenden Augen'—Ber. *gvèrōk.*

żvairiù, żvairė́ti 'schielen'—Ber. *gvèrōk.* Cf. Lesk. Abl. 293.

żvaizdė̃ 'Stern'—see *żvaigżdė̃.*

żvãkė 'Licht, Kerze; (Lalis also) icicle'—B. I, 312. II, 1, 221; (W. *faciēs*); Boi. παιφάσσω.

żvalgaũ, żvalgýti 'mehrfach umherblicken, spähen; etwas ansehen, anschauen; in Unterhandlungen wegen einer Heirat stehen, zur Brautschau reisen'—Boi. θέλγω. See *żvelgiù* & Lesk. Abl. 359.

żvëgiù, żvẽgti 'quieken, in Angst kreischen (bes. von Schweinen)'—Ber. *gvižd̆žǫ.* Cf. Lesk. Abl. 290.

żvelgiù, żvel̃gti 'blicken, sehen'; **żvìlgiu** (B. **żvil̃giu**), **żvilgė́ti** 'schnell hinsehen, einen Blick werfen'; **żvìlgu** (B. **żvil̃gu**), **żvilgė́ti** (Kur. 529, Lalis 439) 'glänzen'—B. I, 260.331.556; Boi. θέλγω, (φυλακός). Cf. Lesk. Abl. 358-9.

żvėrënà 'Wildbret'—F. *ahmeins;* B. II, 1, 273.275.277.278. 665. Cf. Lesk. Nom. 413.

żvėrìs 'wildes Tier, Raubtier' (Ness. 554*: "bes. der Wolf") —B. I, 295.312.321.568. II, 1, 138.141.171. 2, 276; W. *ferus;* Boi. θήρ. Cf. Kur. DLWb. s.v. Thier; Lesk. Nom. 235.

żvygiù, żvỹgti 'quiekend schreien' (bes. von Schweinen)—Ber. *gvižd̆žǫ.* Cf. Lesk. Abl. 290.

żvigù, żvìgti 'aufquieken'—see *żvingù.*

żvìlgiu, żvilgė́ti 'hinsehen'; **żvìlgu, żvilgė́ti** 'glänzen'—see *żvelgiù.*

żvilůti 'schaukeln, wiegen'; **żvilti** id.; **żvilti** 'blasen, sausen' (vom Winde) (?)—Boi. φάλος. Cf. Geitler LS. 123; Bezz. BGLS. 343; Lesk. Abl. 349.

żvingù (żvigù), żvìgti 'aufquieken, aufschreien' (bes. von Schweinen)—Ber. *gvižděǫ*. Cf. Ness. 554*; Donalitius 331; Lesk. Abl. 290.

żvìrblis masc. 'Sperling'—(Boi. κόραξ (note)). Cf. Lesk. Nom. 457.

Zeitfracht Medien GmbH
Ferdinand-Jühlke-Straße 7
99095 Erfurt, Deutschland
produktsicherheit@kolibri360.de